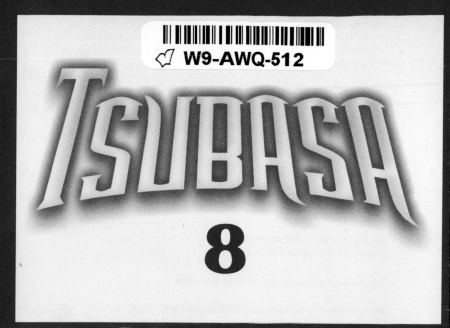

TSUBASA

8

CLAMP

TRANSLATED AND ADAPTED BY
William Flanagan

LETTERED BY
Dana Hayward

BALLANTINE BOOKS • NEW YORK

Tsubasa crosses over with *xxxHOLiC*. Although it isn't necessary to read *xxxHOLiC* to understand the events in *Tsubasa*, you'll get to see the same events from different perspectives if you read both!

Honorifics Explained

Throughout the Del Rey Manga books, you will find Japanese honorifics left intact in the translations. For those not familiar with how the Japanese use honorifics and, more important, how they differ from American honorifics, we present this brief overview.

Politeness has always been a critical facet of Japanese culture. Ever since the feudal era, when Japan was a highly stratified society, use of honorifics — which can be defined as polite speech that indicates relationship or status — has played an essential role in the Japanese language. When addressing someone in Japanese, an honorific usually takes the form of a suffix attached to one's name (example: "Asuna-san"), or as a title at the end of one's name or in place of the name itself (example: "Negi-sensei," or simply "Sensei!").

Honorifics can be expressions of respect or endearment. In the context of manga and anime, honorifics give insight into the nature of the relationship between characters. Many translations into English leave out these important honorifics, and therefore distort the "feel" of the original Japanese. Because Japanese honorifics contain nuances that English honorifics lack, it is our policy at Del Rey not to translate them. Here, instead, is a guide to some of the honorifics you may encounter in Del Rey Manga.

-san: This is the most common honorific, and is equivalent to Mr., Miss, Ms., Mrs., etc. It is the all-purpose honorific and can be used in any situation where politeness is required.

-sama: This is one level higher than "-san." It is used to confer great respect.

-dono: This comes from the word "tono," which means "lord." It is an even higher level than "-sama" and confers utmost respect.

-kun: This suffix is used at the end of boys' names to express familiarity or endearment. It is also sometimes used by men among friends, or when addressing someone younger or of a lower station.

-chan: This is used to express endearment, mostly toward girls. It is also used for little boys, pets, and even among lovers. It gives a sense of childish cuteness.

Bozu: This is an informal way to refer to a boy, similar to the English term "kid" or "squirt."

Sempai/senpai: This title suggests that the addressee is one's senior in a group or organization. It is most often used in a school setting, where underclassmen refer to their upperclassmen as "sempai." It can also be used in the workplace, such as when a newer employee addresses an employee who has seniority in the company.

Kohai: This is the opposite of "sempai," and is used toward underclassmen in school or newcomers in the workplace. It connotes that the addressee is of lower station.

Sensei: Literally meaning "one who has come before," this title is used for teachers, doctors, or masters of any profession or art.

-[blank]: Usually forgotten in these lists, but perhaps the most significant difference between Japanese and English. The lack of honorific means that the speaker has permission to address the person in a very intimate way. Usually, only family, spouses, or very close friends have this kind of permission. Known as *yobisute*, it can be gratifying when someone who has earned the intimacy starts to call one by one's name without an honorific. But when that intimacy hasn't been earned, it can also be very insulting.

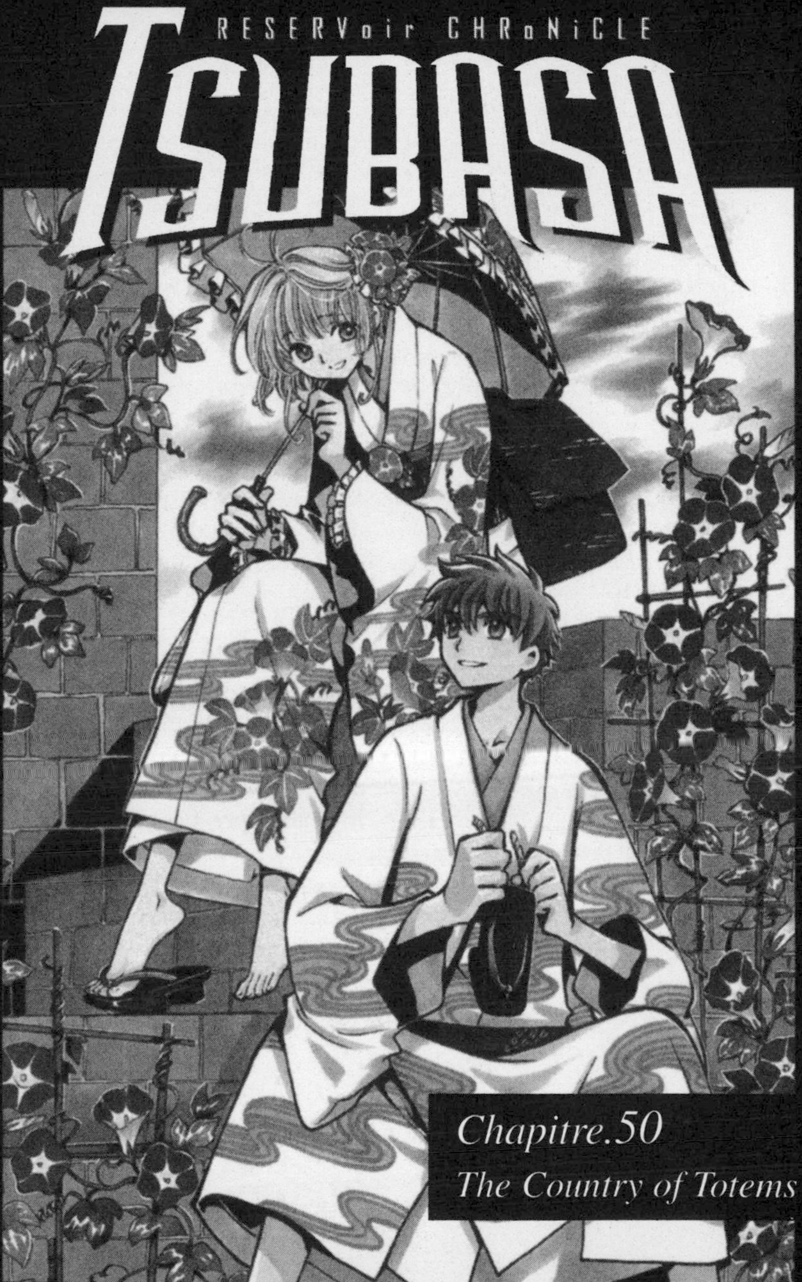
RESERVoir CHRoNiCLE
TSUBASA
Chapitre.50
The Country of Totems

ツバサ

RESERVoir CHRoNiCLE

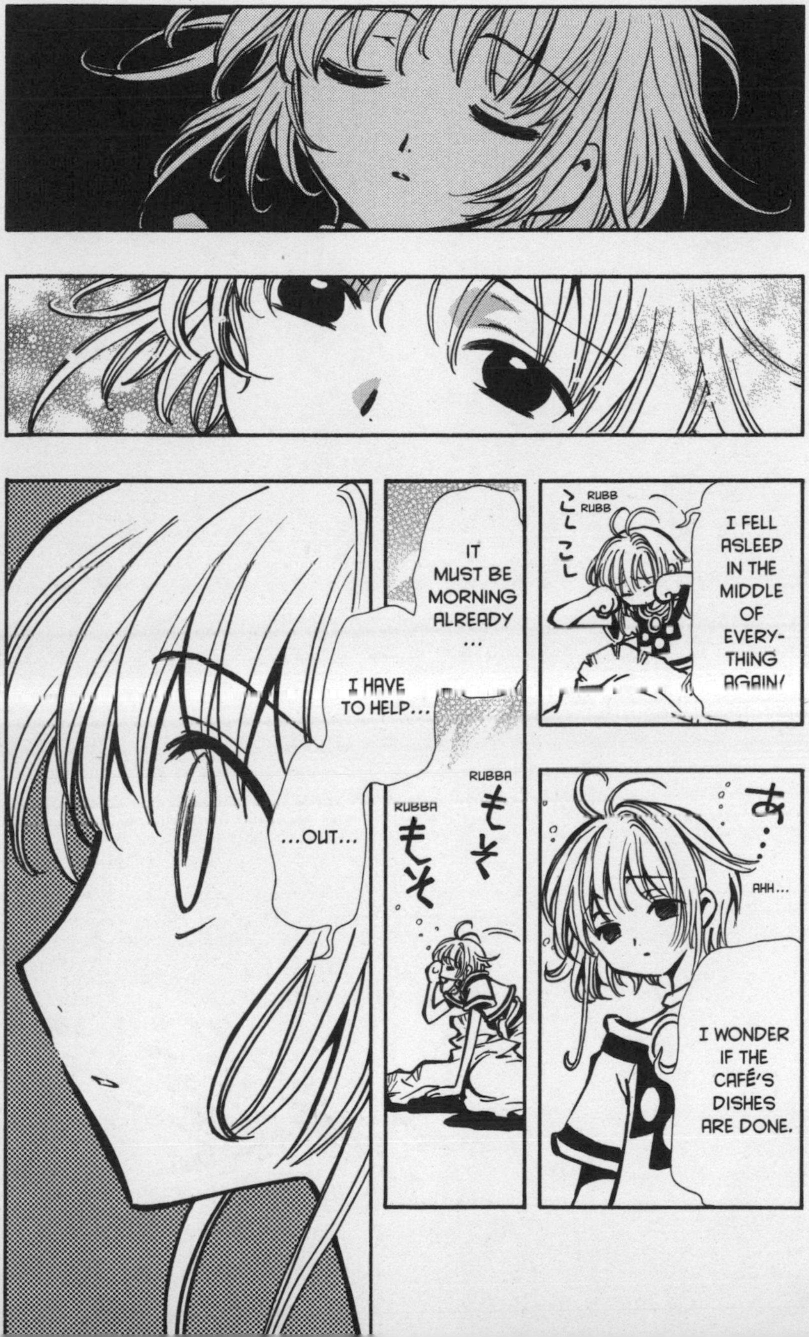
RUBB RUBB
こしこし
I FELL ASLEEP IN THE MIDDLE OF EVERY-THING AGAIN!
あ…
AHH…
I WONDER IF THE CAFÉ'S DISHES ARE DONE.
IT MUST BE MORNING ALREADY…
RUBBA
もそ
RUBBA
もそ
I HAVE TO HELP…
…OUT…

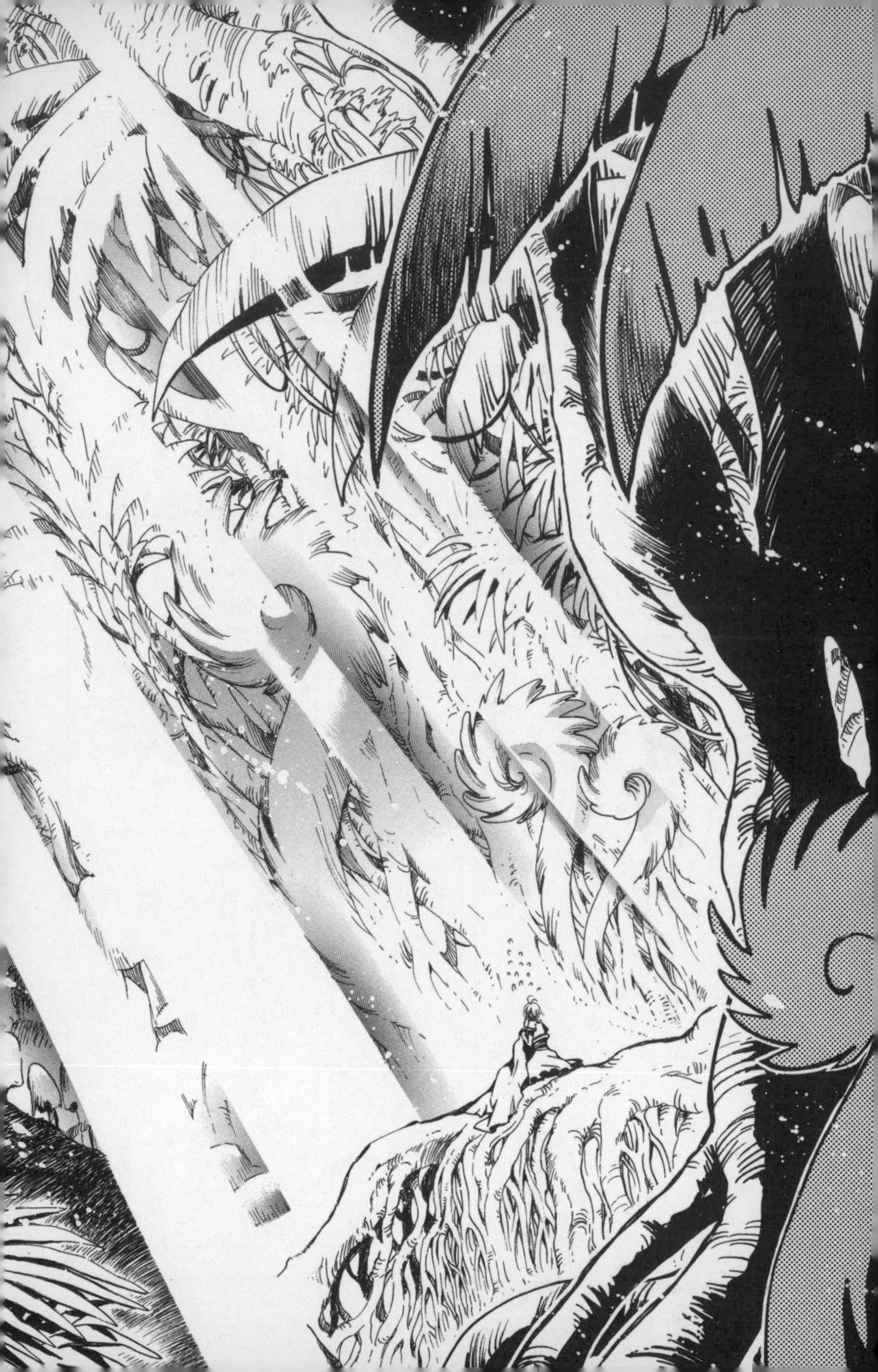

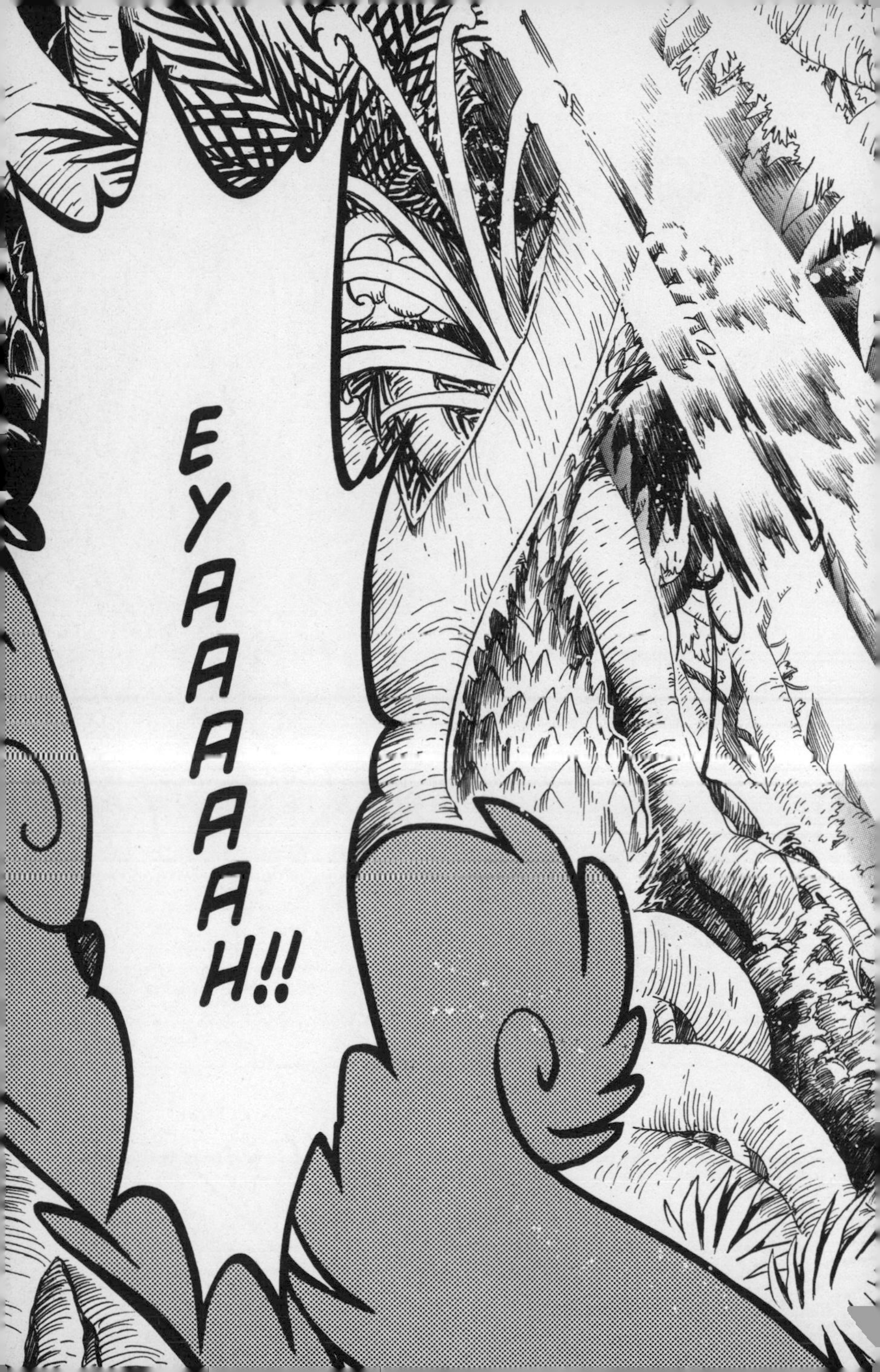
EYAAAAAH!!

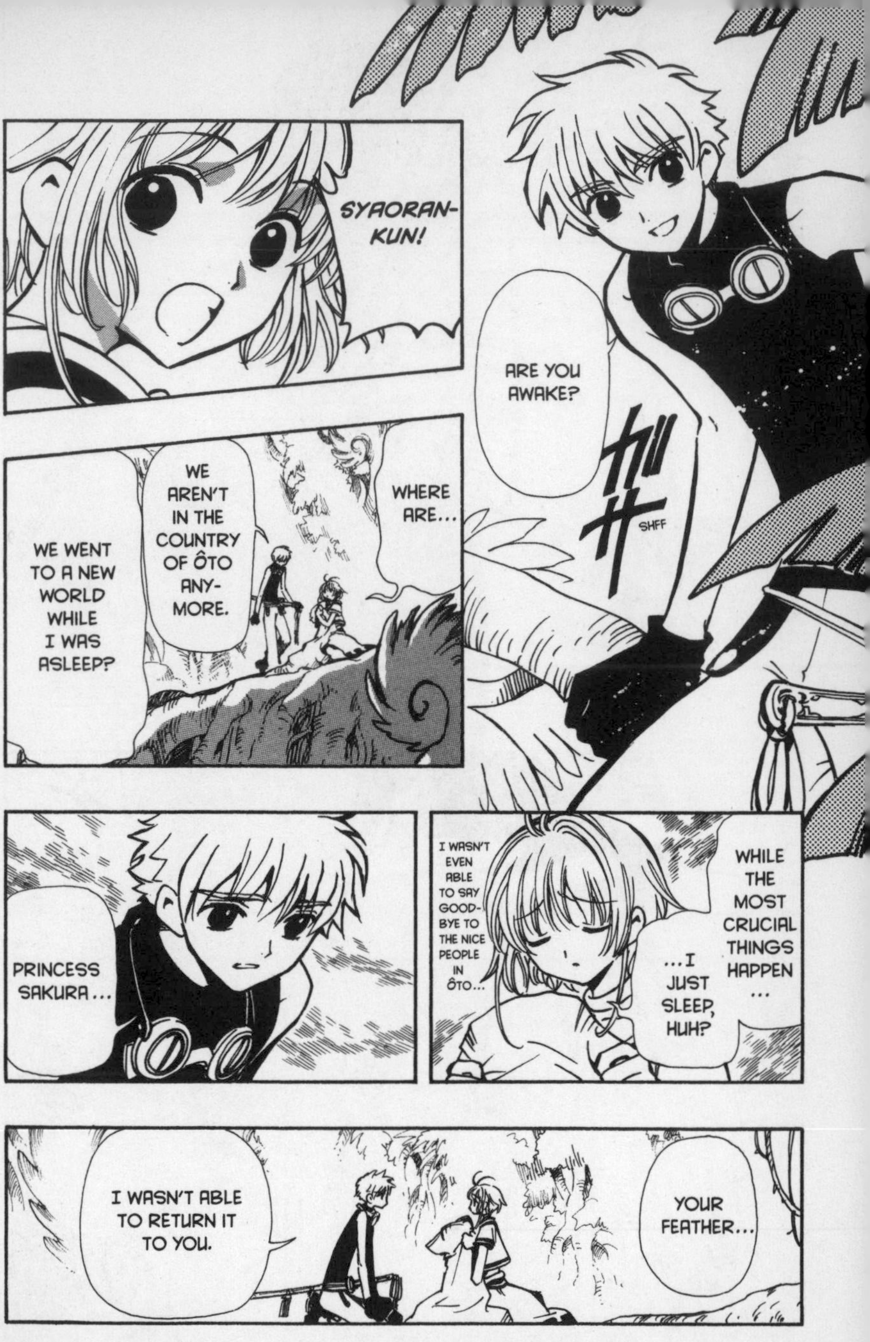
ARE YOU AWAKE?
ガサ
SHFF
SYAORAN-KUN!
WHERE ARE...
WE AREN'T IN THE COUNTRY OF ÔTO ANYMORE.
WE WENT TO A NEW WORLD WHILE I WAS ASLEEP?
WHILE THE MOST CRUCIAL THINGS HAPPEN...
...I JUST SLEEP, HUH?
I WASN'T EVEN ABLE TO SAY GOODBYE TO THE NICE PEOPLE IN ÔTO...
PRINCESS SAKURA...
YOUR FEATHER...
I WASN'T ABLE TO RETURN IT TO YOU.

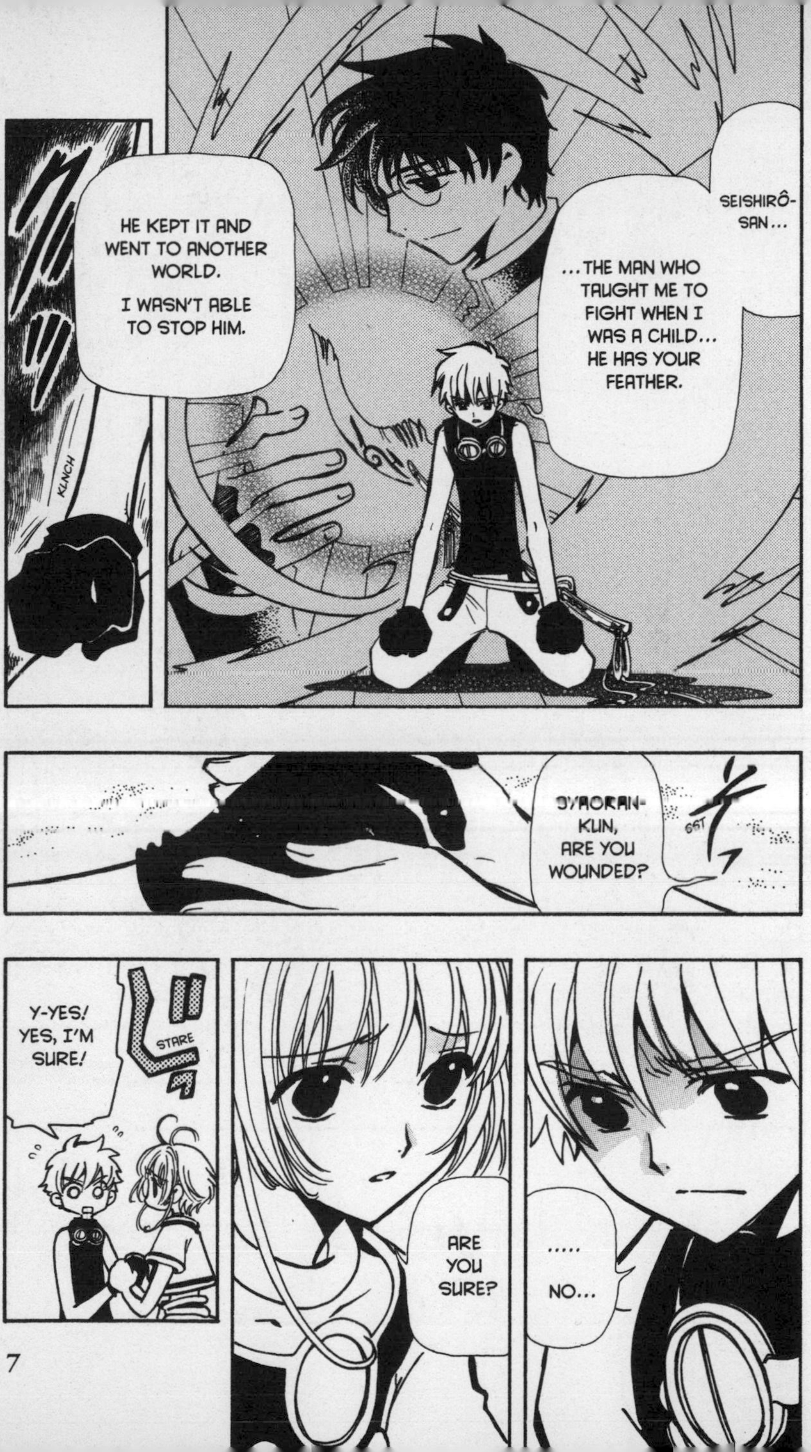
SEISHIRÔ-SAN...
...THE MAN WHO TAUGHT ME TO FIGHT WHEN I WAS A CHILD... HE HAS YOUR FEATHER.
HE KEPT IT AND WENT TO ANOTHER WORLD.
I WASN'T ABLE TO STOP HIM.
KLINCH
GST
SYAORAN-KUN, ARE YOU WOUNDED?
..... NO...
ARE YOU SURE?
STARE
Y-YES! YES, I'M SURE!

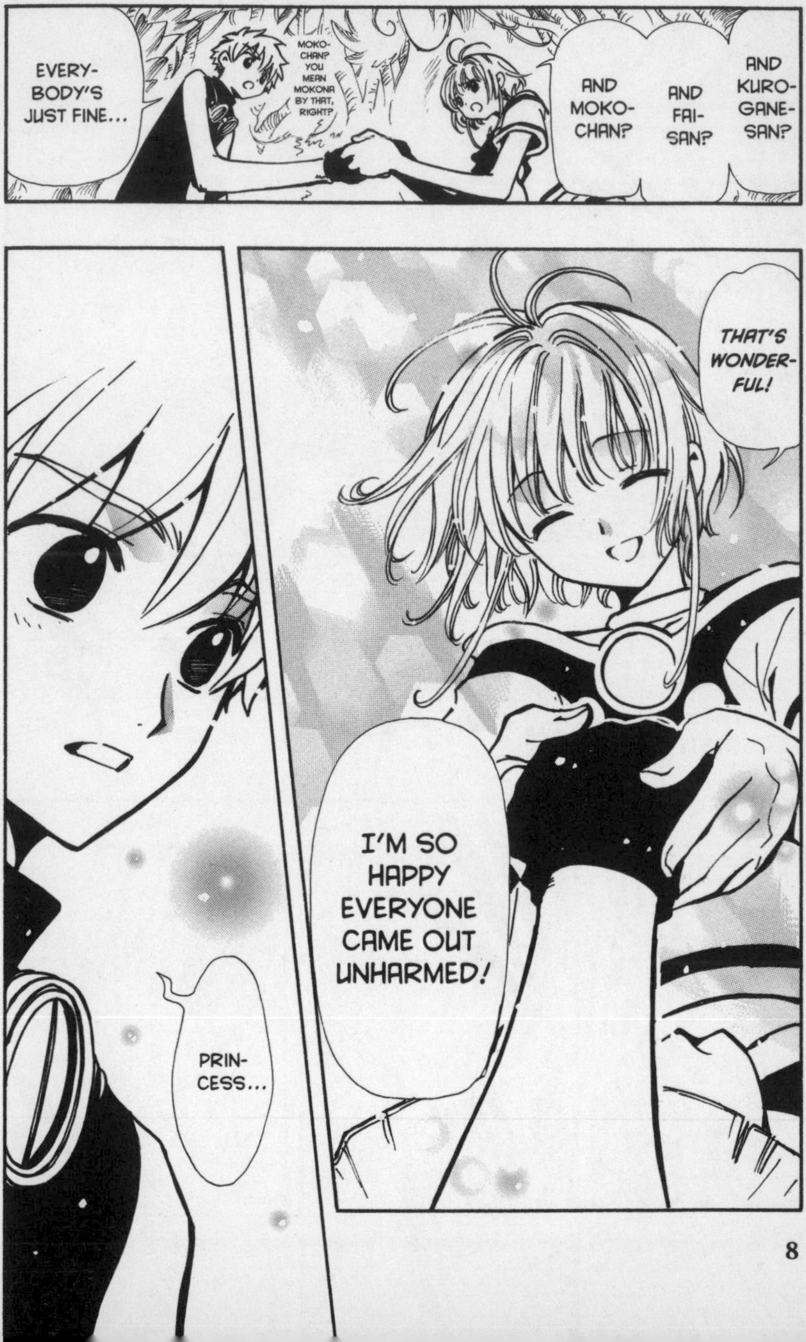
AND KUROGANE-SAN?
AND FAI-SAN?
AND MOKO-CHAN?
MOKO-CHAN? YOU MEAN MOKONA BY THAT, RIGHT?
EVERYBODY'S JUST FINE...
THAT'S WONDERFUL!
I'M SO HAPPY EVERYONE CAME OUT UNHARMED!
PRINCESS...

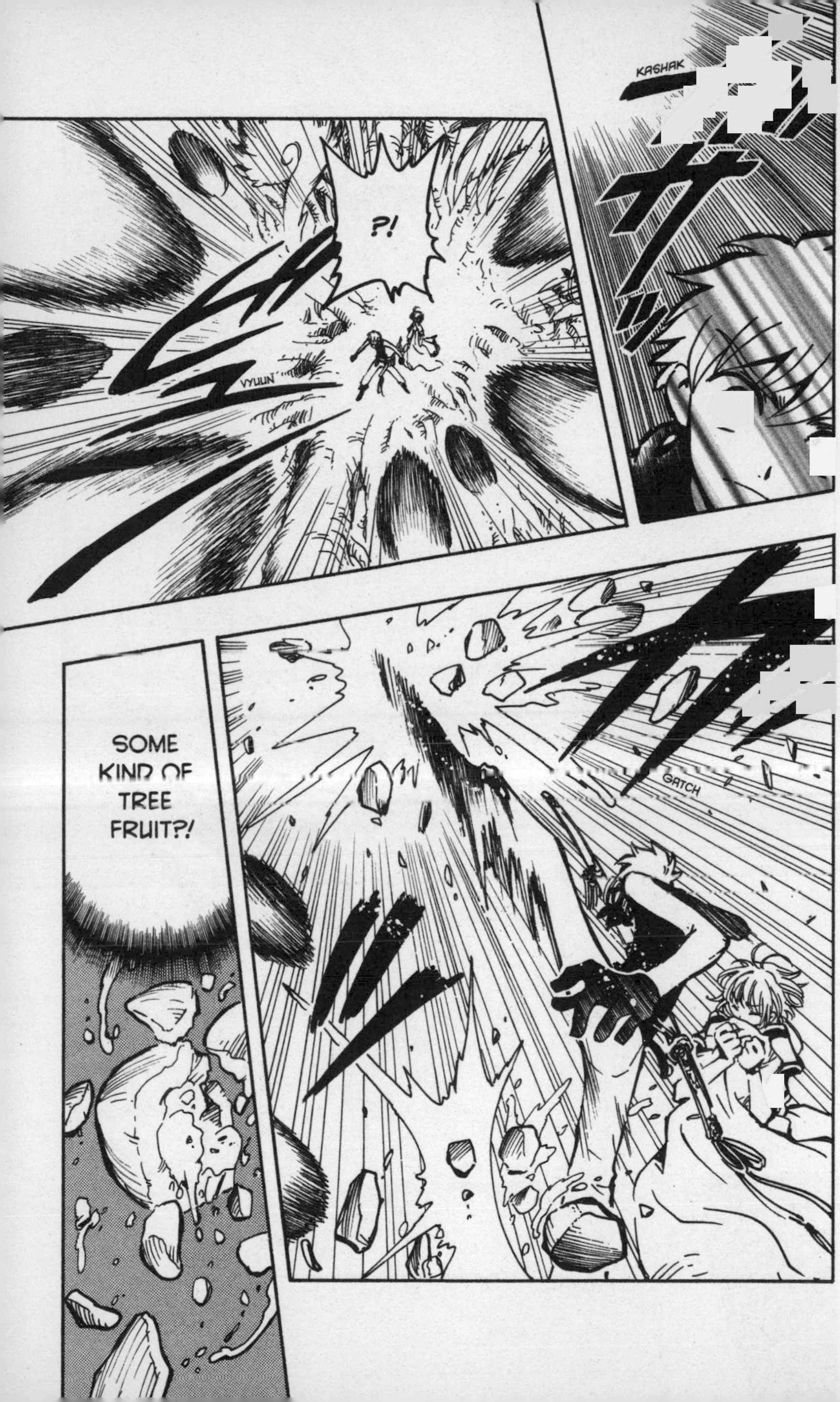
KASHAK
?!
VYUUN
GATCH
SOME KIND OF TREE FRUIT?!

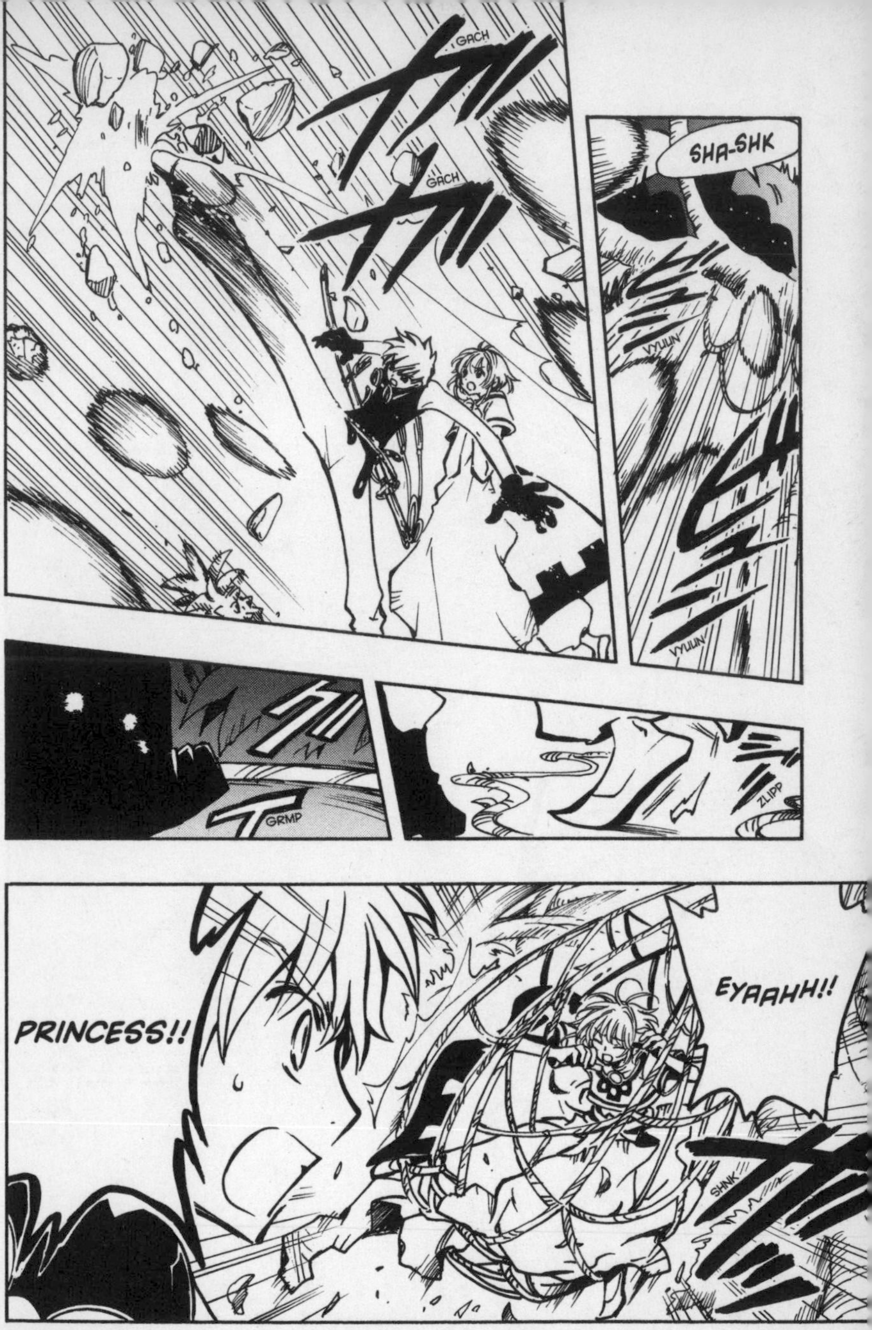
SHA-SHK
VYUUN
VYUUN
GACH
GACH
ZLIPP
GRMP
EYAAHH!!
PRINCESS!!
SHNIK

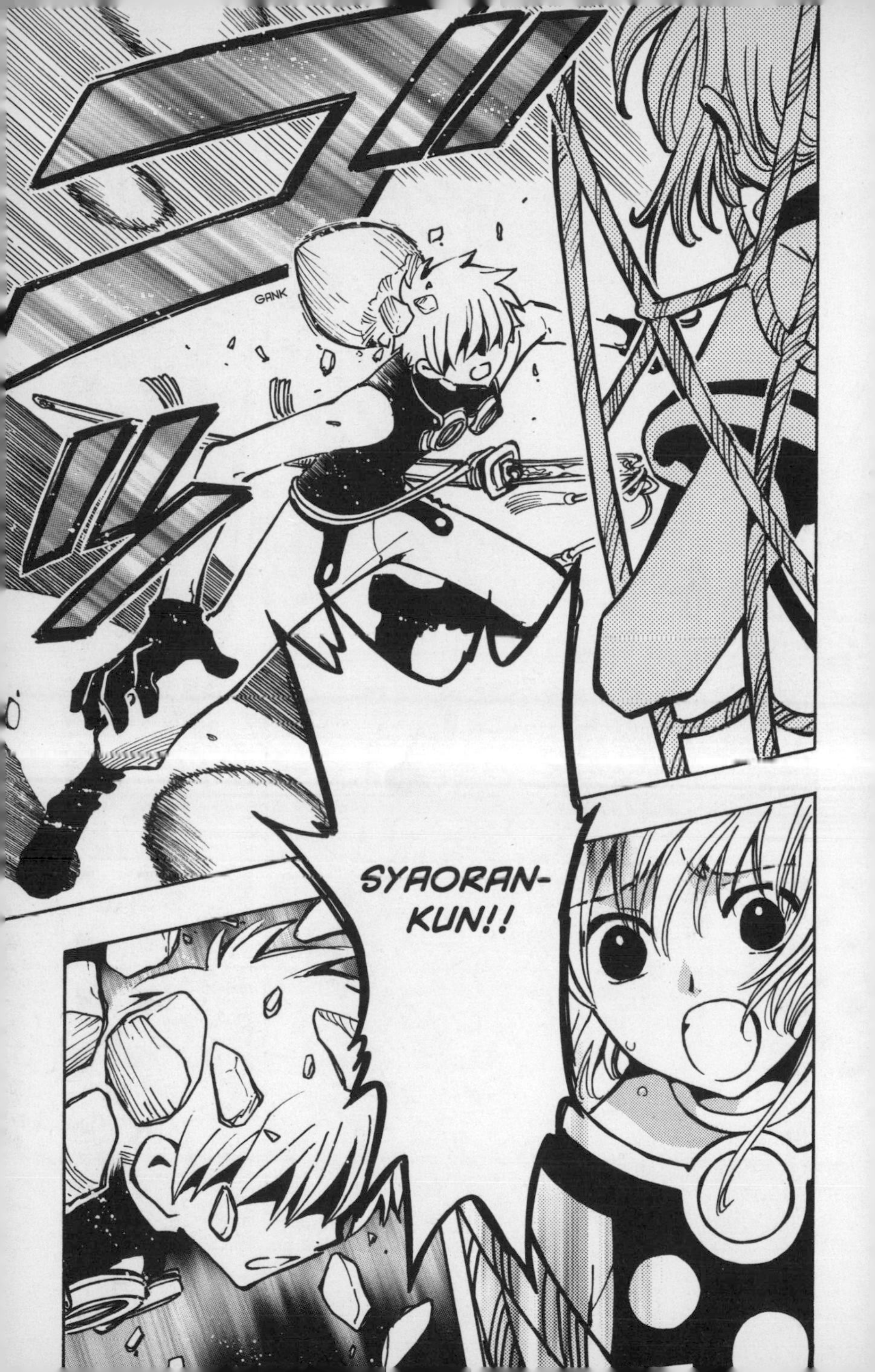
GANK
SYAORAN-
KUN!!

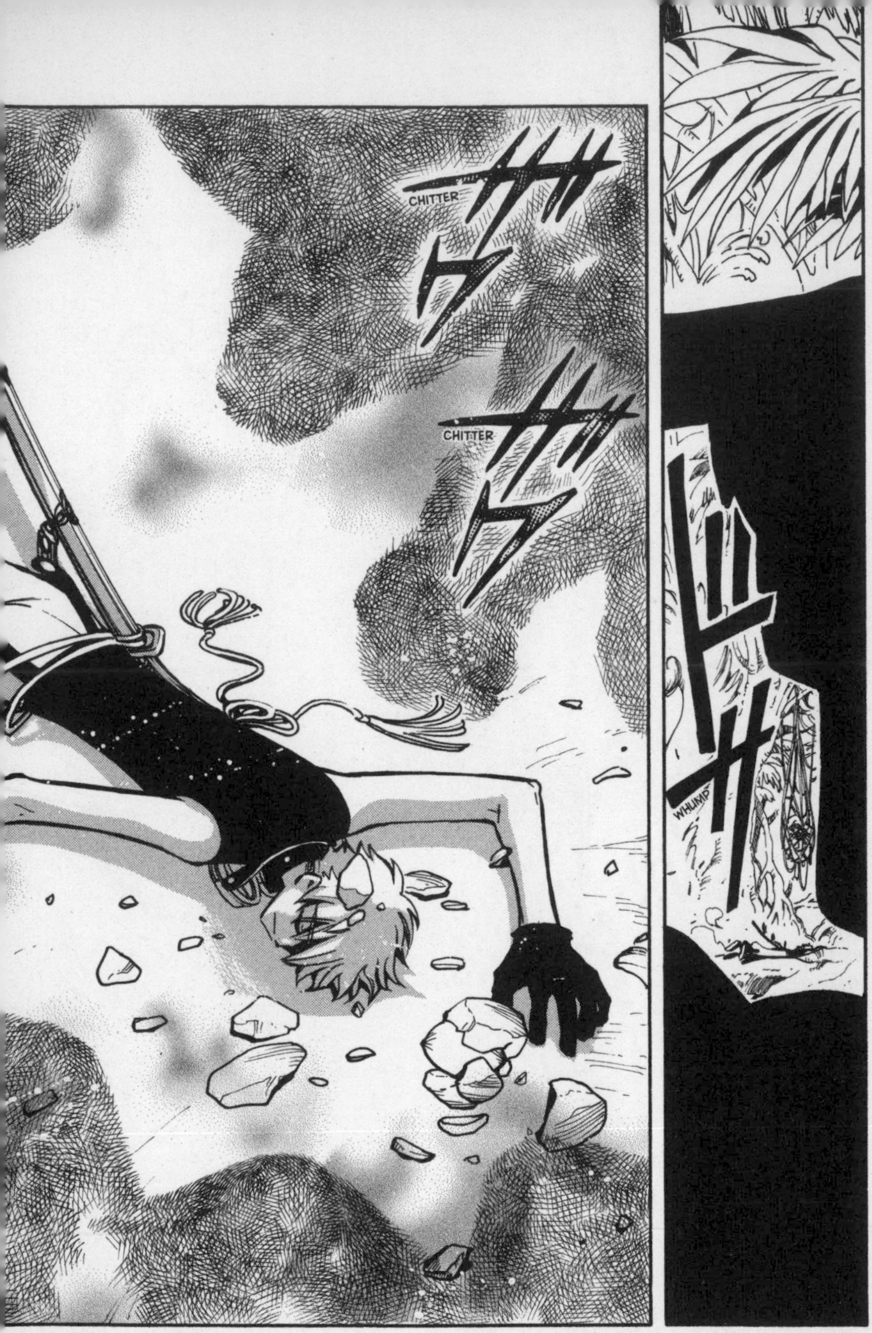
WHUMP
CHITTER
CHITTER

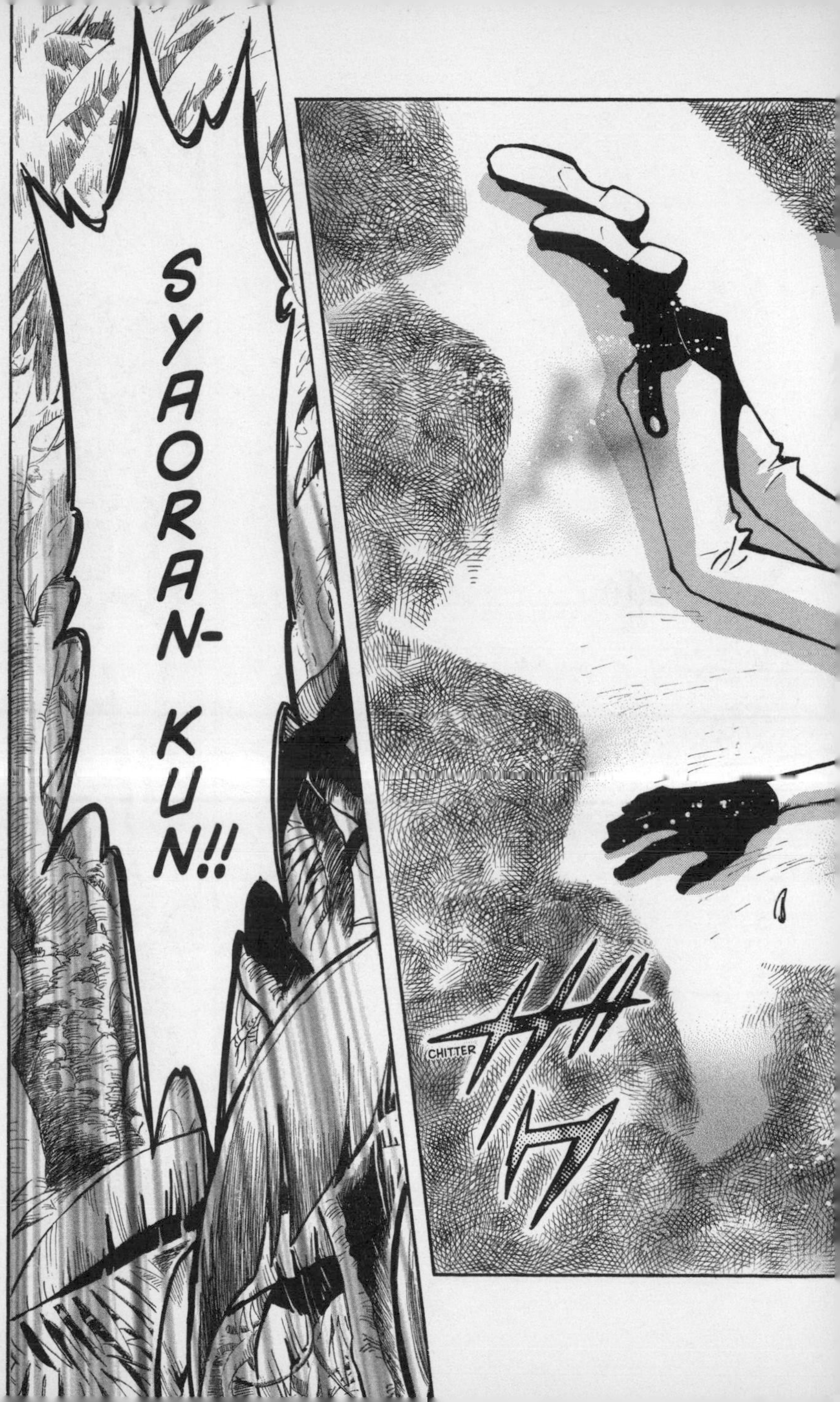
CHITTER
SYAORAN-KUN!!

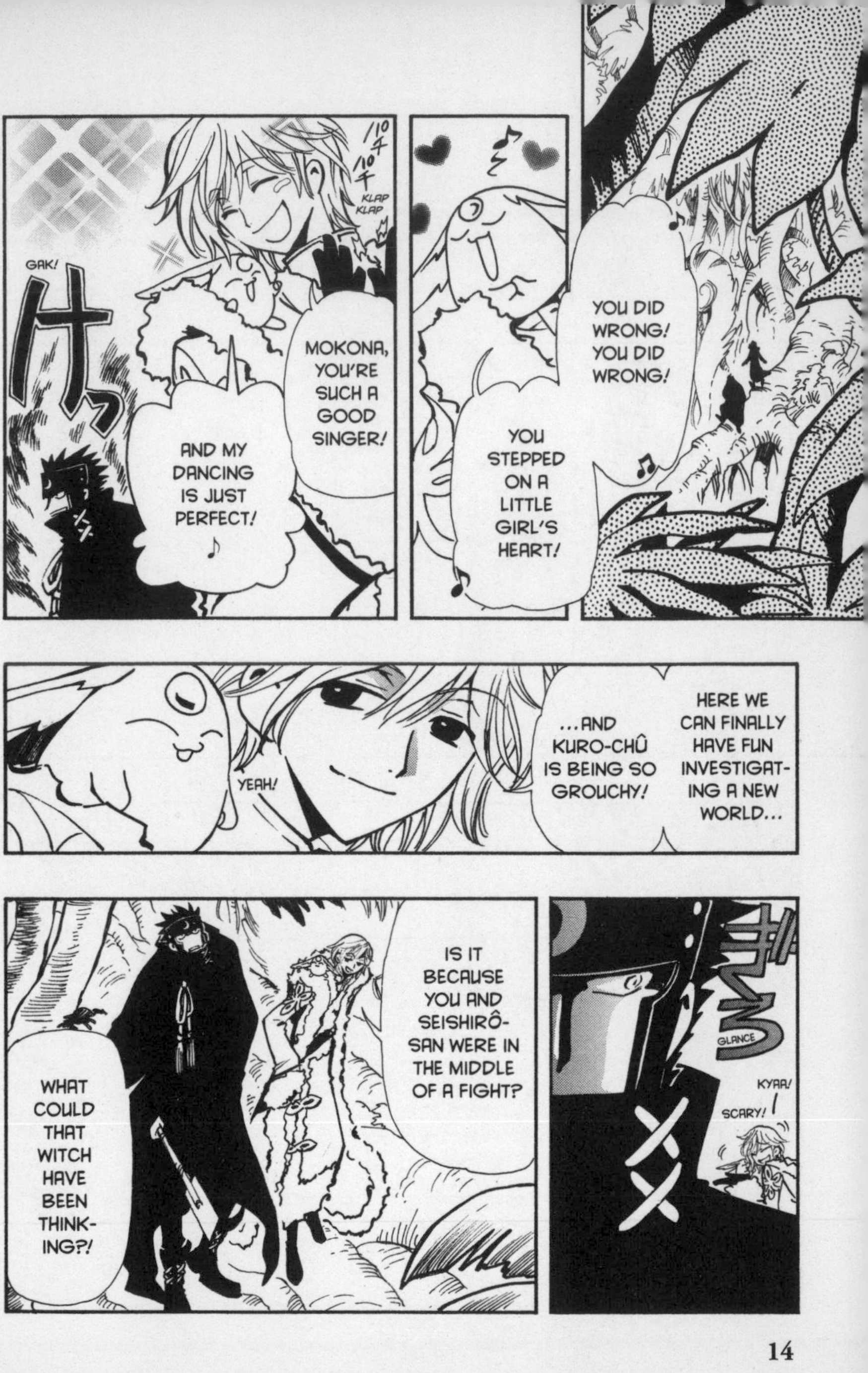
YOU DID WRONG! YOU DID WRONG!
YOU STEPPED ON A LITTLE GIRL'S HEART!
KLAP KLAP
MOKONA, YOU'RE SUCH A GOOD SINGER!
AND MY DANCING IS JUST PERFECT! ♪
GAK!
HERE WE CAN FINALLY HAVE FUN INVESTIGAT-ING A NEW WORLD...
...AND KURO-CHÛ IS BEING SO GROUCHY!
YEAH!
GLANCE
KYAA!
SCARY!
IS IT BECAUSE YOU AND SEISHIRÔ-SAN WERE IN THE MIDDLE OF A FIGHT?
WHAT COULD THAT WITCH HAVE BEEN THINK-ING?!

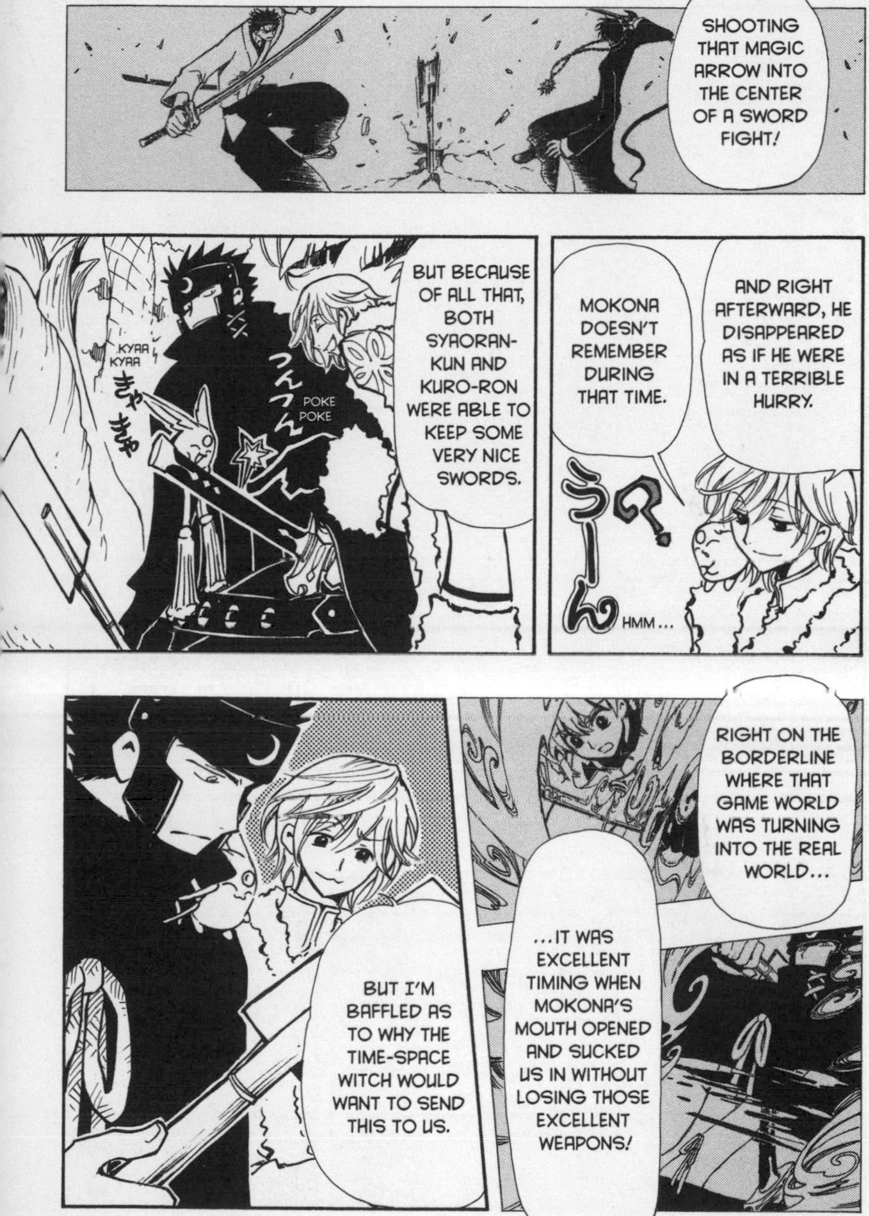
SHOOTING THAT MAGIC ARROW INTO THE CENTER OF A SWORD FIGHT!
AND RIGHT AFTERWARD, HE DISAPPEARED AS IF HE WERE IN A TERRIBLE HURRY.
MOKONA DOESN'T REMEMBER DURING THAT TIME.
うーん
HMM...
BUT BECAUSE OF ALL THAT, BOTH SYAORAN-KUN AND KURO-RON WERE ABLE TO KEEP SOME VERY NICE SWORDS.
つんつん
POKE POKE
きゃきゃ
KYAA KYAA
RIGHT ON THE BORDERLINE WHERE THAT GAME WORLD WAS TURNING INTO THE REAL WORLD...
...IT WAS EXCELLENT TIMING WHEN MOKONA'S MOUTH OPENED AND SUCKED US IN WITHOUT LOSING THOSE EXCELLENT WEAPONS!
BUT I'M BAFFLED AS TO WHY THE TIME-SPACE WITCH WOULD WANT TO SEND THIS TO US.

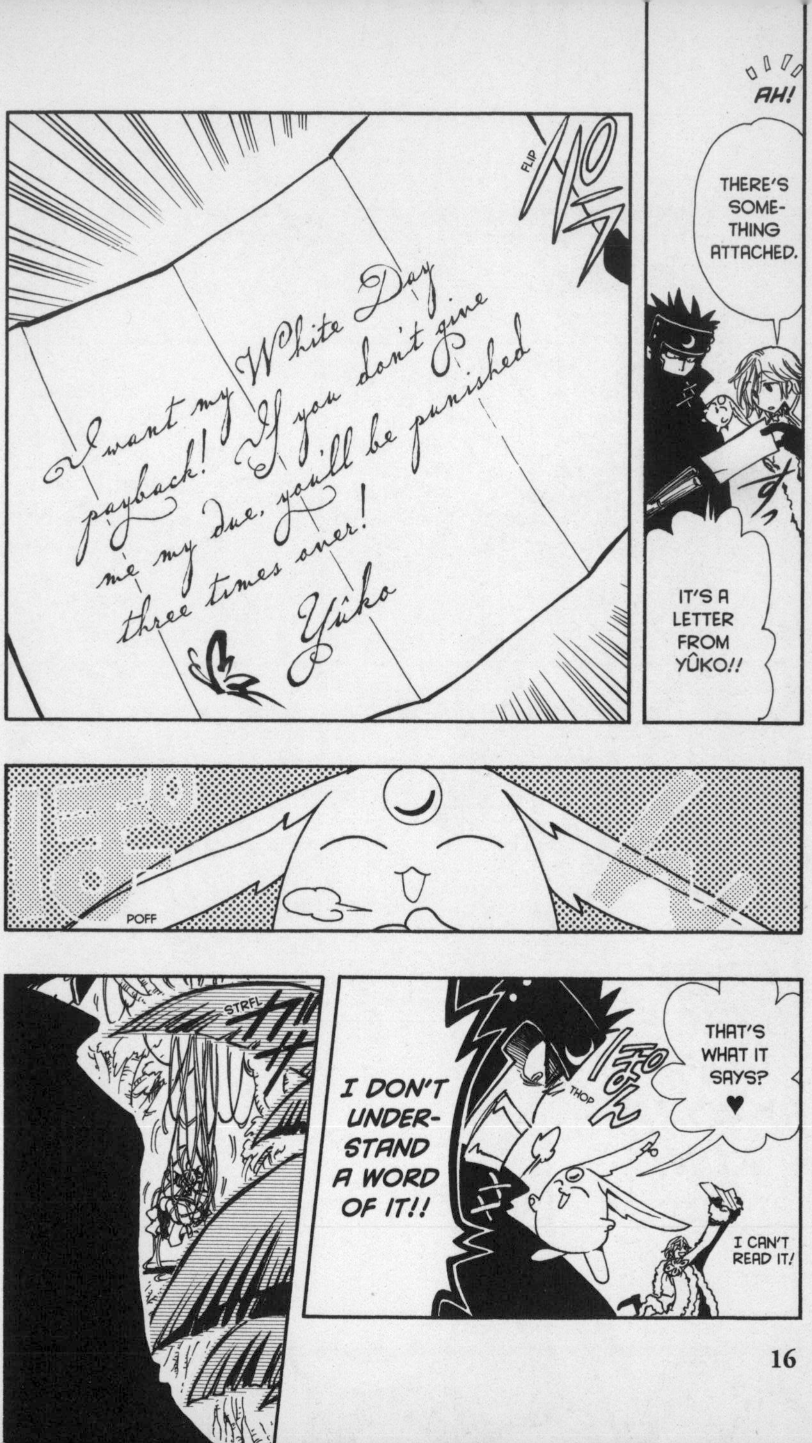
AH!
THERE'S SOME-THING ATTACHED.
IT'S A LETTER FROM YÛKO!!
FLIP
I want my White Day payback! If you don't give me my due, you'll be punished three times over!
Yûko
POFF
THAT'S WHAT IT SAYS? ♥
THOP
I DON'T UNDER-STAND A WORD OF IT!!
I CAN'T READ IT!
STRFL

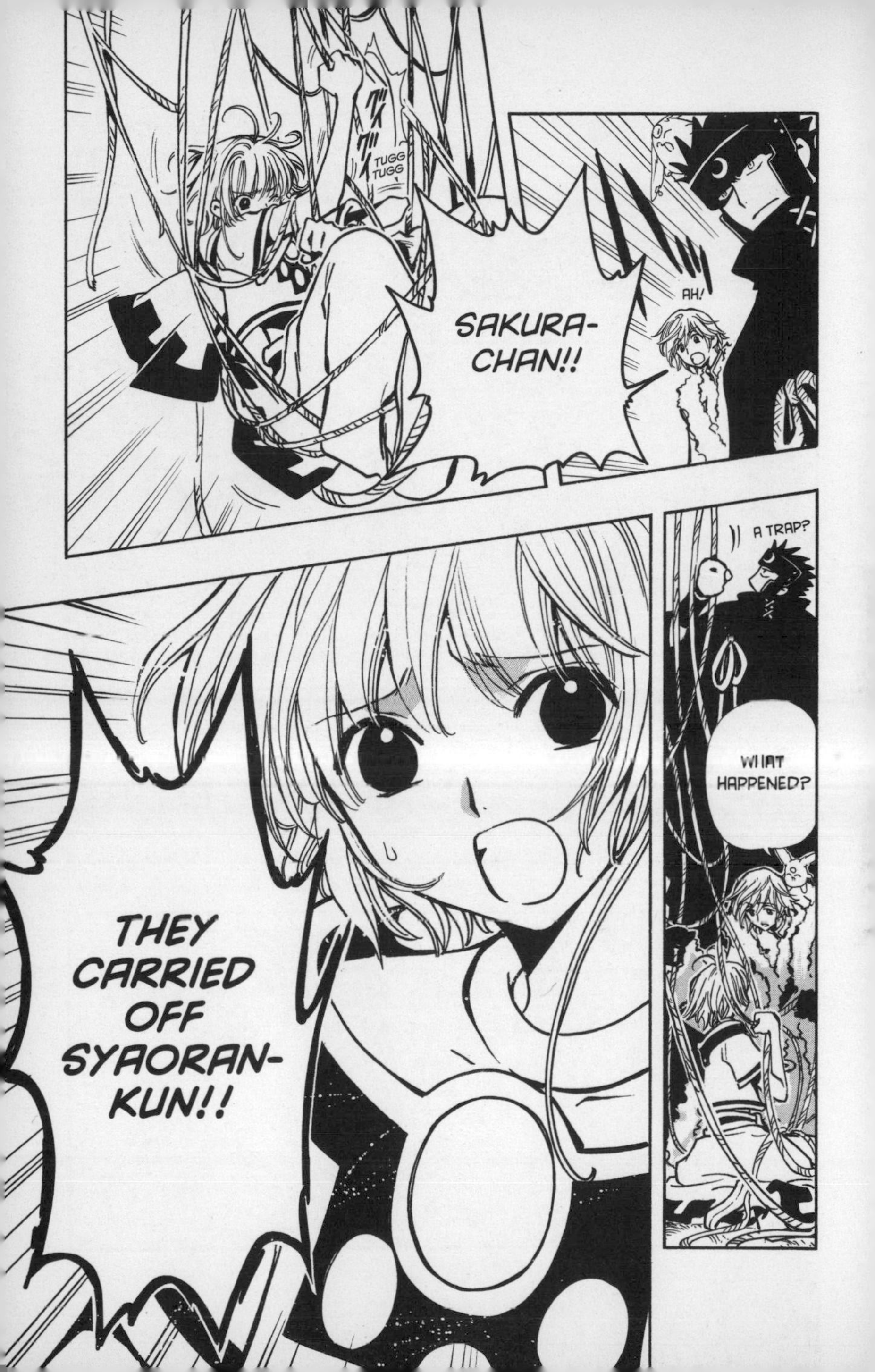
AH!
SAKURA-CHAN!!
TUGG TUGG
A TRAP?
WHAT HAPPENED?
THEY CARRIED OFF SYAORAN-KUN!!

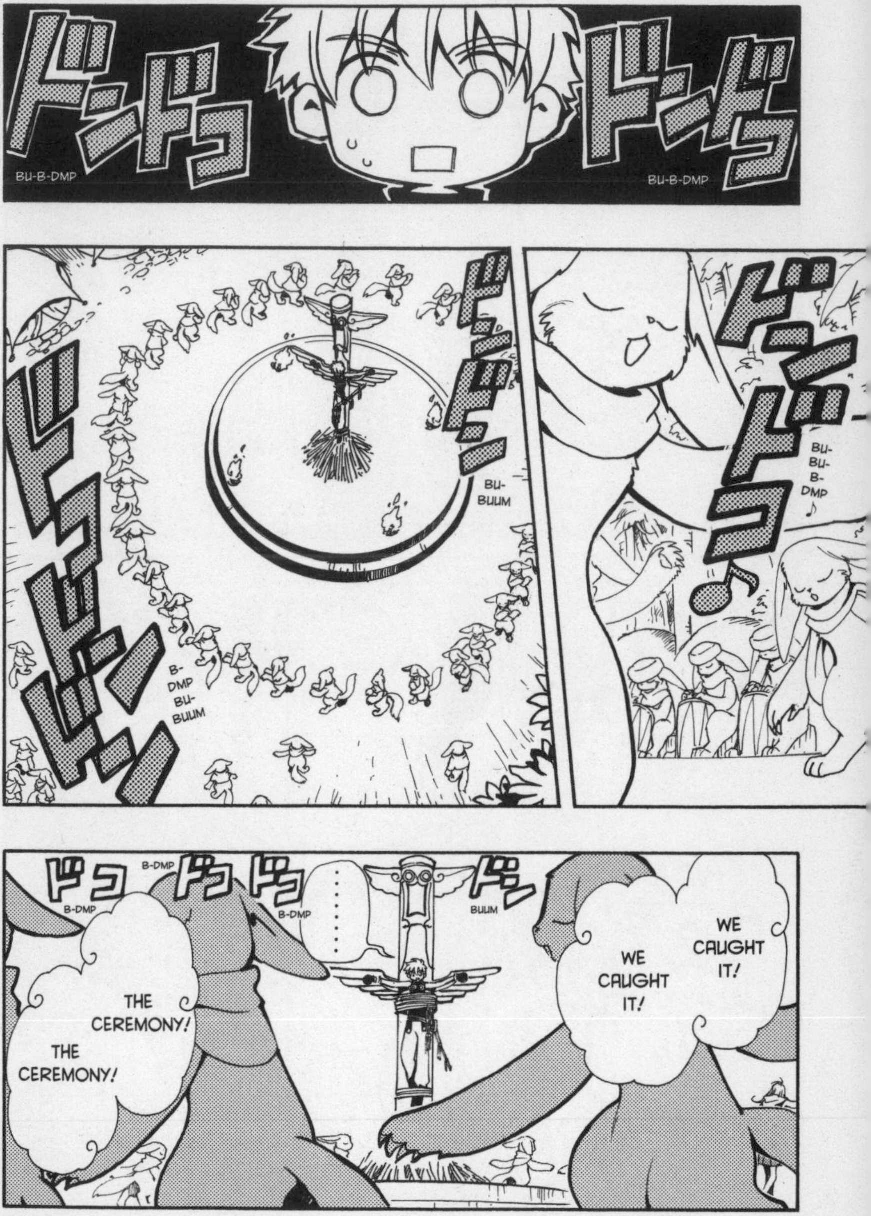
BU-B-DMP
BU-B-DMP
BU-BU-B-DMP ♪
BU-BUUM
B-DMP BU-BUUM
WE CAUGHT IT!
WE CAUGHT IT!
BUUM
......
B-DMP
B-DMP
THE CEREMONY!
THE CEREMONY!
B-DMP

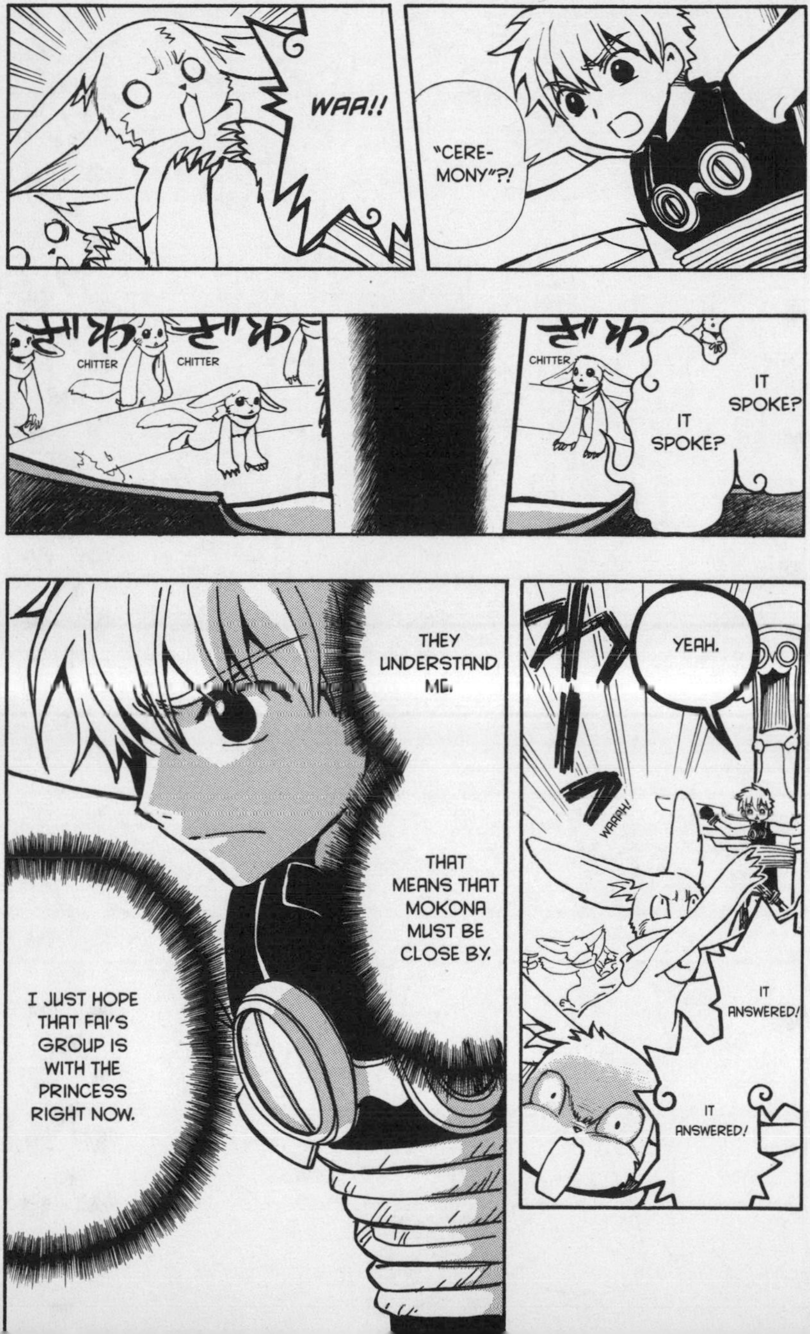
"CERE-MONY"?!
WAA!!
ざわ
IT SPOKE?
IT SPOKE?
CHITTER
ざわ ざわ
CHITTER
CHITTER
YEAH.
WAAAH!
IT ANSWERED!
IT ANSWERED!
THEY UNDERSTAND ME.
THAT MEANS THAT MOKONA MUST BE CLOSE BY.
I JUST HOPE THAT FAI'S GROUP IS WITH THE PRINCESS RIGHT NOW.

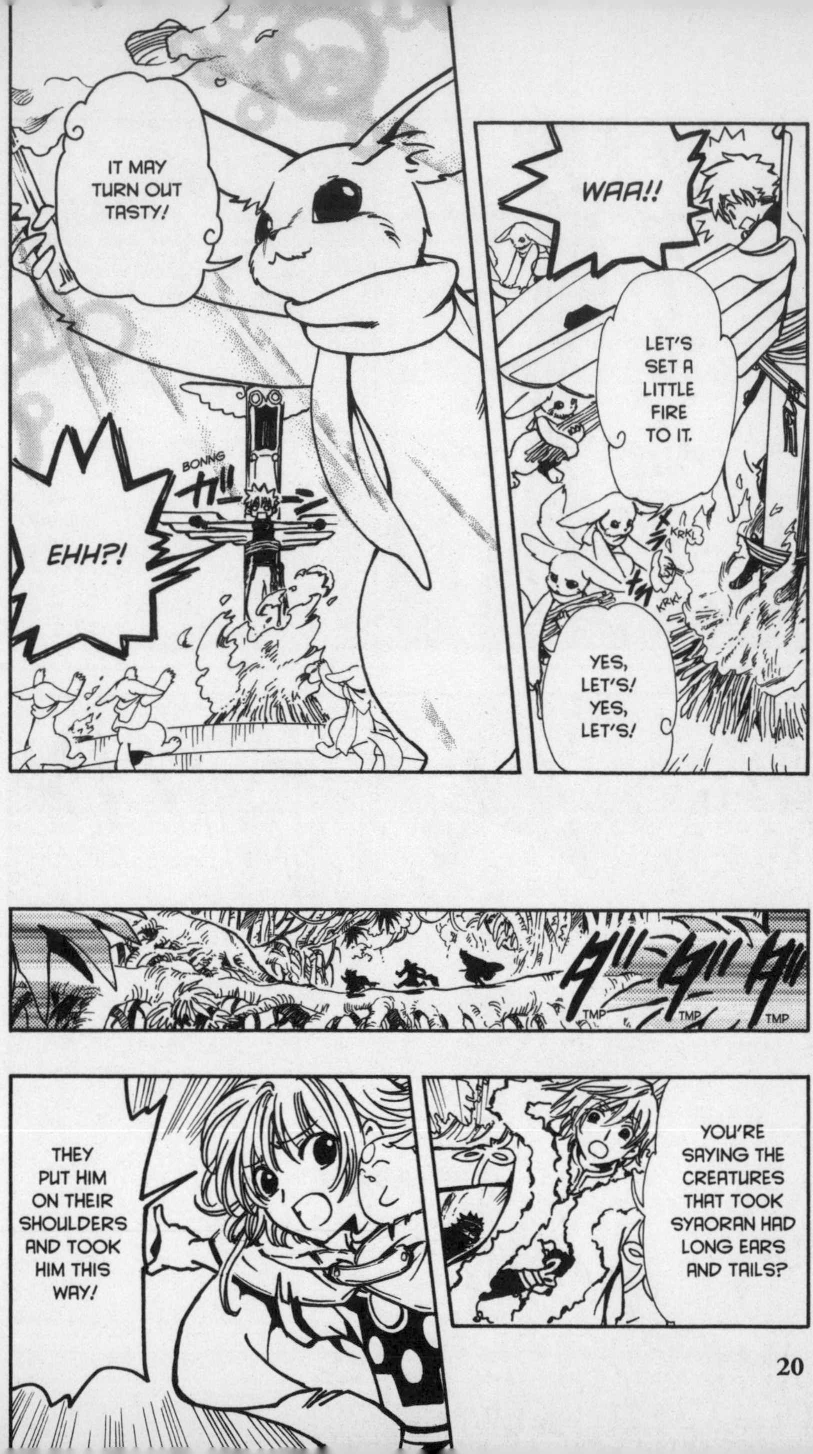
WAA!!
LET'S SET A LITTLE FIRE TO IT.
KRKL
KRKL
YES, LET'S! YES, LET'S!
IT MAY TURN OUT TASTY!
BONNG
EHH?!
TMP
TMP
TMP
YOU'RE SAYING THE CREATURES THAT TOOK SYAORAN HAD LONG EARS AND TAILS?
THEY PUT HIM ON THEIR SHOULDERS AND TOOK HIM THIS WAY!

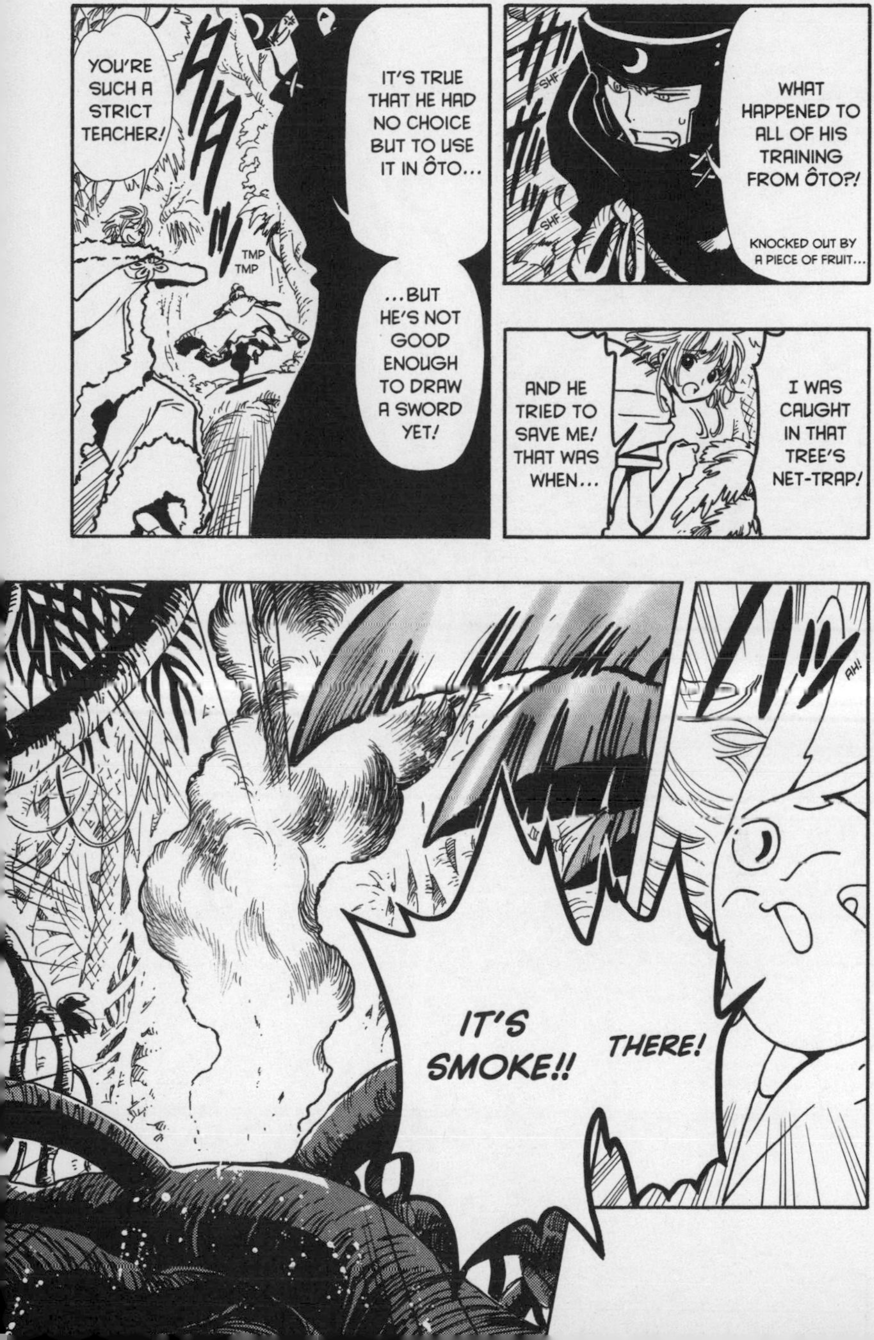
SHF
SHF
WHAT HAPPENED TO ALL OF HIS TRAINING FROM ÔTO?!
KNOCKED OUT BY A PIECE OF FRUIT...
I WAS CAUGHT IN THAT TREE'S NET-TRAP!
AND HE TRIED TO SAVE ME! THAT WAS WHEN...
IT'S TRUE THAT HE HAD NO CHOICE BUT TO USE IT IN ÔTO...
...BUT HE'S NOT GOOD ENOUGH TO DRAW A SWORD YET!
YOU'RE SUCH A STRICT TEACHER!
TMP TMP
AH!
THERE!
IT'S SMOKE!!

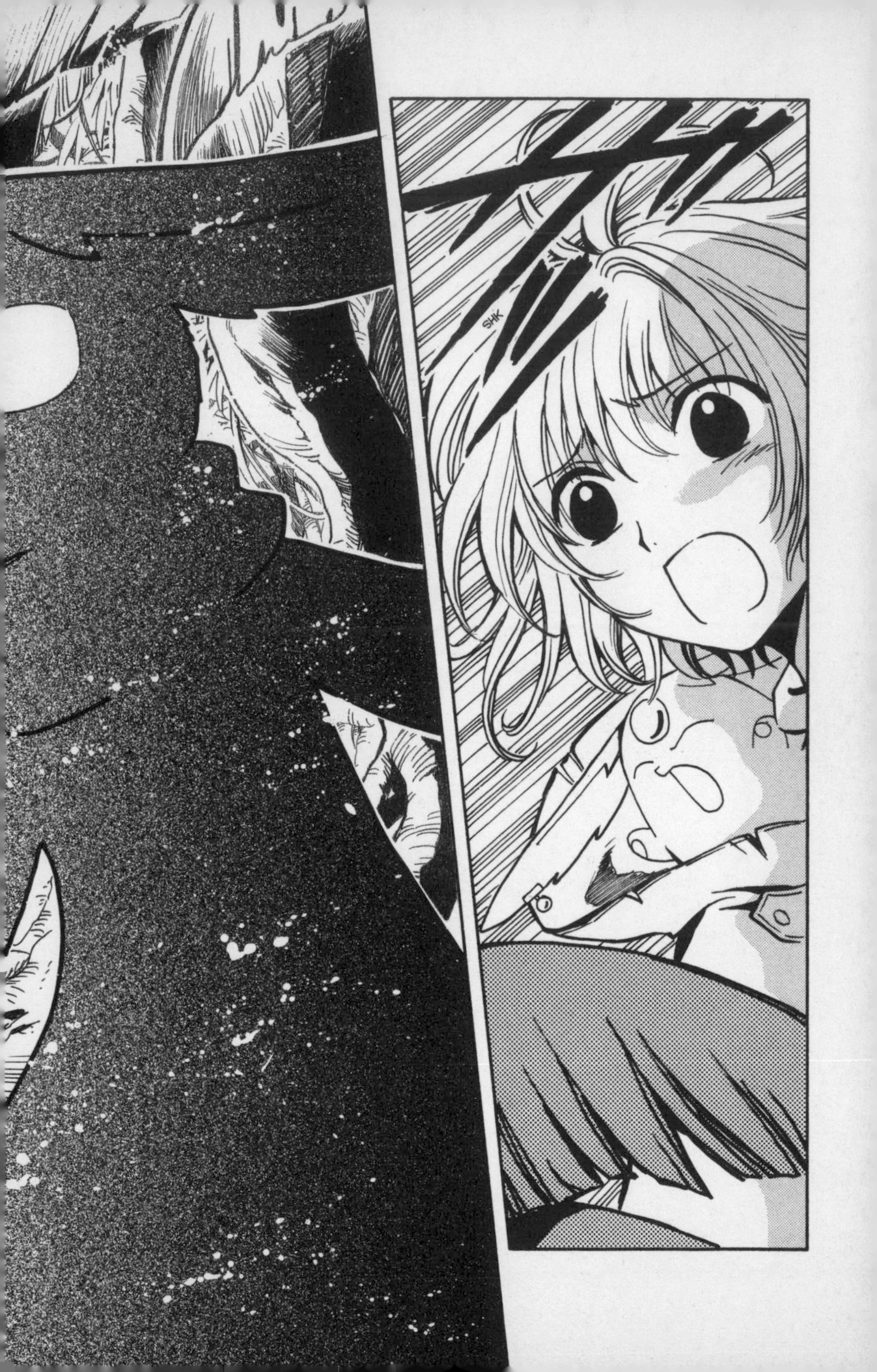
SHK

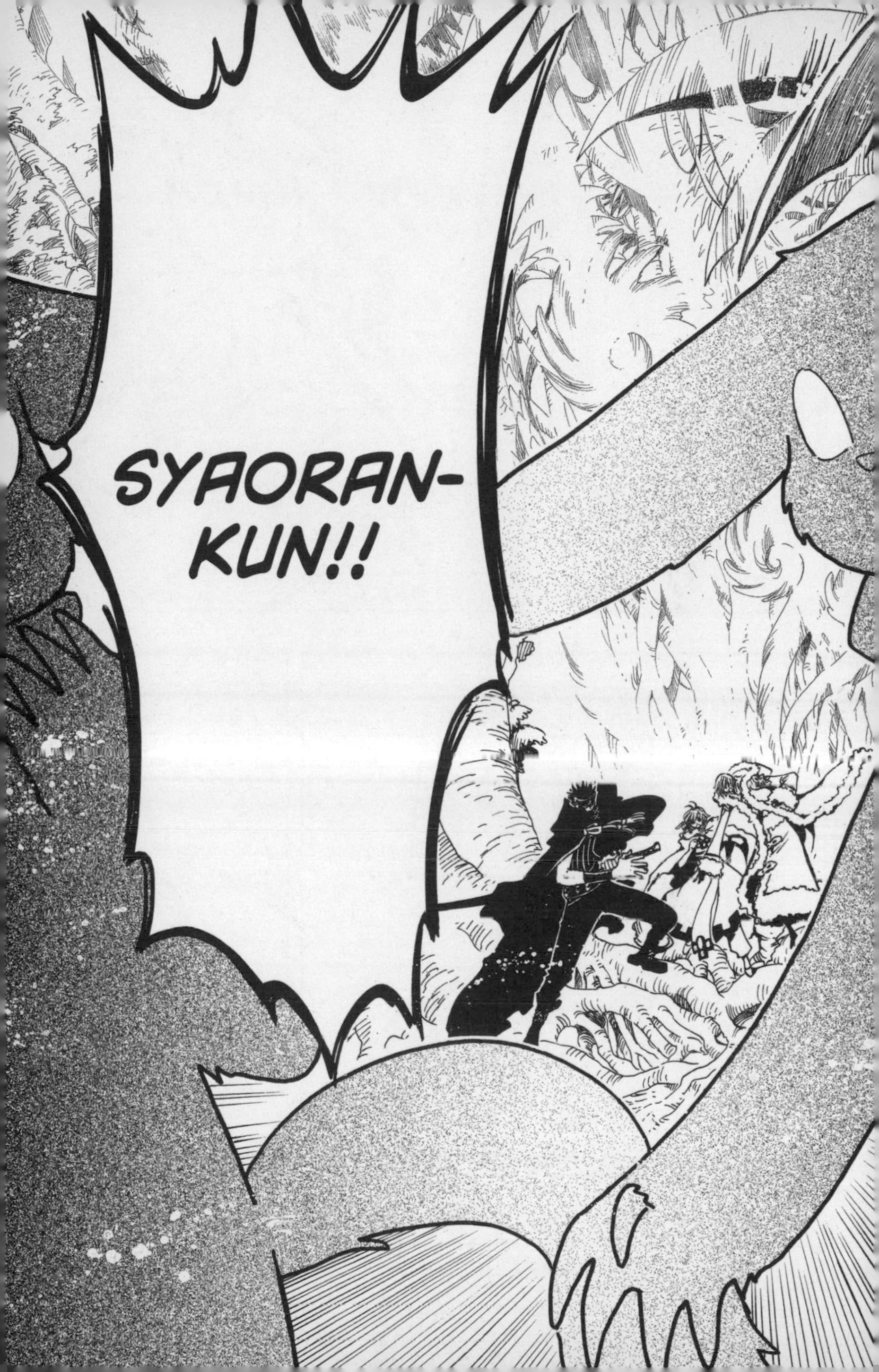
SYAORAN-KUN!!

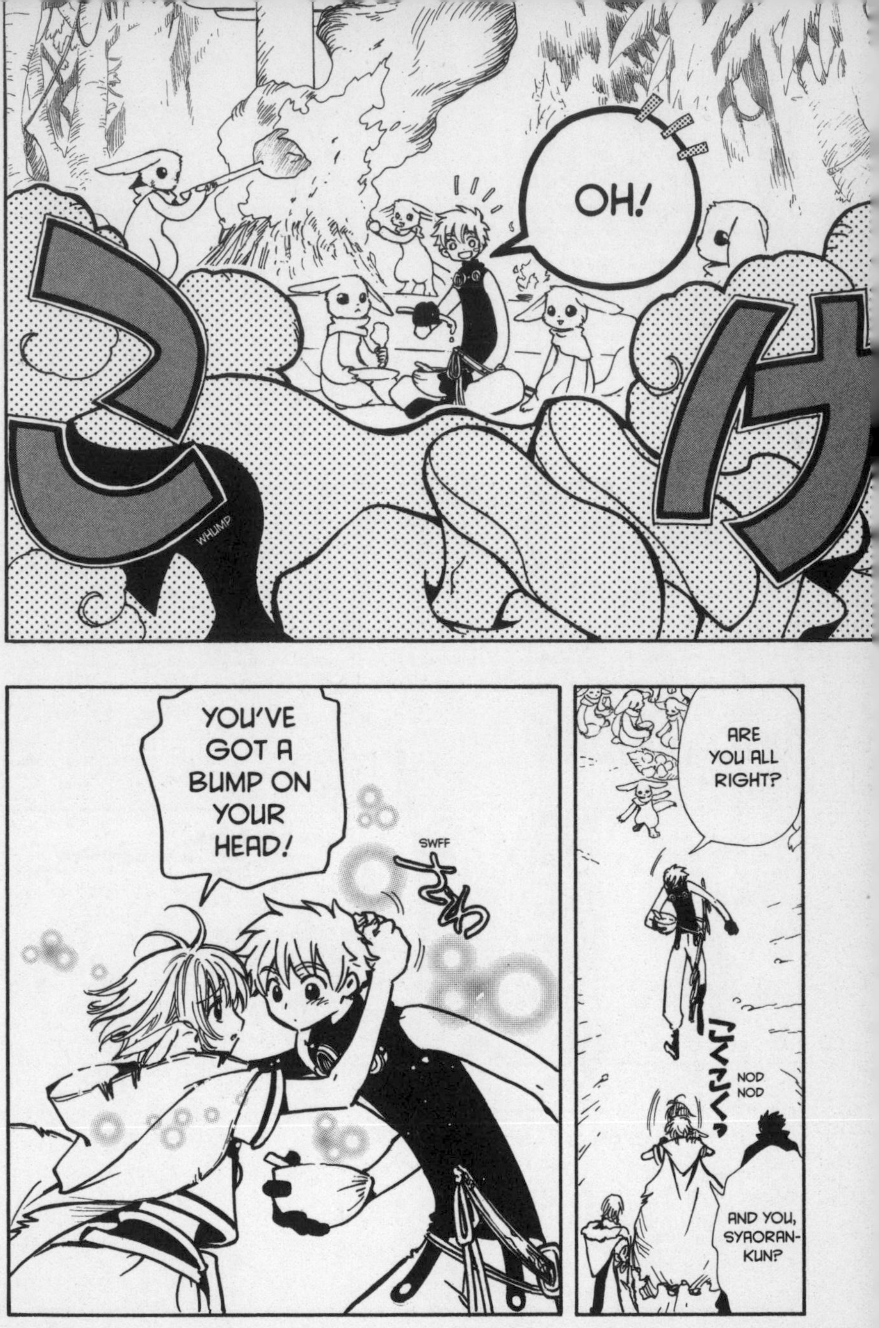
OH!
WHUMP
ARE YOU ALL RIGHT?
NOD NOD
AND YOU, SYAORAN-KUN?
YOU'VE GOT A BUMP ON YOUR HEAD!
SWFF

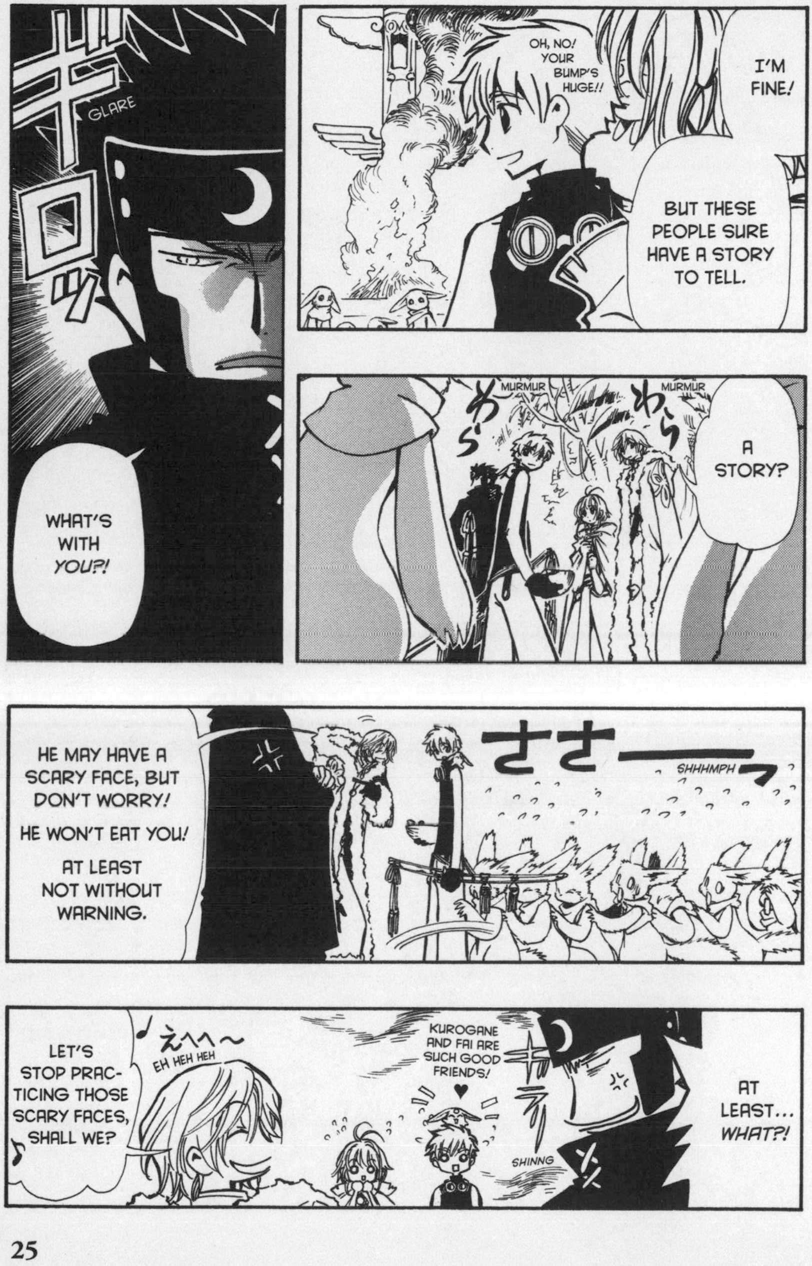
I'M FINE!
OH, NO! YOUR BUMP'S HUGE!!
BUT THESE PEOPLE SURE HAVE A STORY TO TELL.
わら
MURMUR
A STORY?
わら
MURMUR
ギロッ
GLARE
WHAT'S WITH *YOU?!*
さ さー
SHHHMPH
HE MAY HAVE A SCARY FACE, BUT DON'T WORRY!
HE WON'T EAT YOU!
AT LEAST NOT WITHOUT WARNING.
AT LEAST... *WHAT?!*
SHINNG
KUROGANE AND FAI ARE SUCH GOOD FRIENDS!
えへへ～
EH HEH HEH
LET'S STOP PRACTICING THOSE SCARY FACES, SHALL WE?

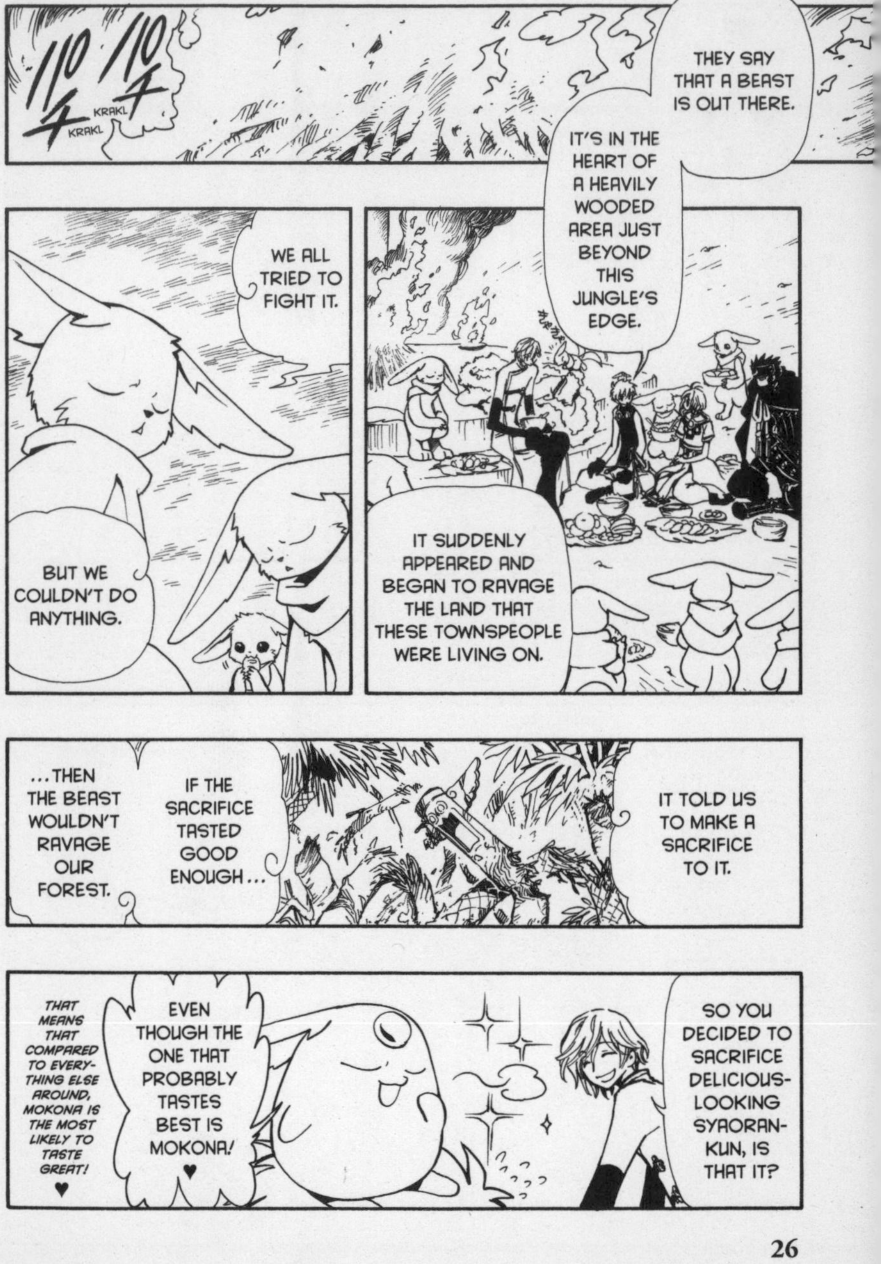
THEY SAY THAT A BEAST IS OUT THERE.
KRAKL
KRAKL
IT'S IN THE HEART OF A HEAVILY WOODED AREA JUST BEYOND THIS JUNGLE'S EDGE.
IT SUDDENLY APPEARED AND BEGAN TO RAVAGE THE LAND THAT THESE TOWNSPEOPLE WERE LIVING ON.
WE ALL TRIED TO FIGHT IT.
BUT WE COULDN'T DO ANYTHING.
IT TOLD US TO MAKE A SACRIFICE TO IT.
IF THE SACRIFICE TASTED GOOD ENOUGH...
...THEN THE BEAST WOULDN'T RAVAGE OUR FOREST.
SO YOU DECIDED TO SACRIFICE DELICIOUS-LOOKING SYAORAN-KUN, IS THAT IT?
EVEN THOUGH THE ONE THAT PROBABLY TASTES BEST IS MOKONA! ♥
THAT MEANS THAT COMPARED TO EVERY-THING ELSE AROUND, MOKONA IS THE MOST LIKELY TO TASTE GREAT! ♥

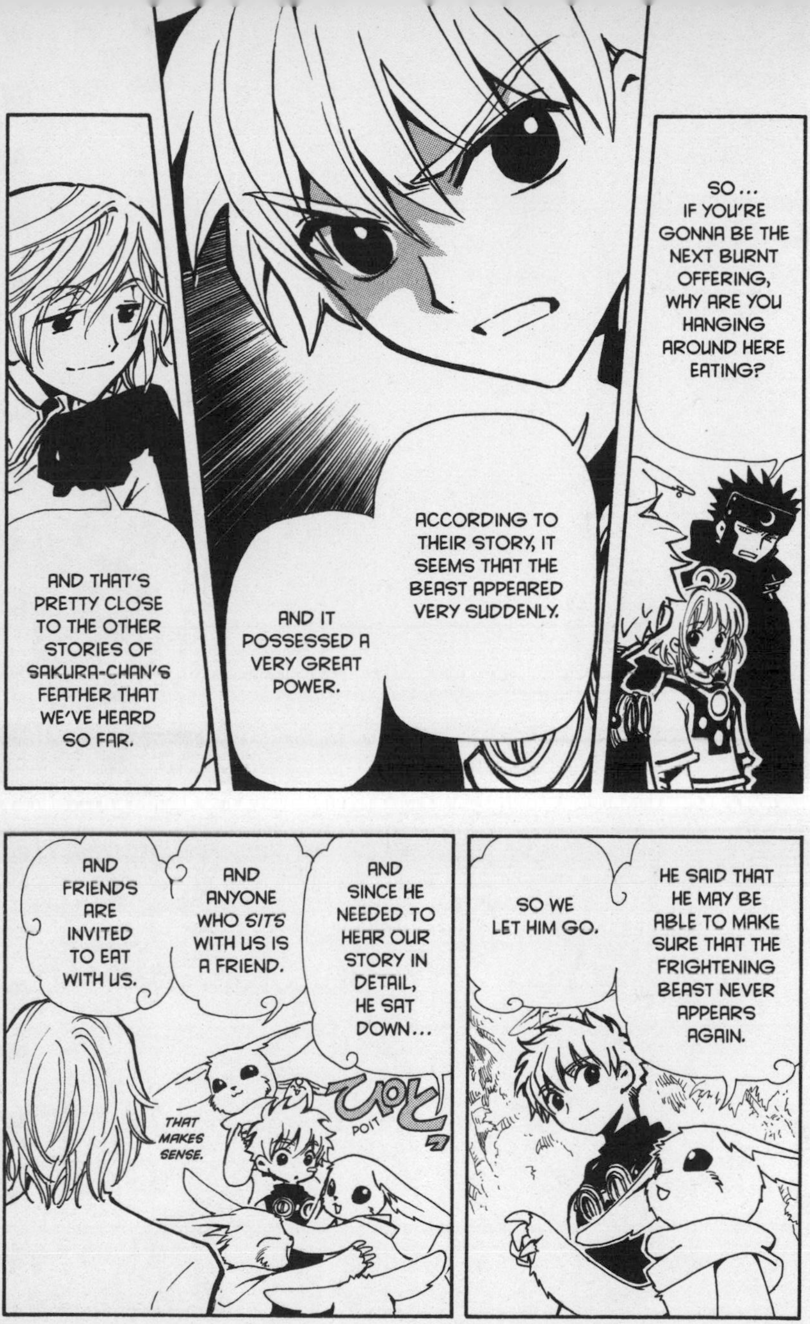
SO... IF YOU'RE GONNA BE THE NEXT BURNT OFFERING, WHY ARE YOU HANGING AROUND HERE EATING?
ACCORDING TO THEIR STORY, IT SEEMS THAT THE BEAST APPEARED VERY SUDDENLY.
AND IT POSSESSED A VERY GREAT POWER.
AND THAT'S PRETTY CLOSE TO THE OTHER STORIES OF SAKURA-CHAN'S FEATHER THAT WE'VE HEARD SO FAR.
HE SAID THAT HE MAY BE ABLE TO MAKE SURE THAT THE FRIGHTENING BEAST NEVER APPEARS AGAIN.
SO WE LET HIM GO.
AND SINCE HE NEEDED TO HEAR OUR STORY IN DETAIL, HE SAT DOWN...
AND ANYONE WHO *SITS* WITH US IS A FRIEND.
AND FRIENDS ARE INVITED TO EAT WITH US.
POIT
THAT MAKES SENSE.

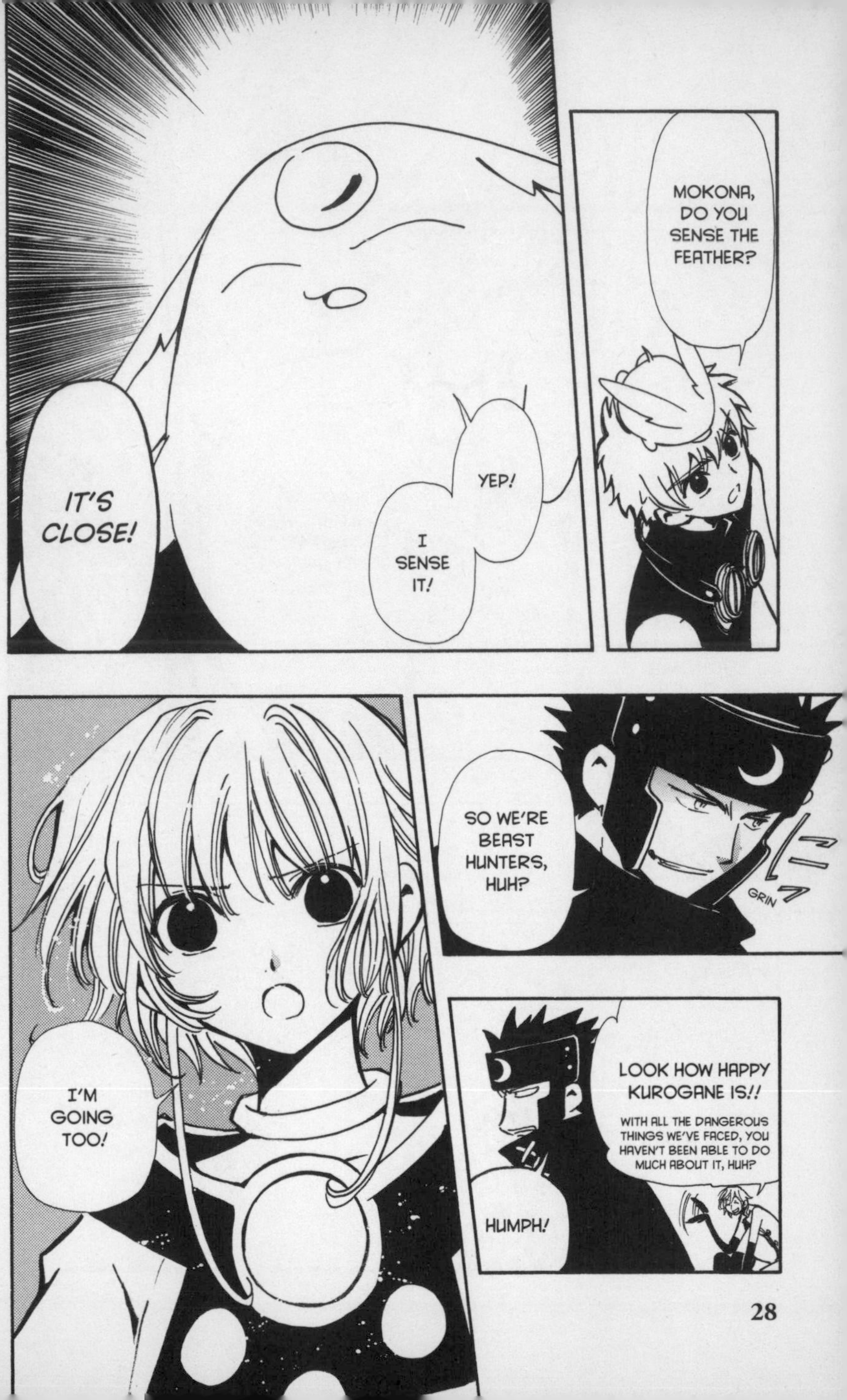
MOKONA, DO YOU SENSE THE FEATHER?
YEP!
I SENSE IT!
IT'S CLOSE!
SO WE'RE BEAST HUNTERS, HUH?
GRIN
LOOK HOW HAPPY KUROGANE IS!!
WITH ALL THE DANGEROUS THINGS WE'VE FACED, YOU HAVEN'T BEEN ABLE TO DO MUCH ABOUT IT, HUH?
HUMPH!
I'M GOING TOO!

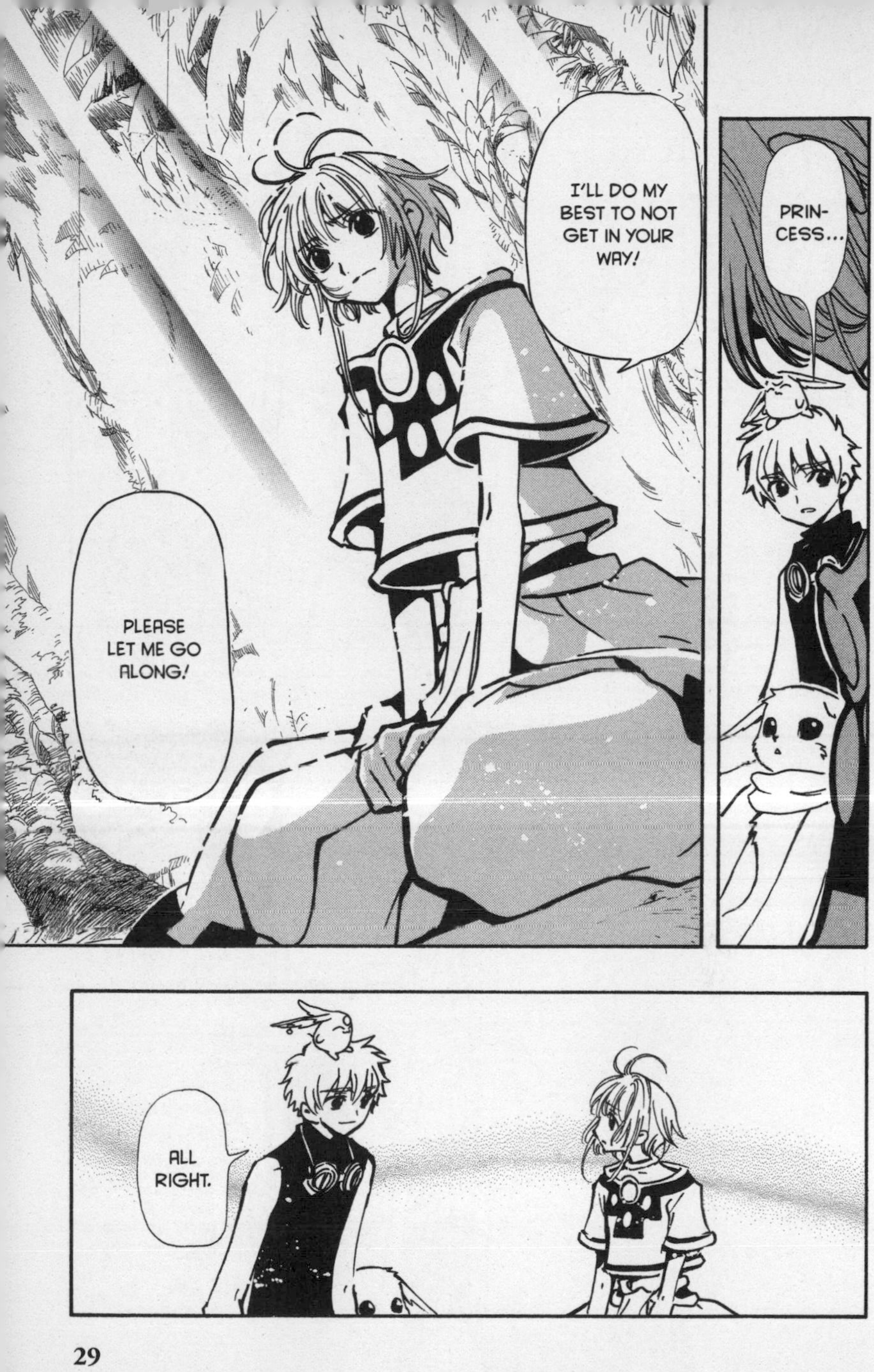
PRIN-CESS...
I'LL DO MY BEST TO NOT GET IN YOUR WAY!
PLEASE LET ME GO ALONG!
ALL RIGHT.

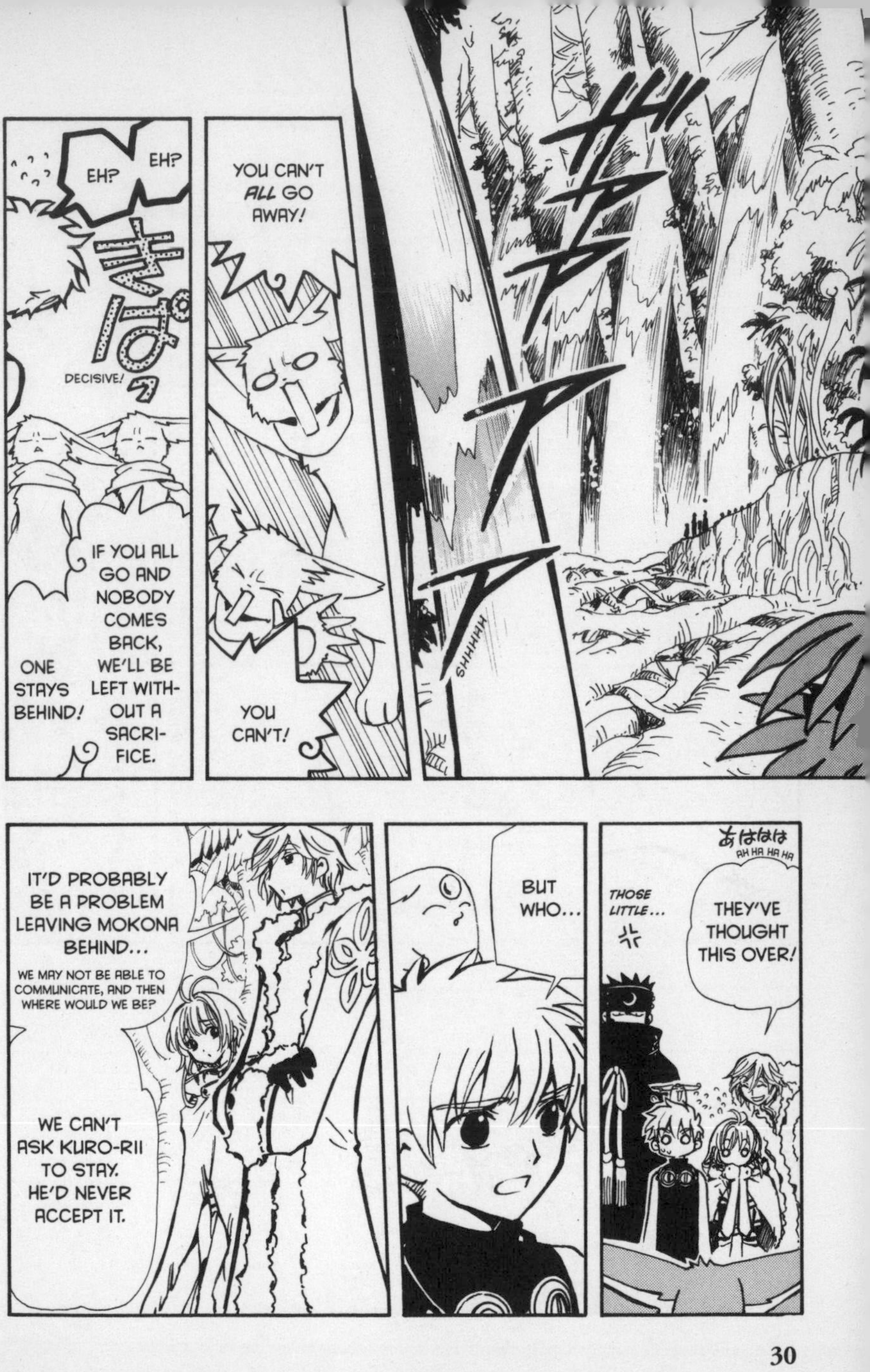
SHHHHH
YOU CAN'T ALL GO AWAY!
YOU CAN'T!
EH?
EH?
きぱっ
DECISIVE!
IF YOU ALL GO AND NOBODY COMES BACK, WE'LL BE LEFT WITH-OUT A SACRI-FICE.
ONE STAYS BEHIND!
あははは
AH HA HA HA
THEY'VE THOUGHT THIS OVER!
THOSE LITTLE...
BUT WHO...
IT'D PROBABLY BE A PROBLEM LEAVING MOKONA BEHIND...
WE MAY NOT BE ABLE TO COMMUNICATE, AND THEN WHERE WOULD WE BE?
WE CAN'T ASK KURO-RII TO STAY. HE'D NEVER ACCEPT IT.

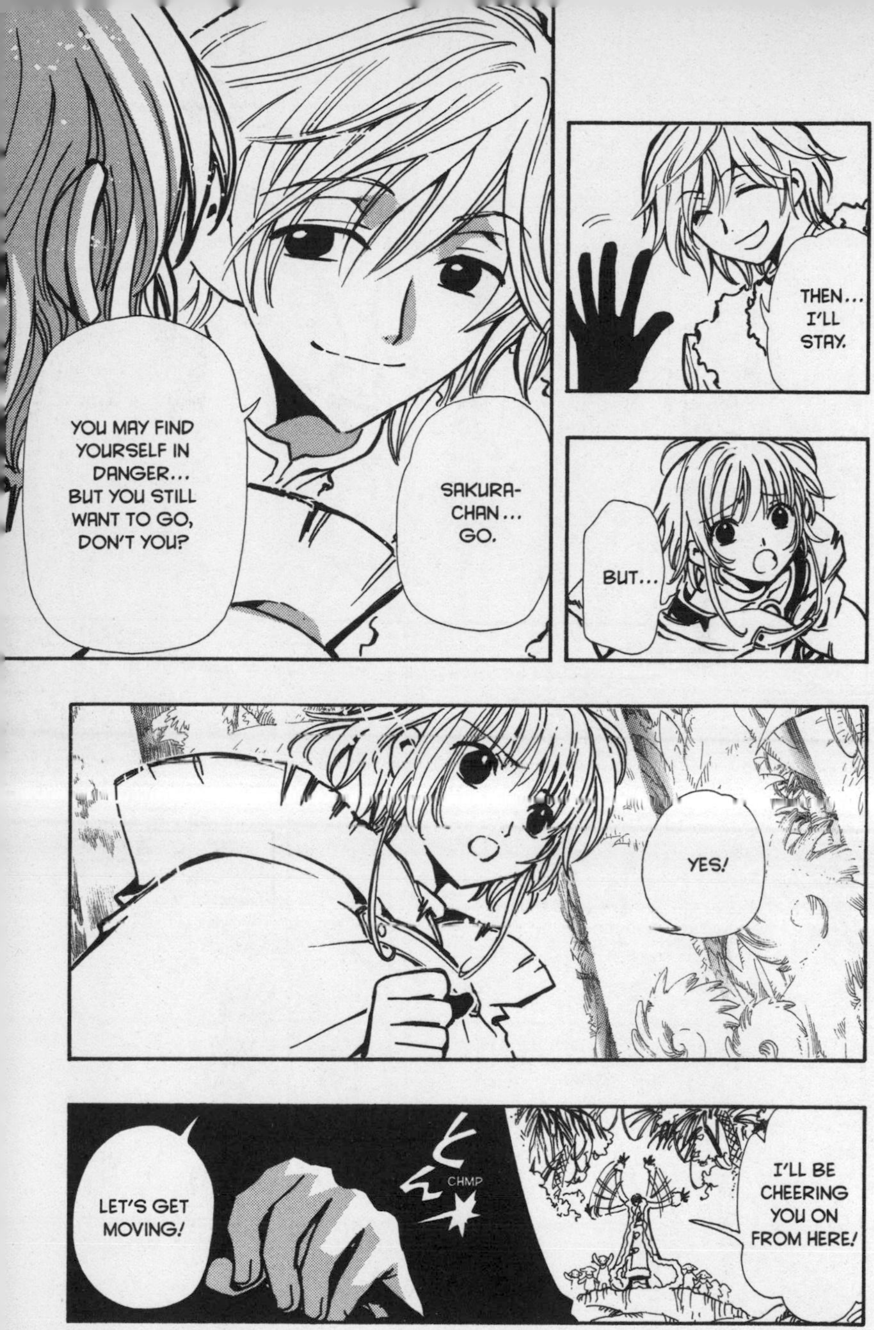
THEN... I'LL STAY.
BUT...
SAKURA-CHAN... GO.
YOU MAY FIND YOURSELF IN DANGER... BUT YOU STILL WANT TO GO, DON'T YOU?
YES!
I'LL BE CHEERING YOU ON FROM HERE!
CHMP
LET'S GET MOVING!

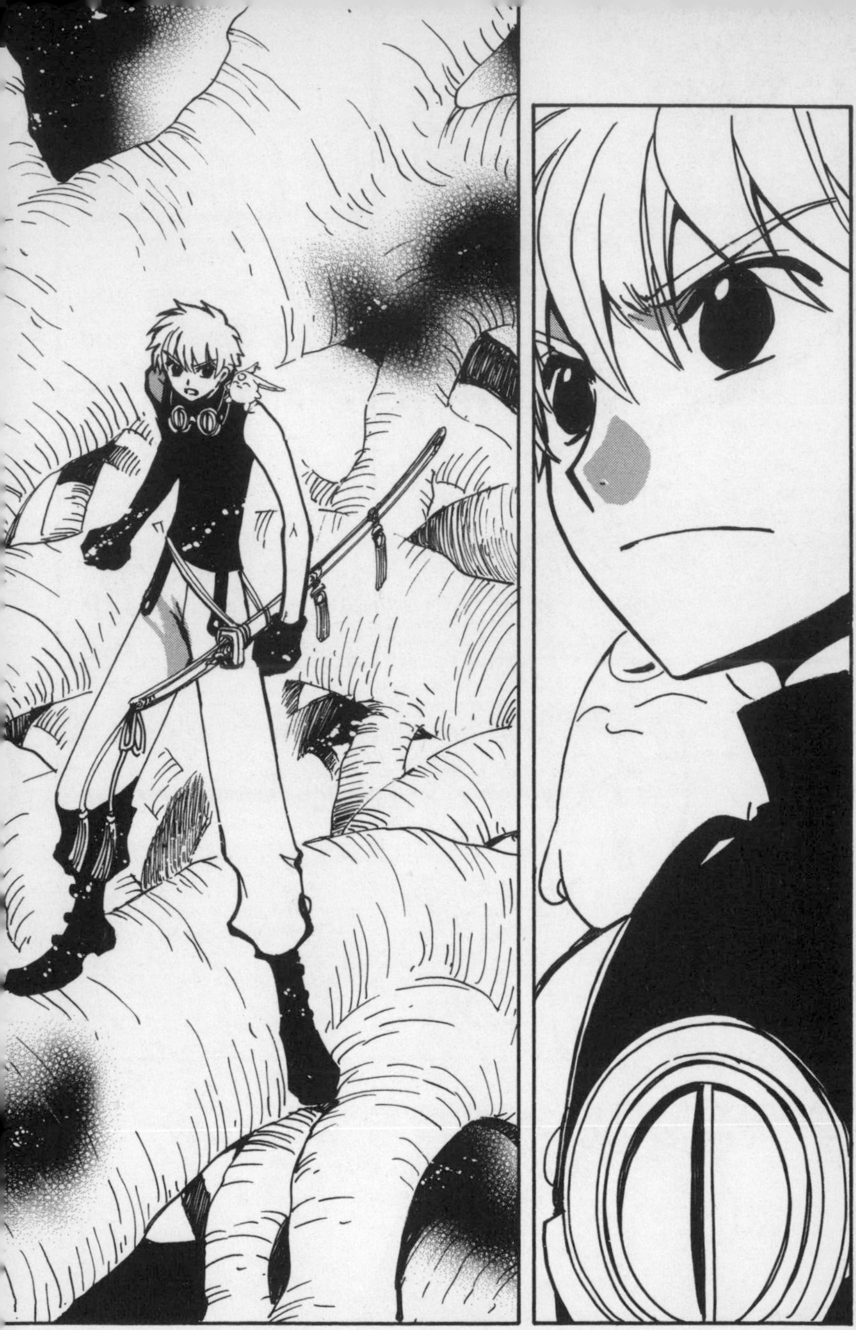

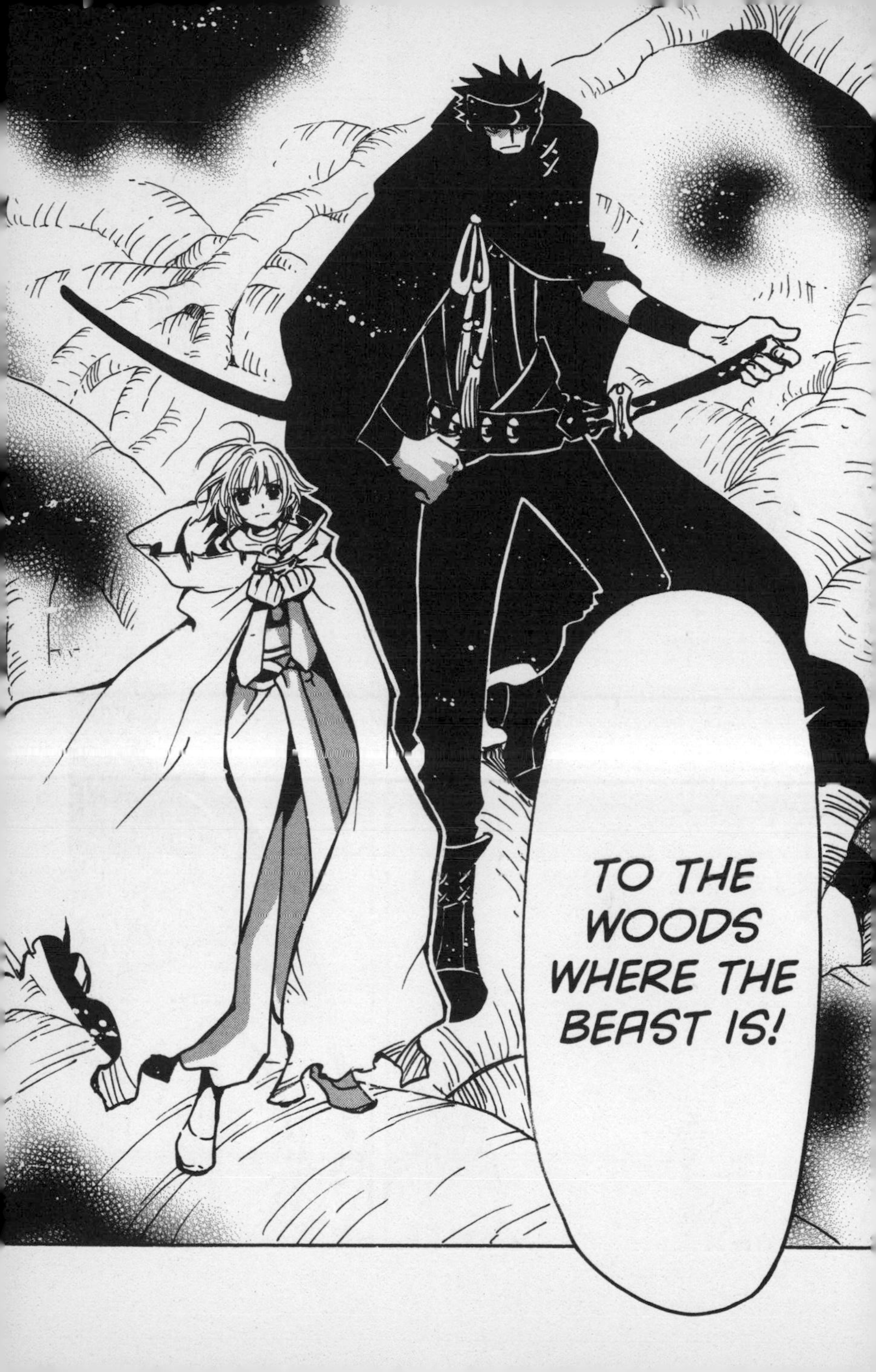
TO THE WOODS WHERE THE BEAST IS!

ツバサ

RESERVoir CHRoNiCLE

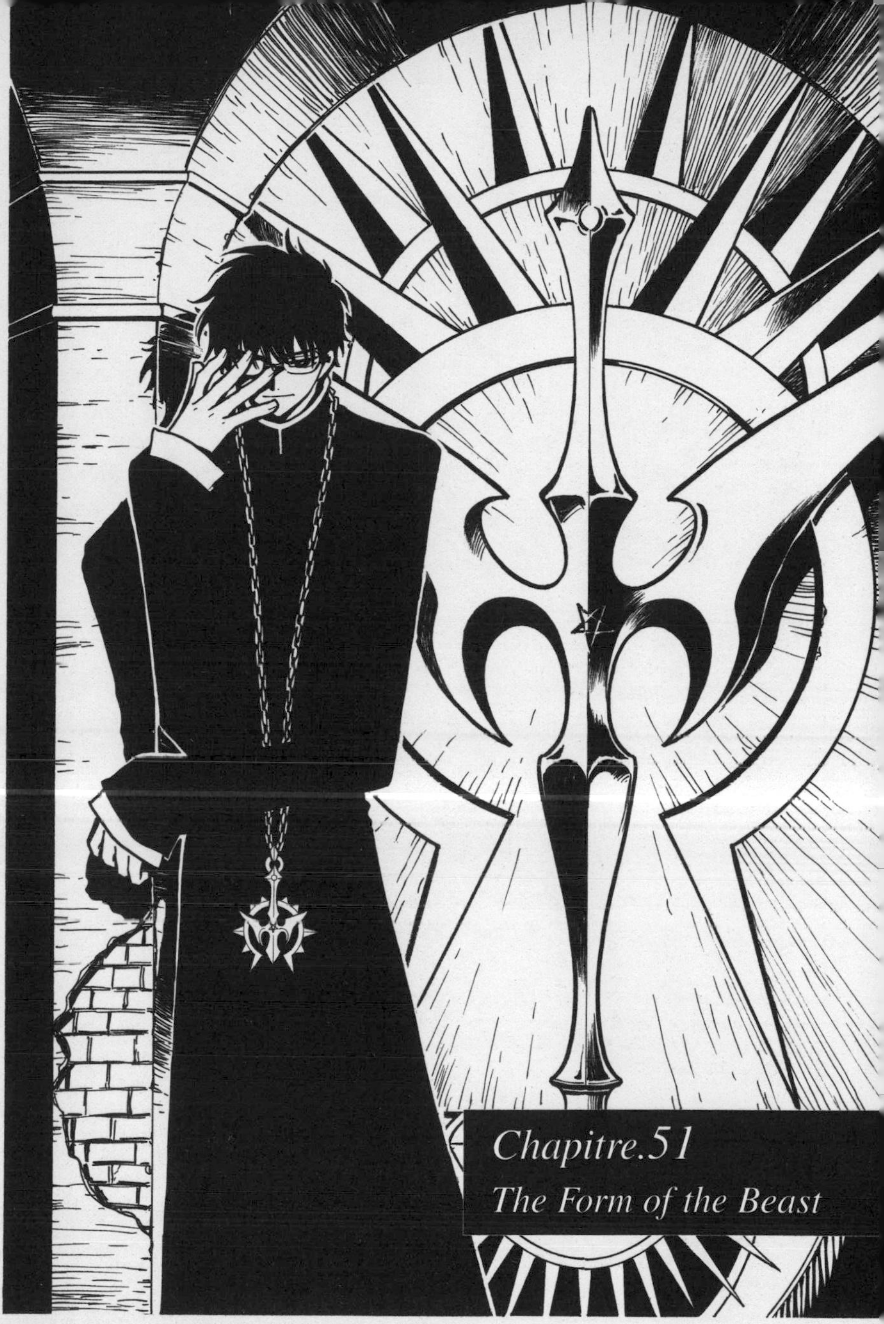
Chapitre.51
The Form of the Beast

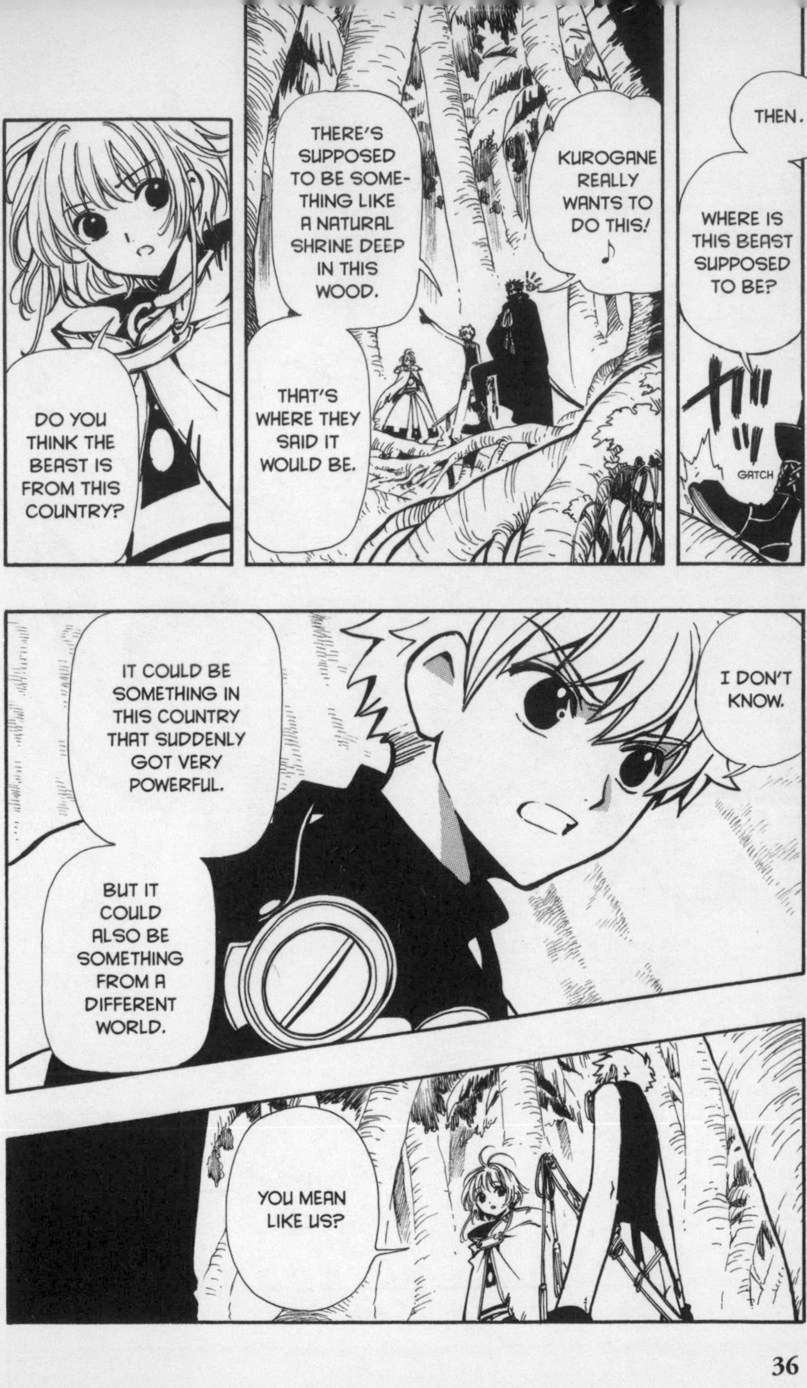
THEN...
WHERE IS THIS BEAST SUPPOSED TO BE?
GATCH
KUROGANE REALLY WANTS TO DO THIS! ♪
THERE'S SUPPOSED TO BE SOME-THING LIKE A NATURAL SHRINE DEEP IN THIS WOOD.
THAT'S WHERE THEY SAID IT WOULD BE.
DO YOU THINK THE BEAST IS FROM THIS COUNTRY?
I DON'T KNOW.
IT COULD BE SOMETHING IN THIS COUNTRY THAT SUDDENLY GOT VERY POWERFUL.
BUT IT COULD ALSO BE SOMETHING FROM A DIFFERENT WORLD.
YOU MEAN LIKE US?

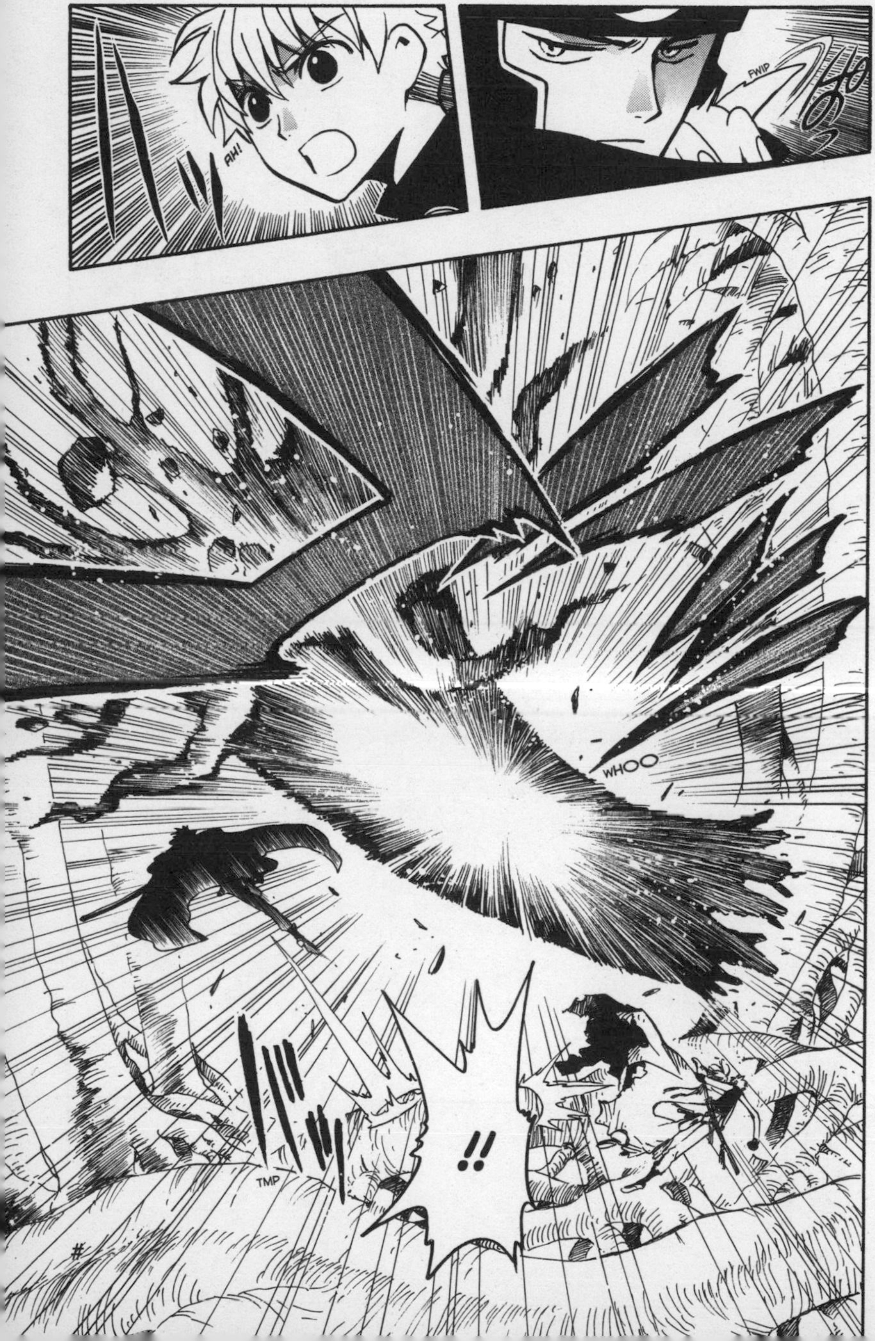
FWIP
AH!
WHOO
TMP
!!

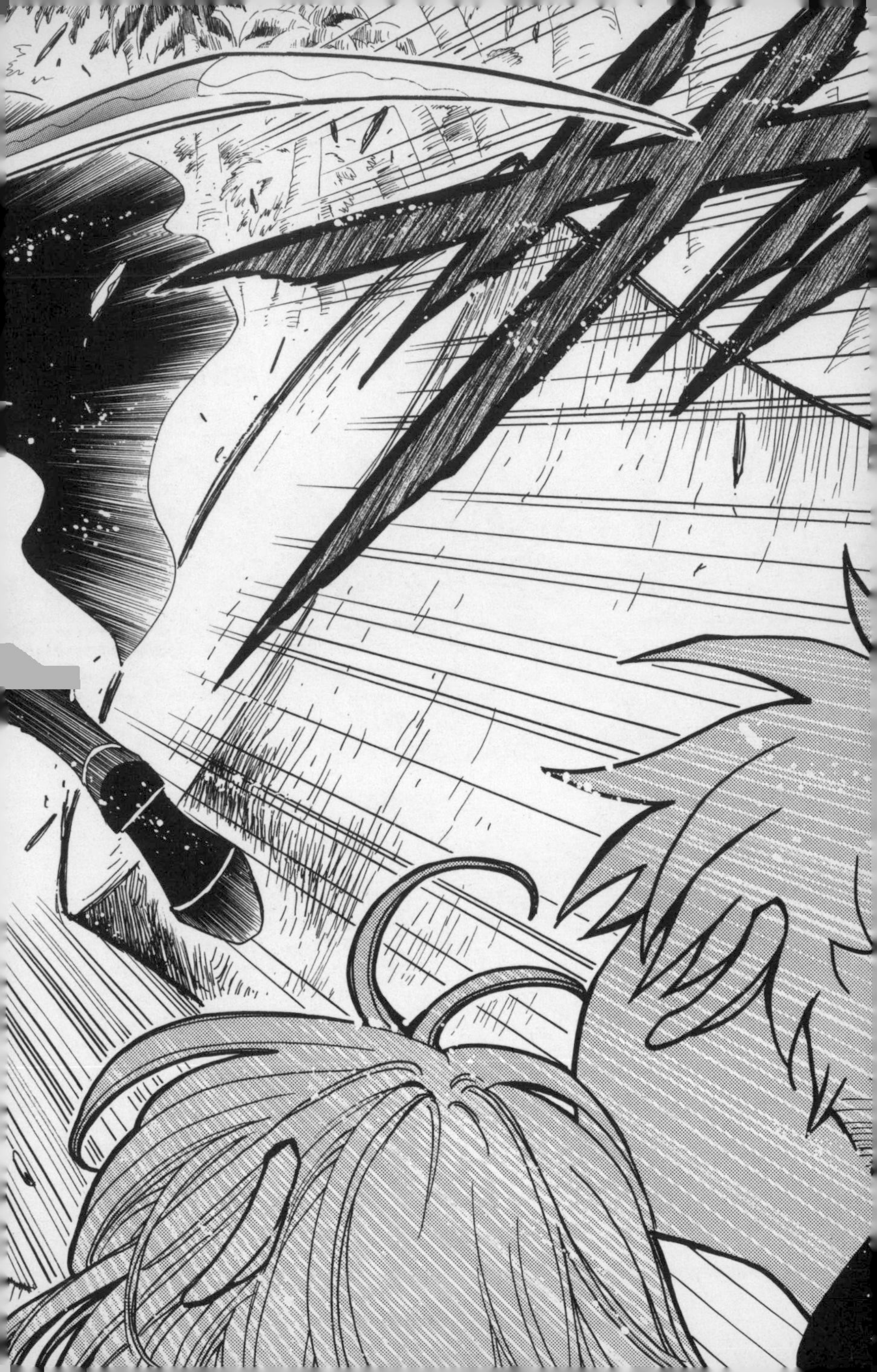

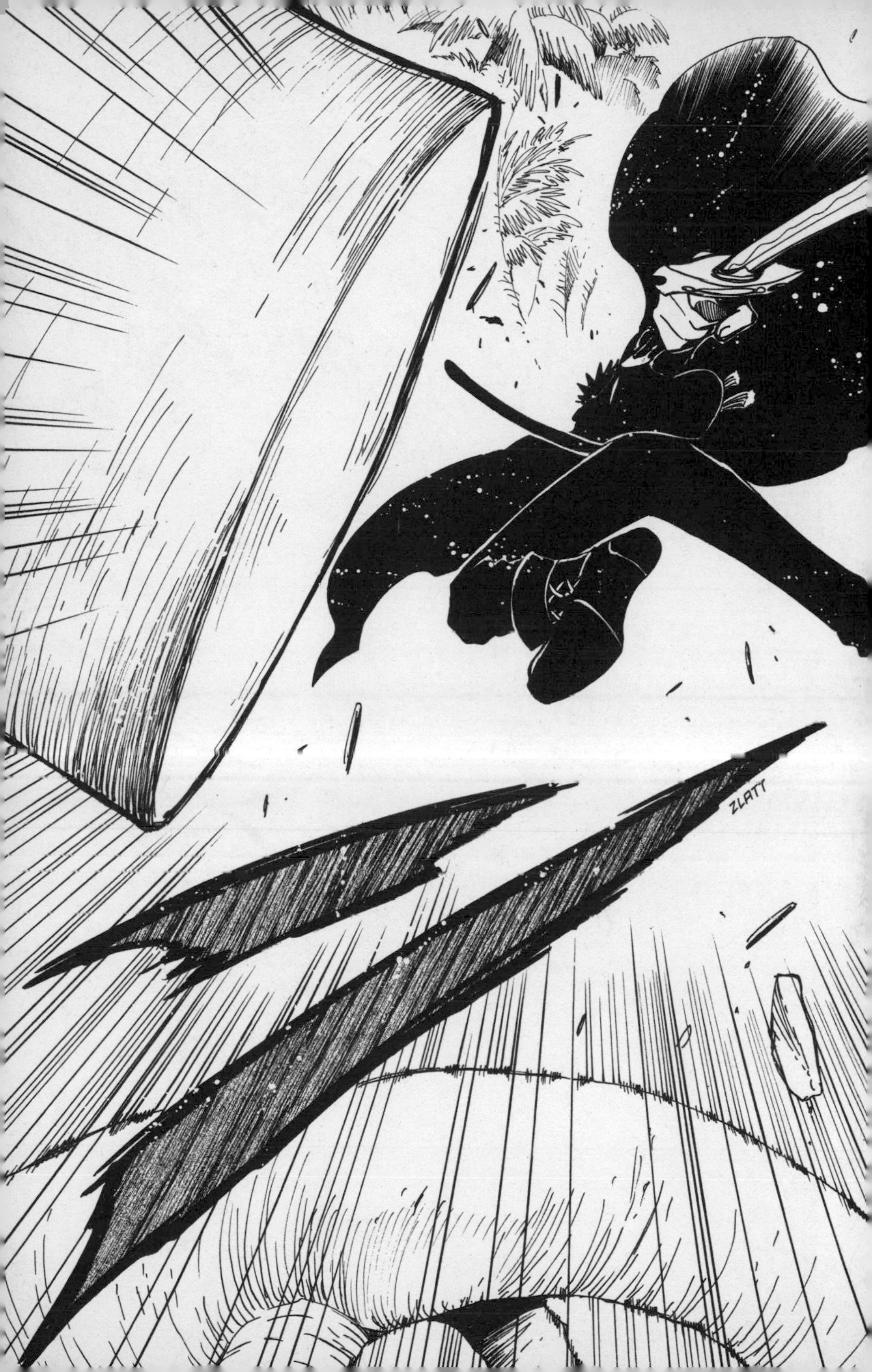
ZLATT

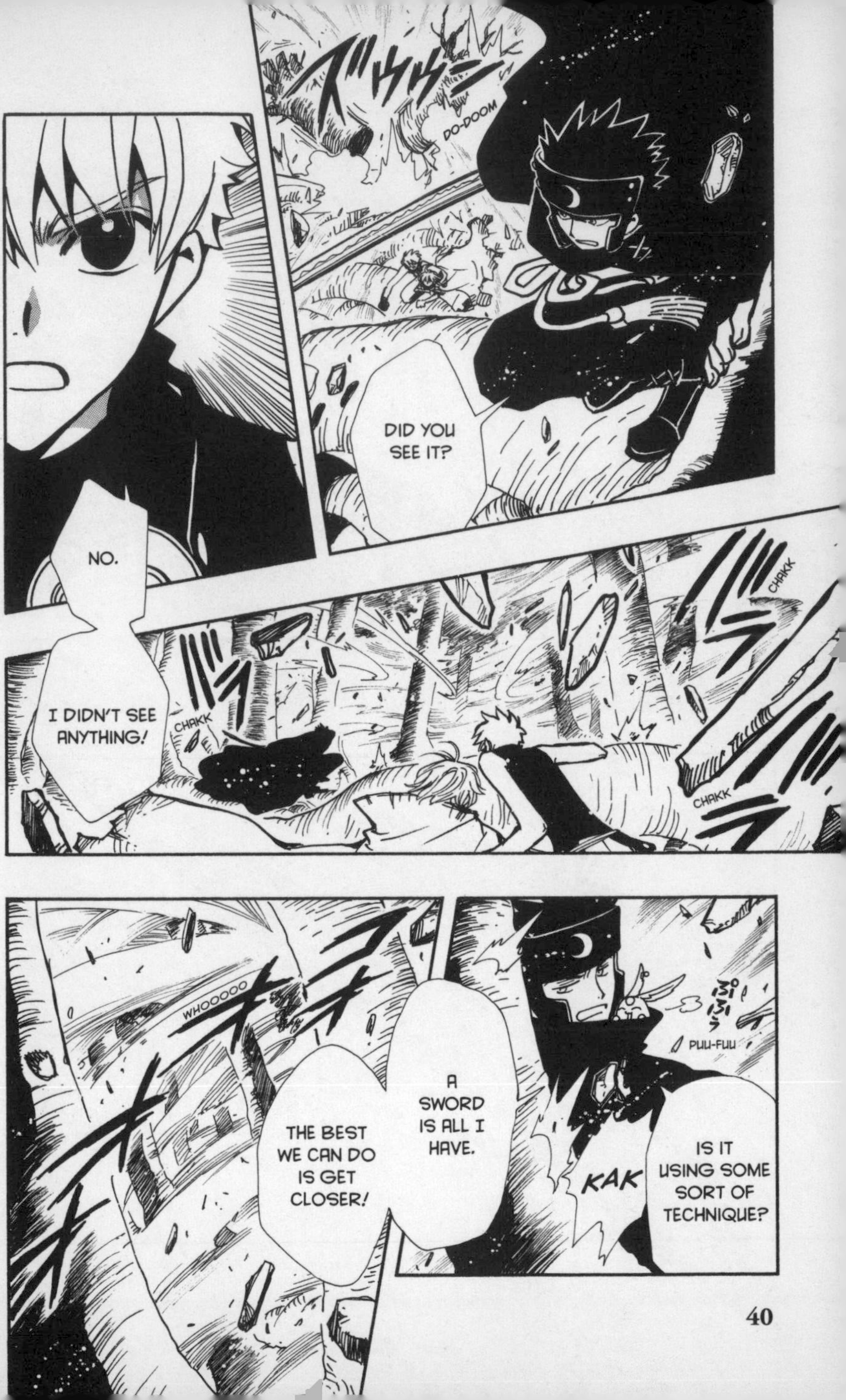
DO-DOOM
DID YOU SEE IT?
NO.
I DIDN'T SEE ANYTHING!
CHAKK
CHAKK
CHAKK
PUU-FUU
IS IT USING SOME SORT OF TECHNIQUE?
KAK
A SWORD IS ALL I HAVE.
WHOOOOO
THE BEST WE CAN DO IS GET CLOSER!

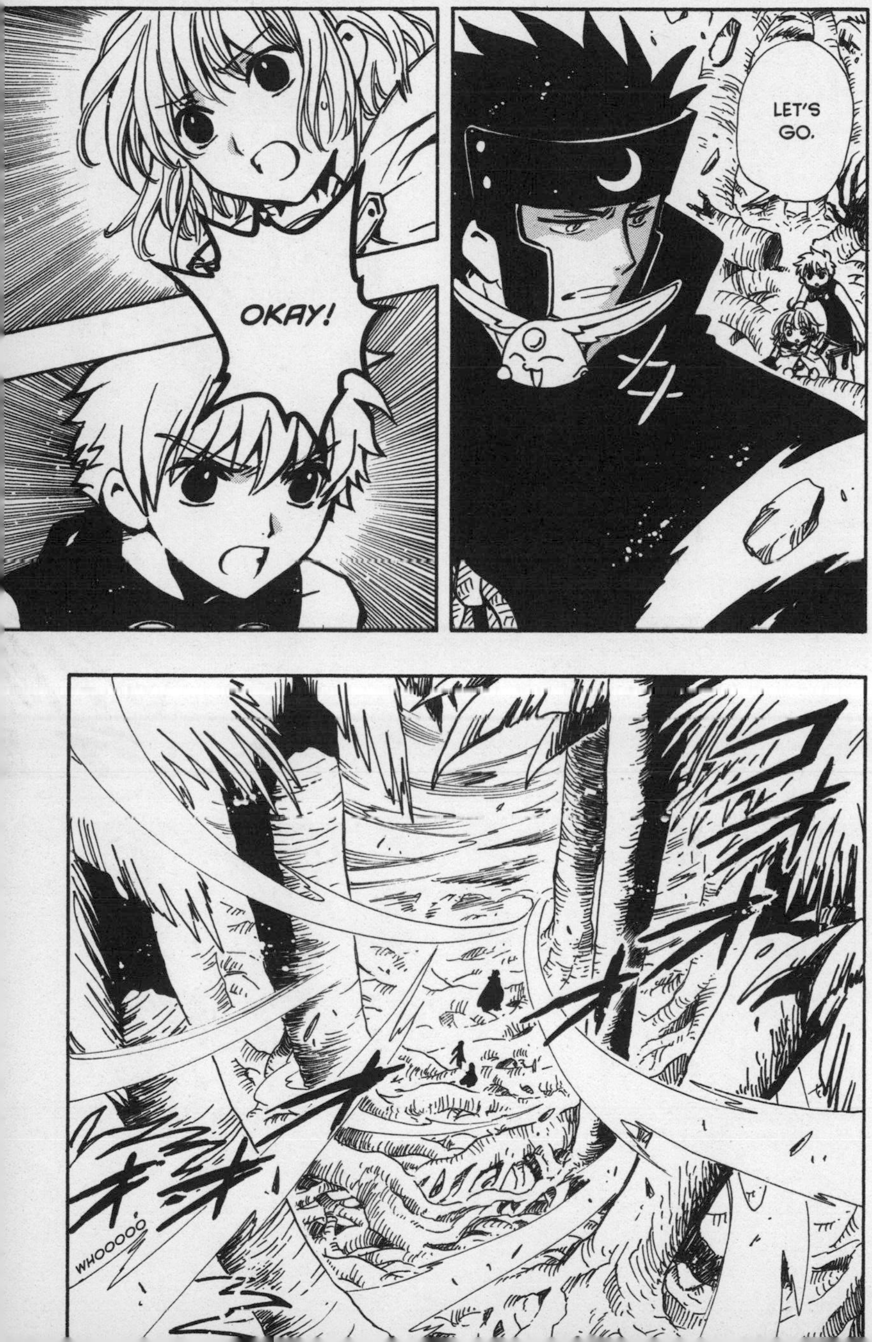
LET'S GO.
OKAY!
WHOOOOO

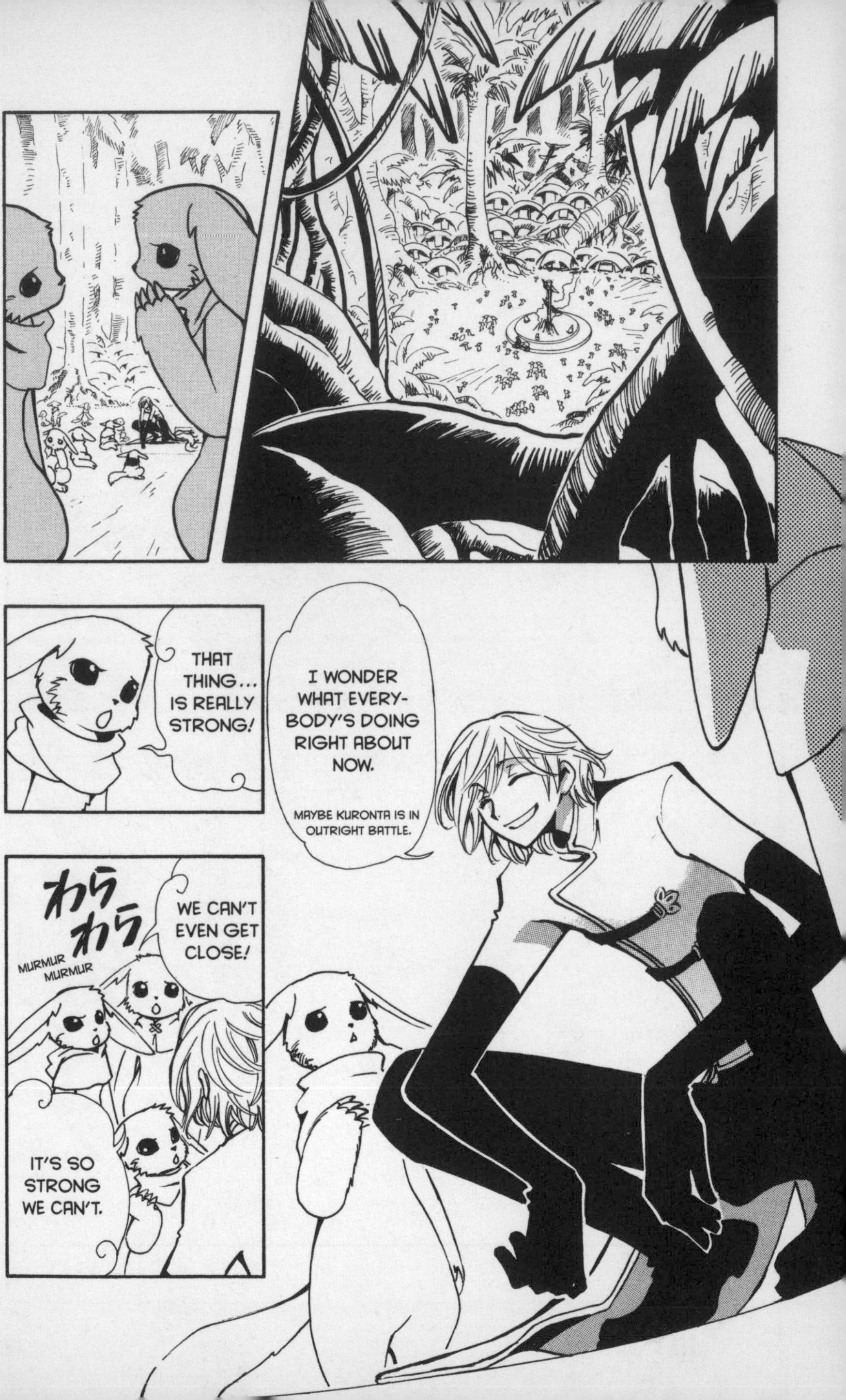
I WONDER WHAT EVERYBODY'S DOING RIGHT ABOUT NOW.
MAYBE KURONTA IS IN OUTRIGHT BATTLE.
THAT THING... IS REALLY STRONG!
わらわら
MURMUR MURMUR
WE CAN'T EVEN GET CLOSE!
IT'S SO STRONG WE CAN'T.

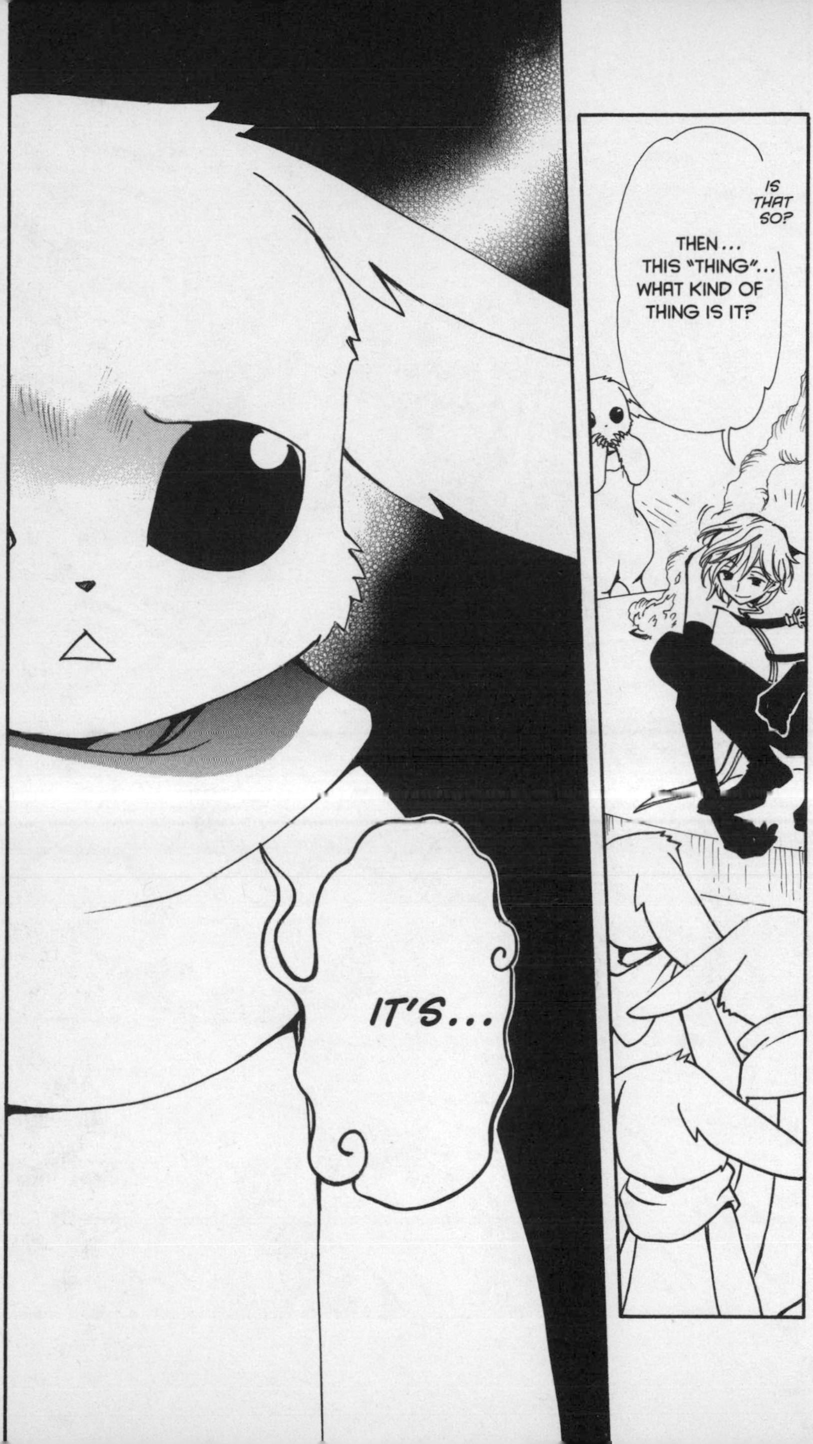
IS THAT SO?
THEN... THIS "THING"... WHAT KIND OF THING IS IT?
IT'S...

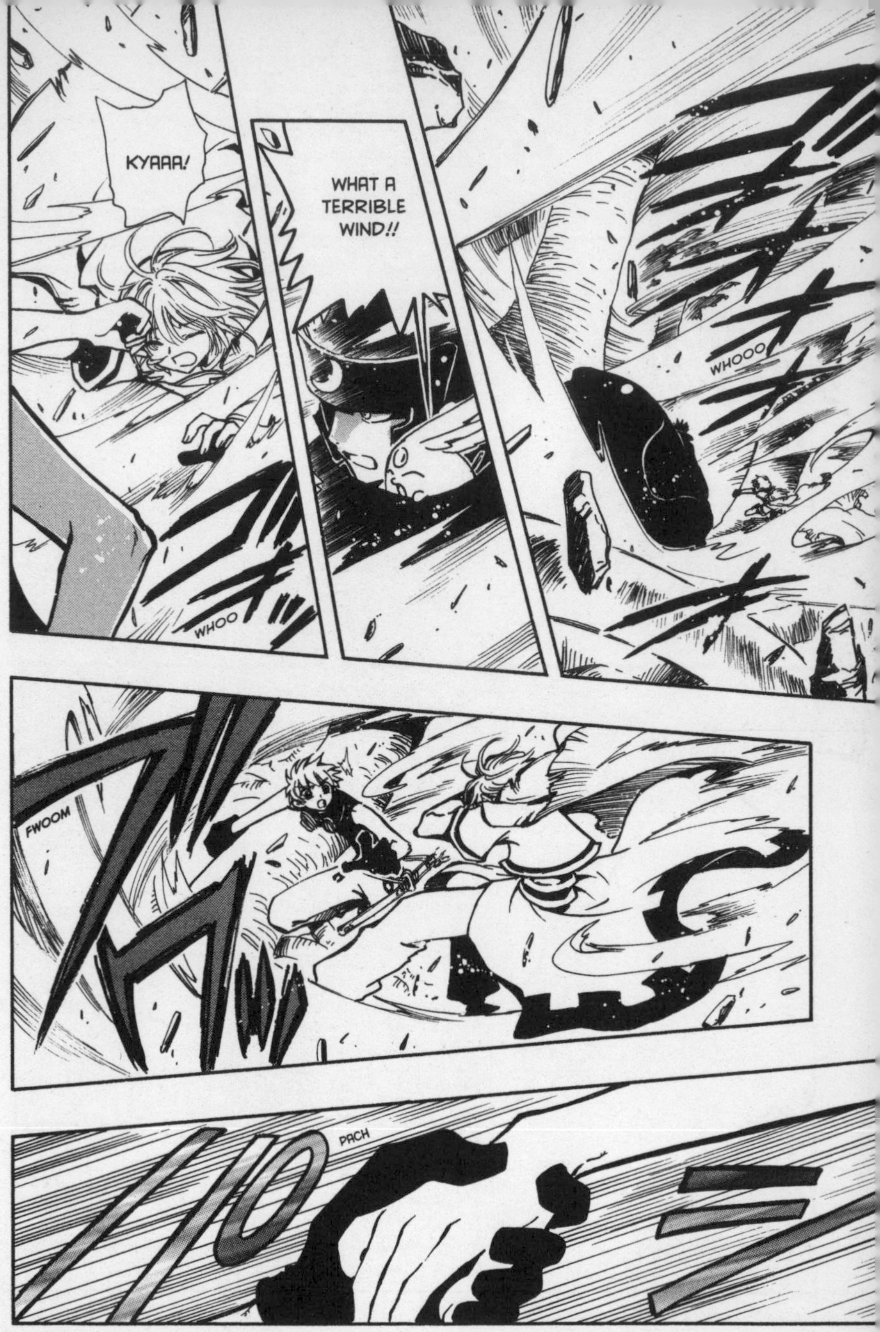
WHOOO
WHAT A TERRIBLE WIND!!
KYAAA!
WHOO
FWOOM
PACH

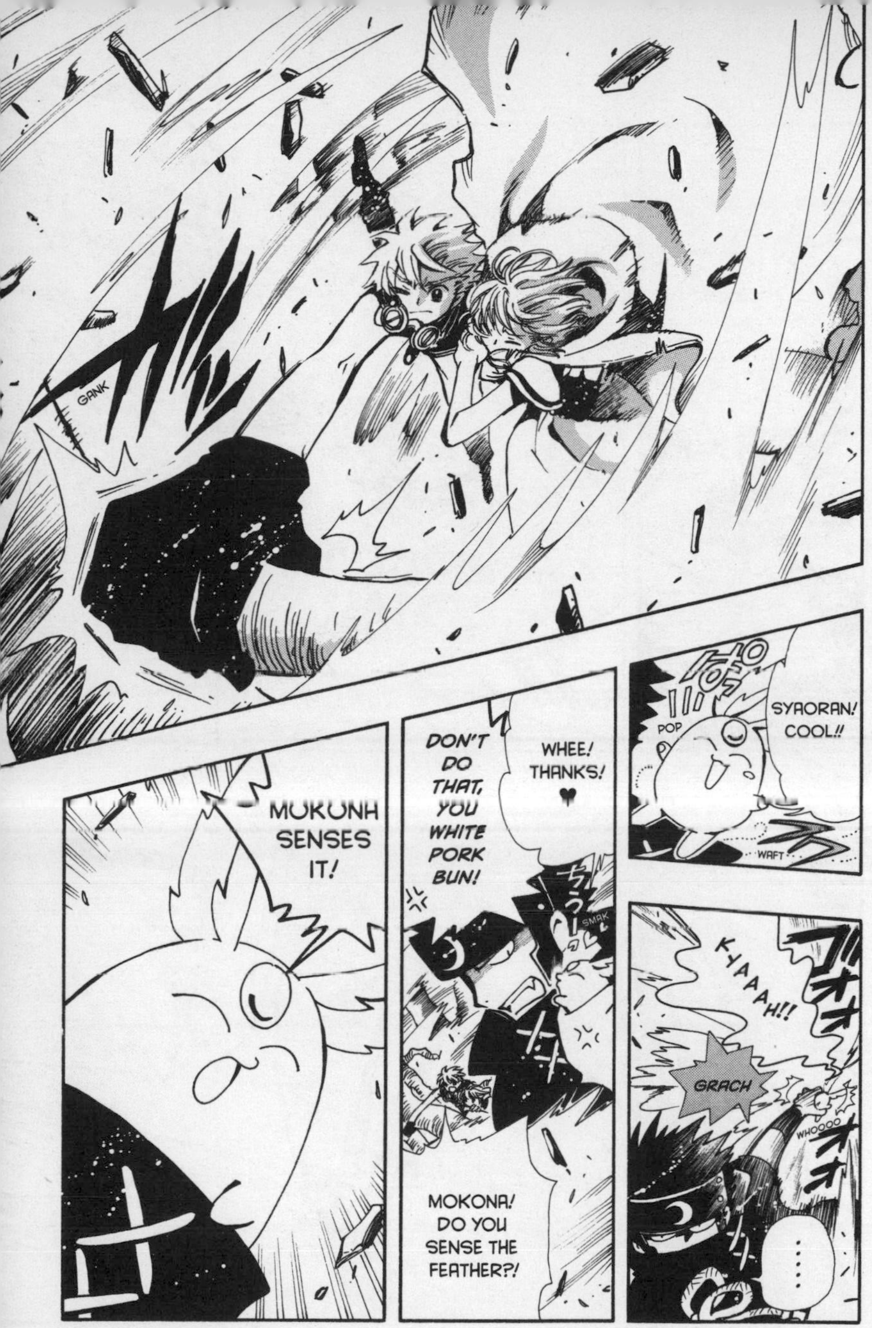
GANK
SYAORAN! COOL!!
POP
WAFT
KYAAAH!!
GRACH
WHOOOO
.....
WHEE! THANKS! ♥
DON'T DO THAT, YOU WHITE PORK BUN!
SMAK
MOKONA! DO YOU SENSE THE FEATHER?!
MOKONA SENSES IT!

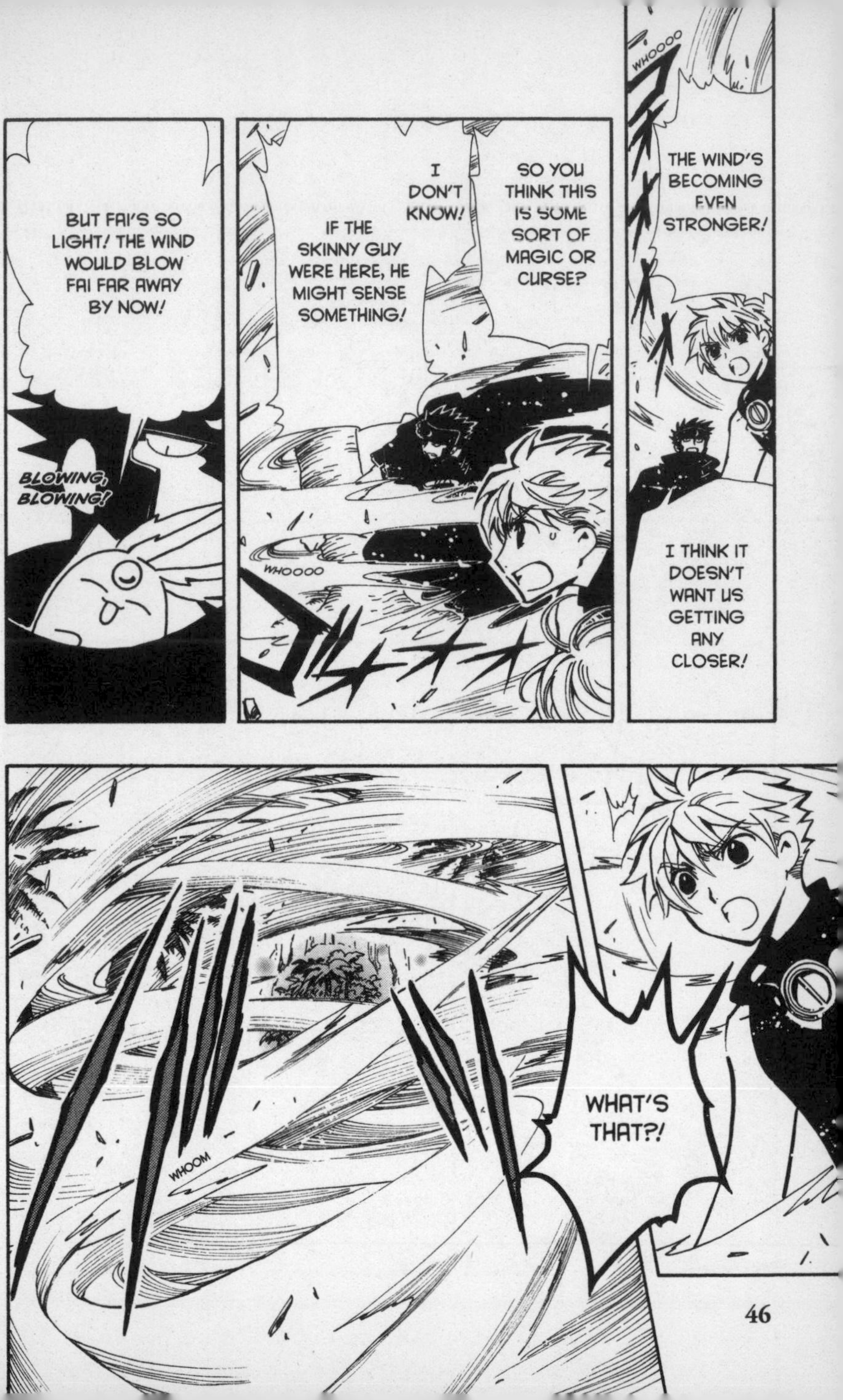
WHOOOO
THE WIND'S BECOMING EVEN STRONGER!
I THINK IT DOESN'T WANT US GETTING ANY CLOSER!
SO YOU THINK THIS IS SOME SORT OF MAGIC OR CURSE?
I DON'T KNOW!
IF THE SKINNY GUY WERE HERE, HE MIGHT SENSE SOMETHING!
WHOOOO
BUT FAI'S SO LIGHT! THE WIND WOULD BLOW FAI FAR AWAY BY NOW!
BLOWING, BLOWING!
WHAT'S THAT?!
WHOOM

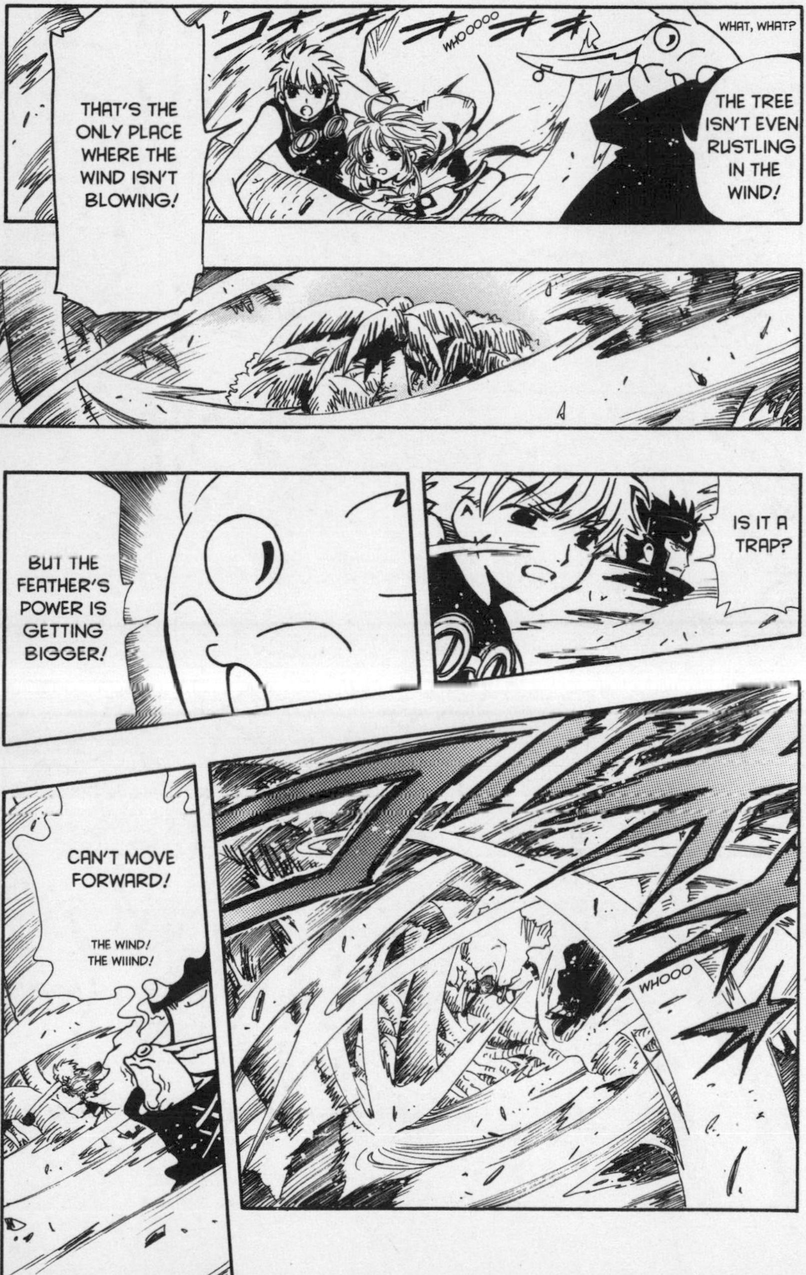
WHOOOOO
WHAT, WHAT?
THE TREE ISN'T EVEN RUSTLING IN THE WIND!
THAT'S THE ONLY PLACE WHERE THE WIND ISN'T BLOWING!
IS IT A TRAP?
BUT THE FEATHER'S POWER IS GETTING BIGGER!
WHOOO
CAN'T MOVE FORWARD!
THE WIND! THE WIIIND!

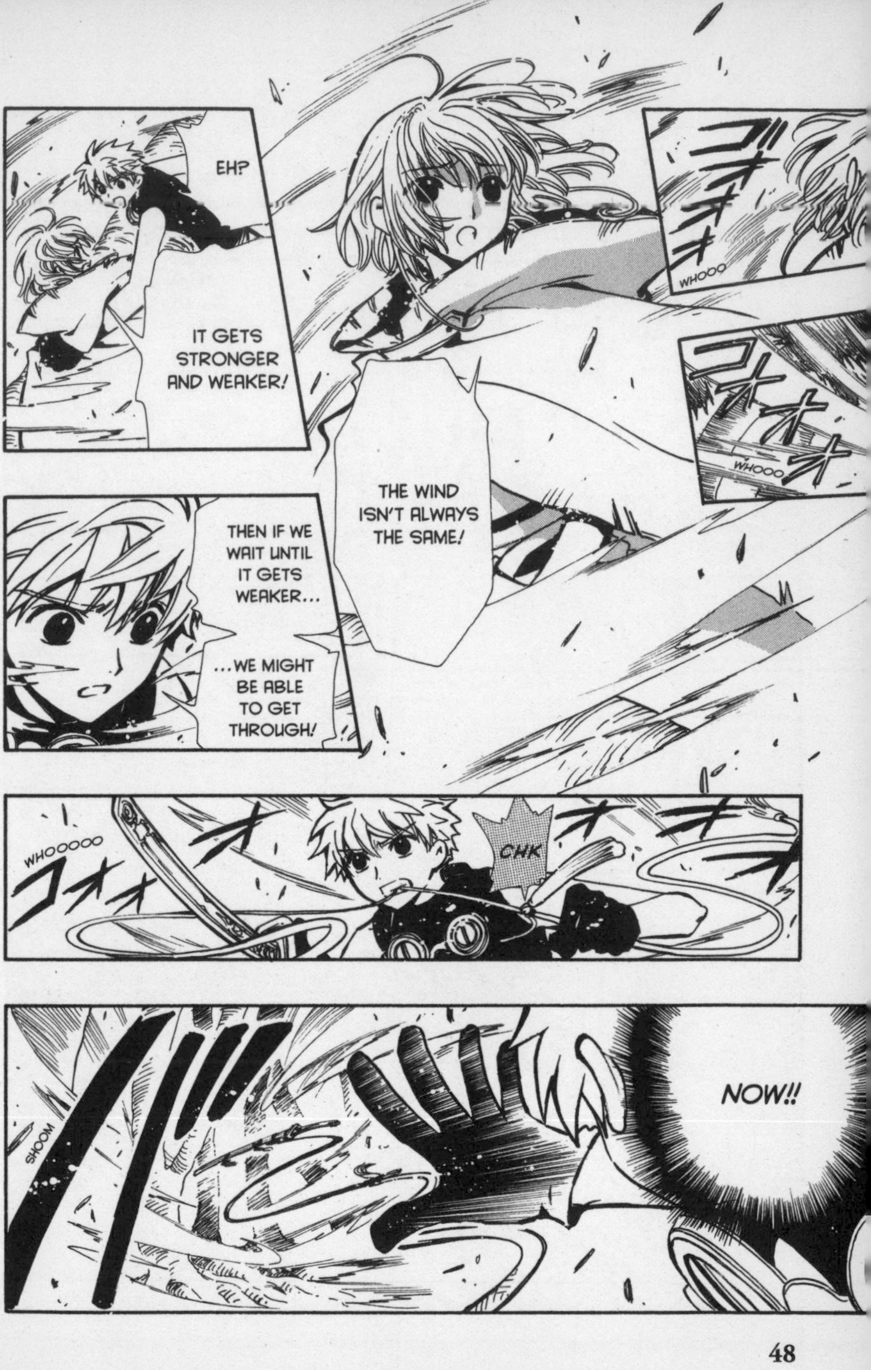
WHOOO
WHOOO
THE WIND ISN'T ALWAYS THE SAME!
EH?
IT GETS STRONGER AND WEAKER!
THEN IF WE WAIT UNTIL IT GETS WEAKER...
...WE MIGHT BE ABLE TO GET THROUGH!
CHK
WHOOOOO
NOW!!
SHOOM

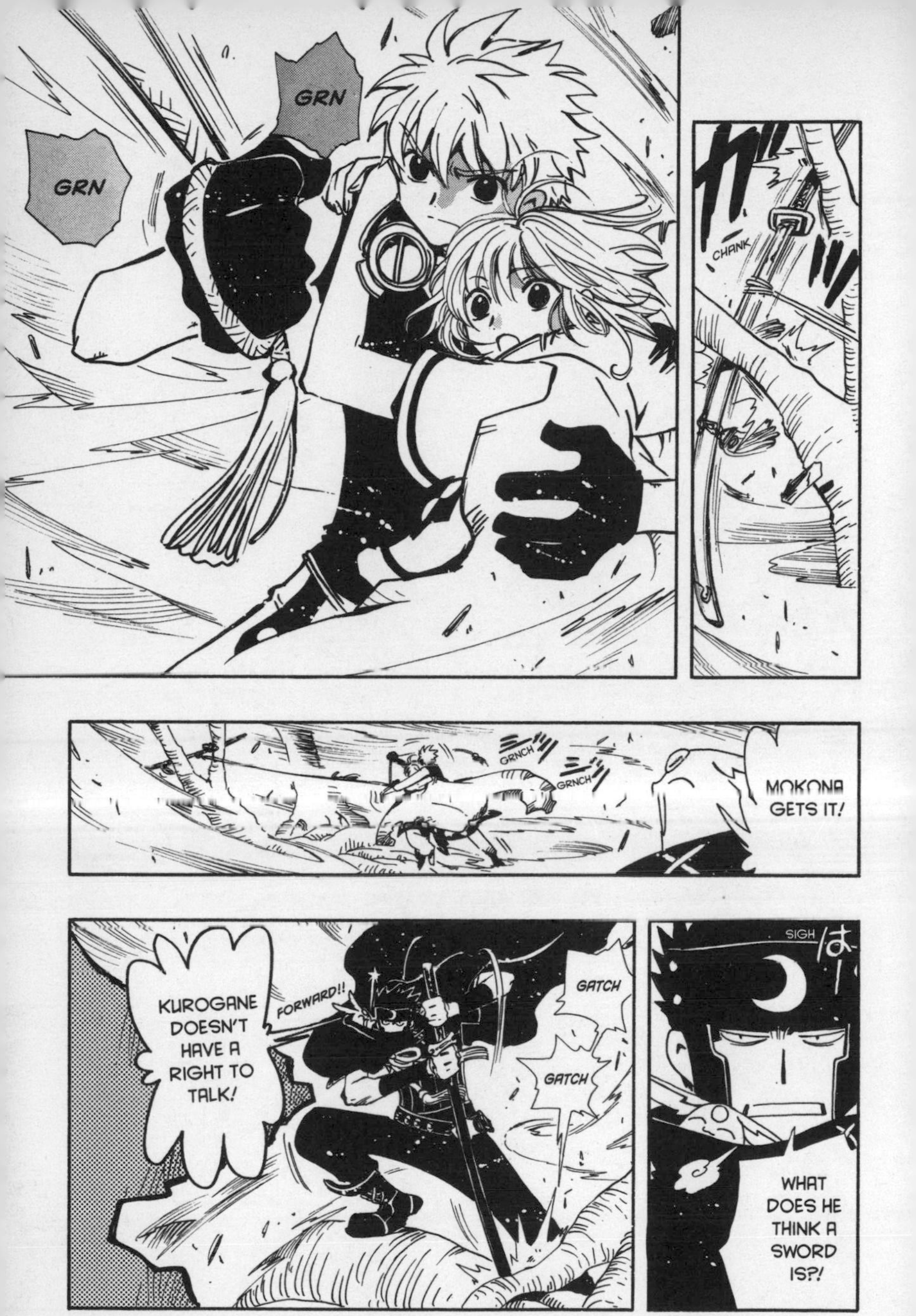
CHANK
GRN
GRN
GRNCH
GRNCH
MOKONA GETS IT!
SIGH
WHAT DOES HE THINK A SWORD IS?!
GATCH
GATCH
FORWARD!!
KUROGANE DOESN'T HAVE A RIGHT TO TALK!

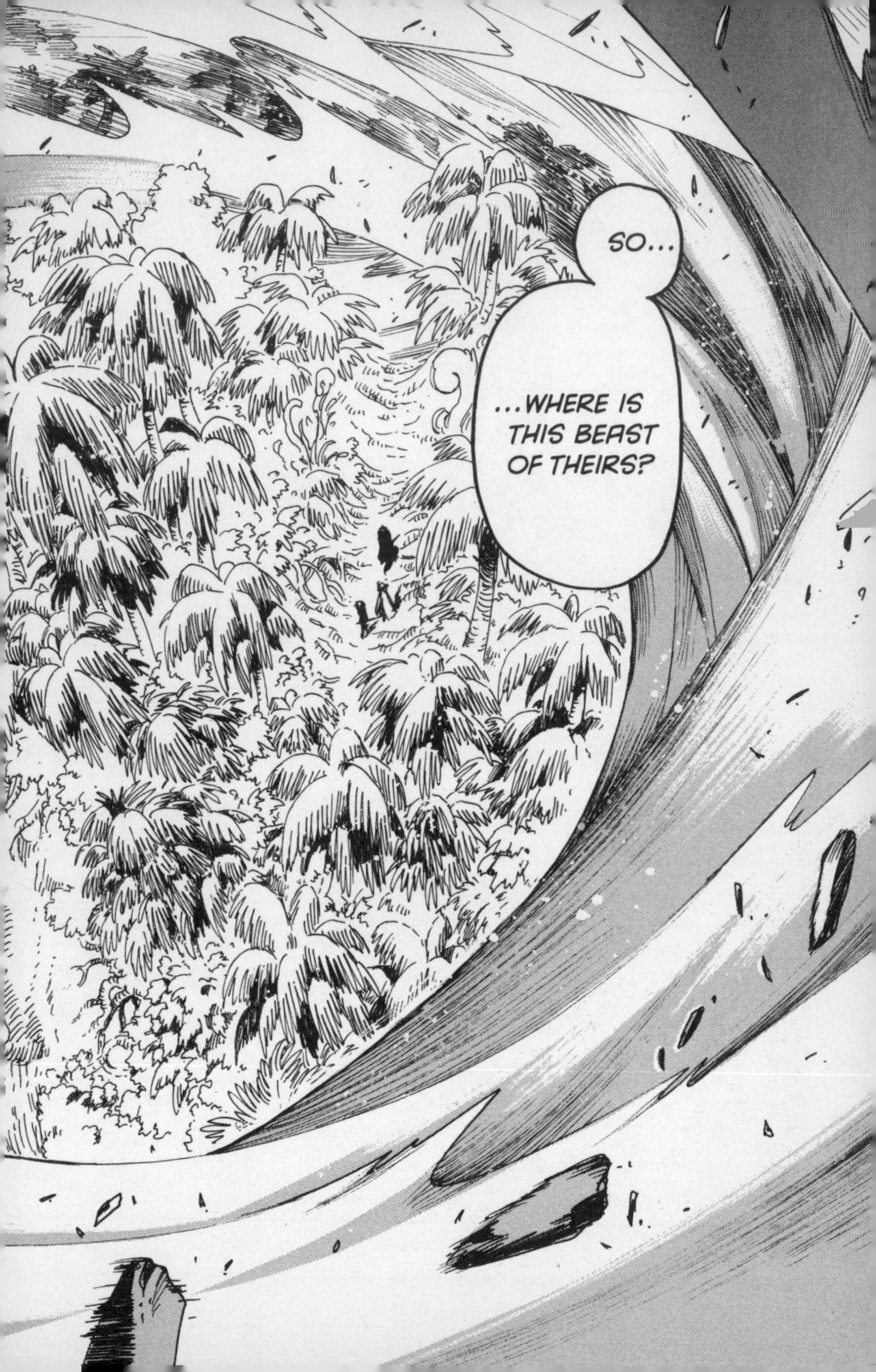
SO...
...WHERE IS THIS BEAST OF THEIRS?

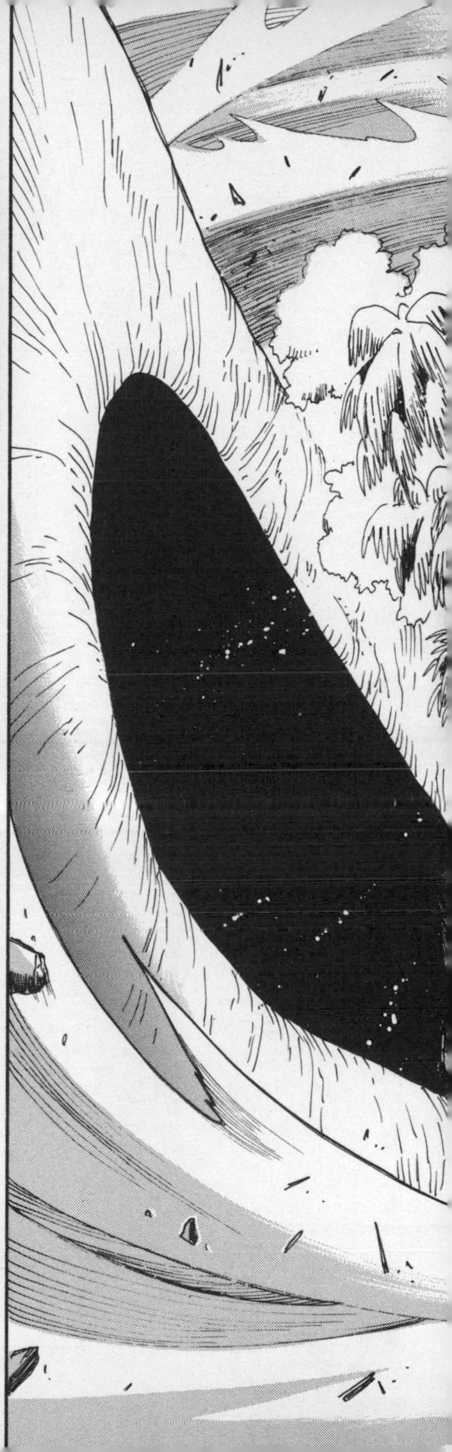

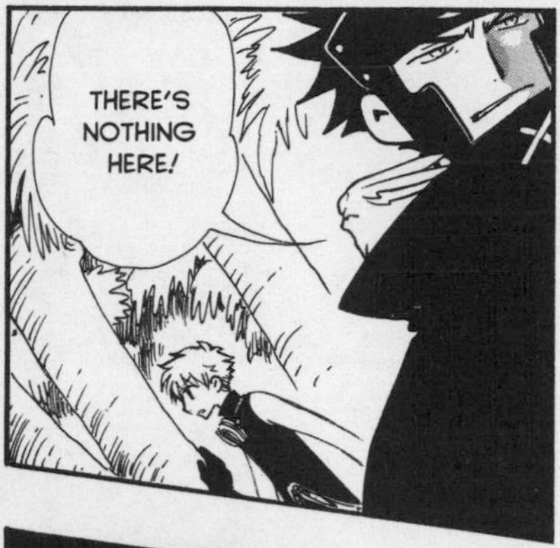
THERE'S NOTHING HERE!

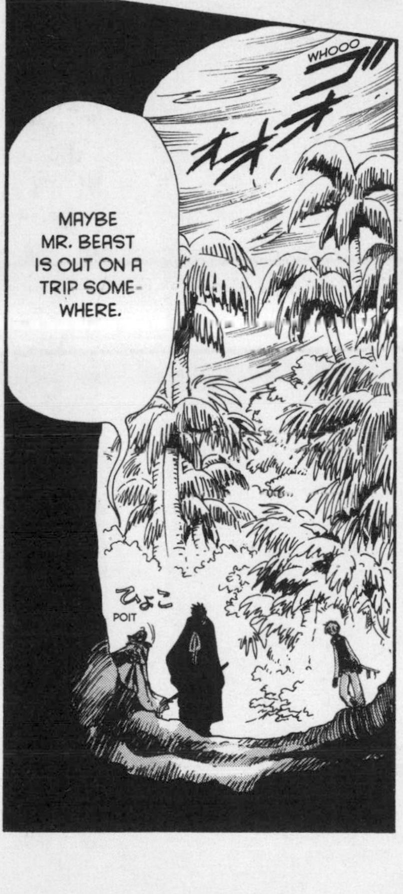
WHOOO
MAYBE MR. BEAST IS OUT ON A TRIP SOME-WHERE.
POIT

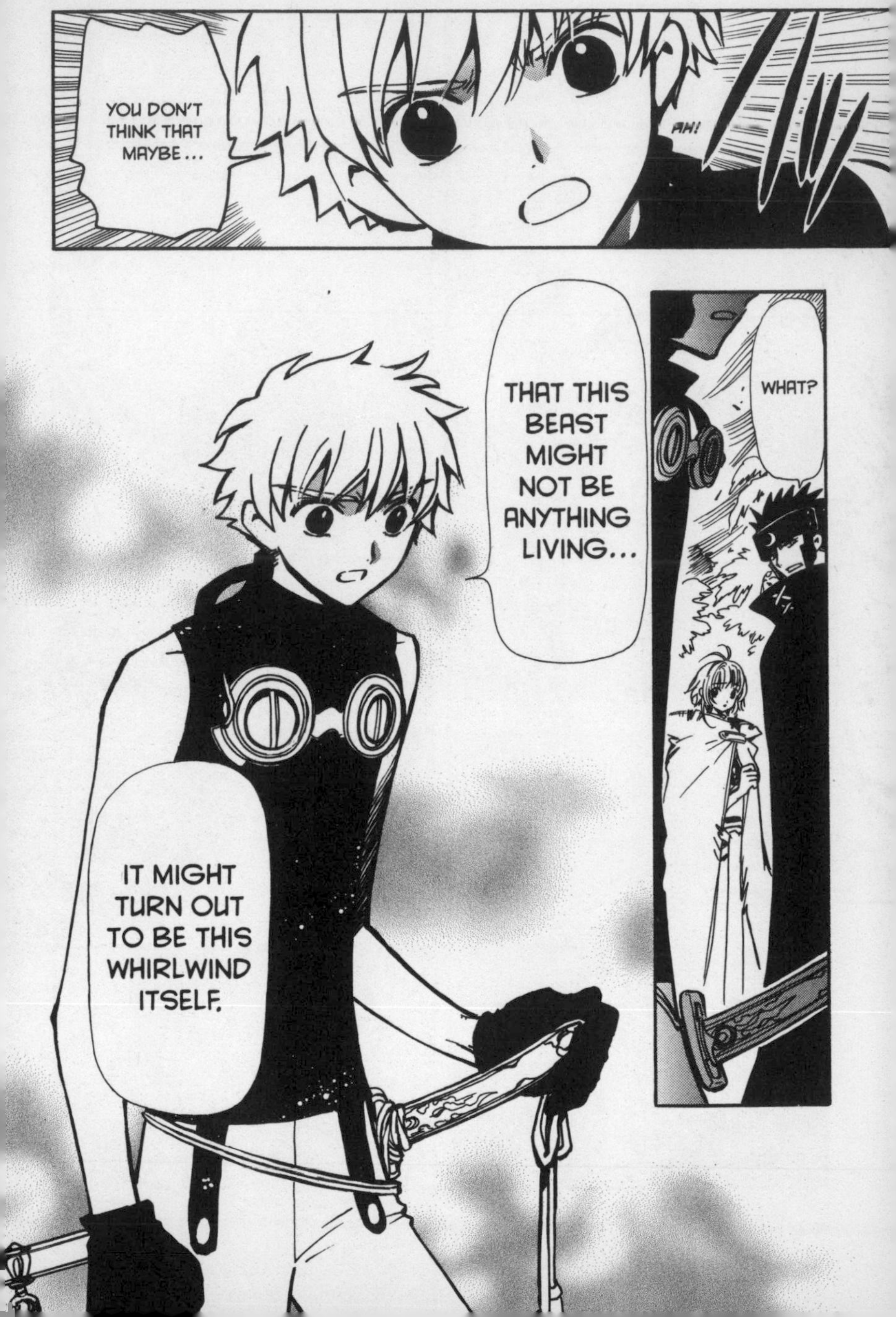
AH!
YOU DON'T THINK THAT MAYBE...
WHAT?
THAT THIS BEAST MIGHT NOT BE ANYTHING LIVING...
IT MIGHT TURN OUT TO BE THIS WHIRLWIND ITSELF.

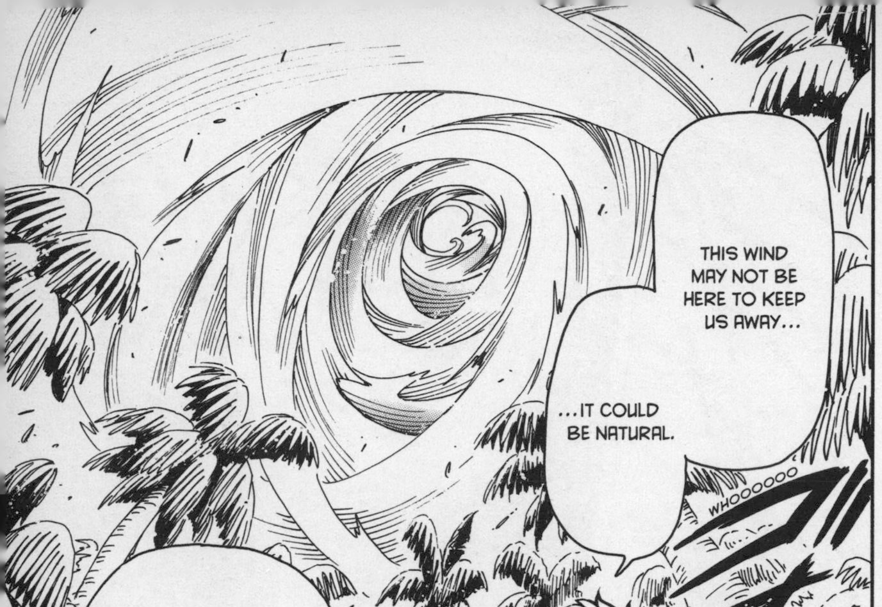
THIS WIND MAY NOT BE HERE TO KEEP US AWAY...
...IT COULD BE NATURAL.
WHOOOOOO
CONSIDERING THAT THIS PLACE IS THE EYE OF THE STORM, THE LOGIC ALL FITS.

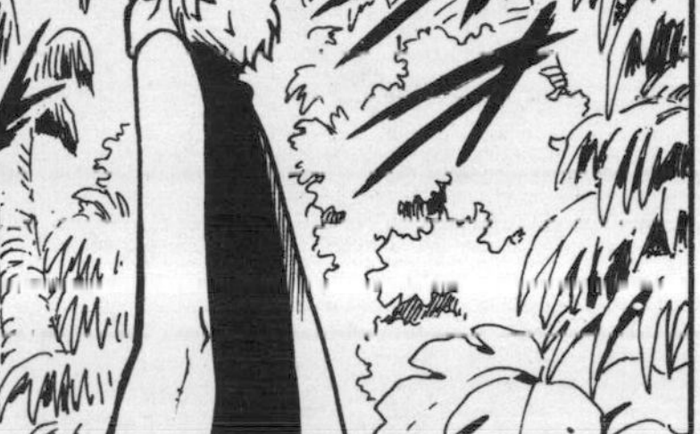
HUH?

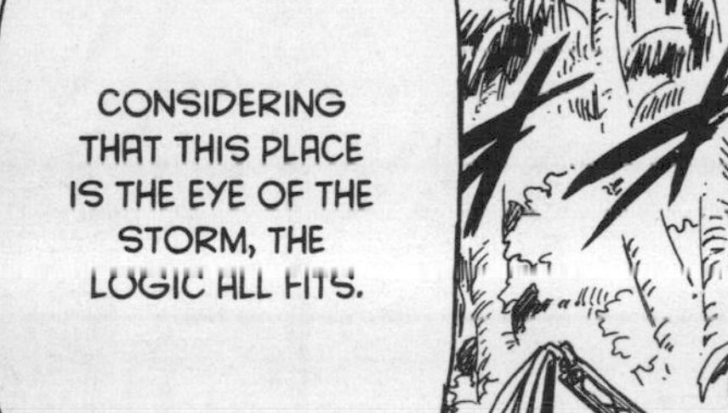
THEN THE WHIRLWIND ITSELF IS THE BEAST THEY WERE TALKING ABOUT?

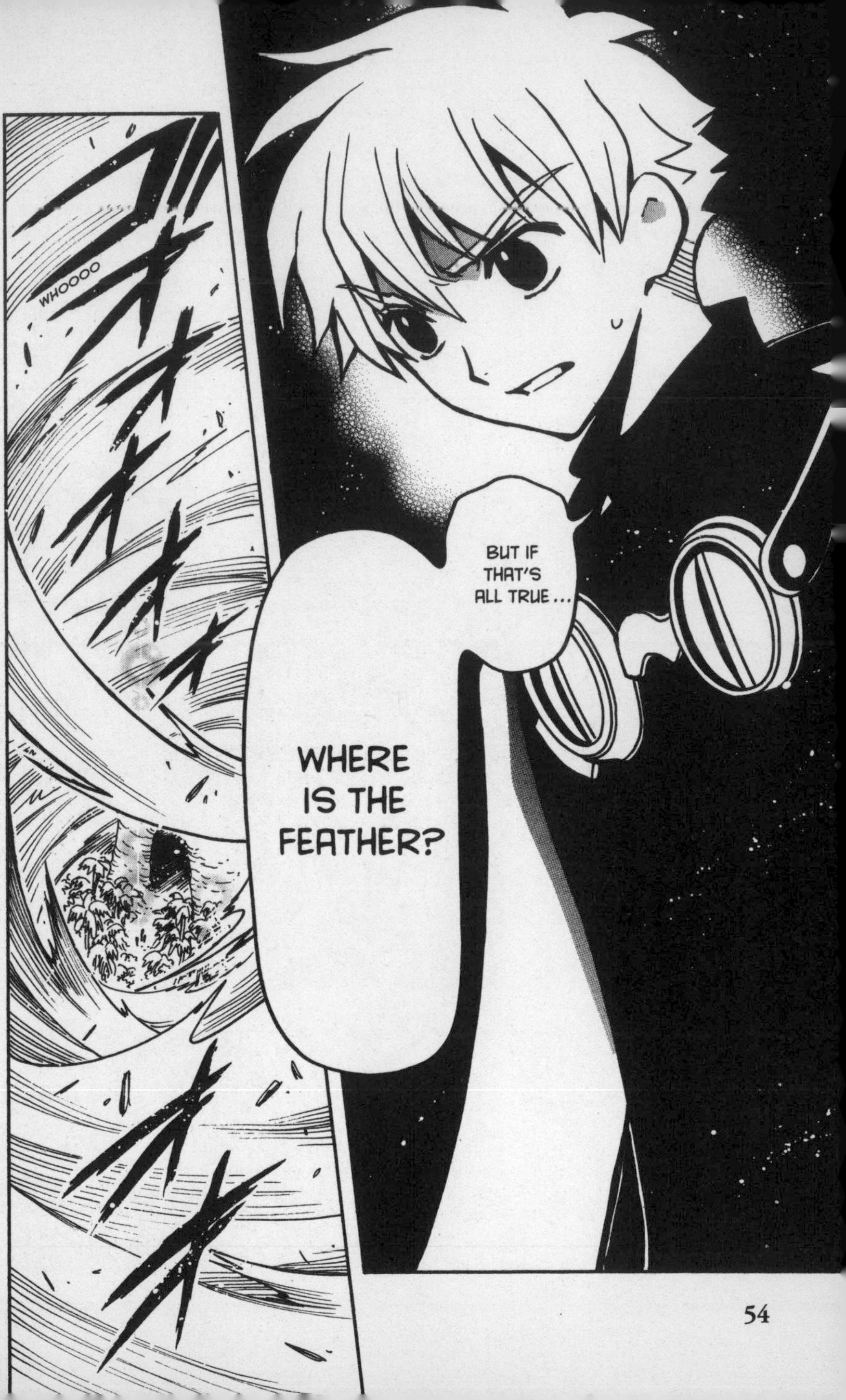
BUT IF THAT'S ALL TRUE...
WHERE IS THE FEATHER?
WHOOOO

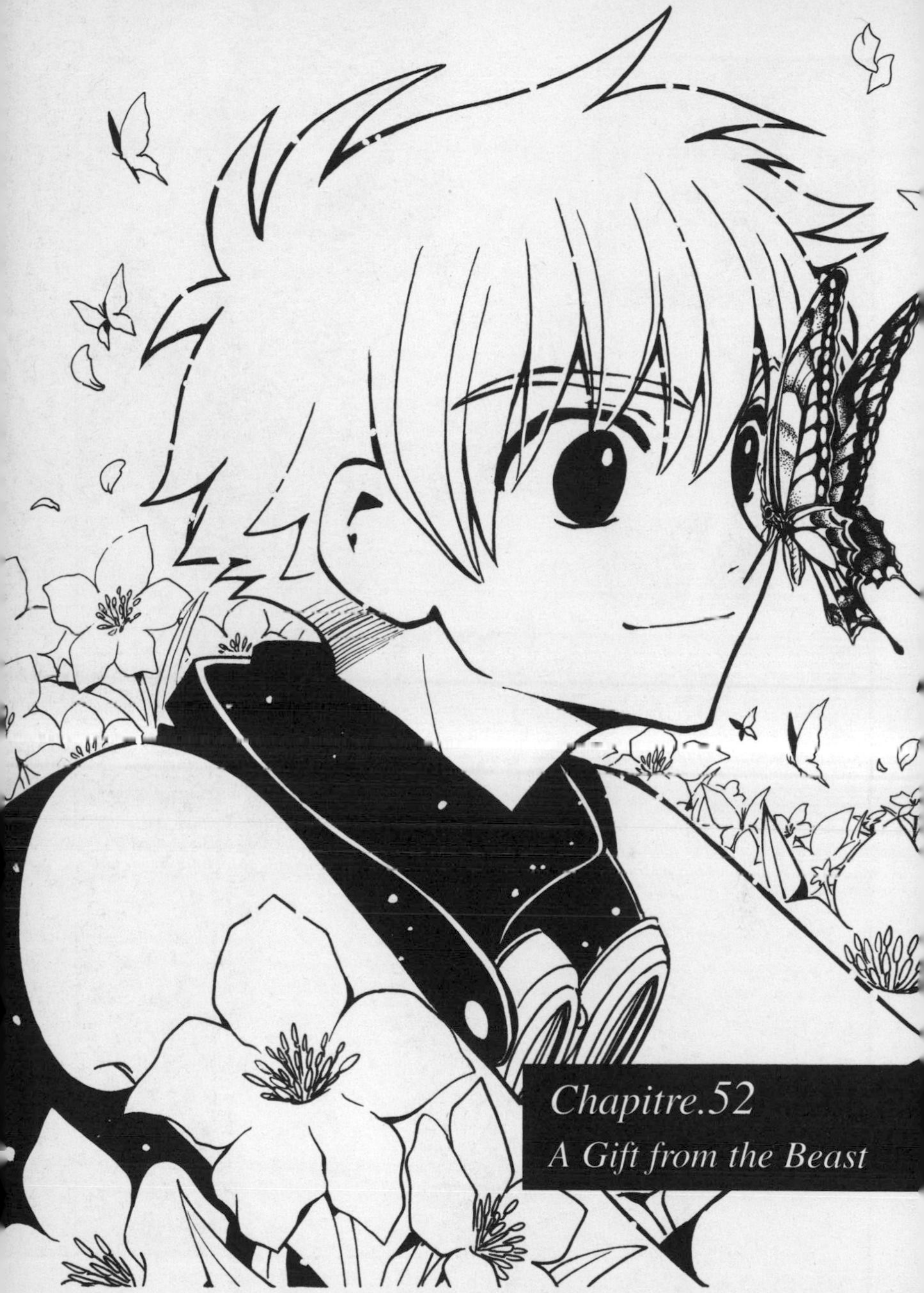
Chapitre.52
A Gift from the Beast

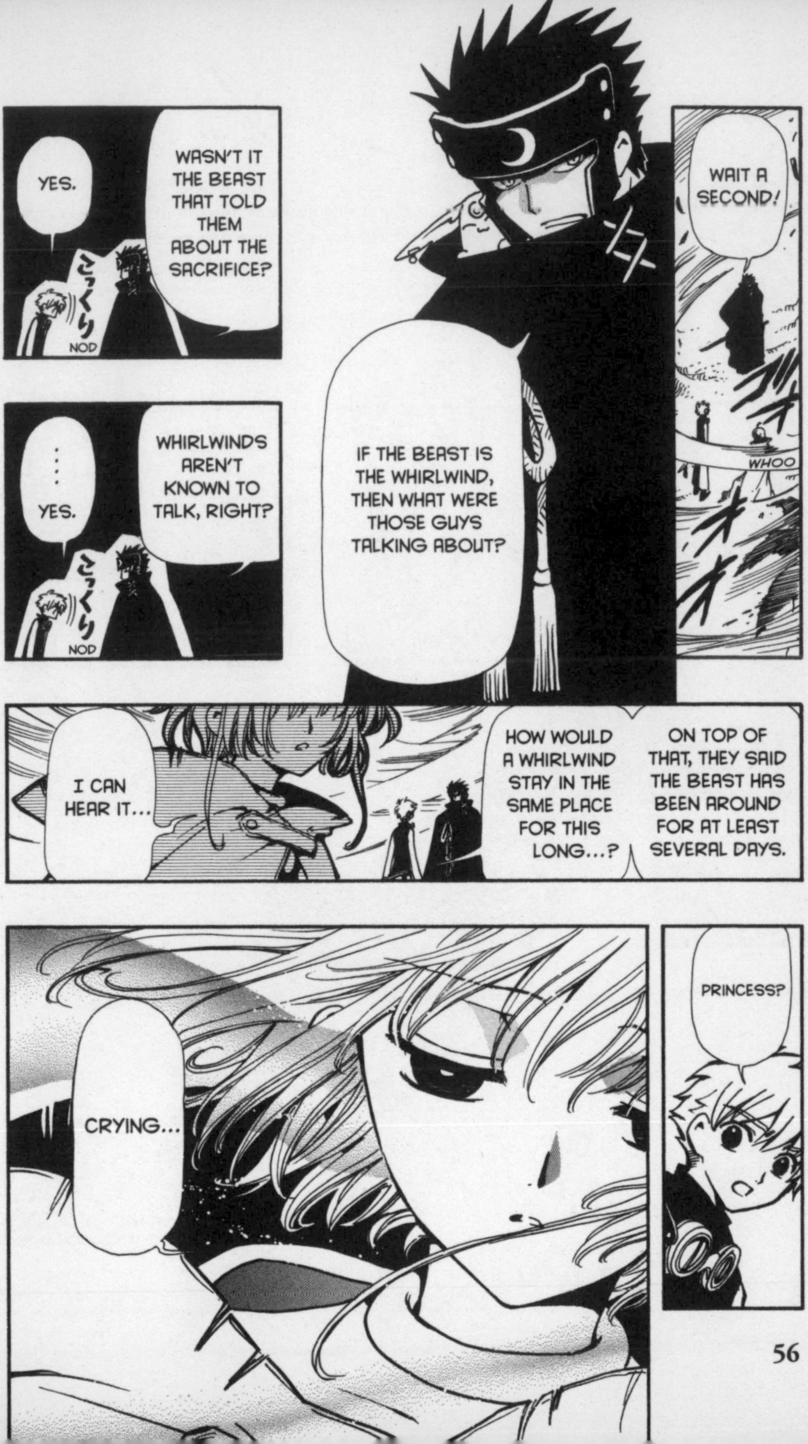
WAIT A SECOND!
WHOO
IF THE BEAST IS THE WHIRLWIND, THEN WHAT WERE THOSE GUYS TALKING ABOUT?
WASN'T IT THE BEAST THAT TOLD THEM ABOUT THE SACRIFICE?
YES.
こっくり
NOD
WHIRLWINDS AREN'T KNOWN TO TALK, RIGHT?
. . . . YES.
こっくり
NOD
ON TOP OF THAT, THEY SAID THE BEAST HAS BEEN AROUND FOR AT LEAST SEVERAL DAYS.
HOW WOULD A WHIRLWIND STAY IN THE SAME PLACE FOR THIS LONG...?
I CAN HEAR IT...
PRINCESS?
CRYING...

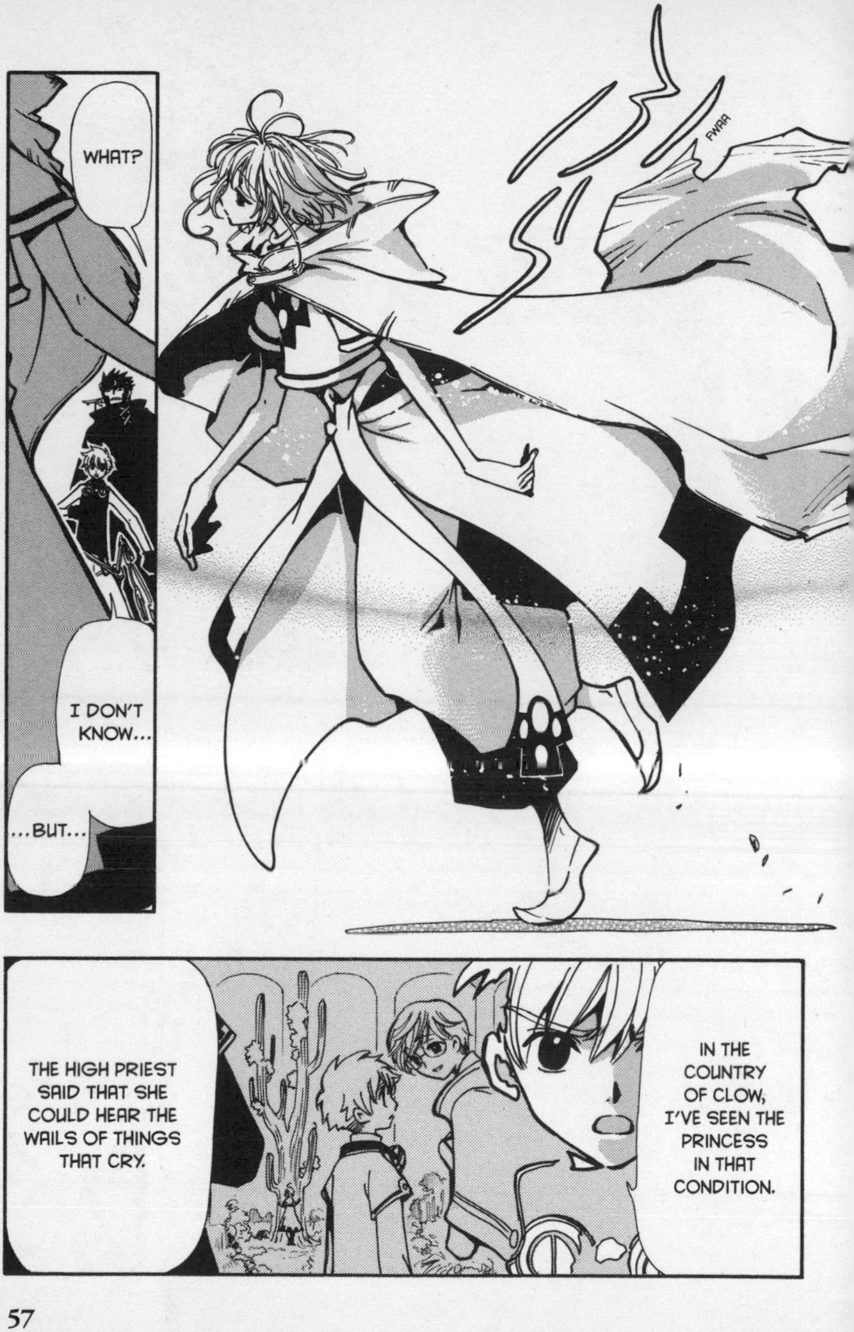
FWAA
WHAT?
I DON'T KNOW...
...BUT...
IN THE COUNTRY OF CLOW, I'VE SEEN THE PRINCESS IN THAT CONDITION.
THE HIGH PRIEST SAID THAT SHE COULD HEAR THE WAILS OF THINGS THAT CRY.

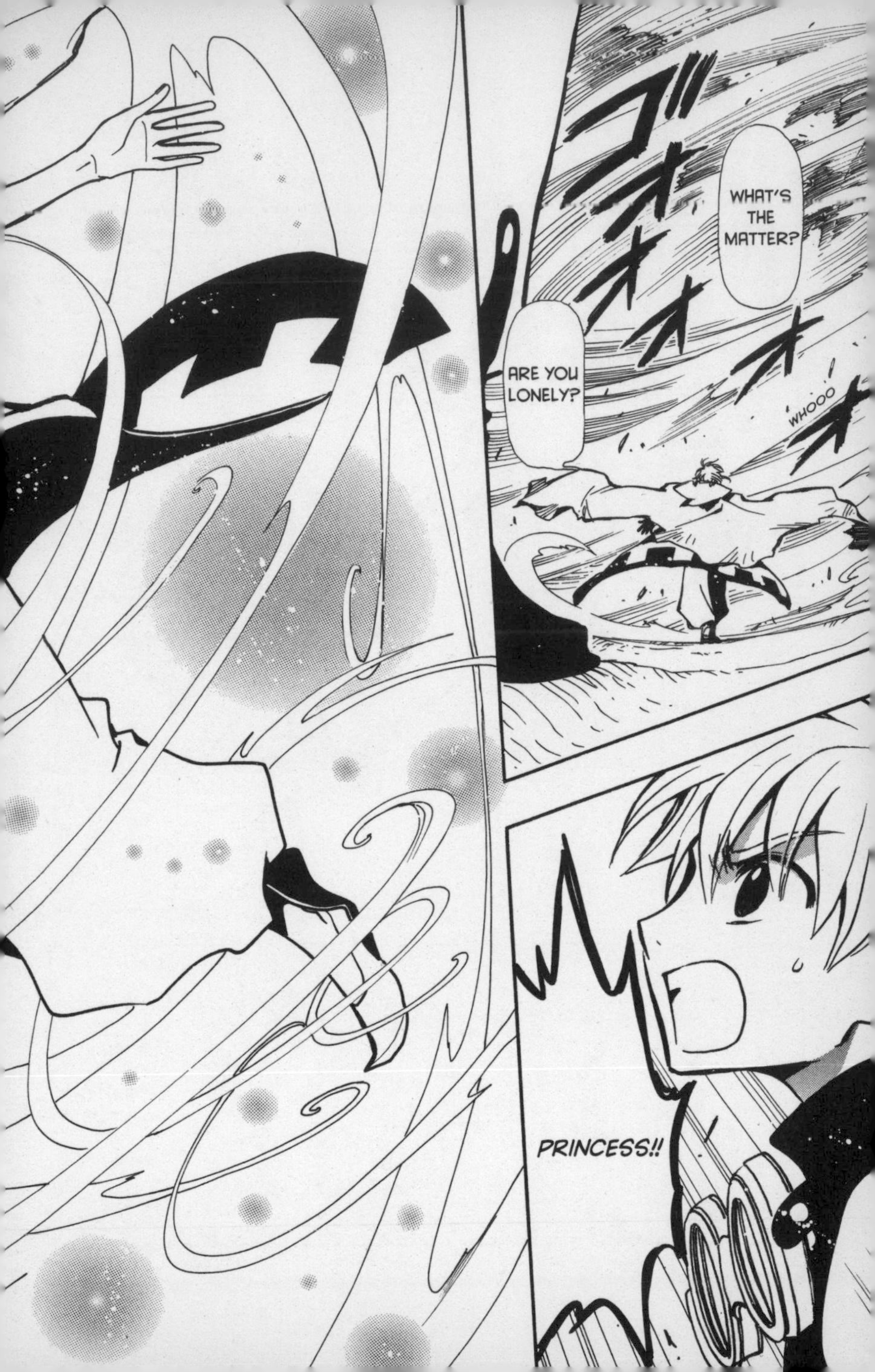
WHAT'S THE MATTER?
ARE YOU LONELY?
WHOOO
PRINCESS!!

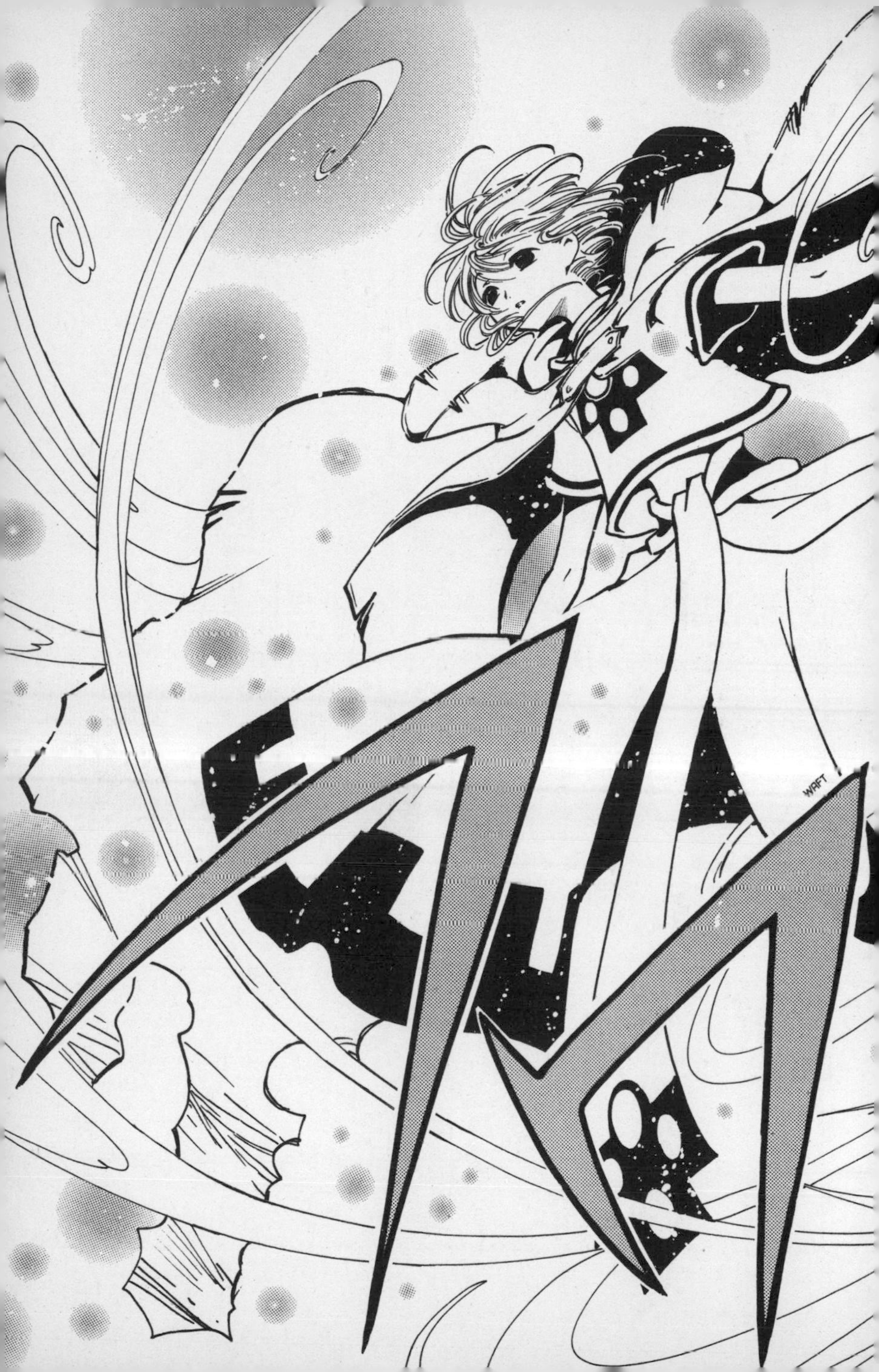
WAFT

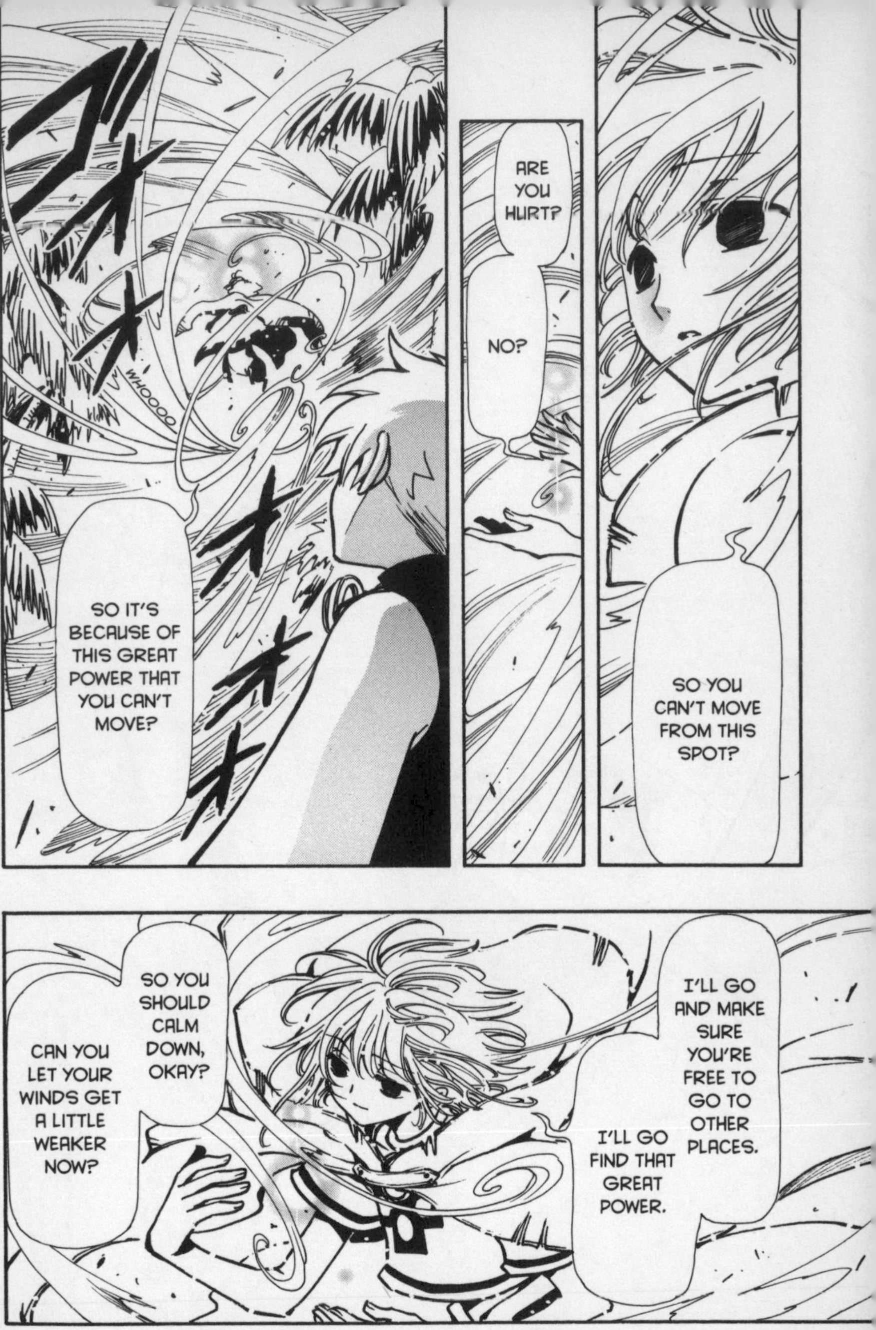

SO YOU CAN'T MOVE FROM THIS SPOT?
ARE YOU HURT?
NO?
WHOOOO
SO IT'S BECAUSE OF THIS GREAT POWER THAT YOU CAN'T MOVE?
I'LL GO AND MAKE SURE YOU'RE FREE TO GO TO OTHER PLACES.
I'LL GO FIND THAT GREAT POWER.
SO YOU SHOULD CALM DOWN, OKAY?
CAN YOU LET YOUR WINDS GET A LITTLE WEAKER NOW?

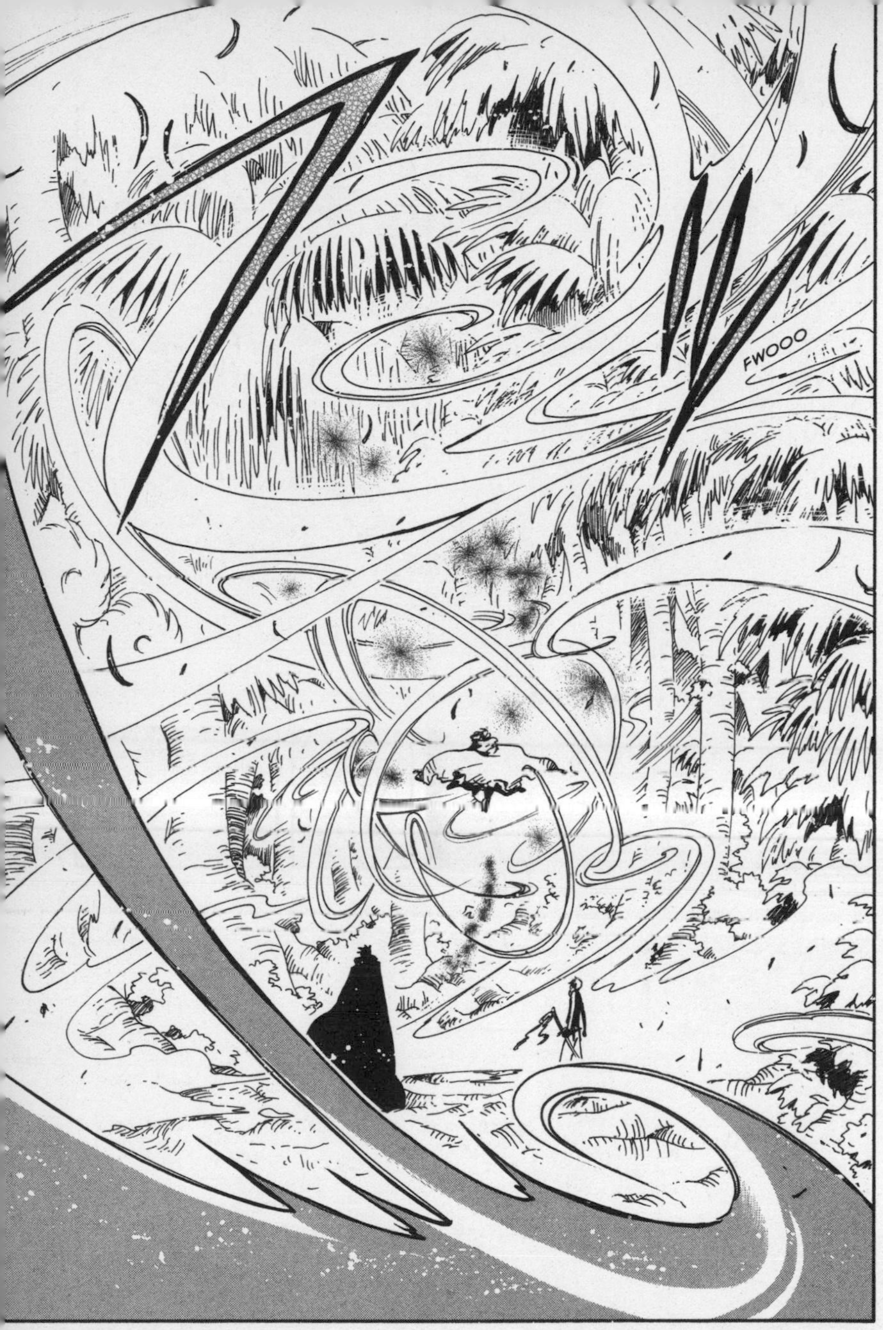
FWOOO

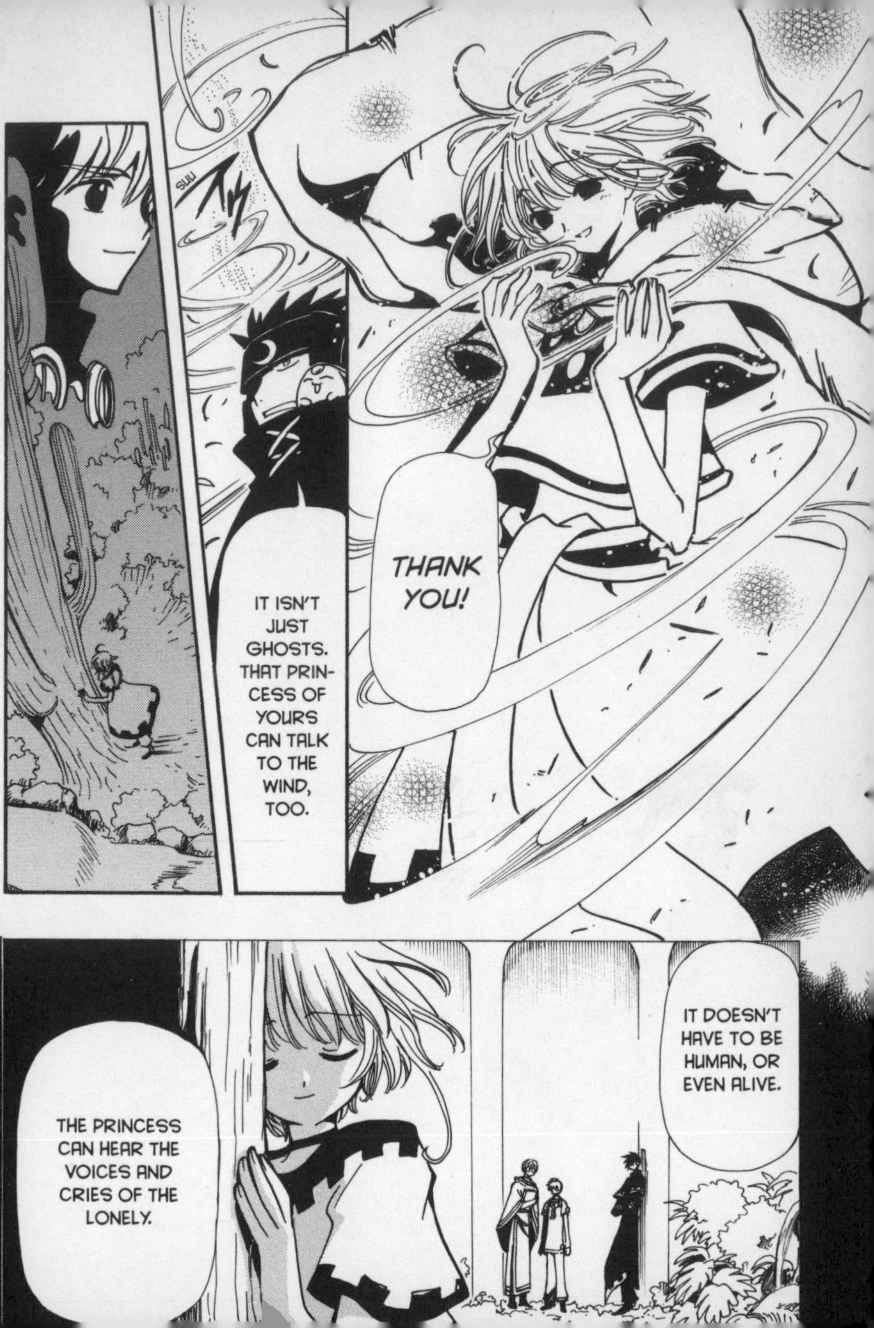
THANK YOU!
SUU
IT ISN'T JUST GHOSTS. THAT PRIN-CESS OF YOURS CAN TALK TO THE WIND, TOO.
IT DOESN'T HAVE TO BE HUMAN, OR EVEN ALIVE.
THE PRINCESS CAN HEAR THE VOICES AND CRIES OF THE LONELY.

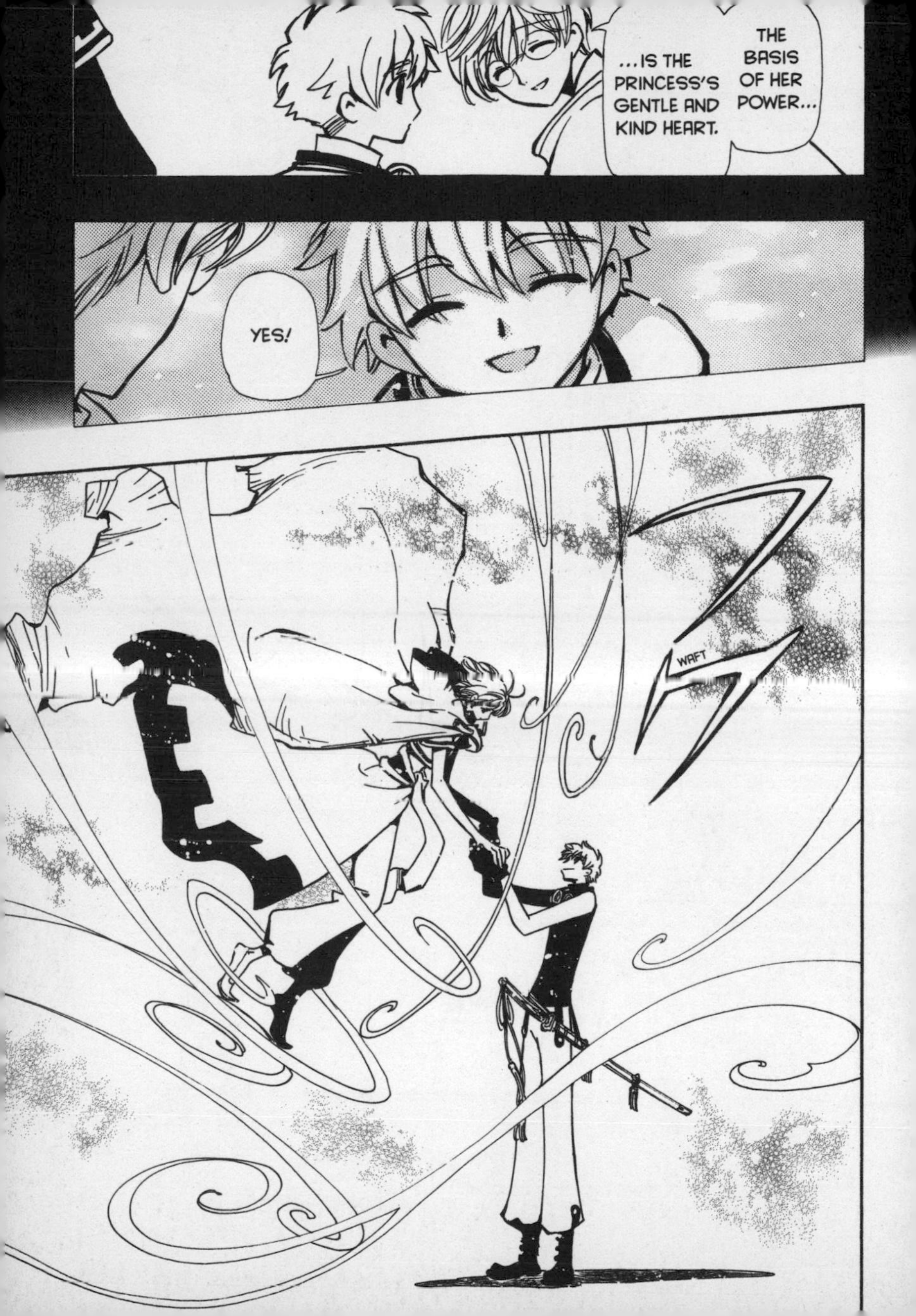
THE BASIS OF HER POWER...
...IS THE PRINCESS'S GENTLE AND KIND HEART.
YES!
WAFT

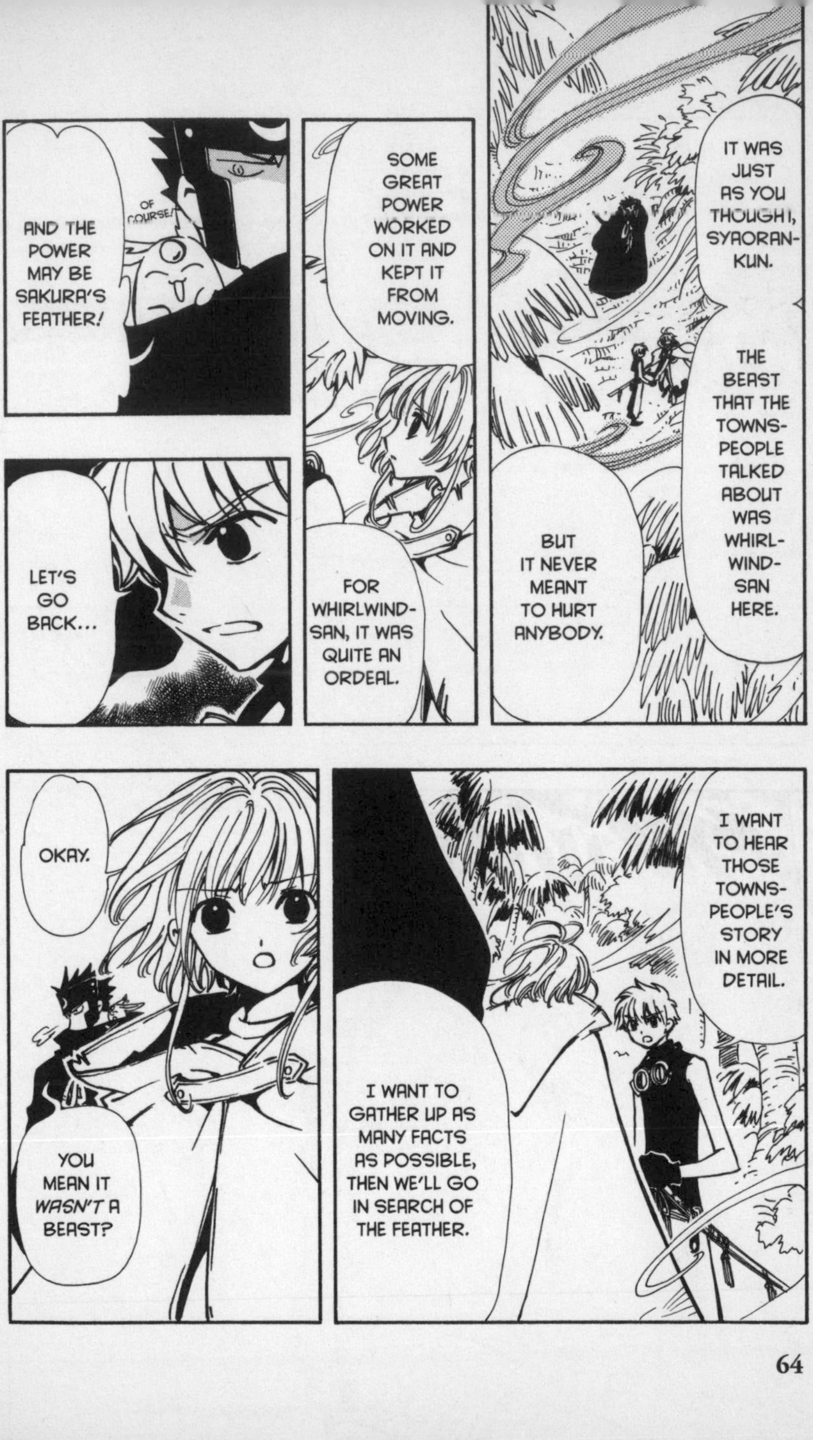

IT WAS JUST AS YOU THOUGHT, SYAORAN-KUN.
THE BEAST THAT THE TOWNSPEOPLE TALKED ABOUT WAS WHIRLWIND-SAN HERE.
BUT IT NEVER MEANT TO HURT ANYBODY.
SOME GREAT POWER WORKED ON IT AND KEPT IT FROM MOVING.
FOR WHIRLWIND-SAN, IT WAS QUITE AN ORDEAL.
OF COURSE!
AND THE POWER MAY BE SAKURA'S FEATHER!
LET'S GO BACK...
I WANT TO HEAR THOSE TOWNSPEOPLE'S STORY IN MORE DETAIL.
I WANT TO GATHER UP AS MANY FACTS AS POSSIBLE, THEN WE'LL GO IN SEARCH OF THE FEATHER.
OKAY.
YOU MEAN IT *WASN'T* A BEAST?

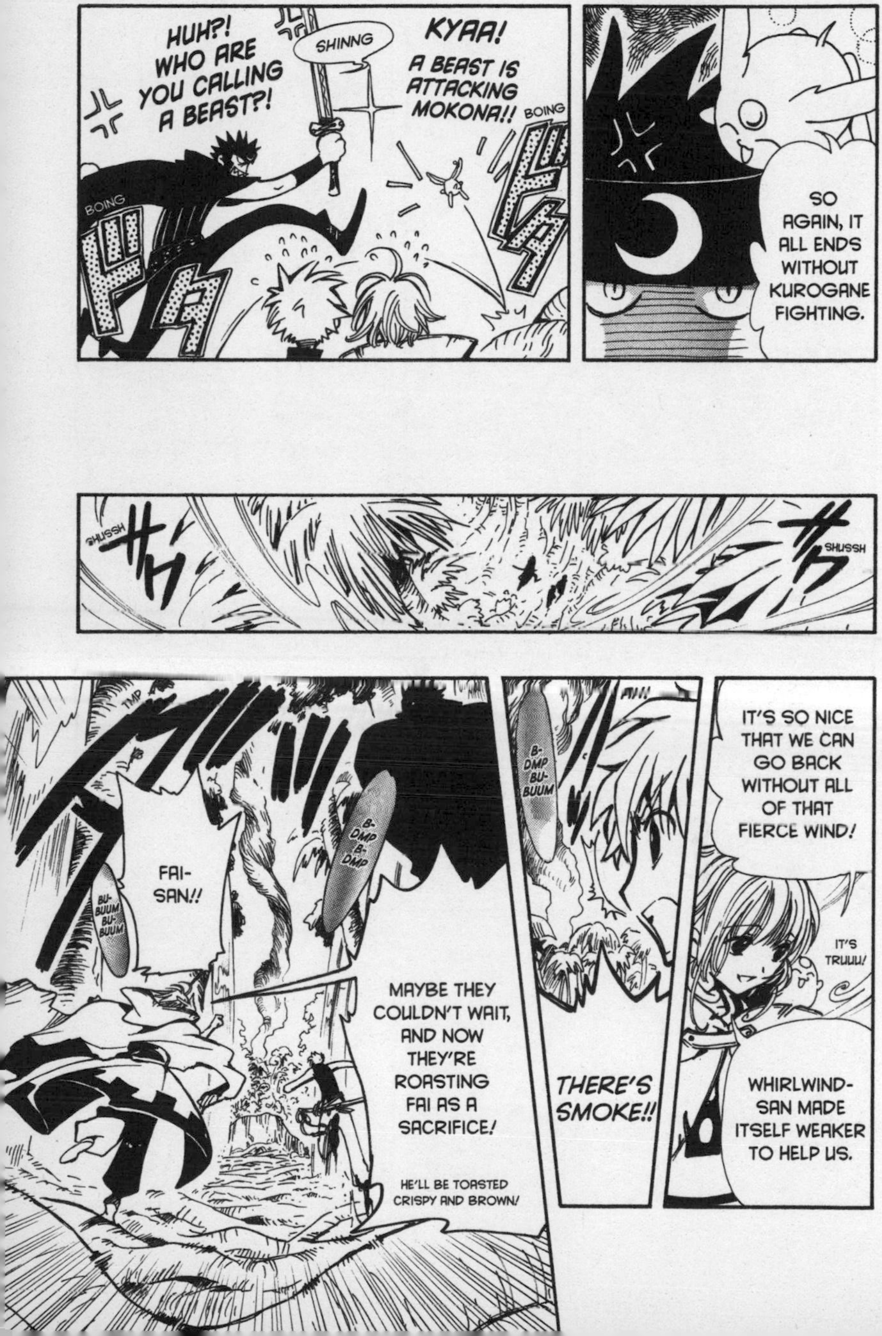
SO AGAIN, IT ALL ENDS WITHOUT KUROGANE FIGHTING.
KYAA! A BEAST IS ATTACKING MOKONA!!
BOING
SHINNG
HUH?! WHO ARE YOU CALLING A BEAST?!
BOING
SHUSSH
SHUSSH
IT'S SO NICE THAT WE CAN GO BACK WITHOUT ALL OF THAT FIERCE WIND!
IT'S TRUUU!
WHIRLWIND-SAN MADE ITSELF WEAKER TO HELP US.
AH!
B-DMP BU-BUUM
THERE'S SMOKE!!
TMP
B-DMP B-DMP
FAI-SAN!!
BU-BUUM BU-BUUM
MAYBE THEY COULDN'T WAIT, AND NOW THEY'RE ROASTING FAI AS A SACRIFICE!
HE'LL BE TOASTED CRISPY AND BROWN!

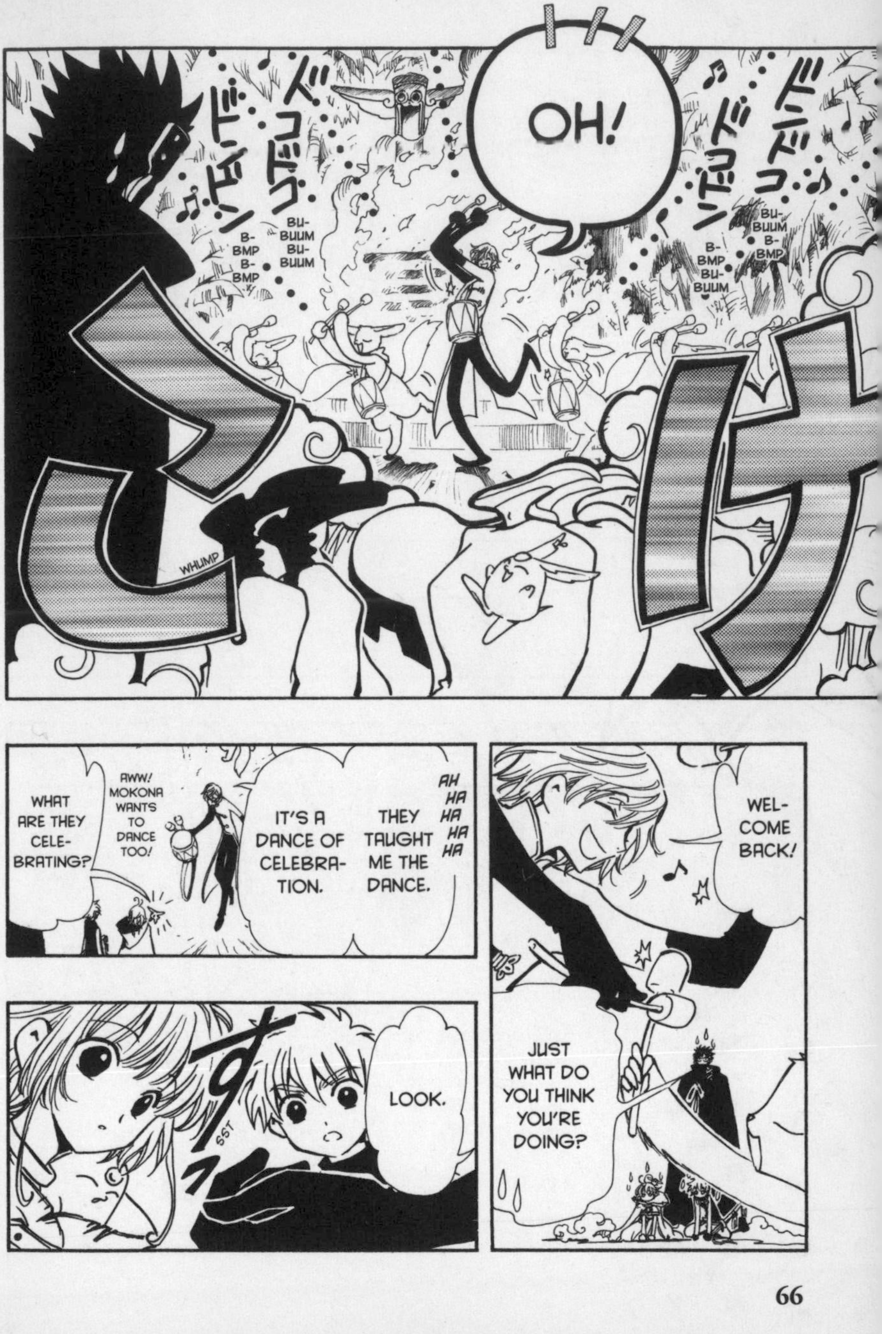
OH!
BU-BUUM B-BMP
B-BMP BU-BUUM
BU-BUUM BU-BUUM
B-BMP B-BMP
WHUMP
WEL-COME BACK!
JUST WHAT DO YOU THINK YOU'RE DOING?
AH HA HA HA HA
THEY TAUGHT ME THE DANCE.
IT'S A DANCE OF CELEBRATION.
AWW! MOKONA WANTS TO DANCE TOO!
WHAT ARE THEY CELEBRATING?
LOOK.
SST

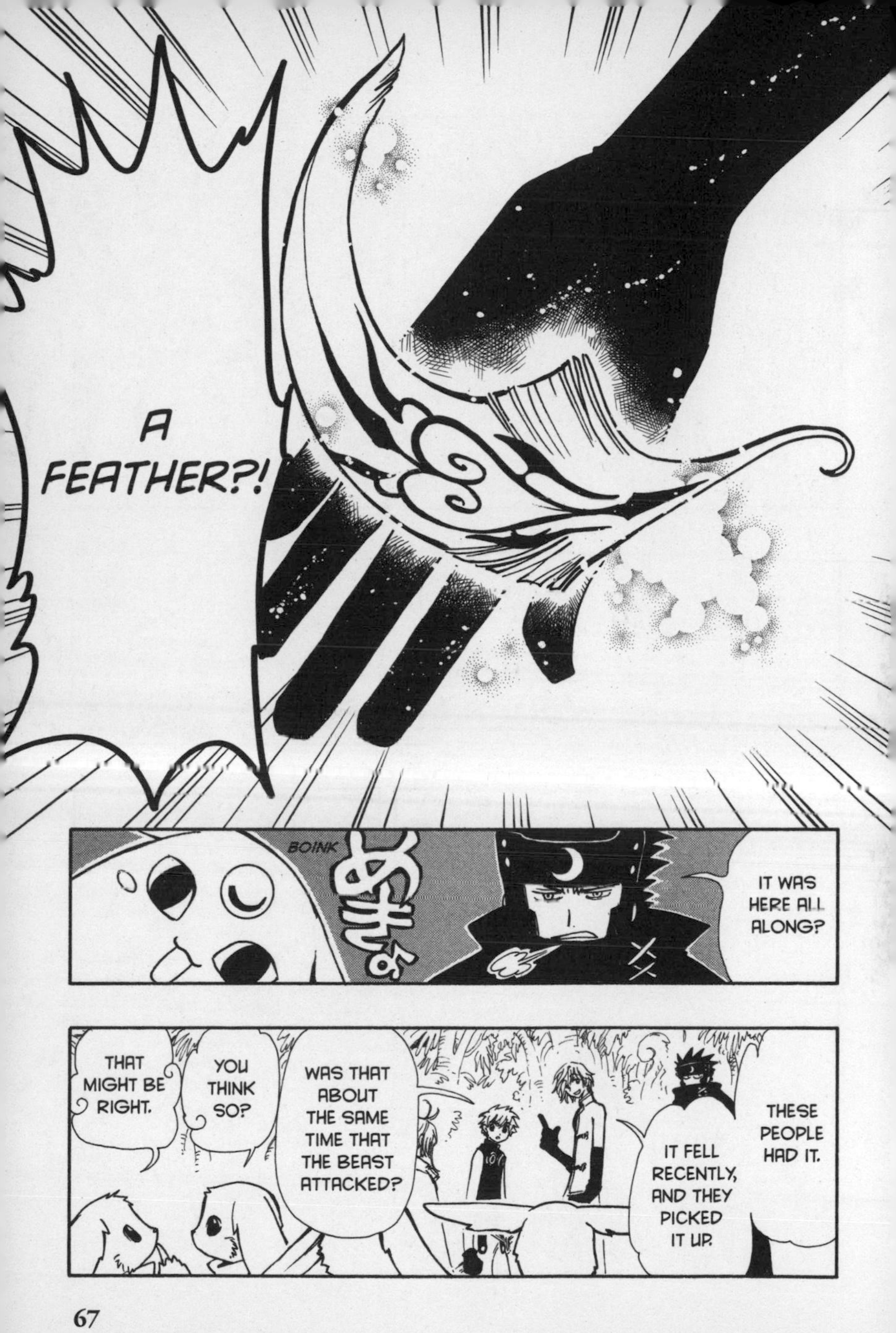
A FEATHER?!
IT WAS HERE ALL ALONG?
BOINK
THESE PEOPLE HAD IT.
IT FELL RECENTLY, AND THEY PICKED IT UP.
WAS THAT ABOUT THE SAME TIME THAT THE BEAST ATTACKED?
YOU THINK SO?
THAT MIGHT BE RIGHT.

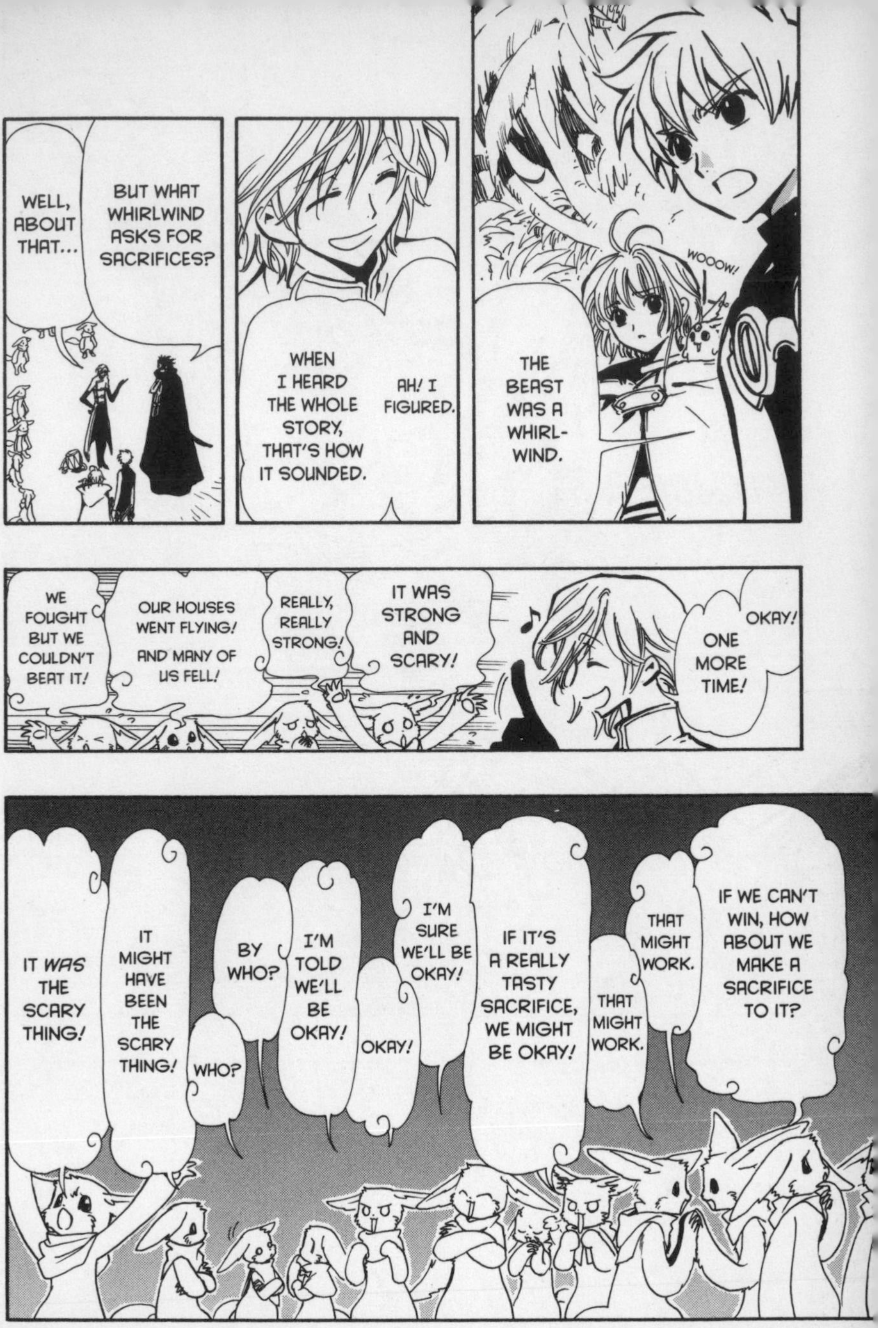
THE BEAST WAS A WHIRLWIND.
WOOOW!
AH! I FIGURED.
WHEN I HEARD THE WHOLE STORY, THAT'S HOW IT SOUNDED.
BUT WHAT WHIRLWIND ASKS FOR SACRIFICES?
WELL, ABOUT THAT...
OKAY! ONE MORE TIME!
IT WAS STRONG AND SCARY!
REALLY, REALLY STRONG!
OUR HOUSES WENT FLYING! AND MANY OF US FELL!
WE FOUGHT BUT WE COULDN'T BEAT IT!
IF WE CAN'T WIN, HOW ABOUT WE MAKE A SACRIFICE TO IT?
THAT MIGHT WORK.
THAT MIGHT WORK.
IF IT'S A REALLY TASTY SACRIFICE, WE MIGHT BE OKAY!
I'M SURE WE'LL BE OKAY!
OKAY!
I'M TOLD WE'LL BE OKAY!
BY WHO?
WHO?
IT MIGHT HAVE BEEN THE SCARY THING!
IT *WAS* THE SCARY THING!

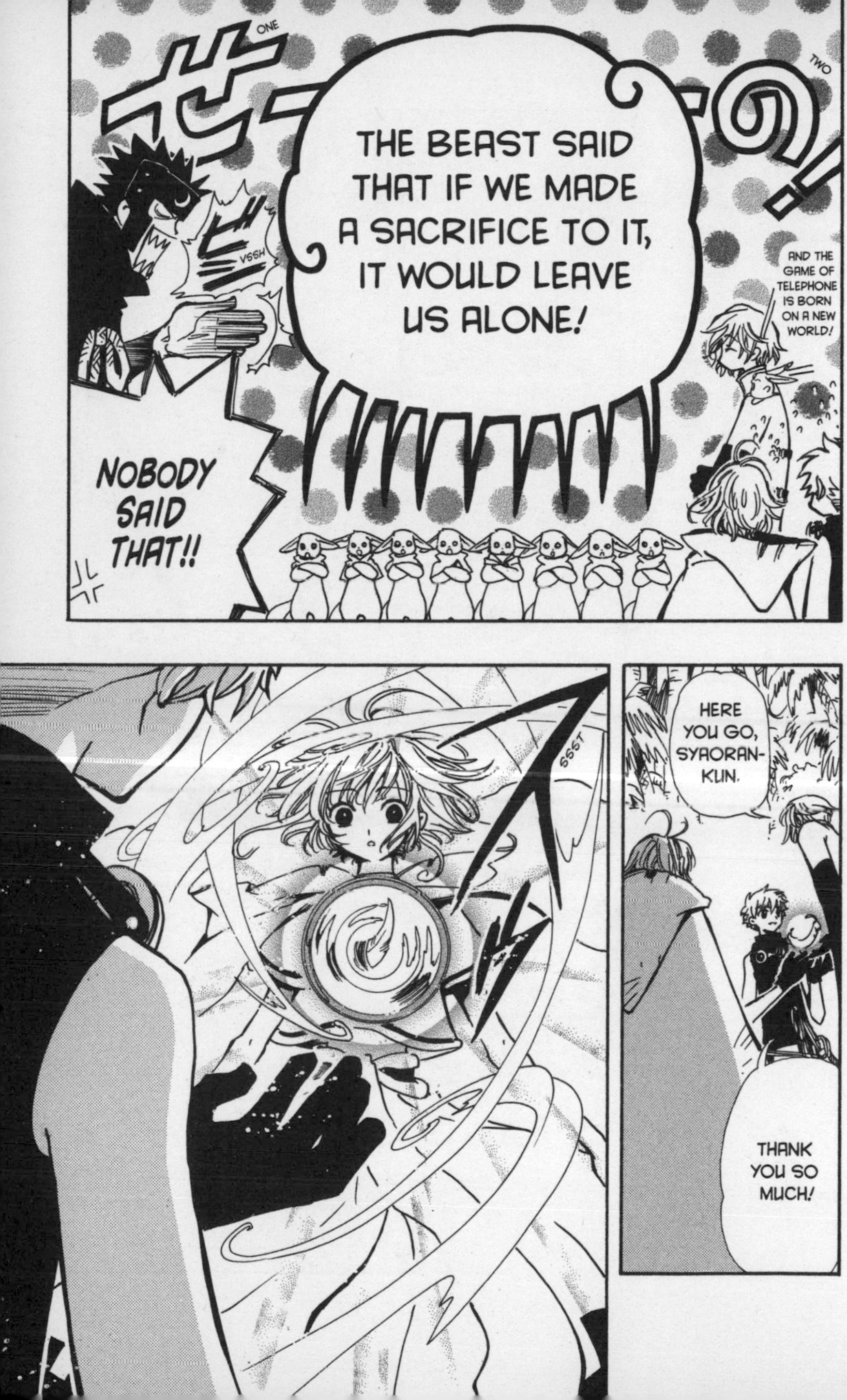
せーの!
ONE
TWO
THE BEAST SAID THAT IF WE MADE A SACRIFICE TO IT, IT WOULD LEAVE US ALONE!
AND THE GAME OF TELEPHONE IS BORN ON A NEW WORLD!
VSSH
NOBODY SAID THAT!!
HERE YOU GO, SYAORAN-KUN.
THANK YOU SO MUCH!
SSST

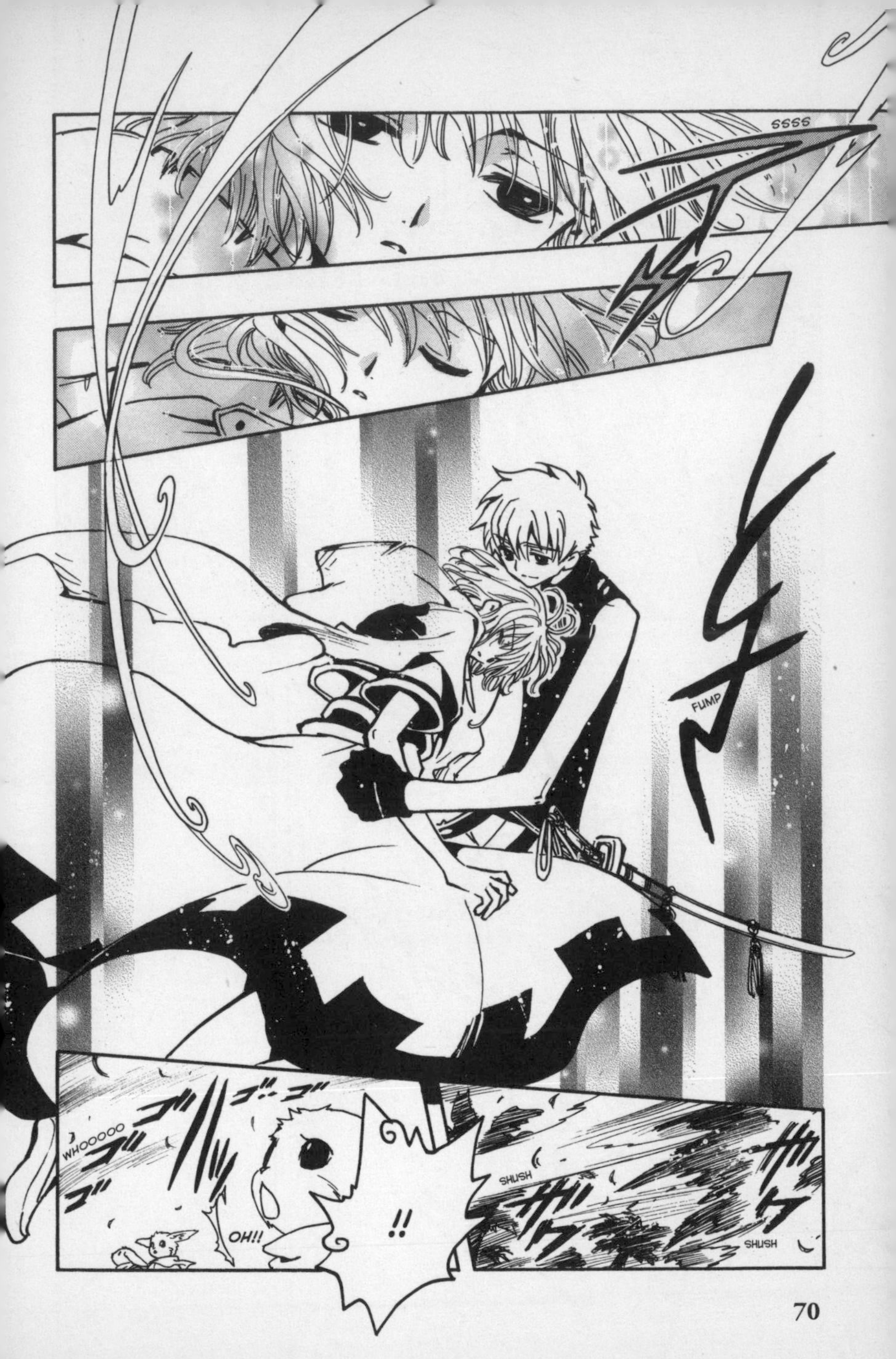
SSSS
FUMP
SHUSH
SHUSH
!!
OH!!
WHOOOOO

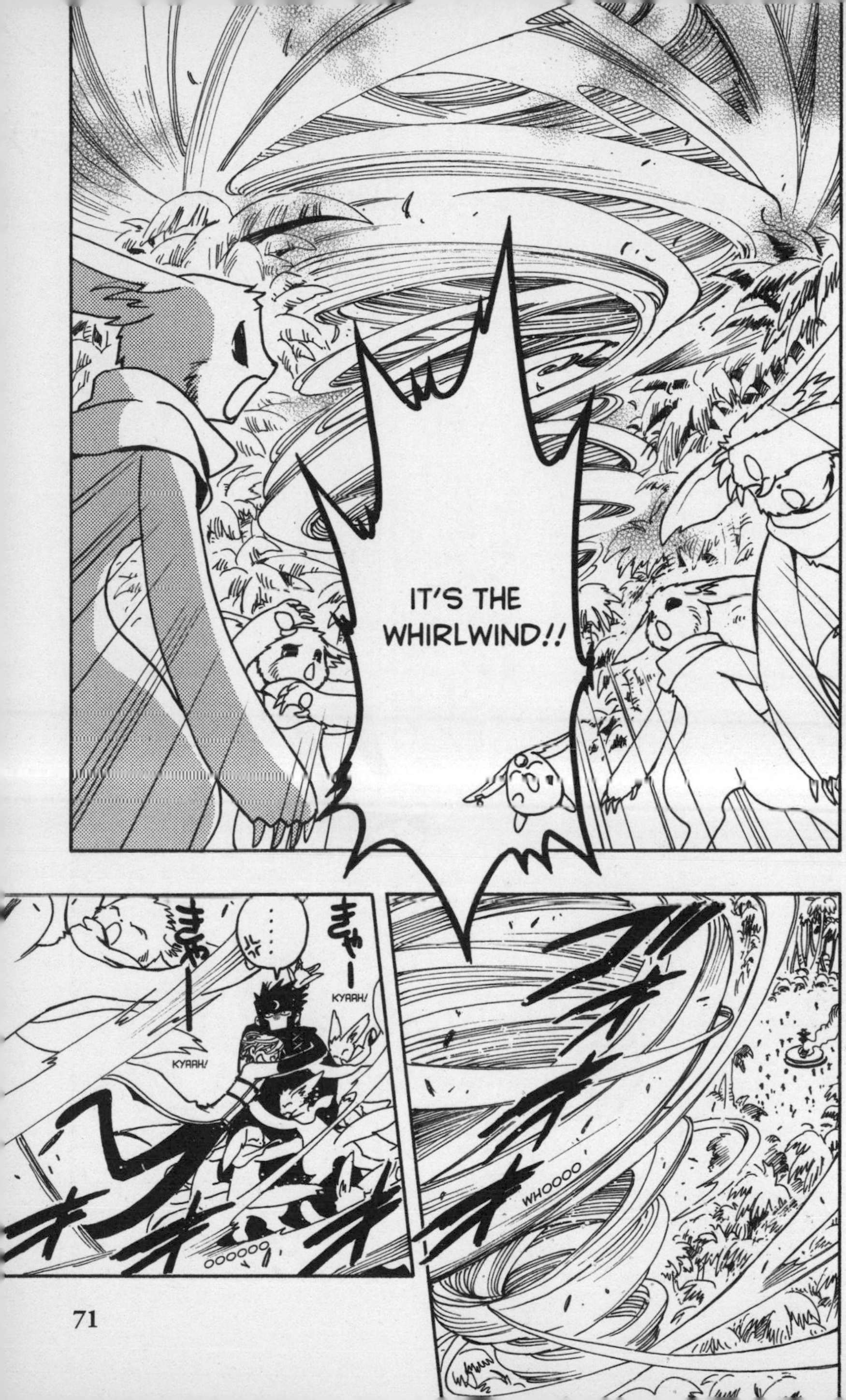
IT'S THE WHIRLWIND!!
WHOOOO
きゃー
KYAAH!
......
きゃー
KYAAH!
OOOOOO

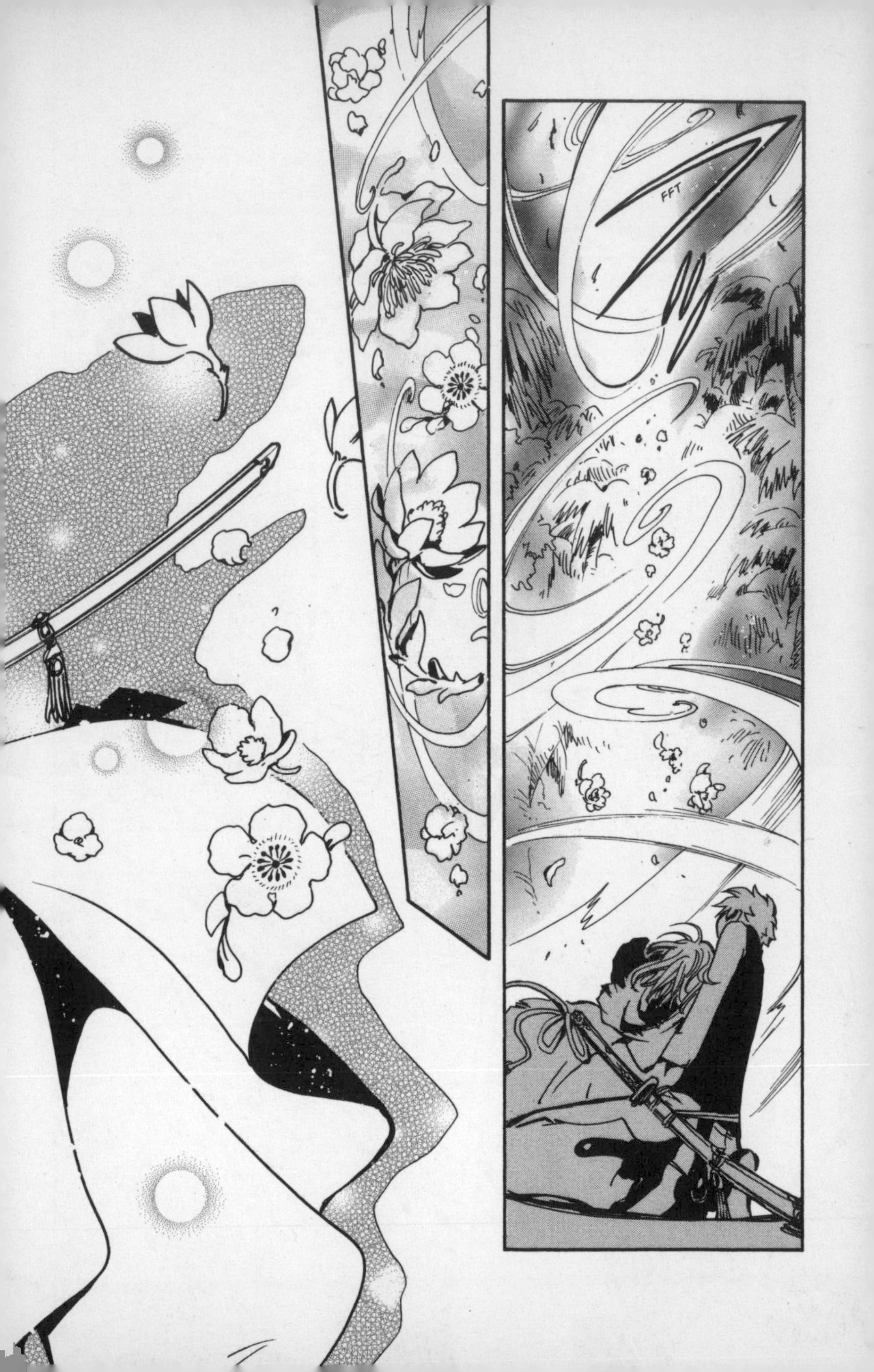
FFT

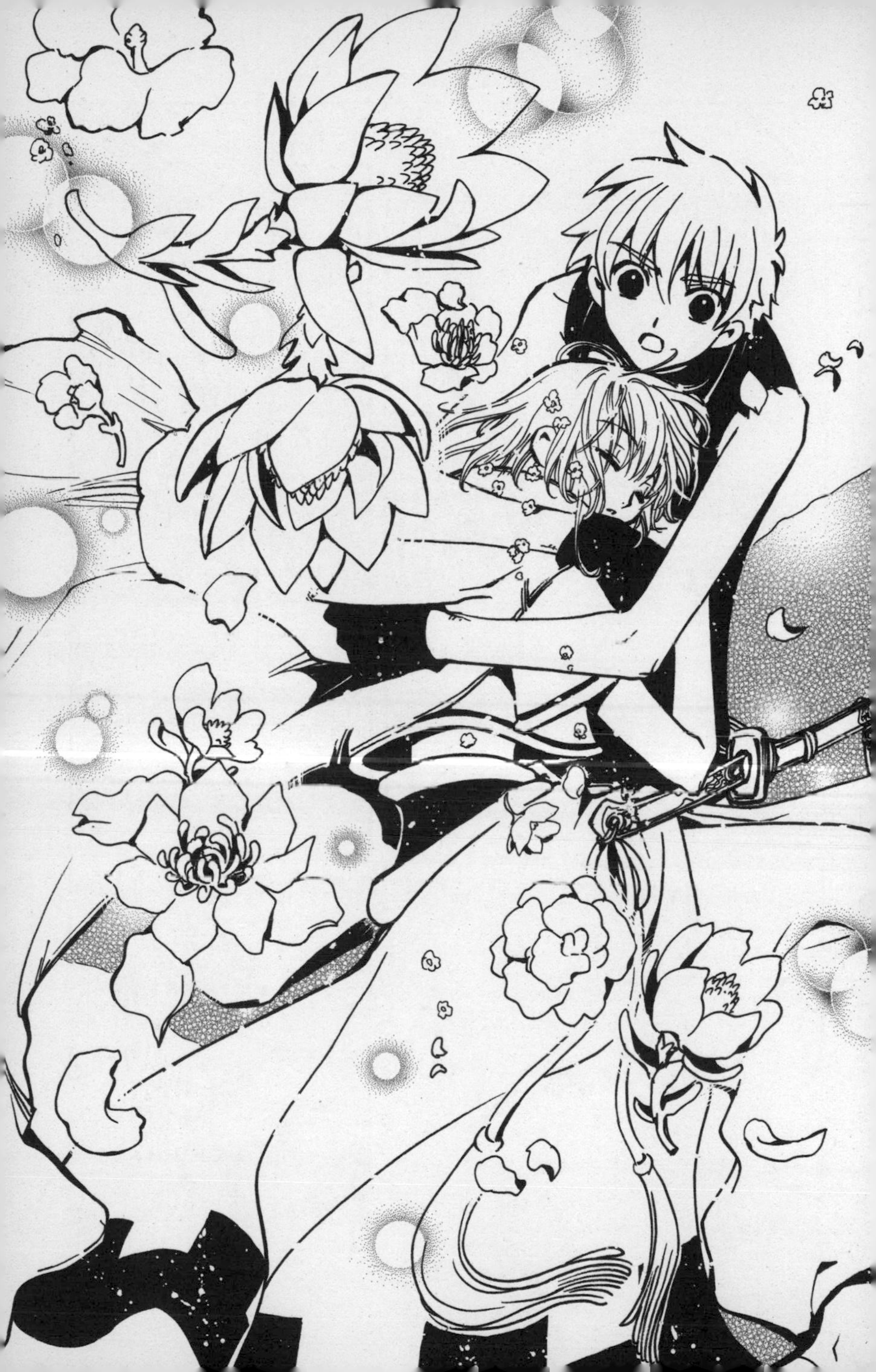

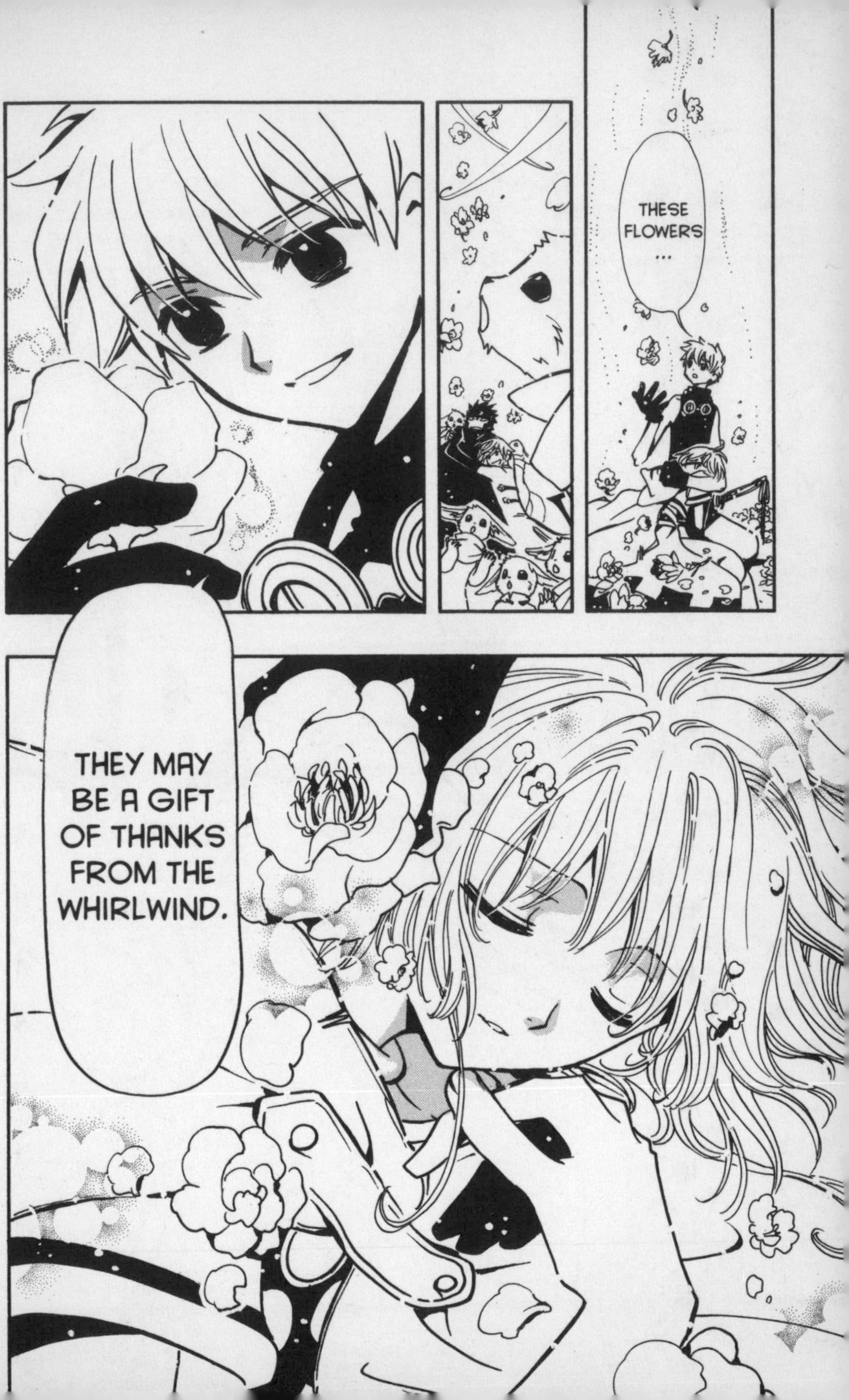
THESE FLOWERS ...
THEY MAY BE A GIFT OF THANKS FROM THE WHIRLWIND.

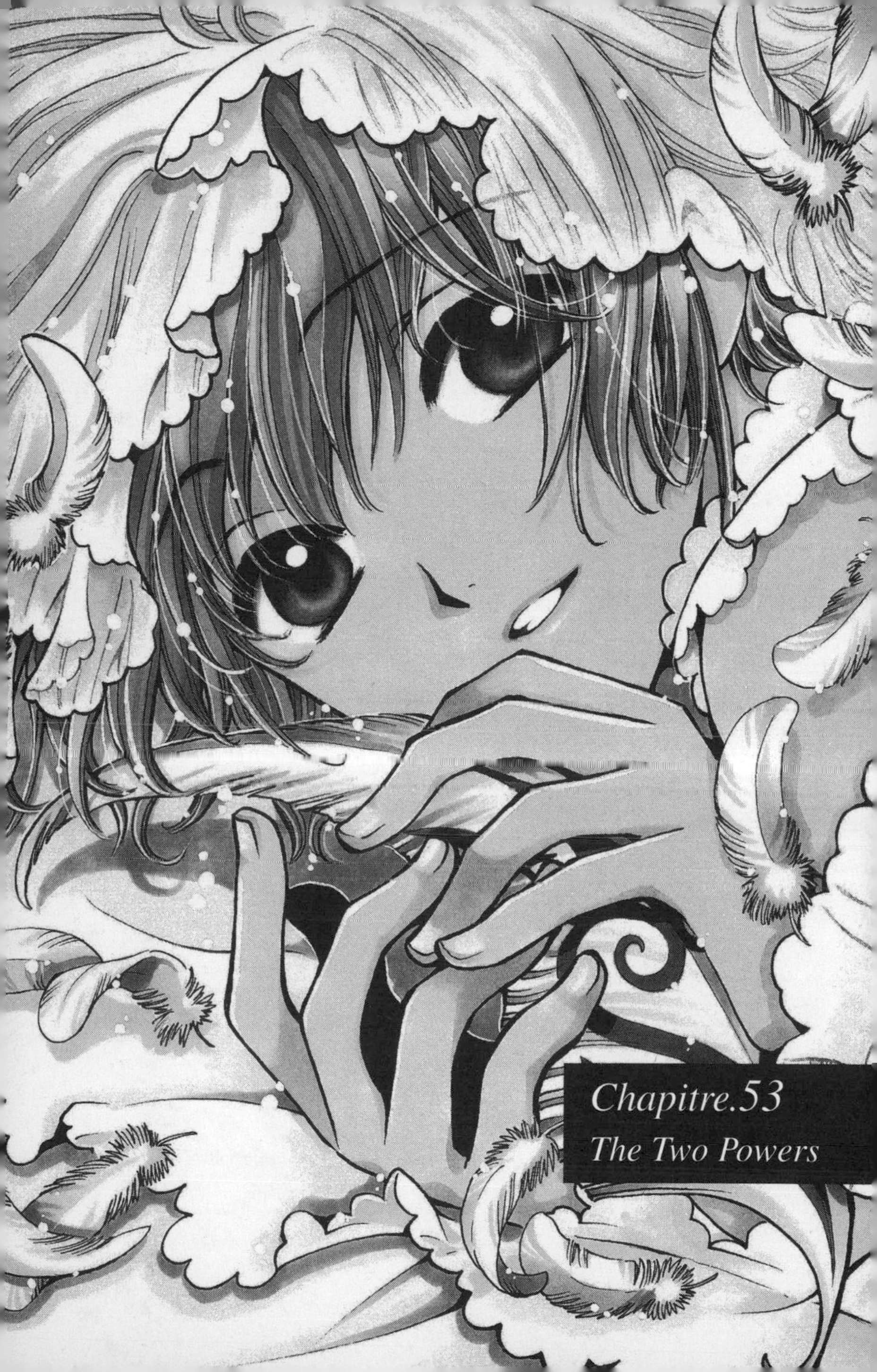

Chapitre.53
The Two Powers

ツバサ

RESERVoir CHRoNiCLE

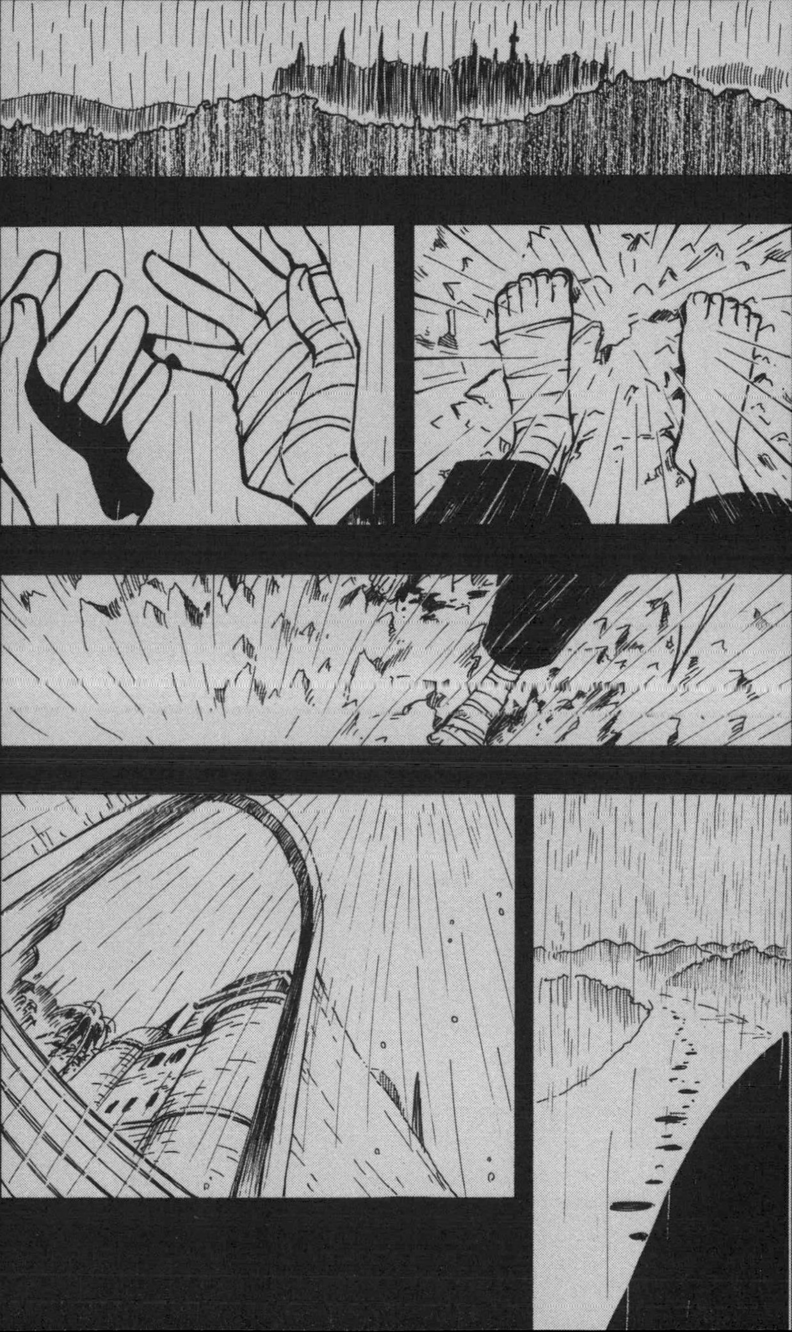

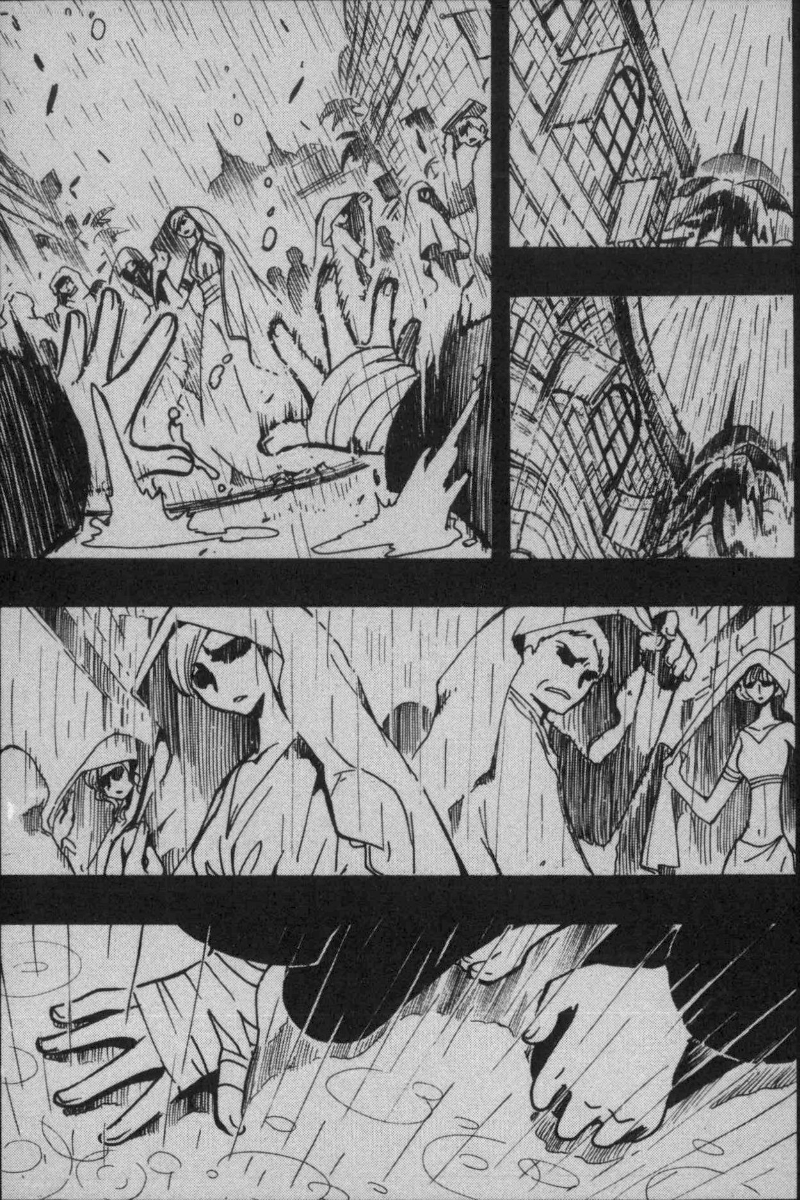

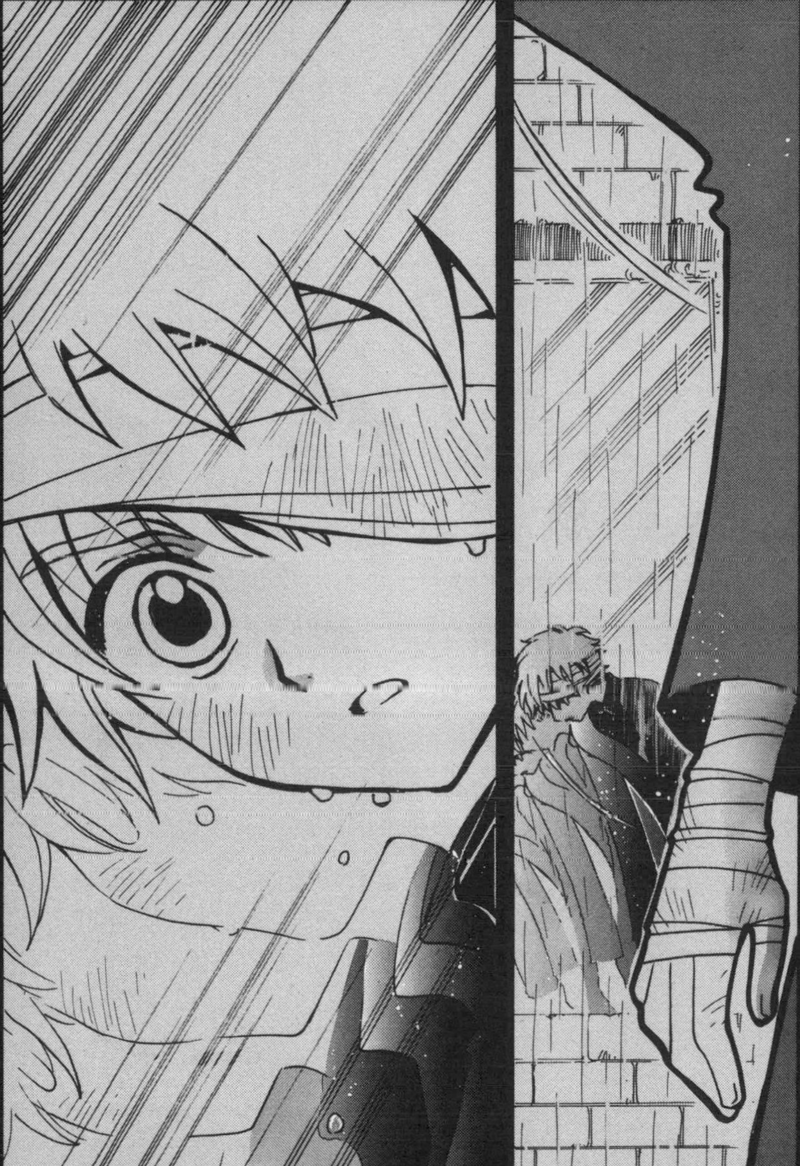

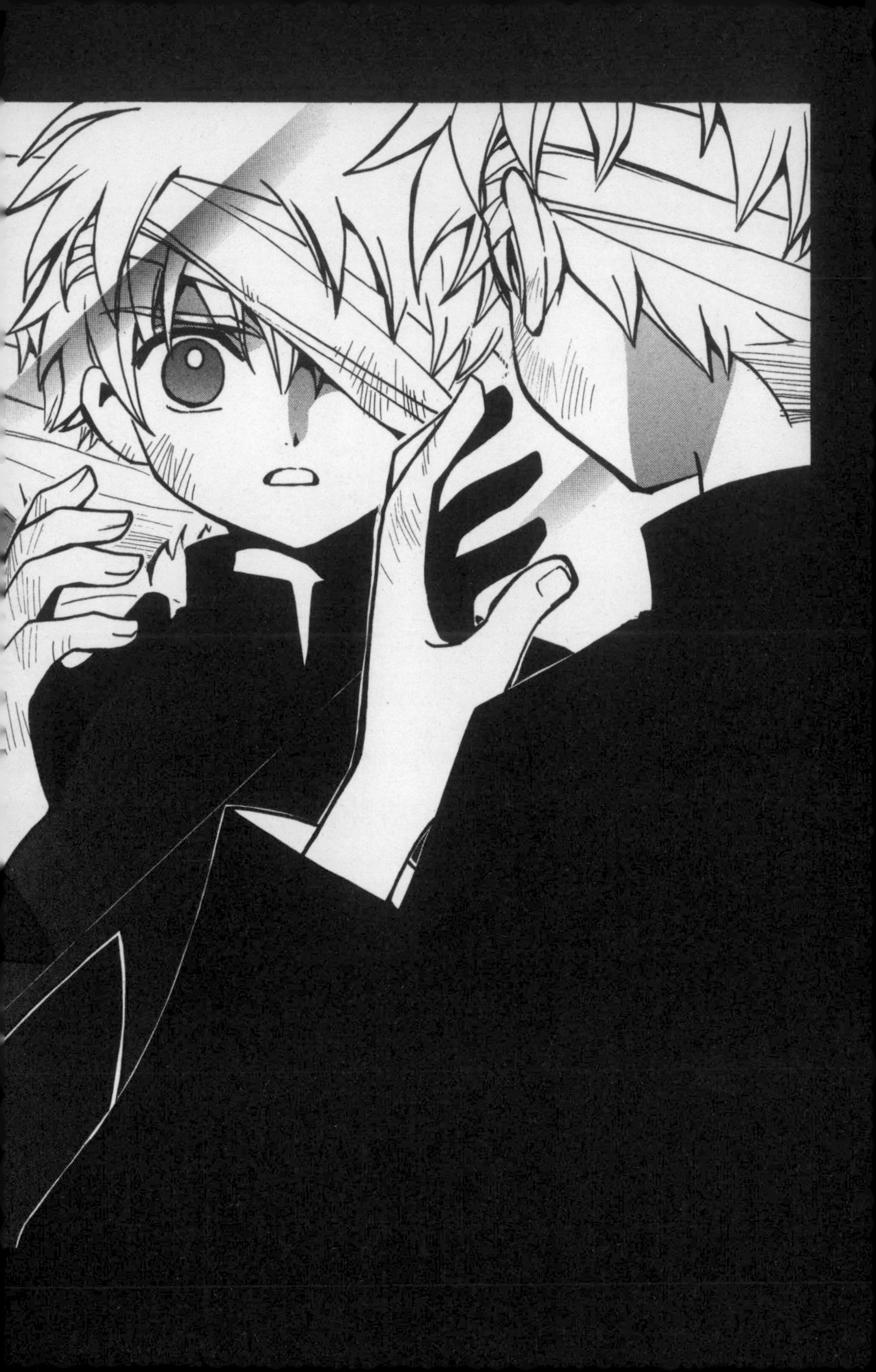

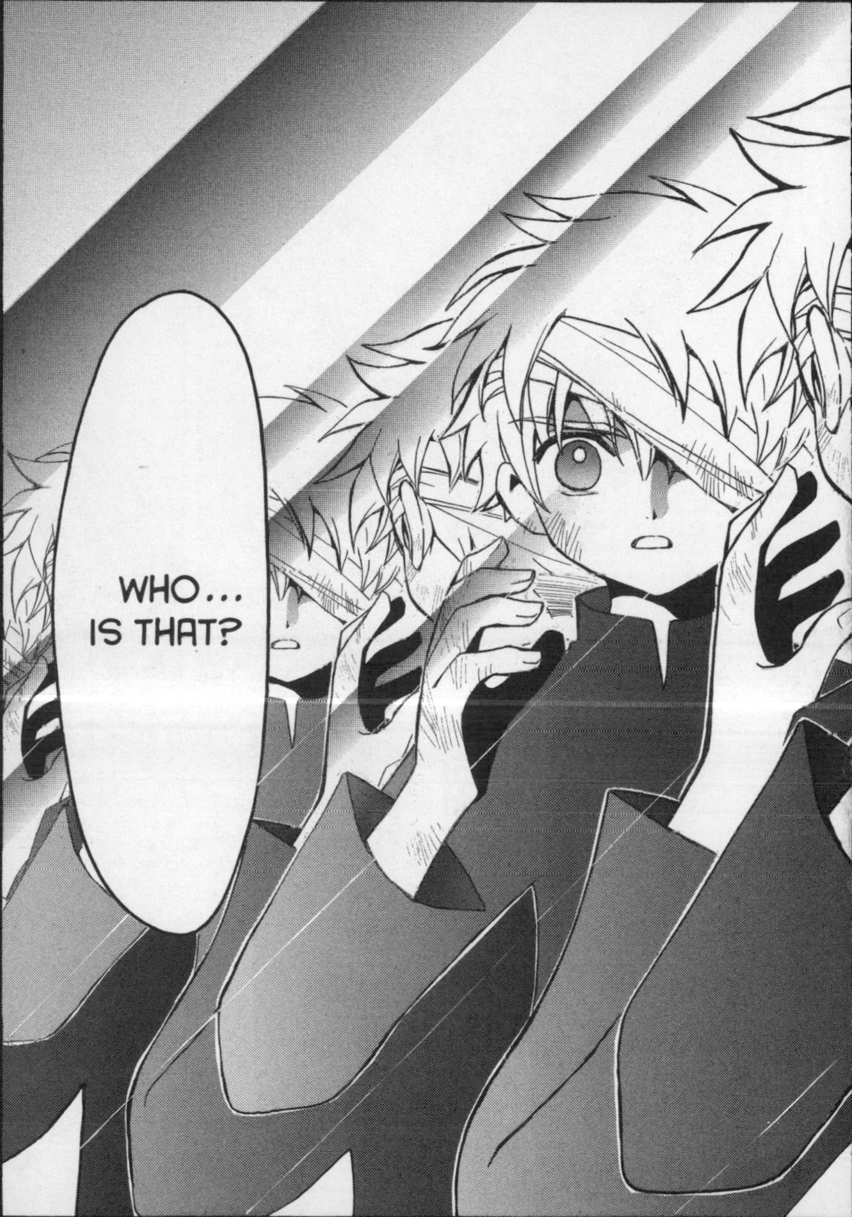
WHO... IS THAT?

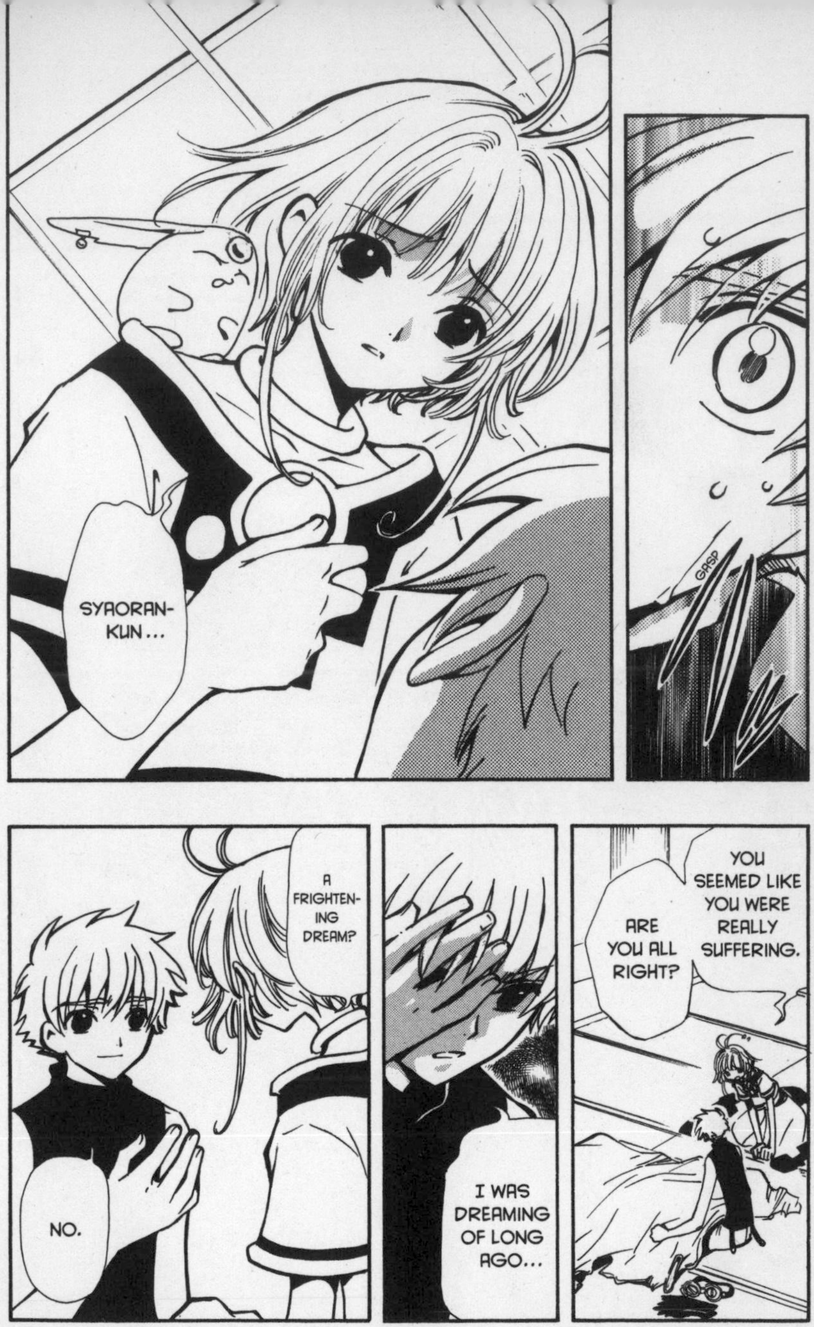
GASP
SYAORAN-KUN...
YOU SEEMED LIKE YOU WERE REALLY SUFFERING.
ARE YOU ALL RIGHT?
I WAS DREAMING OF LONG AGO...
A FRIGHTENING DREAM?
NO.

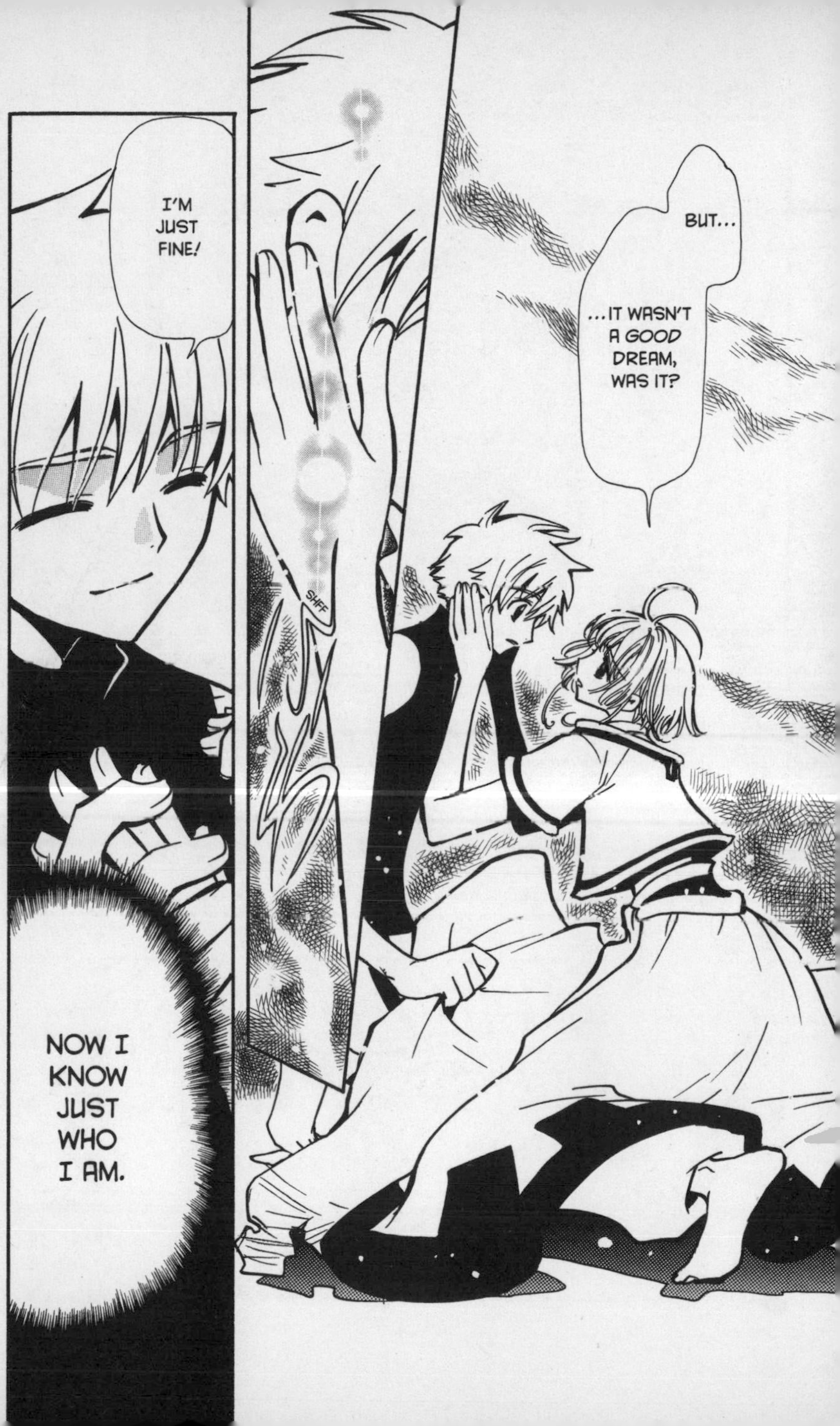
BUT...
...IT WASN'T A *GOOD* DREAM, WAS IT?
SHFF
I'M JUST FINE!
NOW I KNOW JUST WHO I AM.

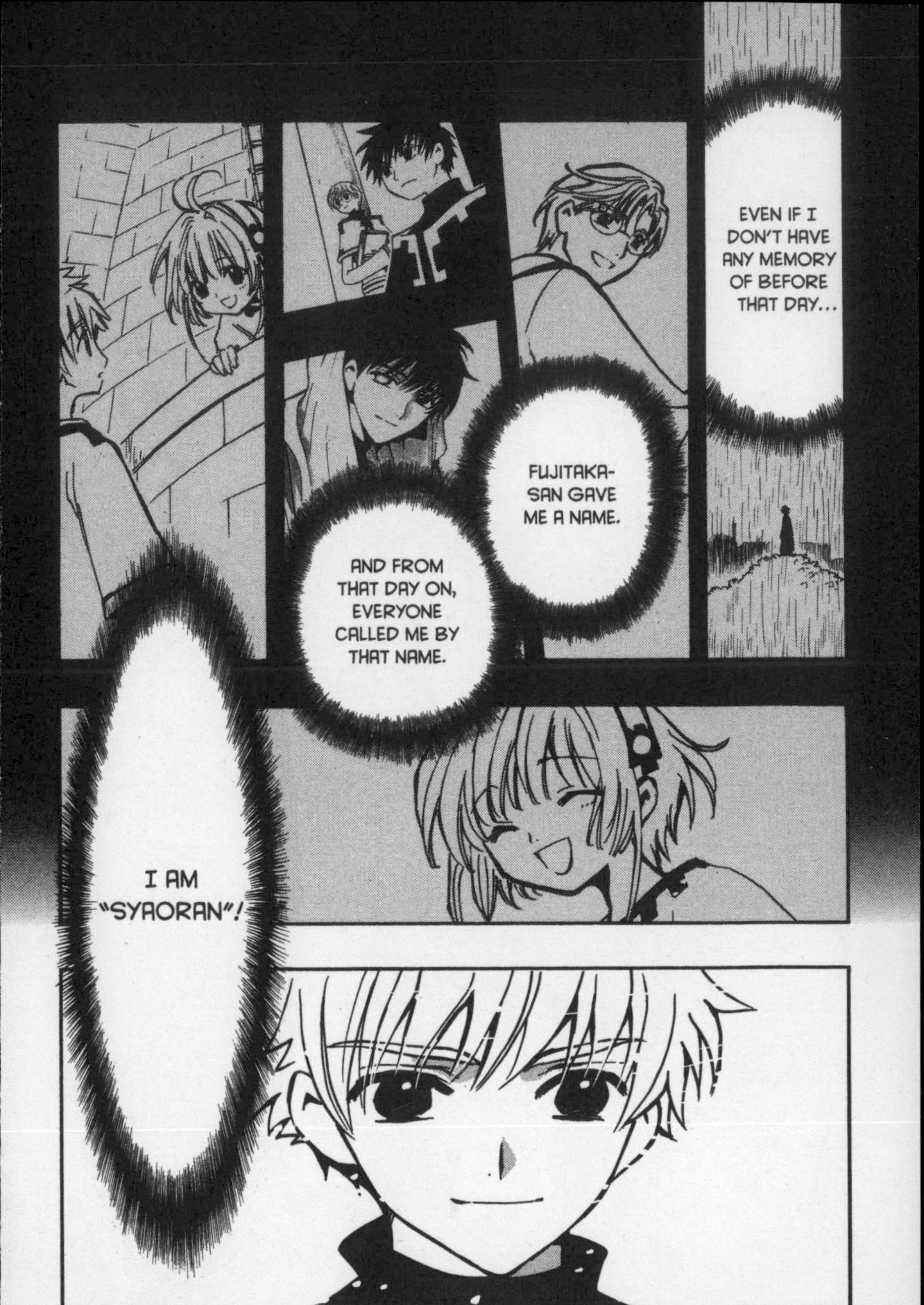
EVEN IF I DON'T HAVE ANY MEMORY OF BEFORE THAT DAY...
FUJITAKA-SAN GAVE ME A NAME.
AND FROM THAT DAY ON, EVERYONE CALLED ME BY THAT NAME.
I AM "SYAORAN"!

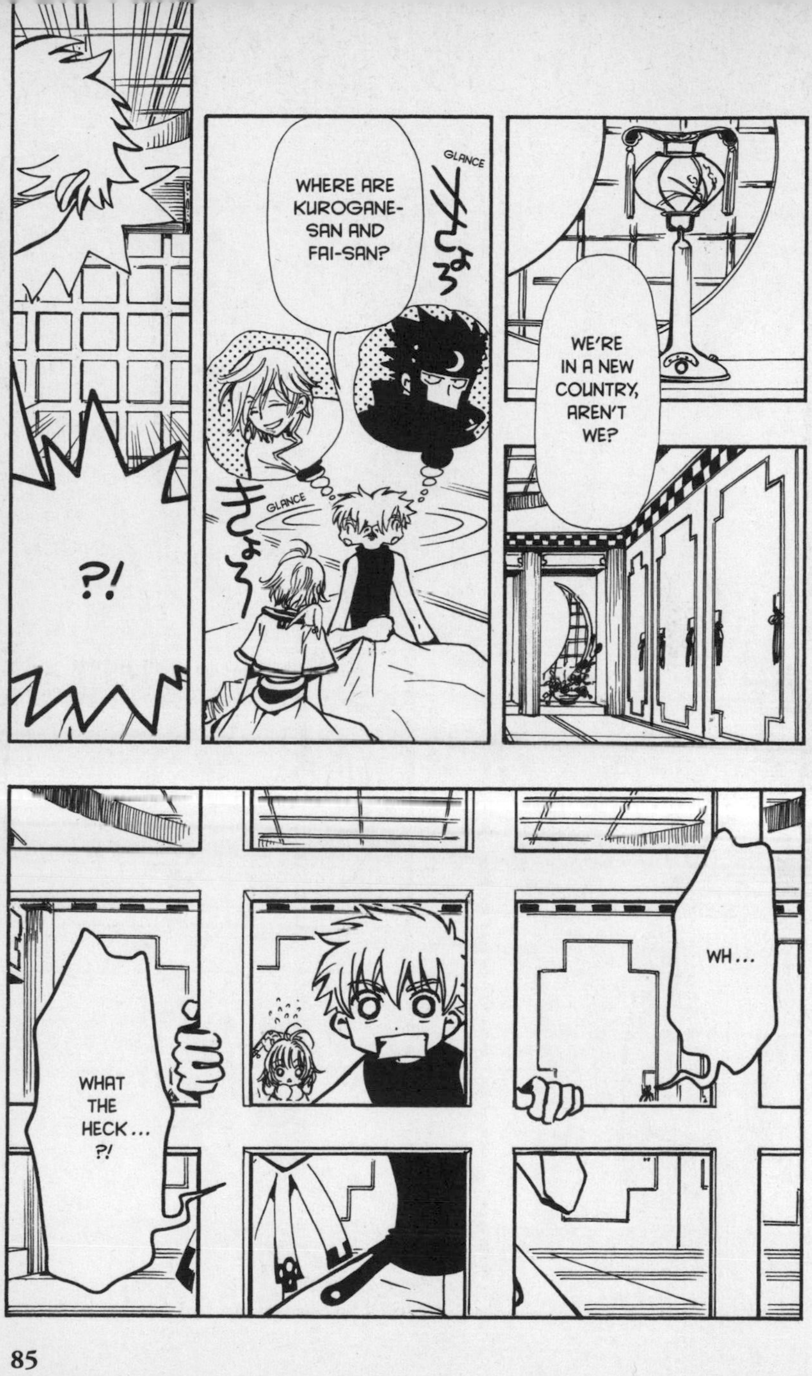
WE'RE IN A NEW COUNTRY, AREN'T WE?
WHERE ARE KUROGANE-SAN AND FAI-SAN?
GLANCE
GLANCE
?!
WH...
WHAT THE HECK...?!

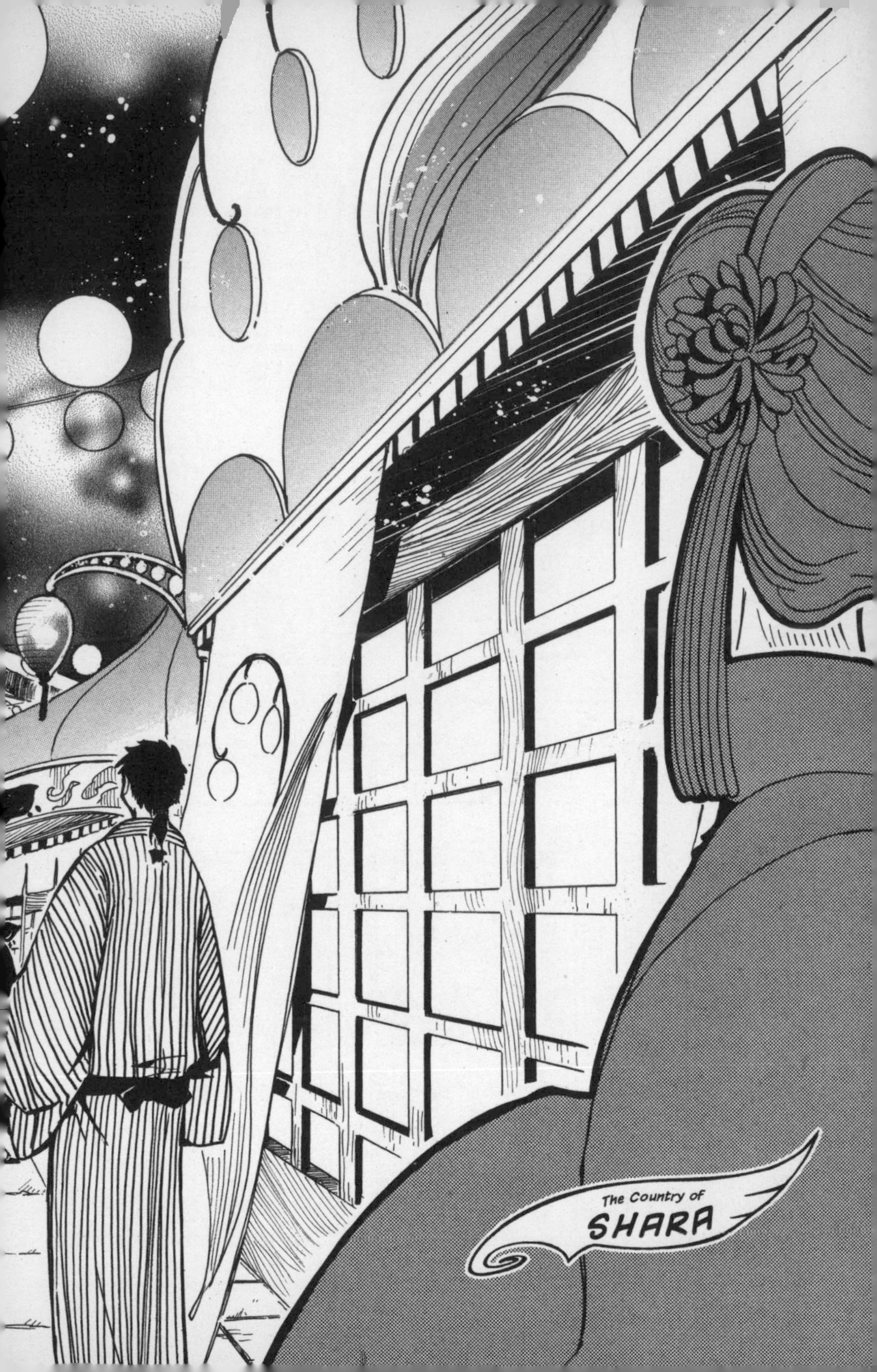
The Country of
SHARA

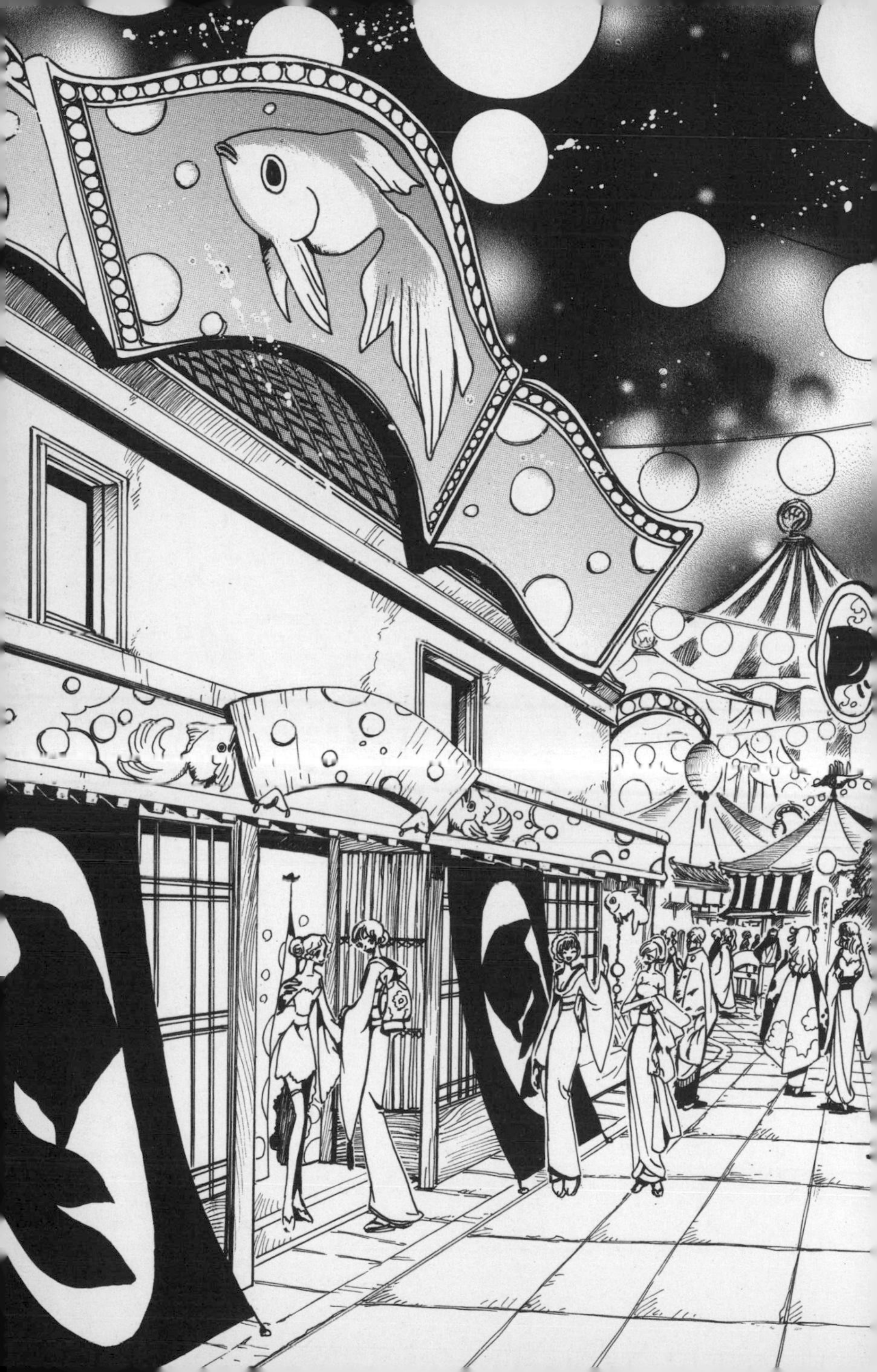

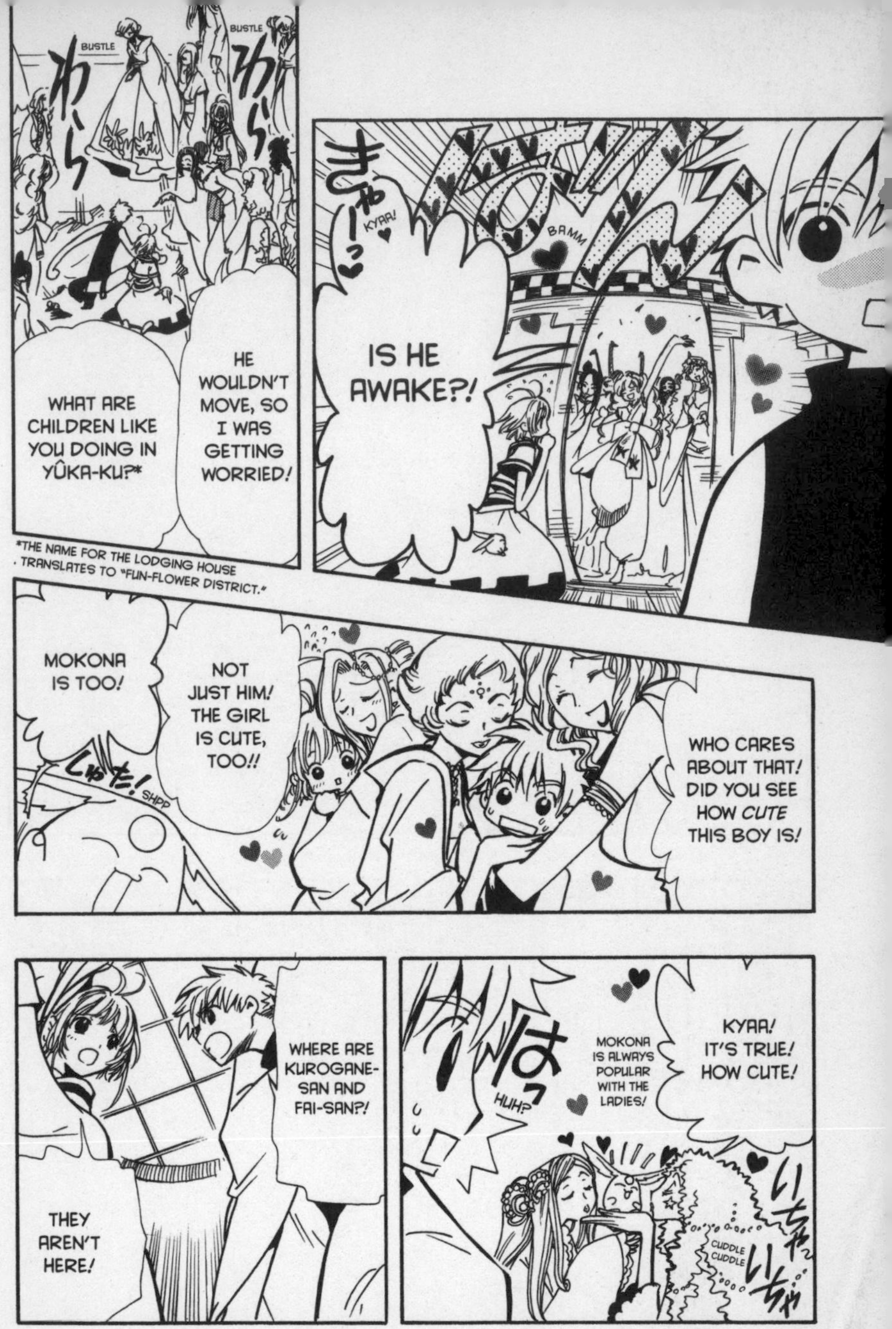
KYAA!
BAMM
IS HE AWAKE?!
BUSTLE
BUSTLE
HE WOULDN'T MOVE, SO I WAS GETTING WORRIED!
WHAT ARE CHILDREN LIKE YOU DOING IN YÛKA-KU?*
WHO CARES ABOUT THAT! DID YOU SEE HOW *CUTE* THIS BOY IS!
NOT JUST HIM! THE GIRL IS CUTE, TOO!!
MOKONA IS TOO!
SHPP
KYAA! IT'S TRUE! HOW CUTE!
MOKONA IS ALWAYS POPULAR WITH THE LADIES!
HUH?
CUDDLE CUDDLE
WHERE ARE KUROGANE-SAN AND FAI-SAN?!
THEY AREN'T HERE!

*THE NAME FOR THE LODGING HOUSE. TRANSLATES TO "FUN-FLOWER DISTRICT."

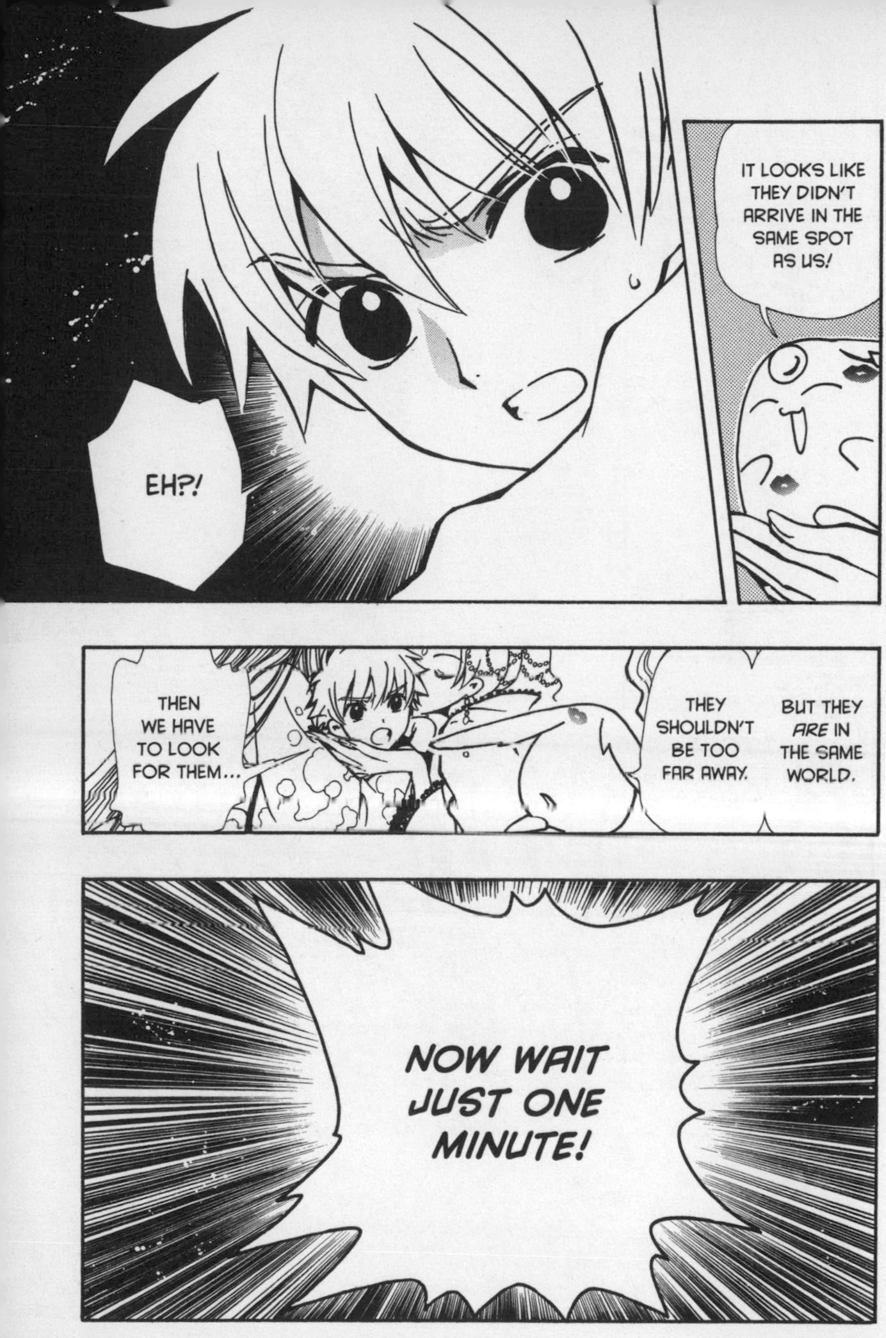
IT LOOKS LIKE THEY DIDN'T ARRIVE IN THE SAME SPOT AS US!
EH?!
BUT THEY *ARE* IN THE SAME WORLD.
THEY SHOULDN'T BE TOO FAR AWAY.
THEN WE HAVE TO LOOK FOR THEM...
NOW WAIT JUST ONE MINUTE!

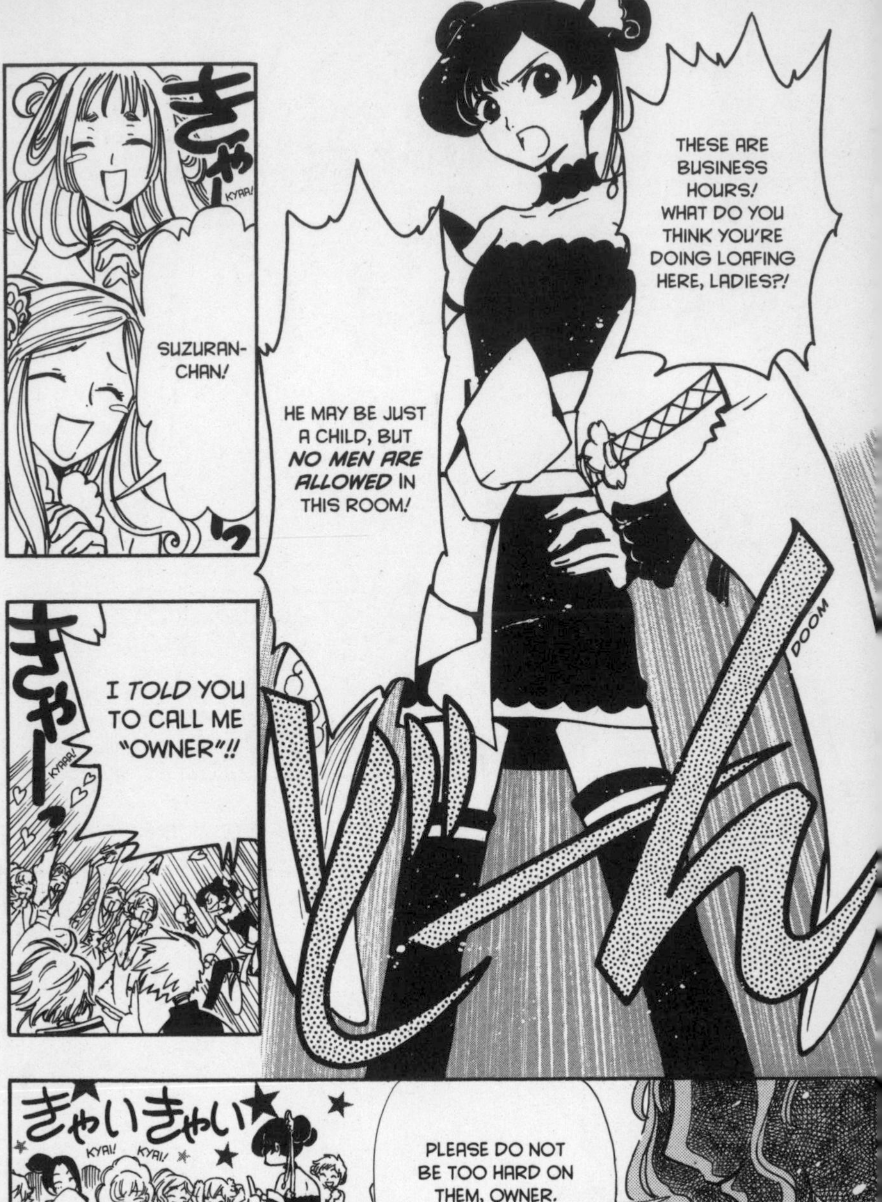
THESE ARE BUSINESS HOURS! WHAT DO YOU THINK YOU'RE DOING LOAFING HERE, LADIES?!
HE MAY BE JUST A CHILD, BUT *NO MEN ARE ALLOWED* IN THIS ROOM!
DOOM
きゃー
KYAA!
SUZURAN-CHAN!
I *TOLD* YOU TO CALL ME "OWNER"!!
きゃー
KYAA!
きゃいきゃい
KYAI! KYAI!
PLEASE DO NOT BE TOO HARD ON THEM, OWNER.

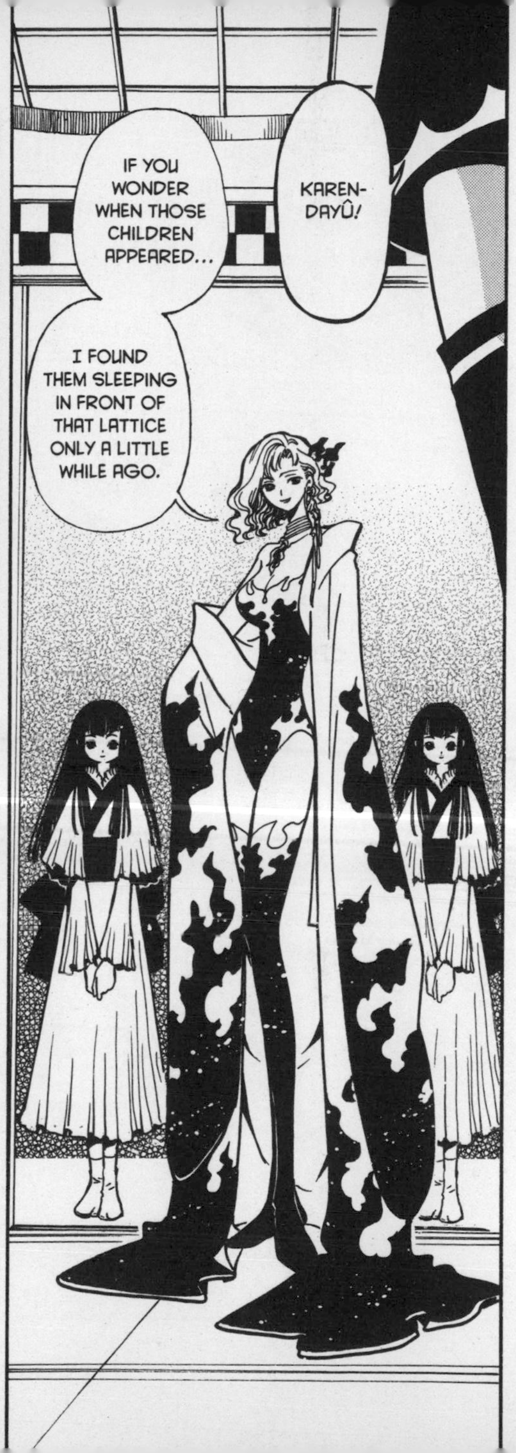
KAREN-DAYÛ!
IF YOU WONDER WHEN THOSE CHILDREN APPEARED...
I FOUND THEM SLEEPING IN FRONT OF THAT LATTICE ONLY A LITTLE WHILE AGO.
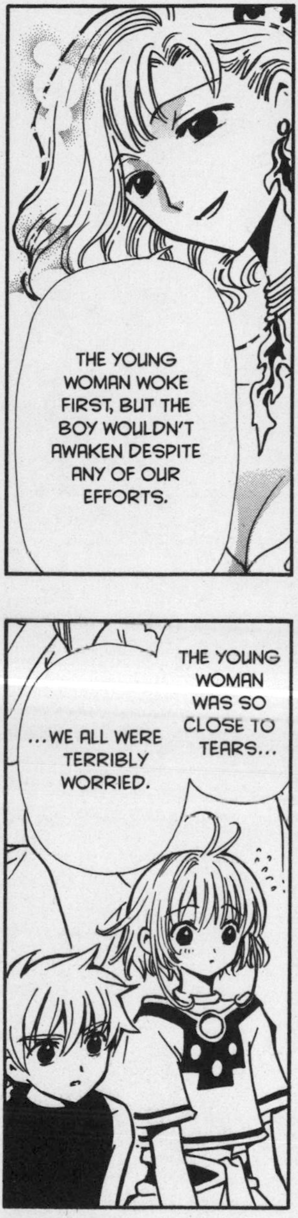
THE YOUNG WOMAN WOKE FIRST, BUT THE BOY WOULDN'T AWAKEN DESPITE ANY OF OUR EFFORTS.
THE YOUNG WOMAN WAS SO CLOSE TO TEARS...
...WE ALL WERE TERRIBLY WORRIED.

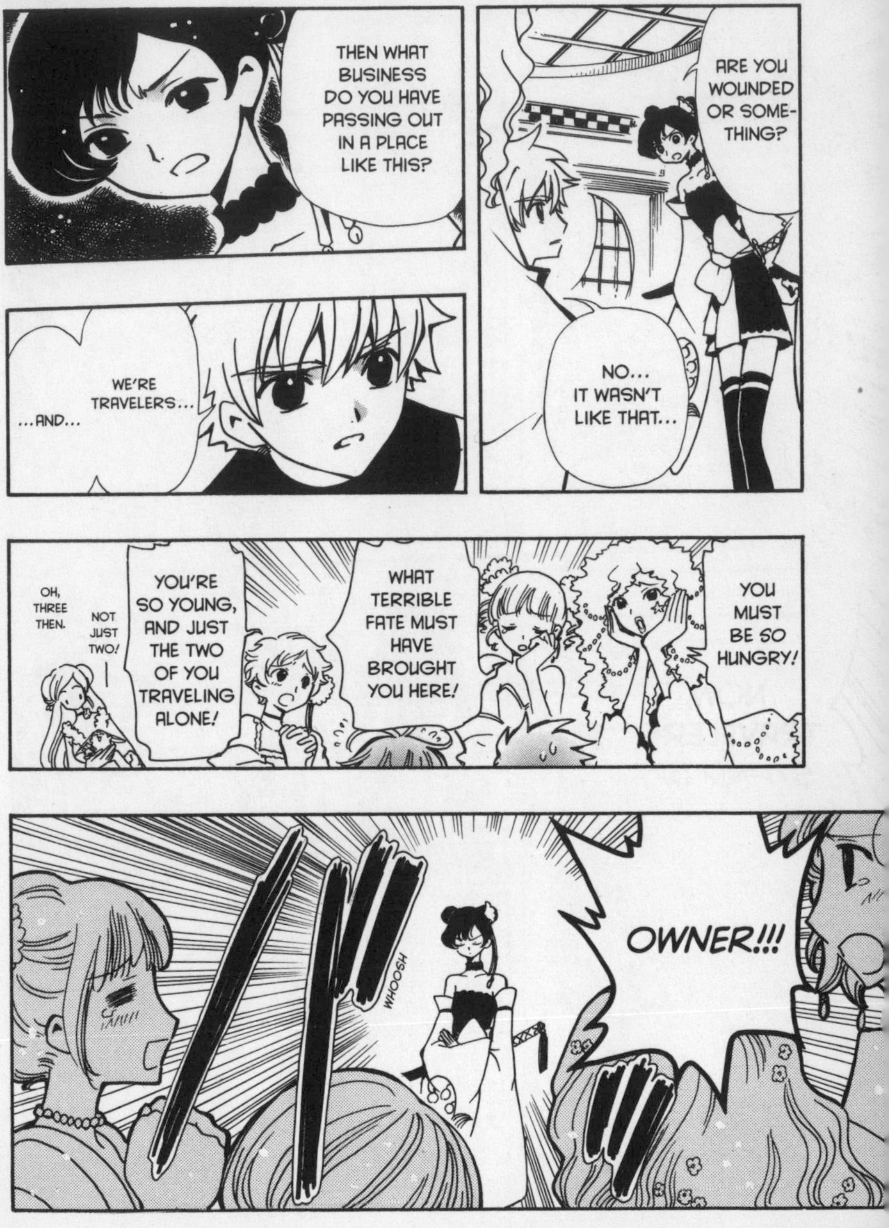

ARE YOU WOUNDED OR SOME-THING?
NO... IT WASN'T LIKE THAT...
THEN WHAT BUSINESS DO YOU HAVE PASSING OUT IN A PLACE LIKE THIS?
WE'RE TRAVELERS...
...AND...
YOU MUST BE SO HUNGRY!
WHAT TERRIBLE FATE MUST HAVE BROUGHT YOU HERE!
YOU'RE SO YOUNG, AND JUST THE TWO OF YOU TRAVELING ALONE!
NOT JUST TWO!
OH, THREE THEN.
OWNER!!!
WHOOSH

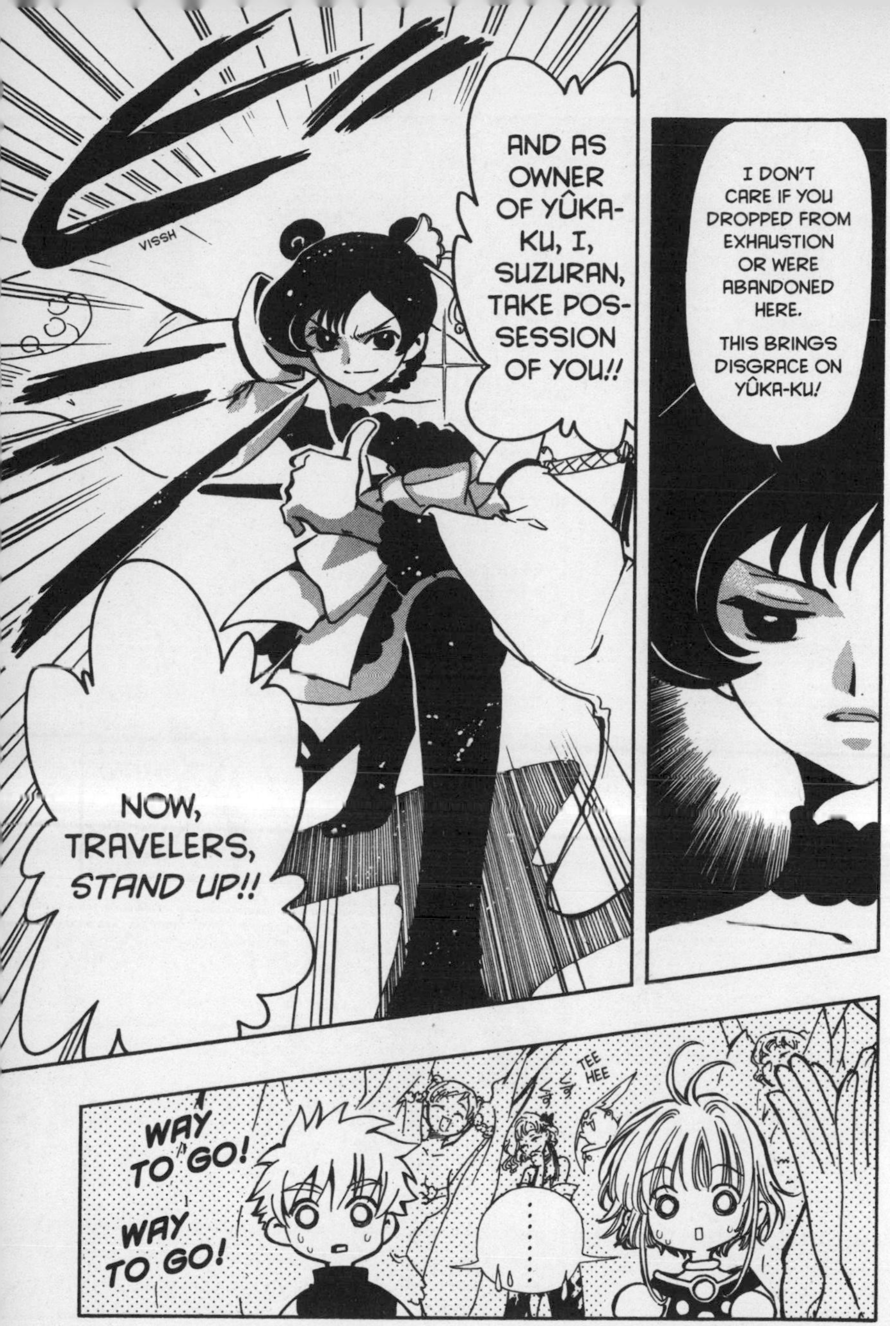
I DON'T CARE IF YOU DROPPED FROM EXHAUSTION OR WERE ABANDONED HERE.
THIS BRINGS DISGRACE ON YÛKA-KU!
AND AS OWNER OF YÛKA-KU, I, SUZURAN, TAKE POSSESSION OF YOU!!
VISSH
NOW, TRAVELERS, STAND UP!!
TEE HEE
WAY TO GO!
WAY TO GO!

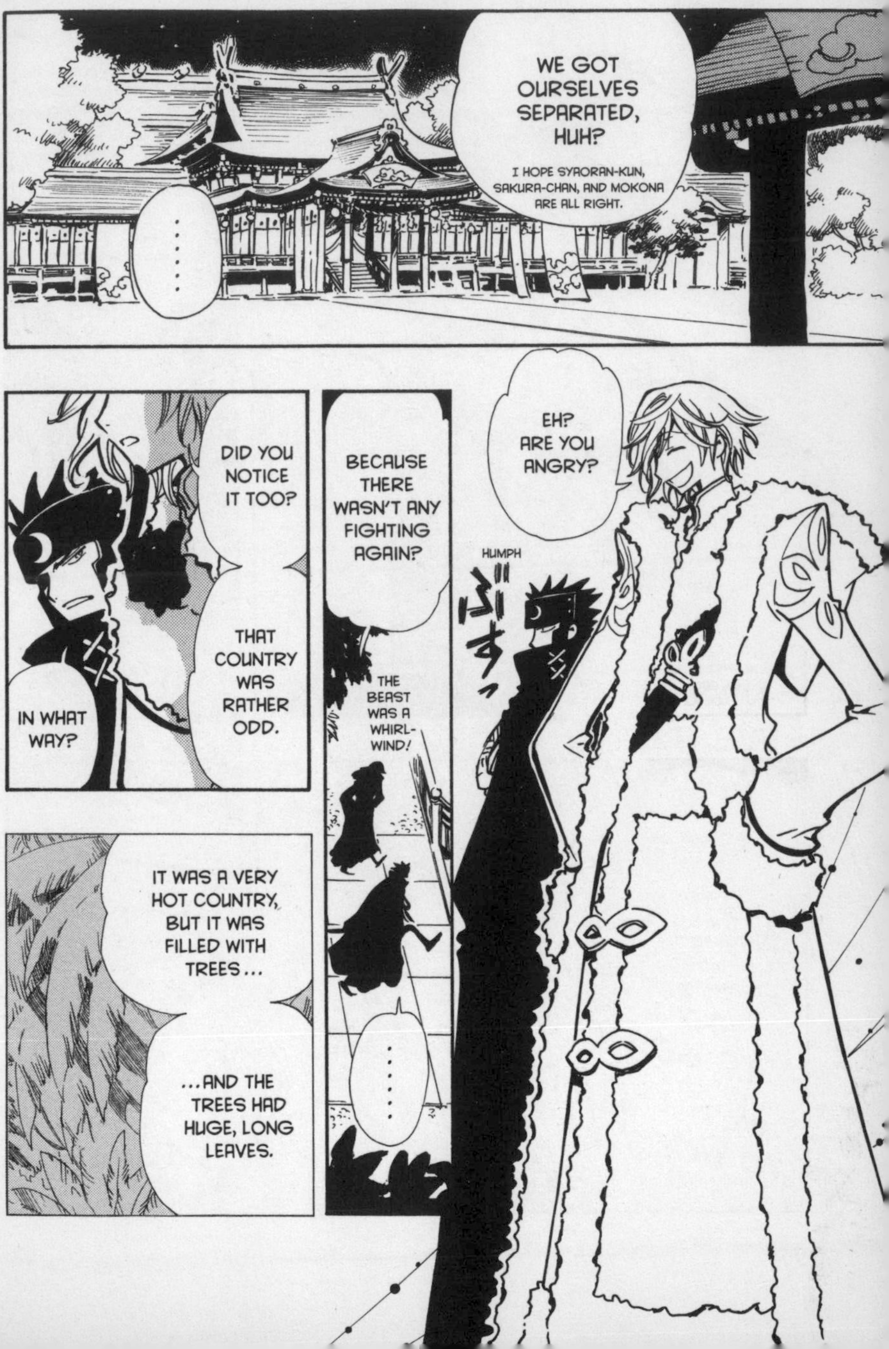
WE GOT OURSELVES SEPARATED, HUH?
I HOPE SYAORAN-KUN, SAKURA-CHAN, AND MOKONA ARE ALL RIGHT.
......
EH? ARE YOU ANGRY?
HUMPH
ぶすっ
BECAUSE THERE WASN'T ANY FIGHTING AGAIN?
THE BEAST WAS A WHIRLWIND!
......
DID YOU NOTICE IT TOO?
THAT COUNTRY WAS RATHER ODD.
IN WHAT WAY?
IT WAS A VERY HOT COUNTRY, BUT IT WAS FILLED WITH TREES...
...AND THE TREES HAD HUGE, LONG LEAVES.

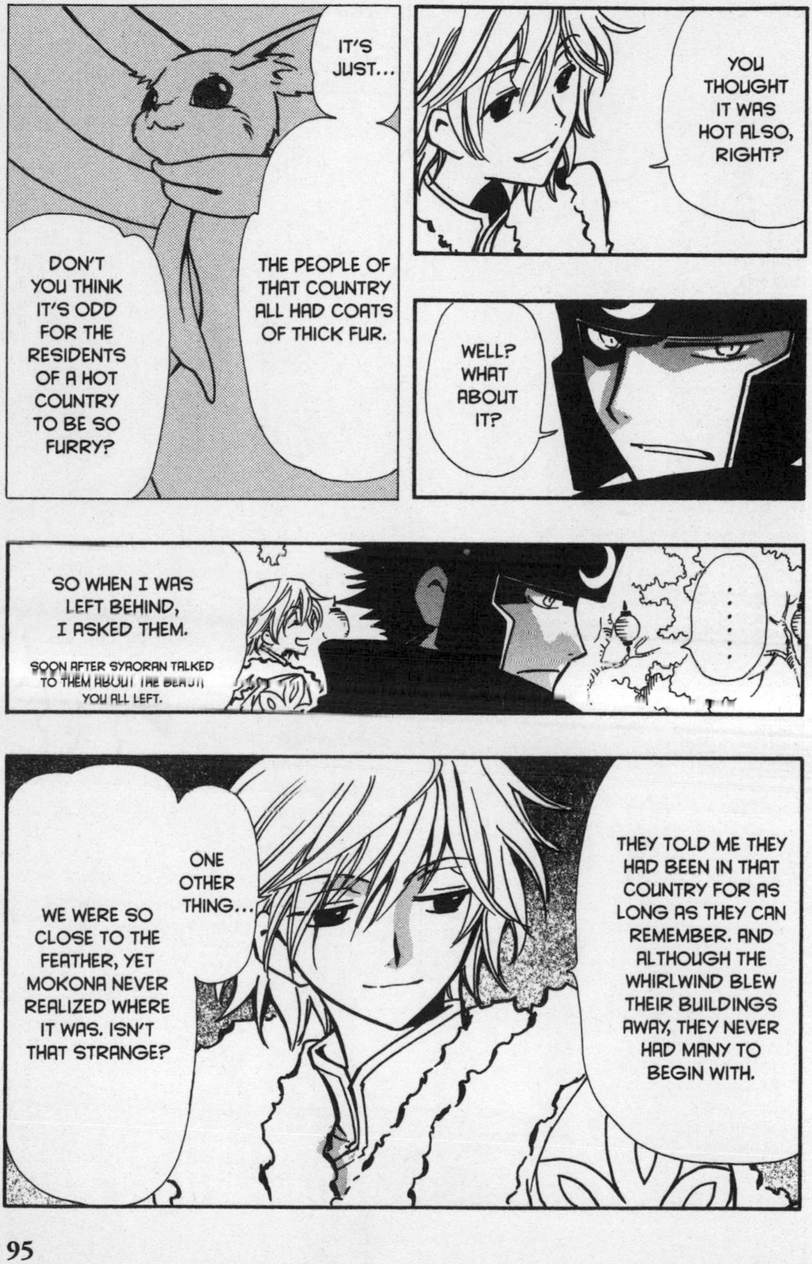
YOU THOUGHT IT WAS HOT ALSO, RIGHT?
WELL? WHAT ABOUT IT?
IT'S JUST...
THE PEOPLE OF THAT COUNTRY ALL HAD COATS OF THICK FUR.
DON'T YOU THINK IT'S ODD FOR THE RESIDENTS OF A HOT COUNTRY TO BE SO FURRY?
......
SO WHEN I WAS LEFT BEHIND, I ASKED THEM.
SOON AFTER SYAORAN TALKED TO THEM ABOUT THE BEAST, YOU ALL LEFT.
THEY TOLD ME THEY HAD BEEN IN THAT COUNTRY FOR AS LONG AS THEY CAN REMEMBER. AND ALTHOUGH THE WHIRLWIND BLEW THEIR BUILDINGS AWAY, THEY NEVER HAD MANY TO BEGIN WITH.
ONE OTHER THING...
WE WERE SO CLOSE TO THE FEATHER, YET MOKONA NEVER REALIZED WHERE IT WAS. ISN'T THAT STRANGE?

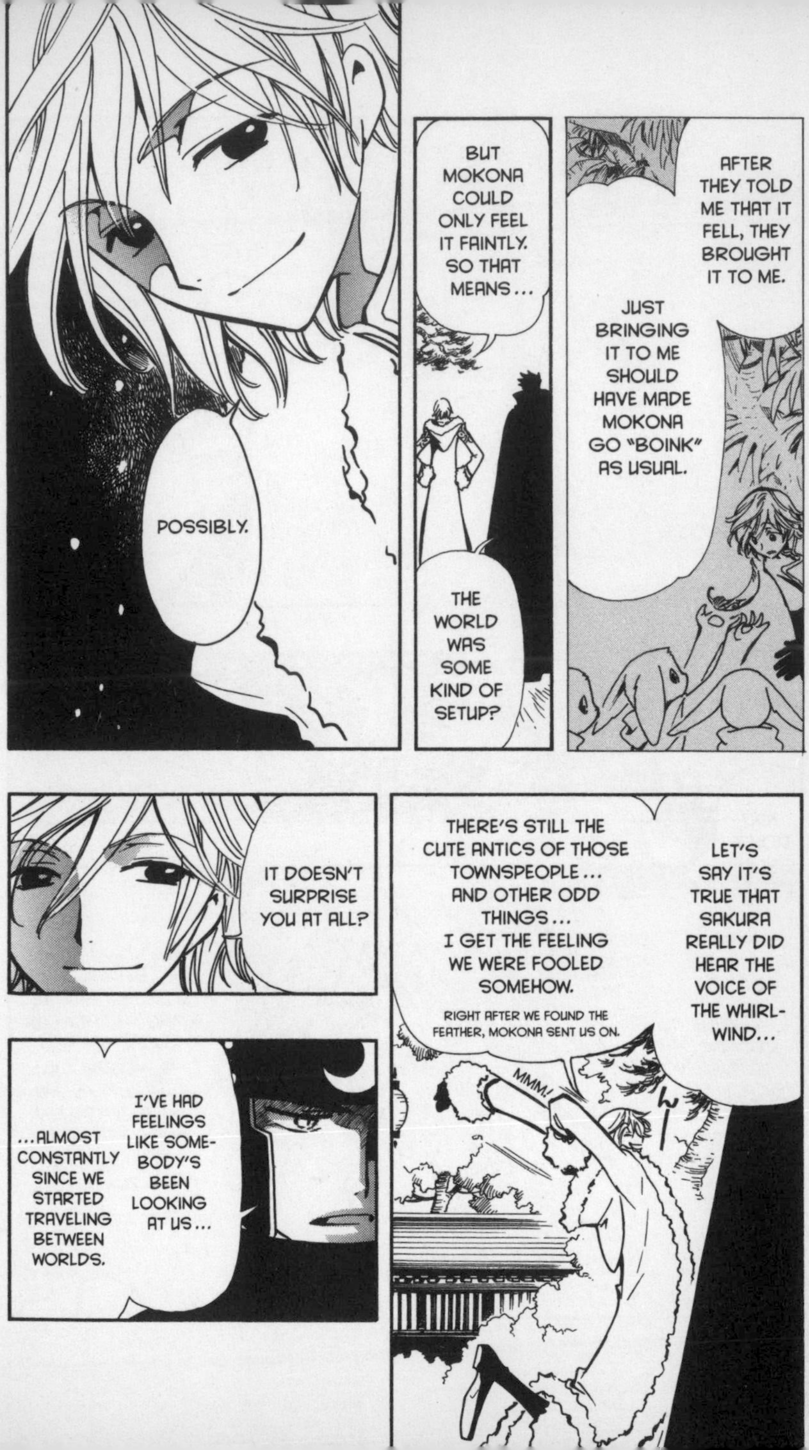
AFTER THEY TOLD ME THAT IT FELL, THEY BROUGHT IT TO ME.
JUST BRINGING IT TO ME SHOULD HAVE MADE MOKONA GO "BOINK" AS USUAL.
BUT MOKONA COULD ONLY FEEL IT FAINTLY. SO THAT MEANS...
THE WORLD WAS SOME KIND OF SETUP?
POSSIBLY.
LET'S SAY IT'S TRUE THAT SAKURA REALLY DID HEAR THE VOICE OF THE WHIRL-WIND...
THERE'S STILL THE CUTE ANTICS OF THOSE TOWNSPEOPLE... AND OTHER ODD THINGS... I GET THE FEELING WE WERE FOOLED SOMEHOW.
RIGHT AFTER WE FOUND THE FEATHER, MOKONA SENT US ON.
MMM!
IT DOESN'T SURPRISE YOU AT ALL?
I'VE HAD FEELINGS LIKE SOME-BODY'S BEEN LOOKING AT US...
...ALMOST CONSTANTLY SINCE WE STARTED TRAVELING BETWEEN WORLDS.

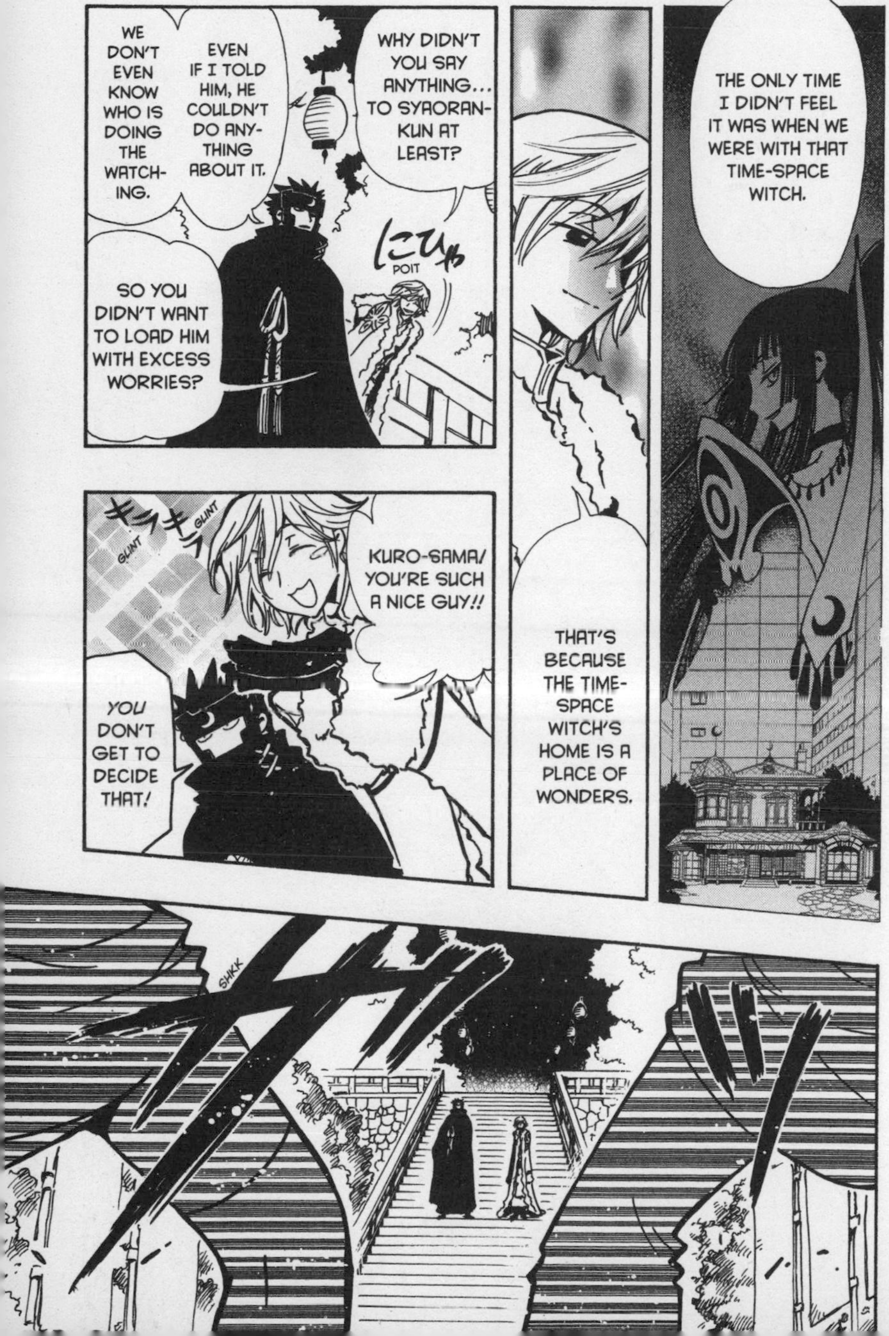
THE ONLY TIME I DIDN'T FEEL IT WAS WHEN WE WERE WITH THAT TIME-SPACE WITCH.
THAT'S BECAUSE THE TIME-SPACE WITCH'S HOME IS A PLACE OF WONDERS.
WHY DIDN'T YOU SAY ANYTHING... TO SYAORAN-KUN AT LEAST?
EVEN IF I TOLD HIM, HE COULDN'T DO ANY-THING ABOUT IT.
WE DON'T EVEN KNOW WHO IS DOING THE WATCH-ING.
にひゃ
POIT
SO YOU DIDN'T WANT TO LOAD HIM WITH EXCESS WORRIES?
KURO-SAMA! YOU'RE SUCH A NICE GUY!!
キラキラ
GLINT GLINT
YOU DON'T GET TO DECIDE THAT!
SHKK

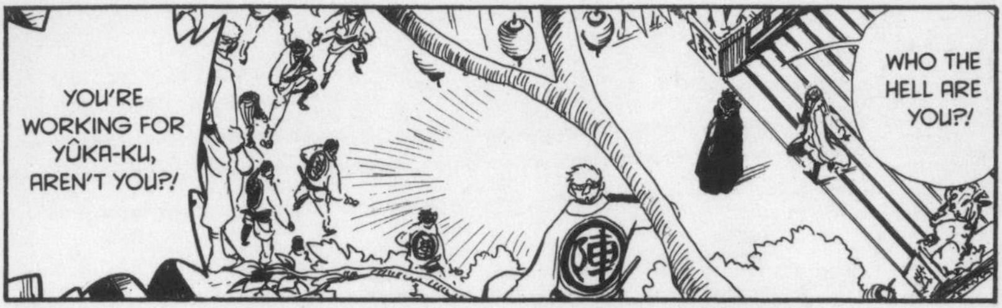
WHO THE HELL ARE YOU?!
YOU'RE WORKING FOR YÛKA-KU, AREN'T YOU?!

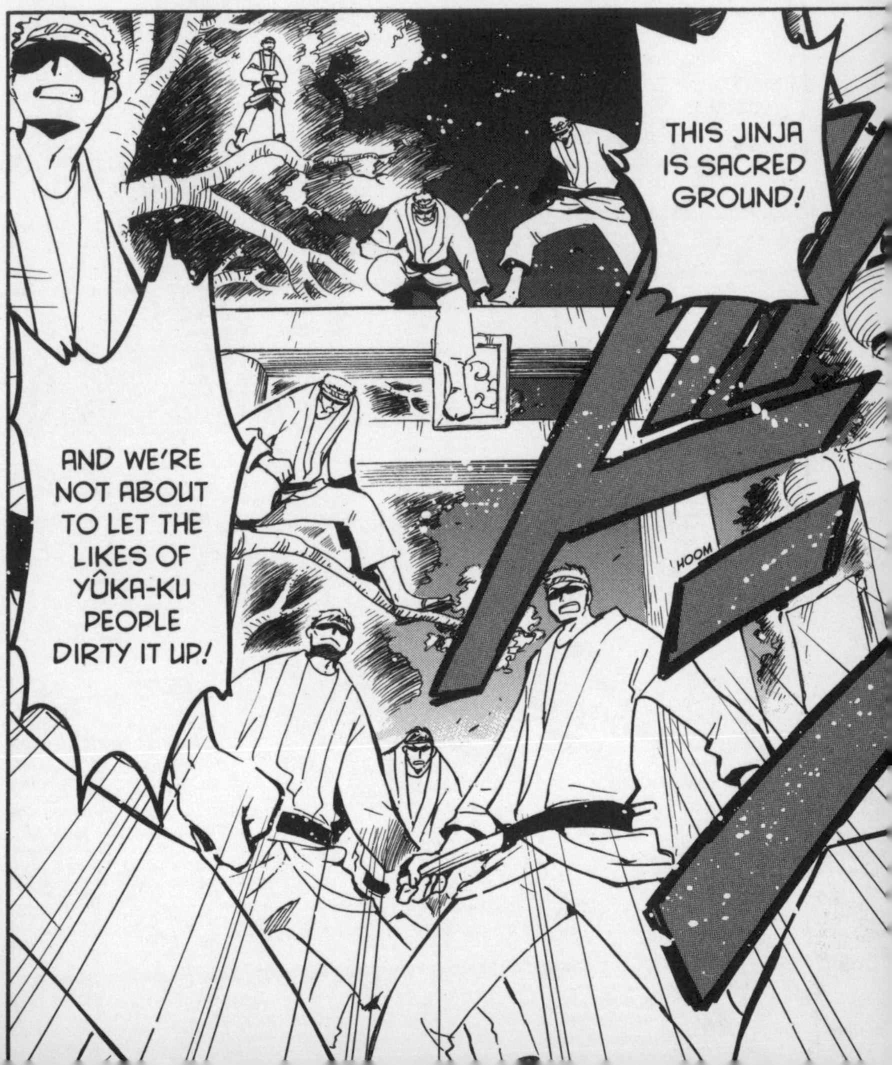
THIS JINJA IS SACRED GROUND!
HOOM
AND WE'RE NOT ABOUT TO LET THE LIKES OF YÛKA-KU PEOPLE DIRTY IT UP!

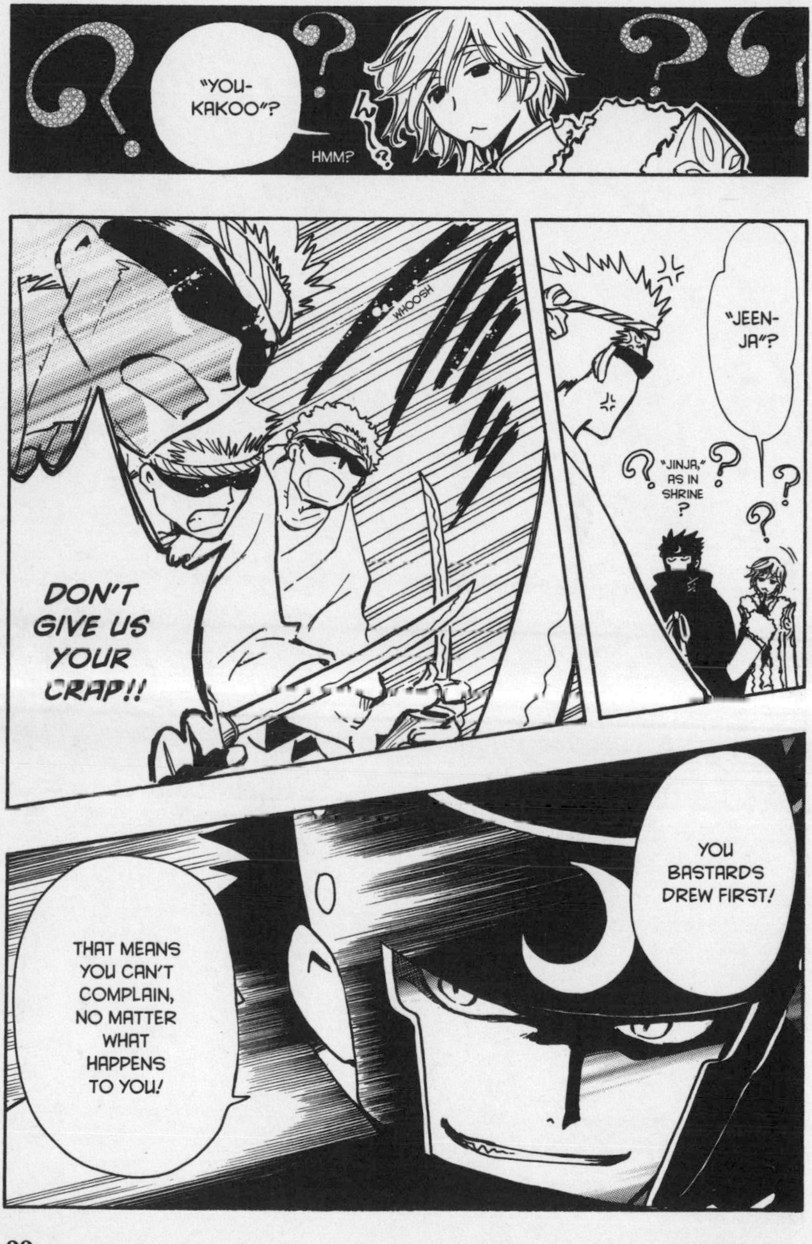
"YOU-KAKOO"?
HMM?
"JEEN-JA"?
"JINJA," AS IN SHRINE?
WHOOSH
DON'T GIVE US YOUR CRAP!!
YOU BASTARDS DREW FIRST!
THAT MEANS YOU CAN'T COMPLAIN, NO MATTER WHAT HAPPENS TO YOU!

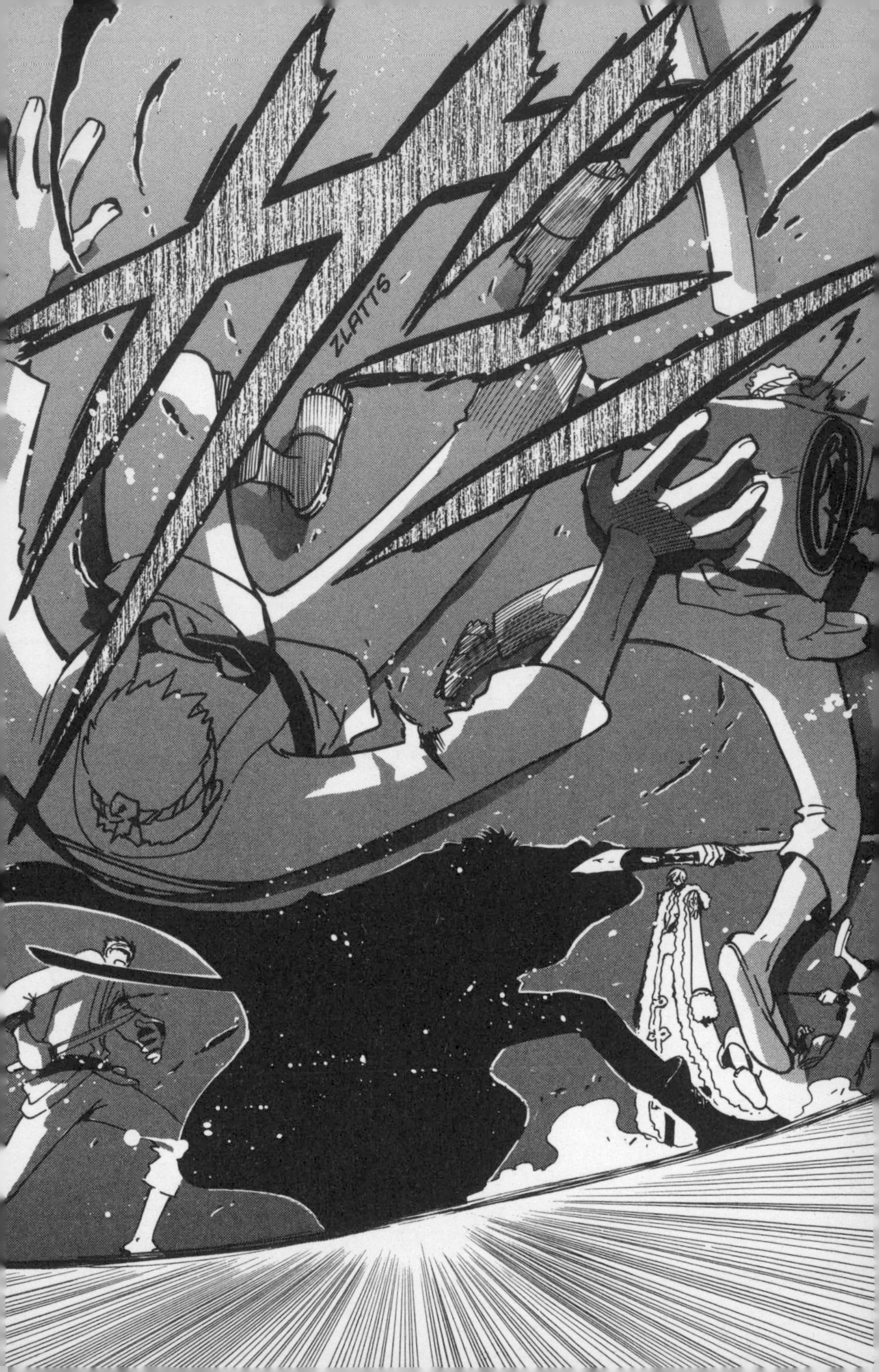
ZLATTS

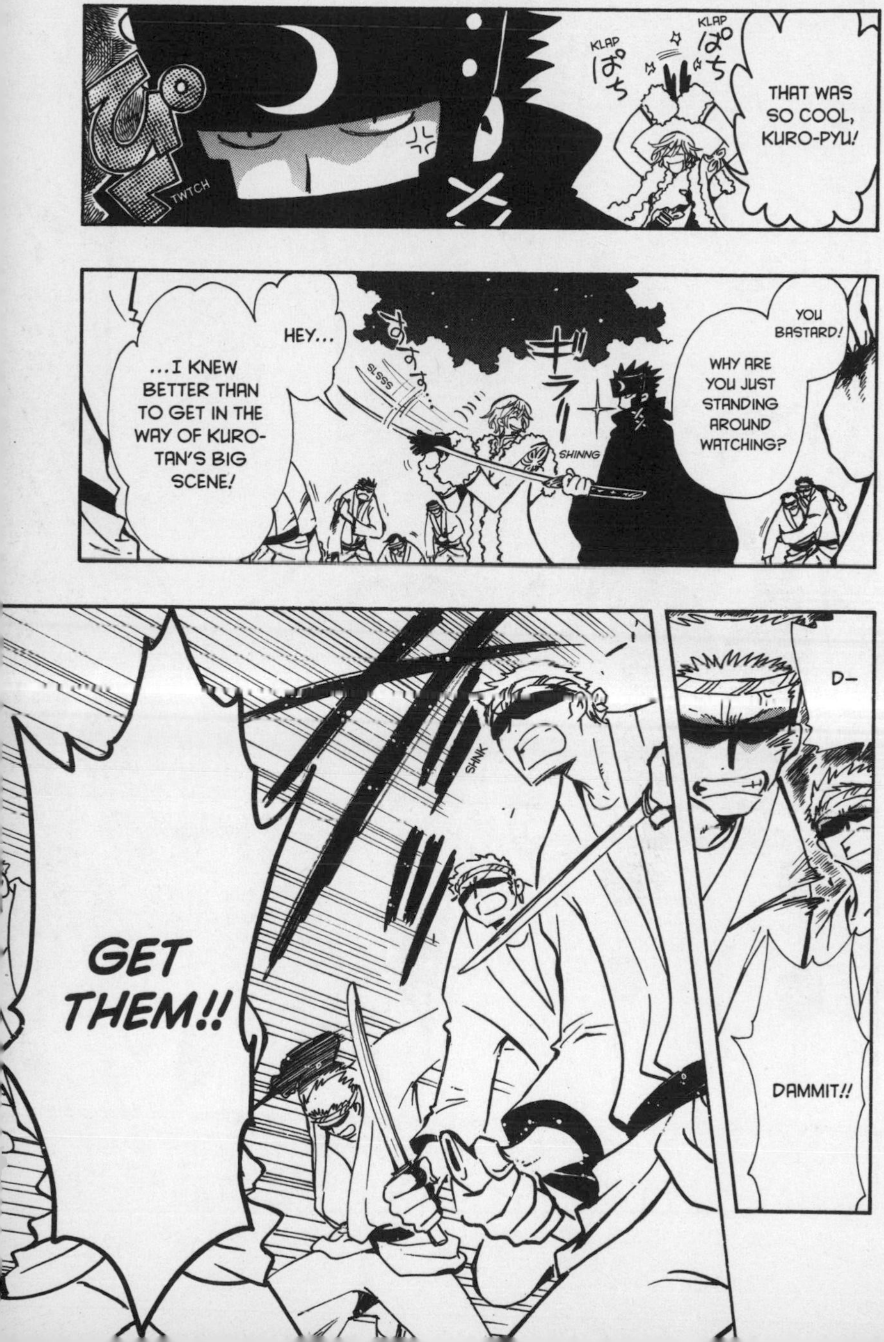
THAT WAS SO COOL, KURO-PYU!
KLAP ぱち
KLAP ぱち
TWTCH
YOU BASTARD!
WHY ARE YOU JUST STANDING AROUND WATCHING?
SHINNG ギラリ
HEY...
...I KNEW BETTER THAN TO GET IN THE WAY OF KURO-TAN'S BIG SCENE!
SLSSS すすす
D–
DAMMIT!!
SHINK
GET THEM!!

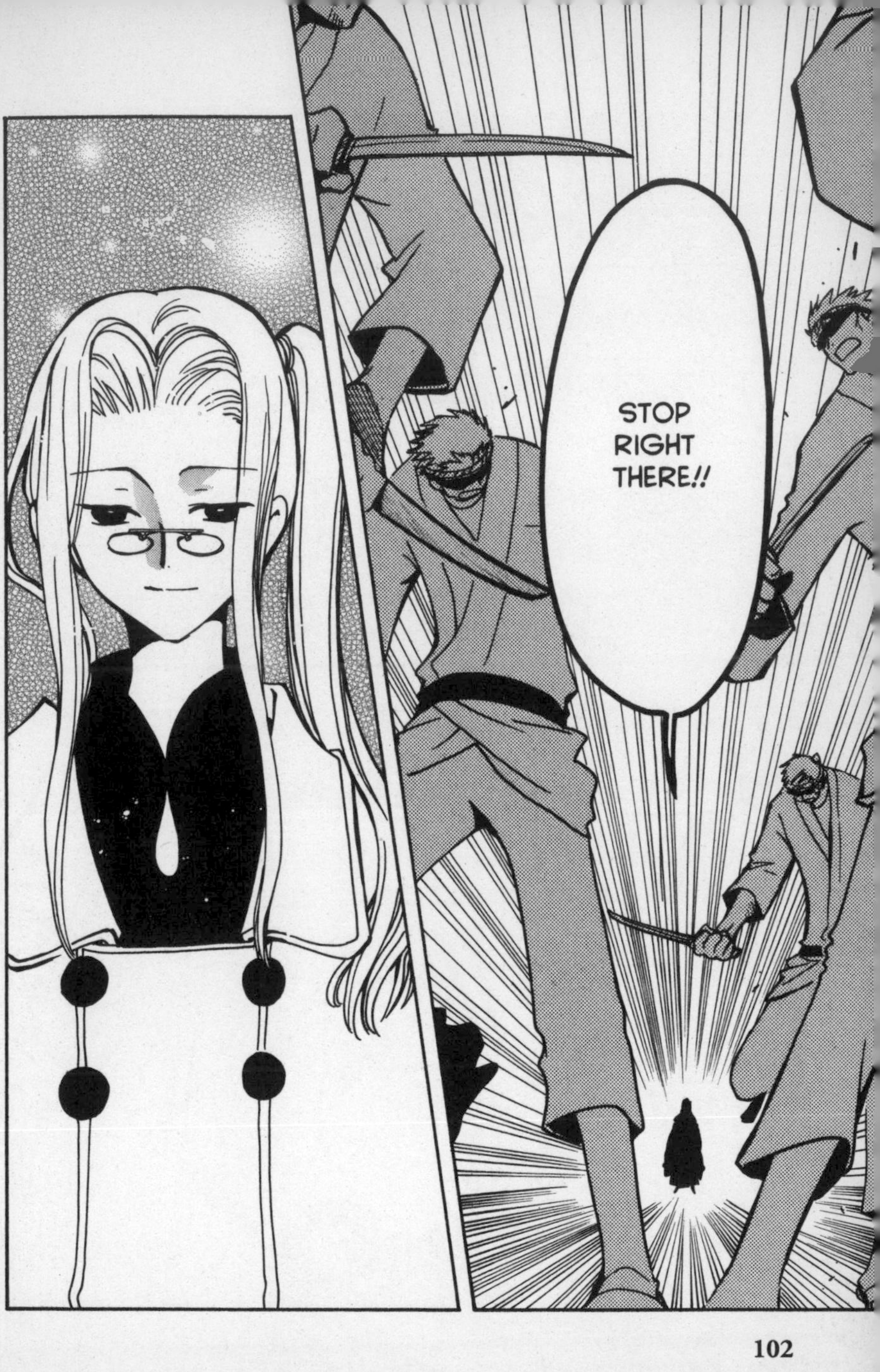
STOP RIGHT THERE!!

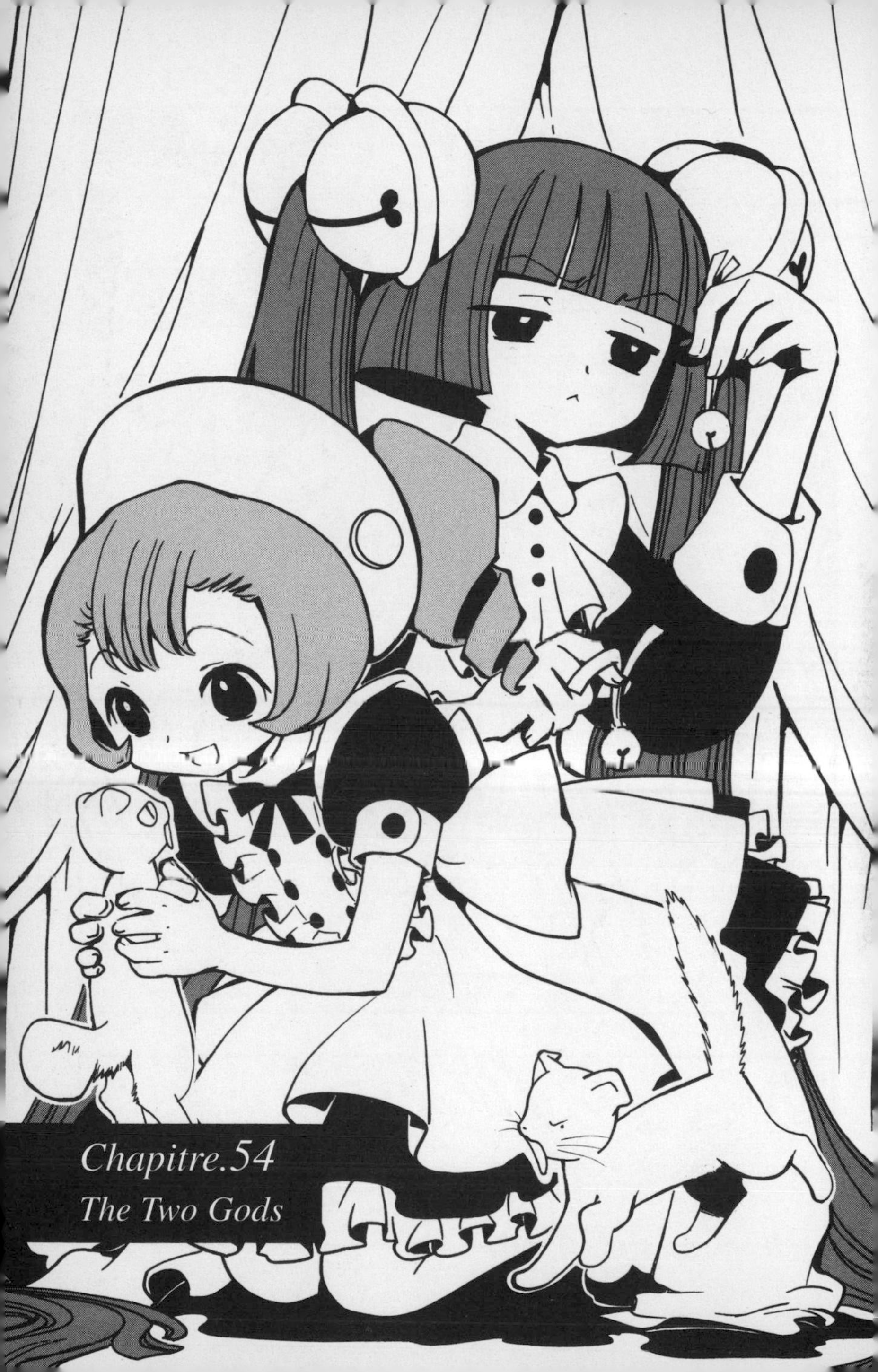
Chapitre.54
The Two Gods

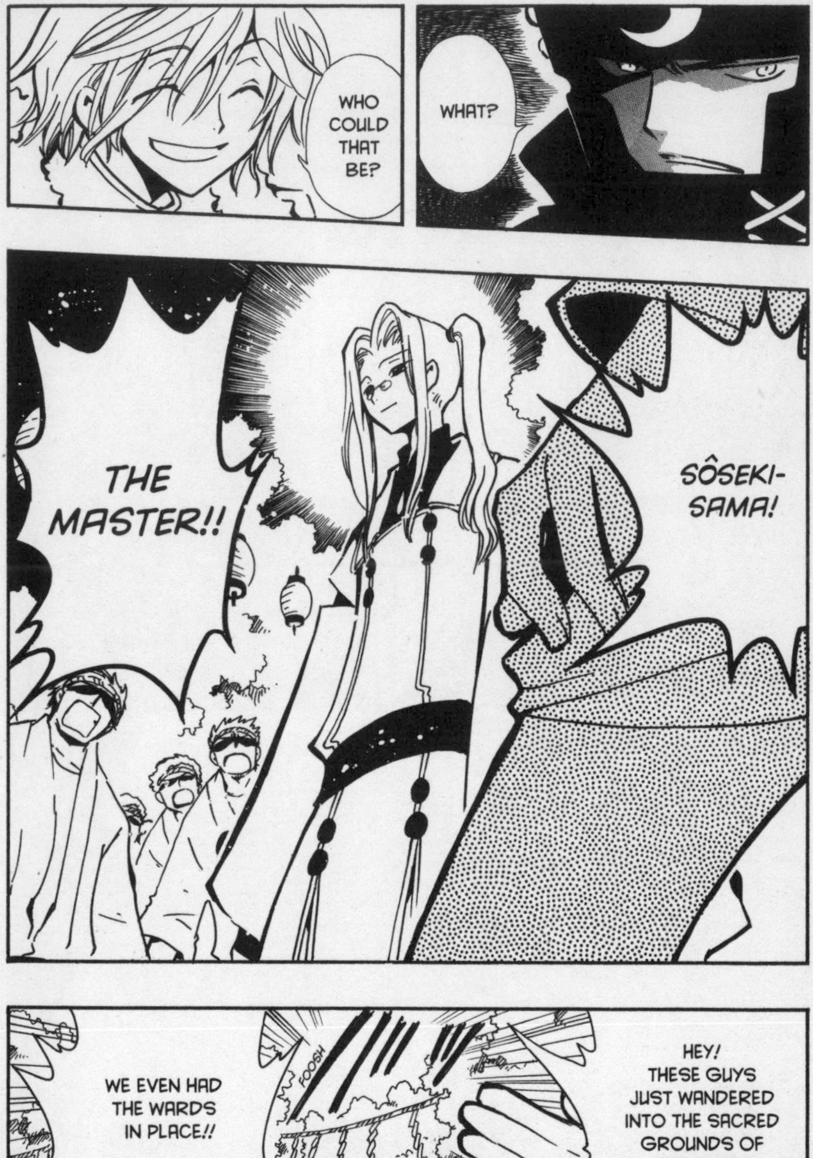
WHAT?
WHO COULD THAT BE?
SÔSEKI-SAMA!
THE MASTER!!
HEY! THESE GUYS JUST WANDERED INTO THE SACRED GROUNDS OF THE JINJA!
FOOSH
WE EVEN HAD THE WARDS IN PLACE!!

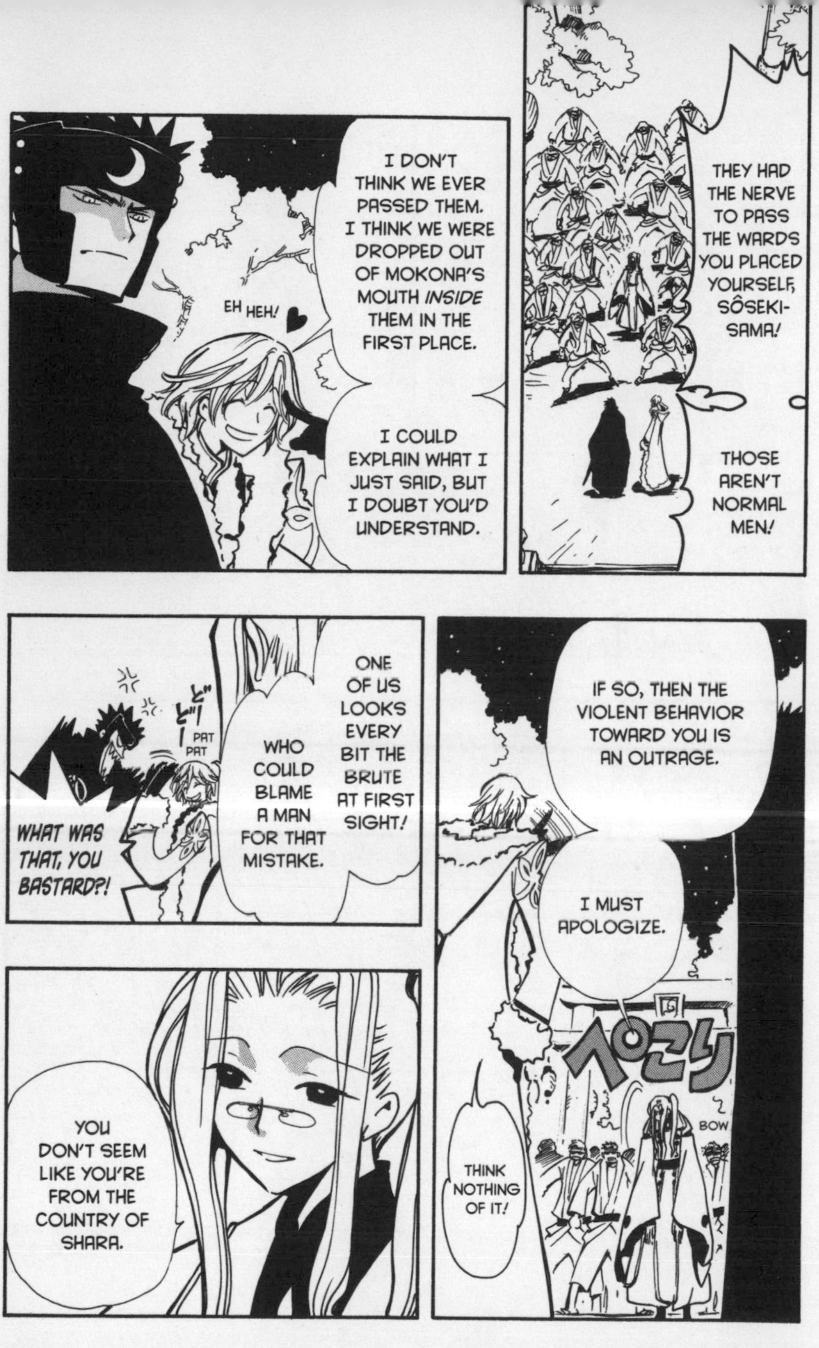
THEY HAD THE NERVE TO PASS THE WARDS YOU PLACED YOURSELF, SÔSEKI-SAMA!
THOSE AREN'T NORMAL MEN!
I DON'T THINK WE EVER PASSED THEM. I THINK WE WERE DROPPED OUT OF MOKONA'S MOUTH *INSIDE* THEM IN THE FIRST PLACE.
EH HEH! ♥
I COULD EXPLAIN WHAT I JUST SAID, BUT I DOUBT YOU'D UNDERSTAND.
IF SO, THEN THE VIOLENT BEHAVIOR TOWARD YOU IS AN OUTRAGE.
I MUST APOLOGIZE.
ぺこり
BOW
THINK NOTHING OF IT!
ONE OF US LOOKS EVERY BIT THE BRUTE AT FIRST SIGHT!
WHO COULD BLAME A MAN FOR THAT MISTAKE.
PAT PAT
WHAT WAS THAT, YOU BASTARD?!
YOU DON'T SEEM LIKE YOU'RE FROM THE COUNTRY OF SHARA.

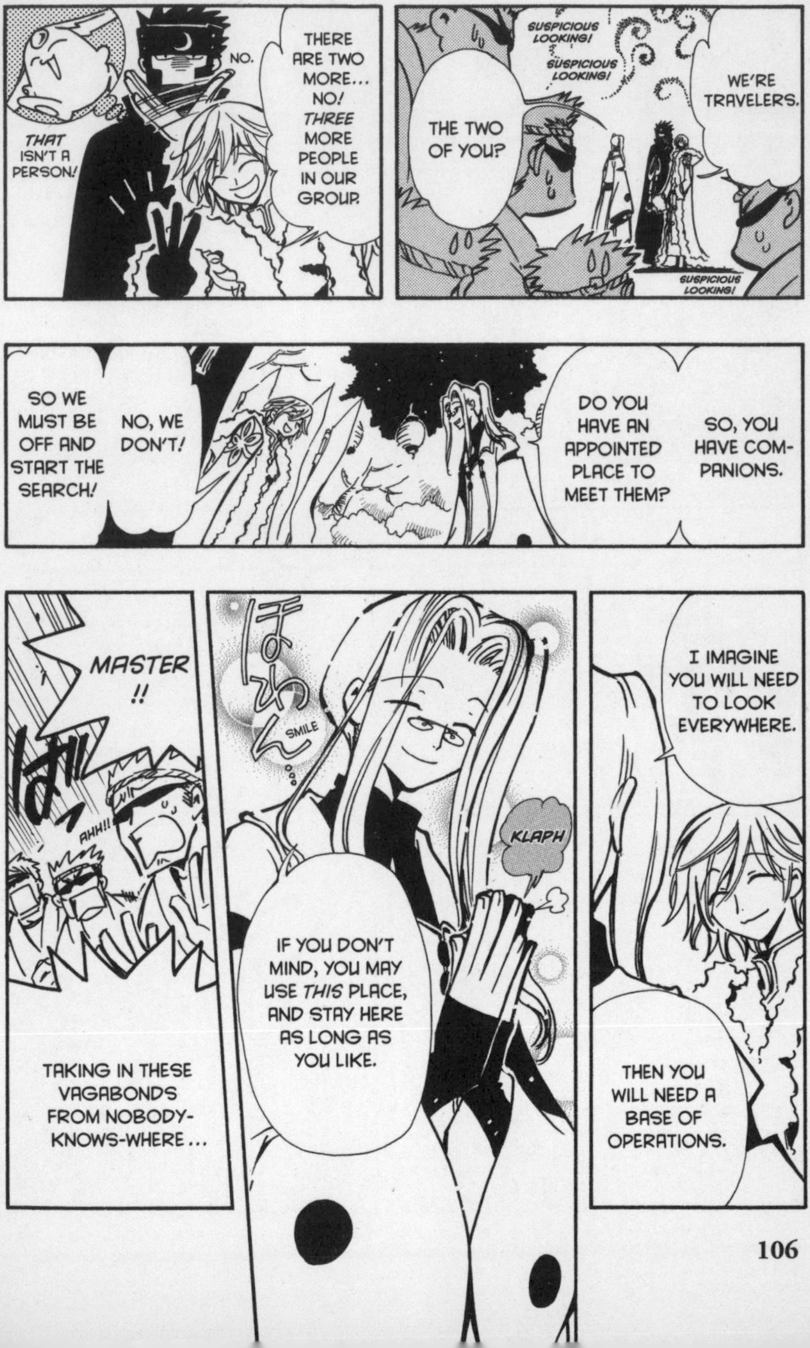
WE'RE TRAVELERS.
SUSPICIOUS LOOKING!
SUSPICIOUS LOOKING!
SUSPICIOUS LOOKING!
THE TWO OF YOU?
THERE ARE TWO MORE... NO! *THREE* MORE PEOPLE IN OUR GROUP.
NO.
THAT ISN'T A PERSON!
SO, YOU HAVE COMPANIONS.
DO YOU HAVE AN APPOINTED PLACE TO MEET THEM?
NO, WE DON'T!
SO WE MUST BE OFF AND START THE SEARCH!
I IMAGINE YOU WILL NEED TO LOOK EVERYWHERE.
THEN YOU WILL NEED A BASE OF OPERATIONS.
ほわん
SMILE
KLAPH
IF YOU DON'T MIND, YOU MAY USE *THIS* PLACE, AND STAY HERE AS LONG AS YOU LIKE.
MASTER!!
AHH!!
TAKING IN THESE VAGABONDS FROM NOBODY-KNOWS-WHERE...

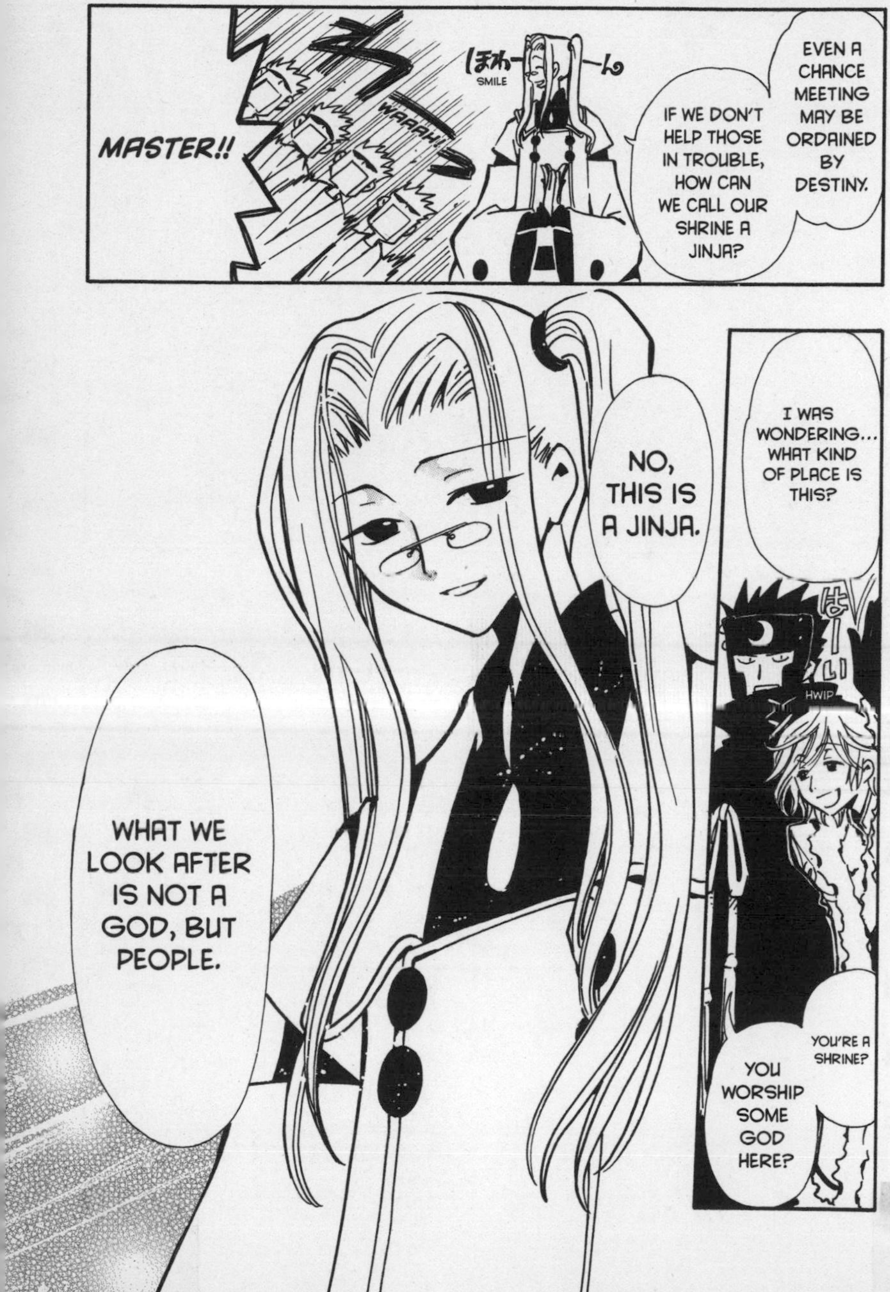
EVEN A CHANCE MEETING MAY BE ORDAINED BY DESTINY.
IF WE DON'T HELP THOSE IN TROUBLE, HOW CAN WE CALL OUR SHRINE A JINJA?
ほわーーん
SMILE
WAAAH!
MASTER!!
I WAS WONDERING... WHAT KIND OF PLACE IS THIS?
はーい
HWIP
YOU'RE A SHRINE?
YOU WORSHIP SOME GOD HERE?
NO, THIS IS A JINJA.
WHAT WE LOOK AFTER IS NOT A GOD, BUT PEOPLE.

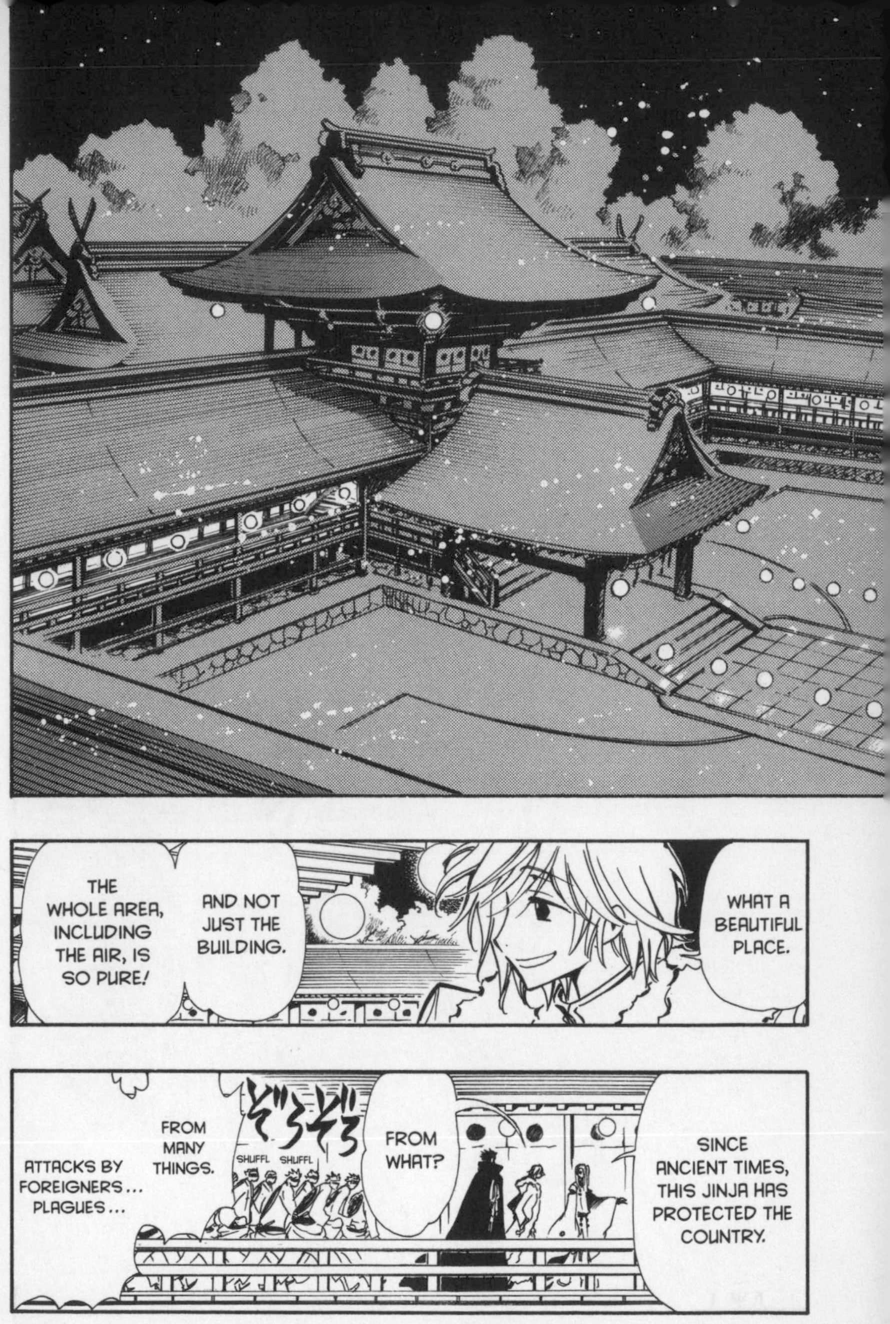
WHAT A BEAUTIFUL PLACE.
AND NOT JUST THE BUILDING.
THE WHOLE AREA, INCLUDING THE AIR, IS SO PURE!
SINCE ANCIENT TIMES, THIS JINJA HAS PROTECTED THE COUNTRY.
FROM WHAT?
ぞろぞろ
SHUFFL SHUFFL
FROM MANY THINGS.
ATTACKS BY FOREIGNERS... PLAGUES...

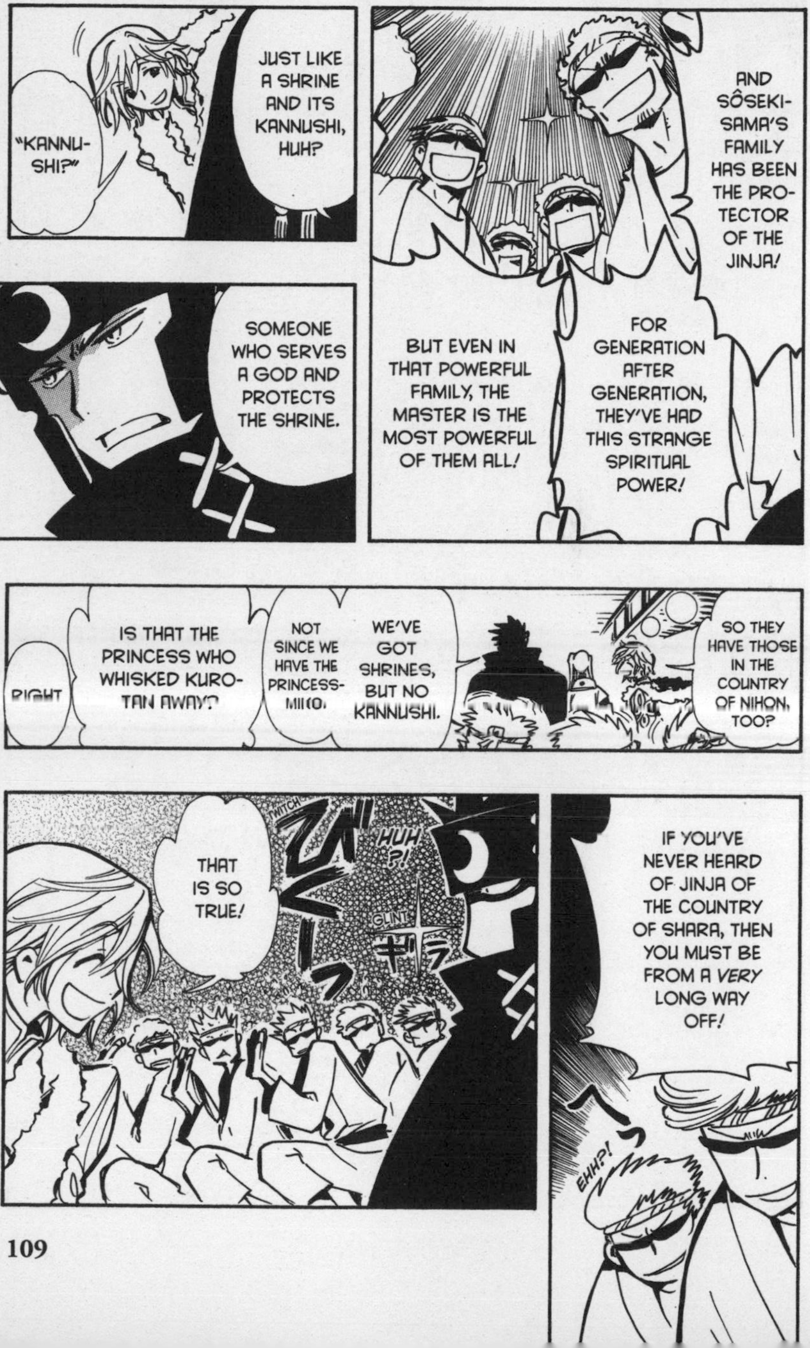
AND SÔSEKI-SAMA'S FAMILY HAS BEEN THE PROTECTOR OF THE JINJA!
FOR GENERATION AFTER GENERATION, THEY'VE HAD THIS STRANGE SPIRITUAL POWER!
BUT EVEN IN THAT POWERFUL FAMILY, THE MASTER IS THE MOST POWERFUL OF THEM ALL!
JUST LIKE A SHRINE AND ITS KANNUSHI, HUH?
"KANNUSHI?"
SOMEONE WHO SERVES A GOD AND PROTECTS THE SHRINE.
SO THEY HAVE THOSE IN THE COUNTRY OF NIHON, TOO?
WE'VE GOT SHRINES, BUT NO KANNUSHI.
NOT SINCE WE HAVE THE PRINCESS-MIKO.
IS THAT THE PRINCESS WHO WHISKED KURO-TAN AWAY?
RIGHT
IF YOU'VE NEVER HEARD OF JINJA OF THE COUNTRY OF SHARA, THEN YOU MUST BE FROM A *VERY* LONG WAY OFF!
EHH?!
HUH?!
TWITCH
GLINT
THAT IS SO TRUE!

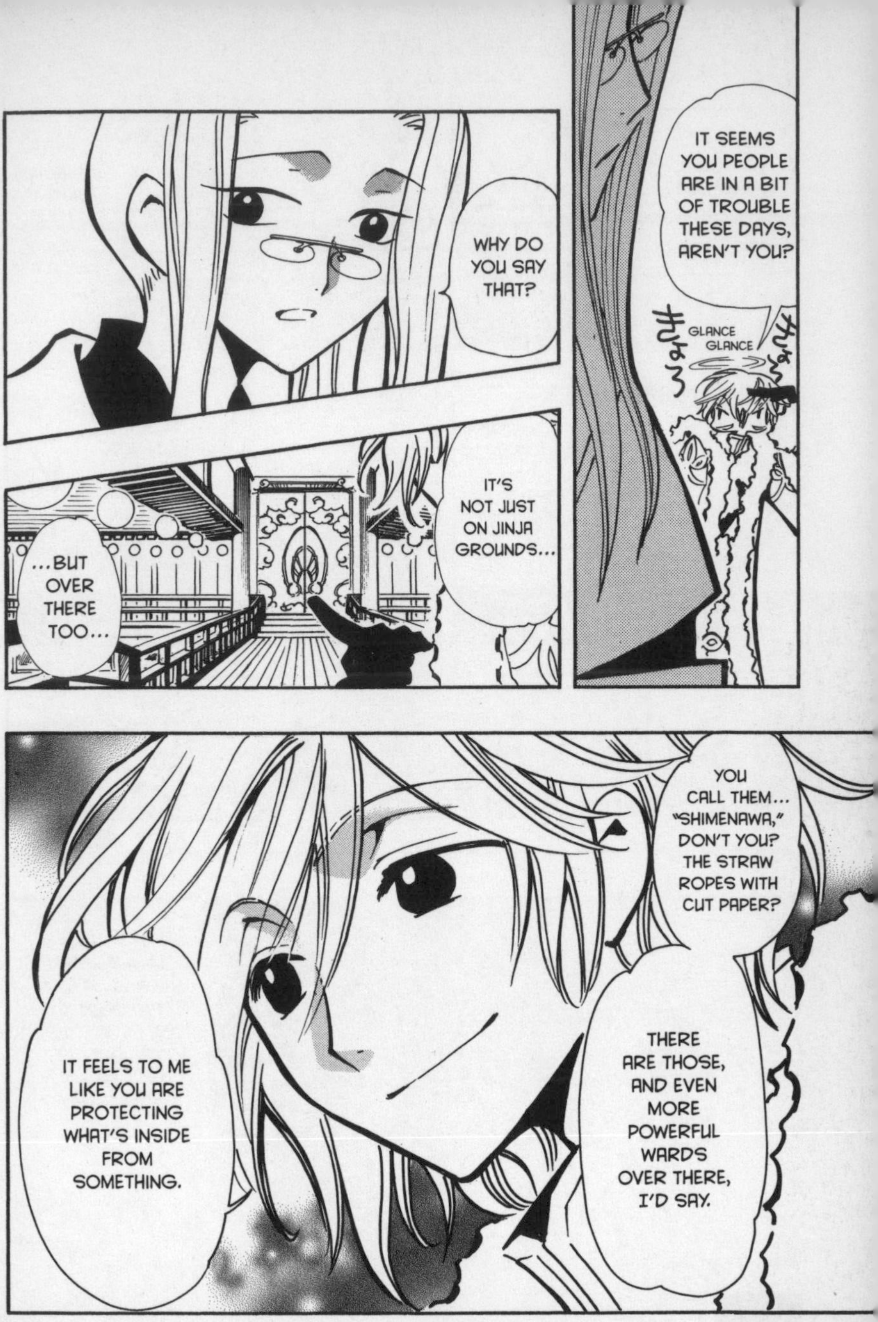
IT SEEMS YOU PEOPLE ARE IN A BIT OF TROUBLE THESE DAYS, AREN'T YOU?
GLANCE GLANCE
WHY DO YOU SAY THAT?
IT'S NOT JUST ON JINJA GROUNDS...
...BUT OVER THERE TOO...
YOU CALL THEM... "SHIMENAWA," DON'T YOU? THE STRAW ROPES WITH CUT PAPER?
THERE ARE THOSE, AND EVEN MORE POWERFUL WARDS OVER THERE, I'D SAY.
IT FEELS TO ME LIKE YOU ARE PROTECTING WHAT'S INSIDE FROM SOMETHING.

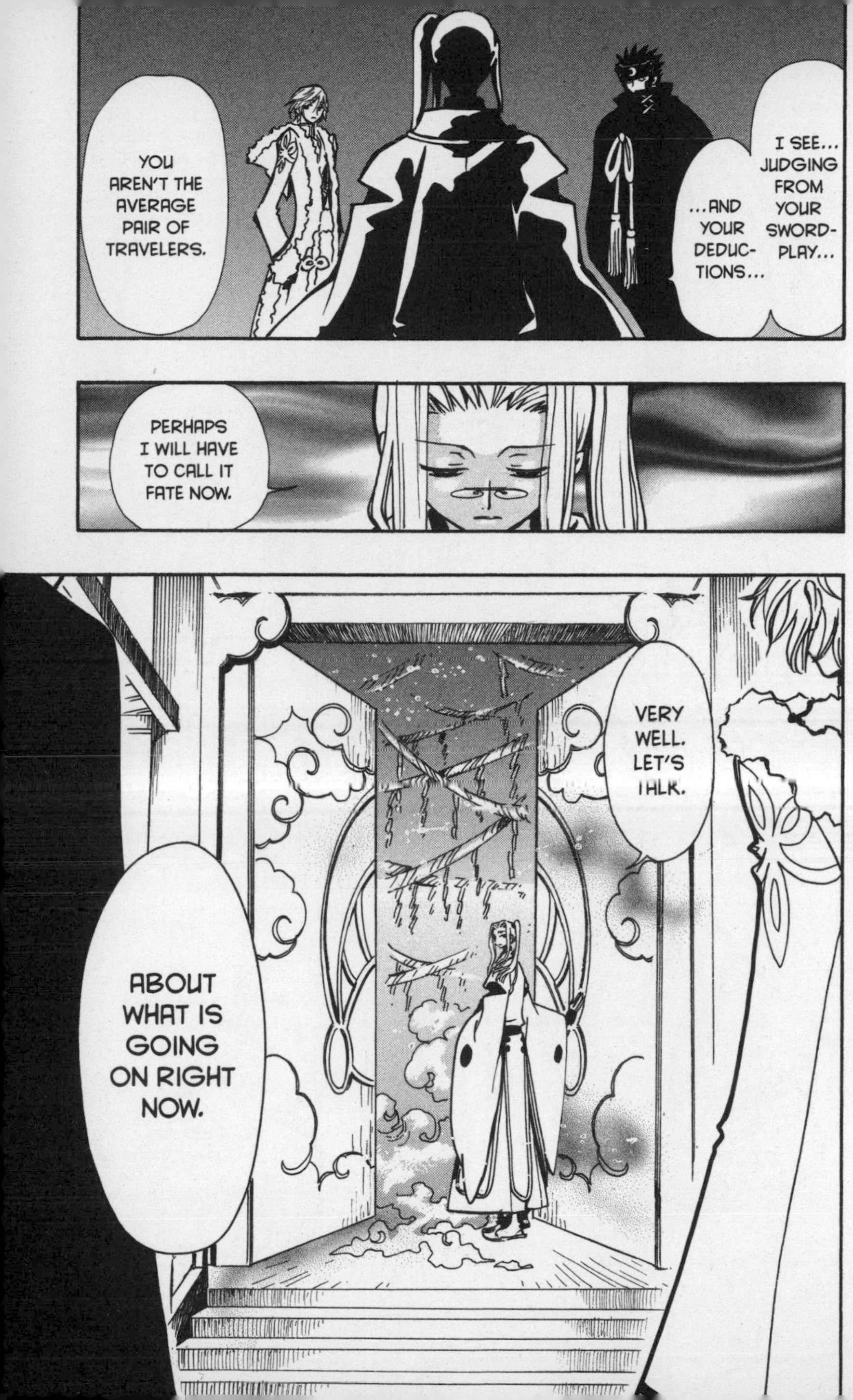
I SEE... JUDGING FROM YOUR SWORD-PLAY...
...AND YOUR DEDUCTIONS...
YOU AREN'T THE AVERAGE PAIR OF TRAVELERS.
PERHAPS I WILL HAVE TO CALL IT FATE NOW.
VERY WELL. LET'S TALK.
ABOUT WHAT IS GOING ON RIGHT NOW.

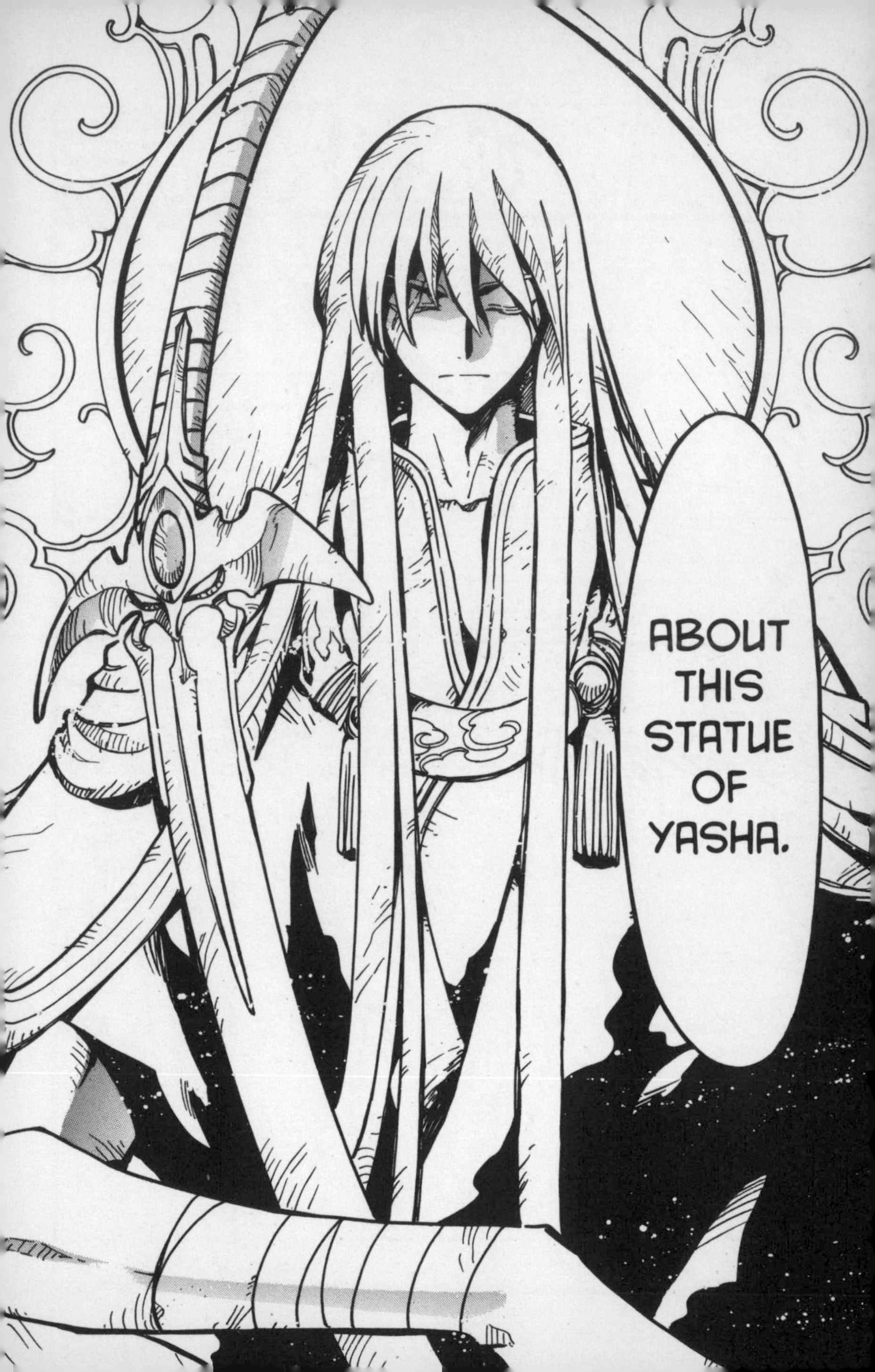
ABOUT THIS STATUE OF YASHA.

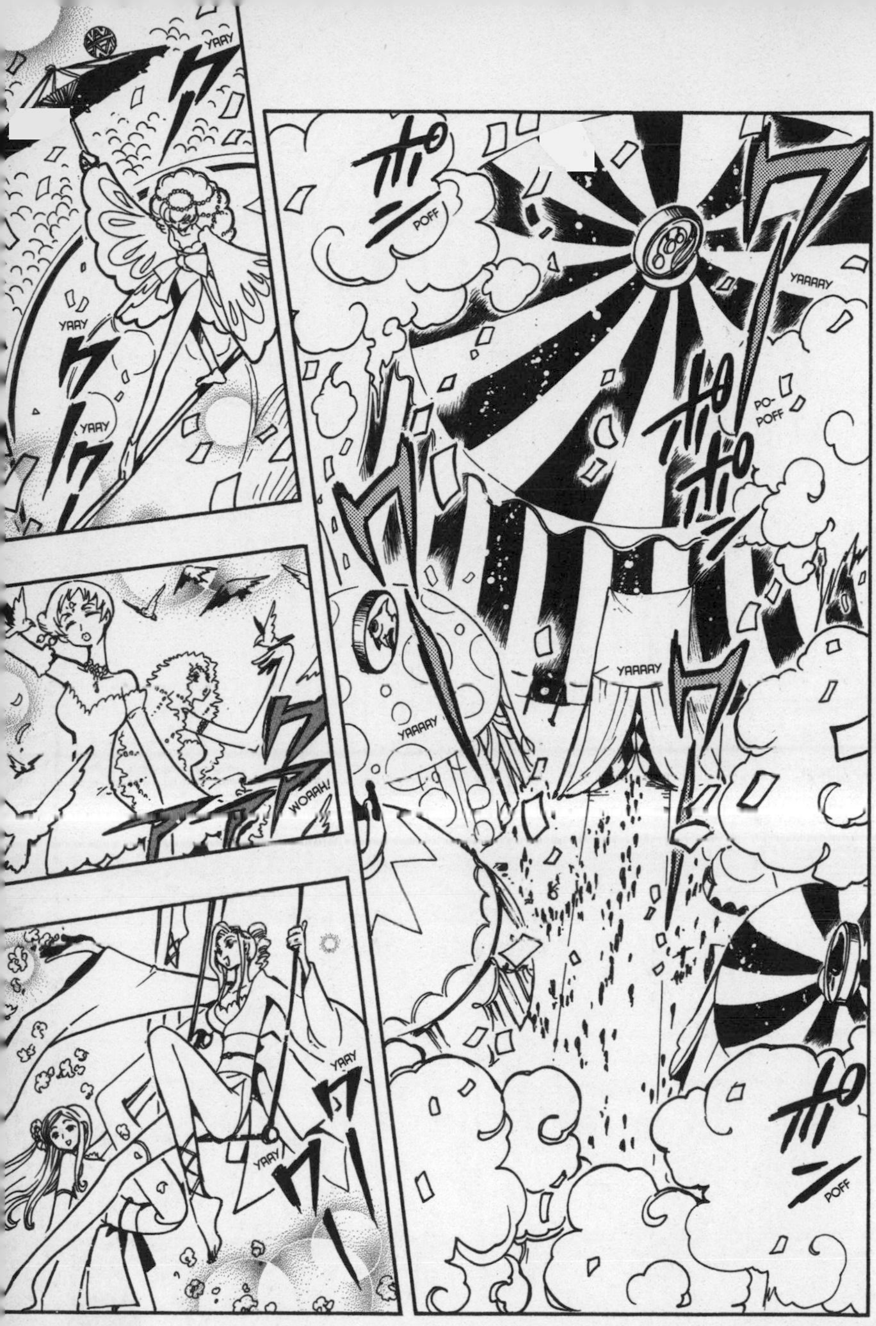
YAAAAY
POFF
PO-
POFF
YAAAAY
YAAAAY
POFF
YAAY
YAAY
YAAY
WOAAH!
YAAY
YAAY

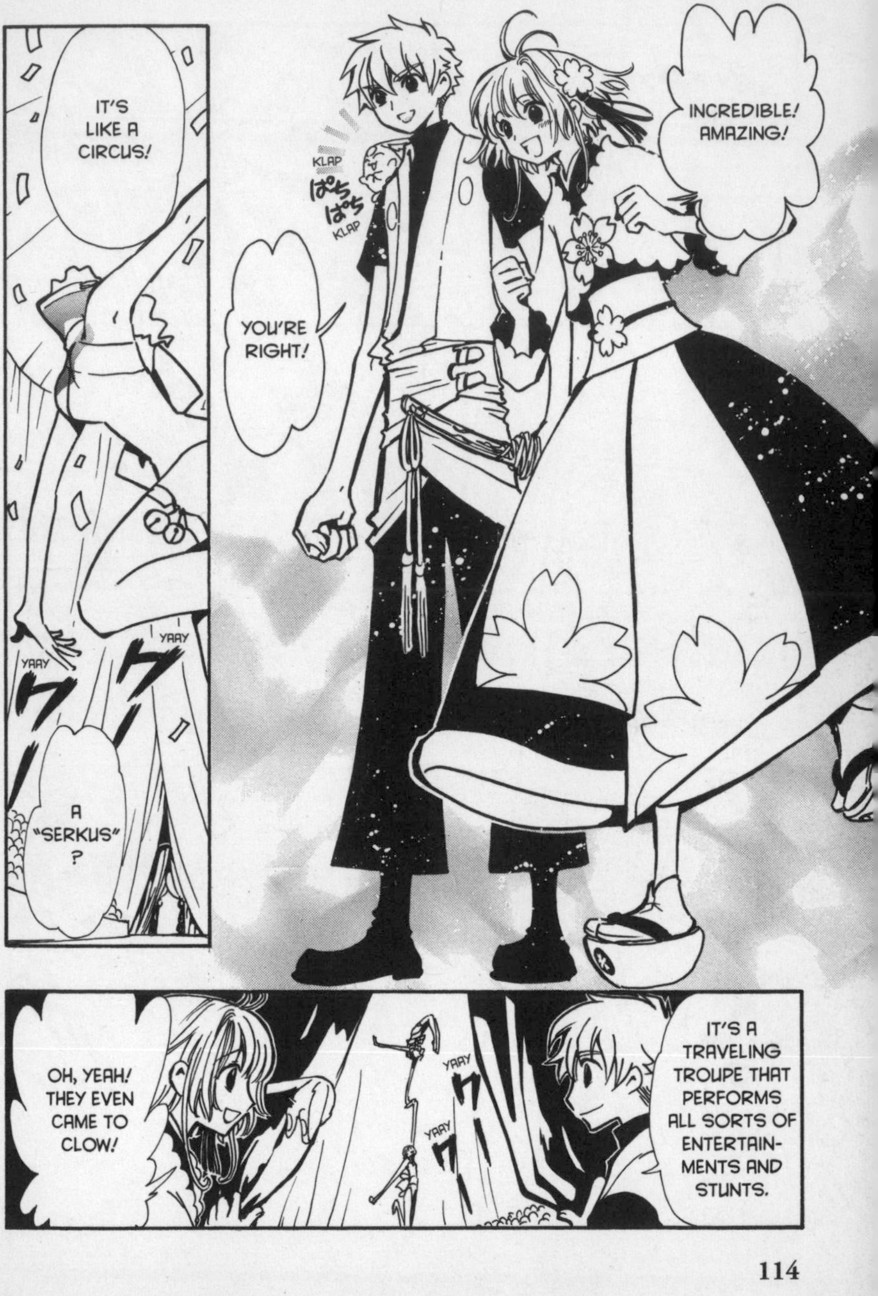
INCREDIBLE! AMAZING!
KLAP ぱちぱち KLAP
YOU'RE RIGHT!
IT'S LIKE A CIRCUS!
YAAY
YAAY
A "SERKUS"?
IT'S A TRAVELING TROUPE THAT PERFORMS ALL SORTS OF ENTERTAIN-MENTS AND STUNTS.
YAAY
YAAY
OH, YEAH! THEY EVEN CAME TO CLOW!

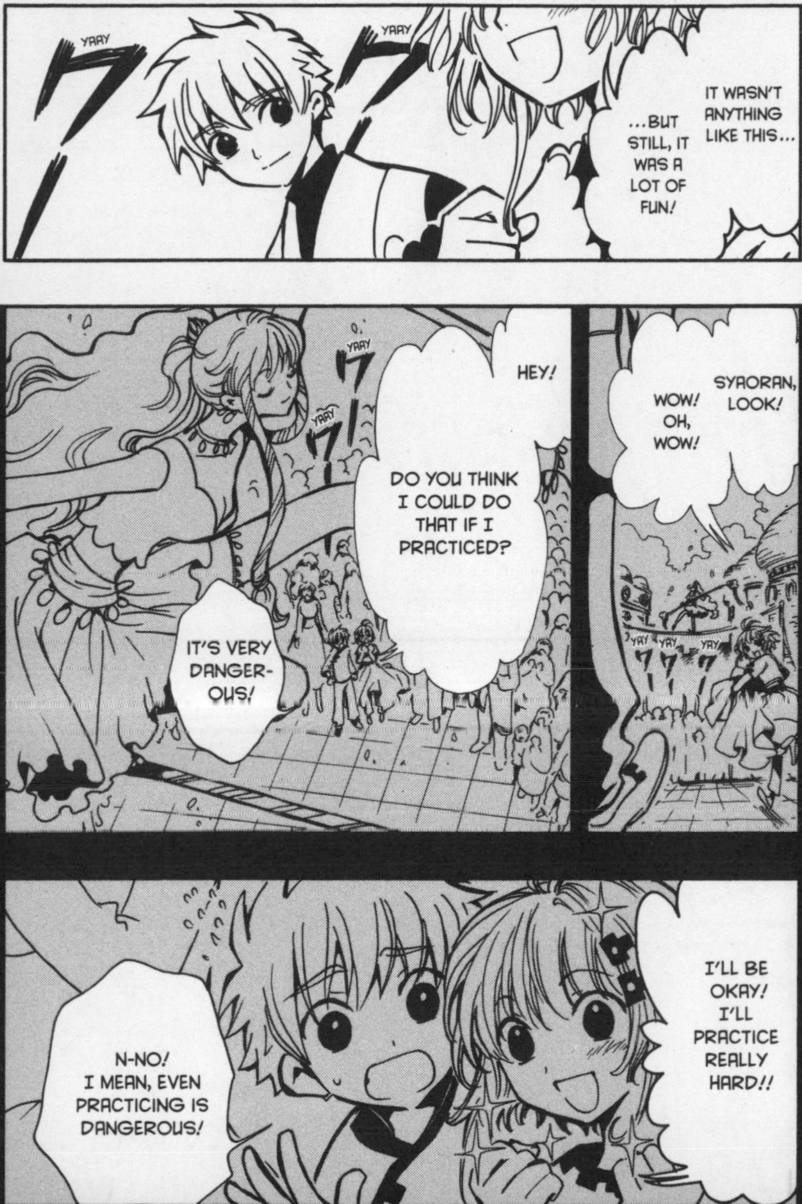
YAAY
YAAY
IT WASN'T ANYTHING LIKE THIS...
...BUT STILL, IT WAS A LOT OF FUN!
SYAORAN, LOOK!
WOW! OH, WOW!
YAY YAY YAY
HEY!
YAAY
YAAY
DO YOU THINK I COULD DO THAT IF I PRACTICED?
IT'S VERY DANGER-OUS!
I'LL BE OKAY! I'LL PRACTICE REALLY HARD!!
N-NO! I MEAN, EVEN PRACTICING IS DANGEROUS!

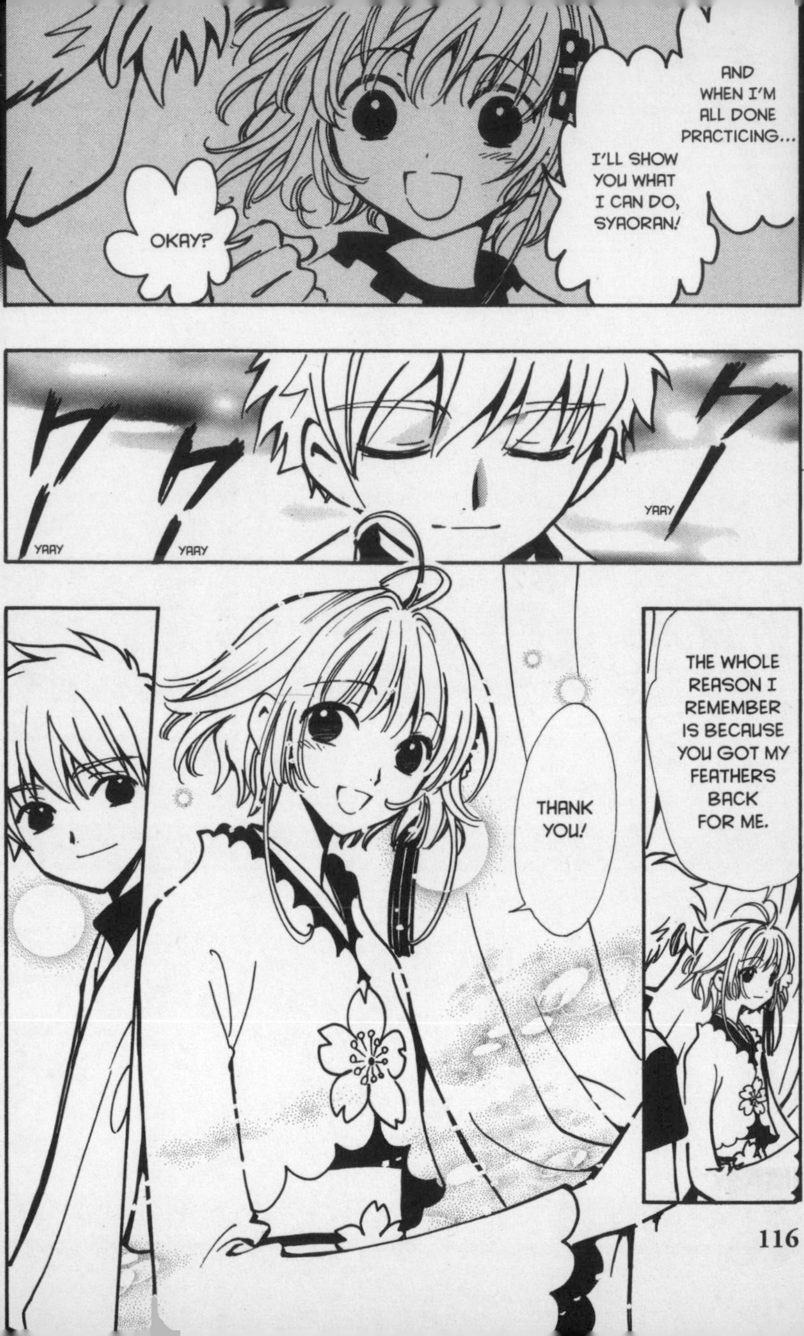
AND WHEN I'M ALL DONE PRACTICING...
I'LL SHOW YOU WHAT I CAN DO, SYAORAN!
OKAY?
YAAY
YAAY
YAAY
THE WHOLE REASON I REMEMBER IS BECAUSE YOU GOT MY FEATHERS BACK FOR ME.
THANK YOU!

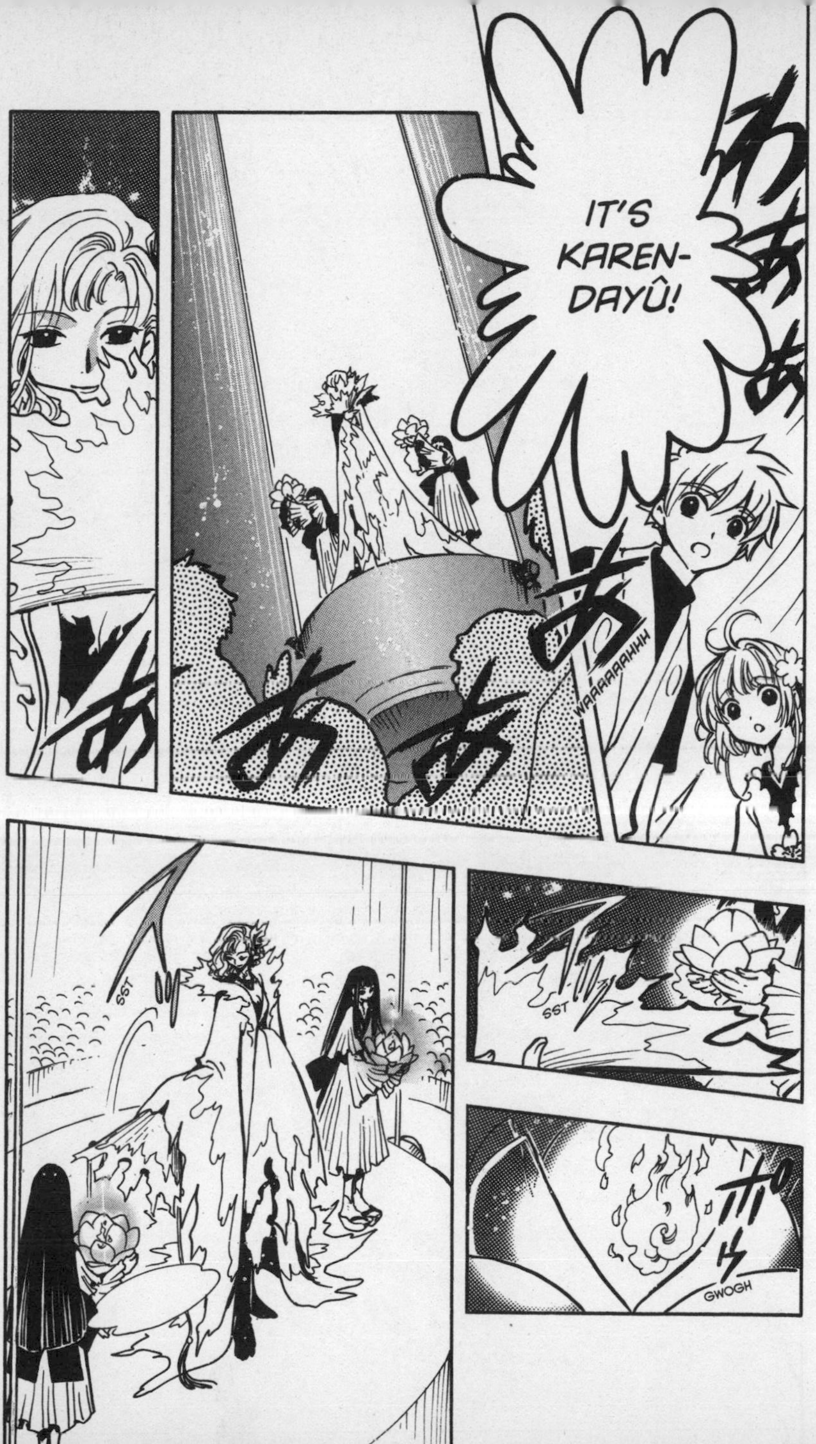
IT'S KAREN-DAYÛ!
WAAAAAAAHHH
SST
GWOGH
SST

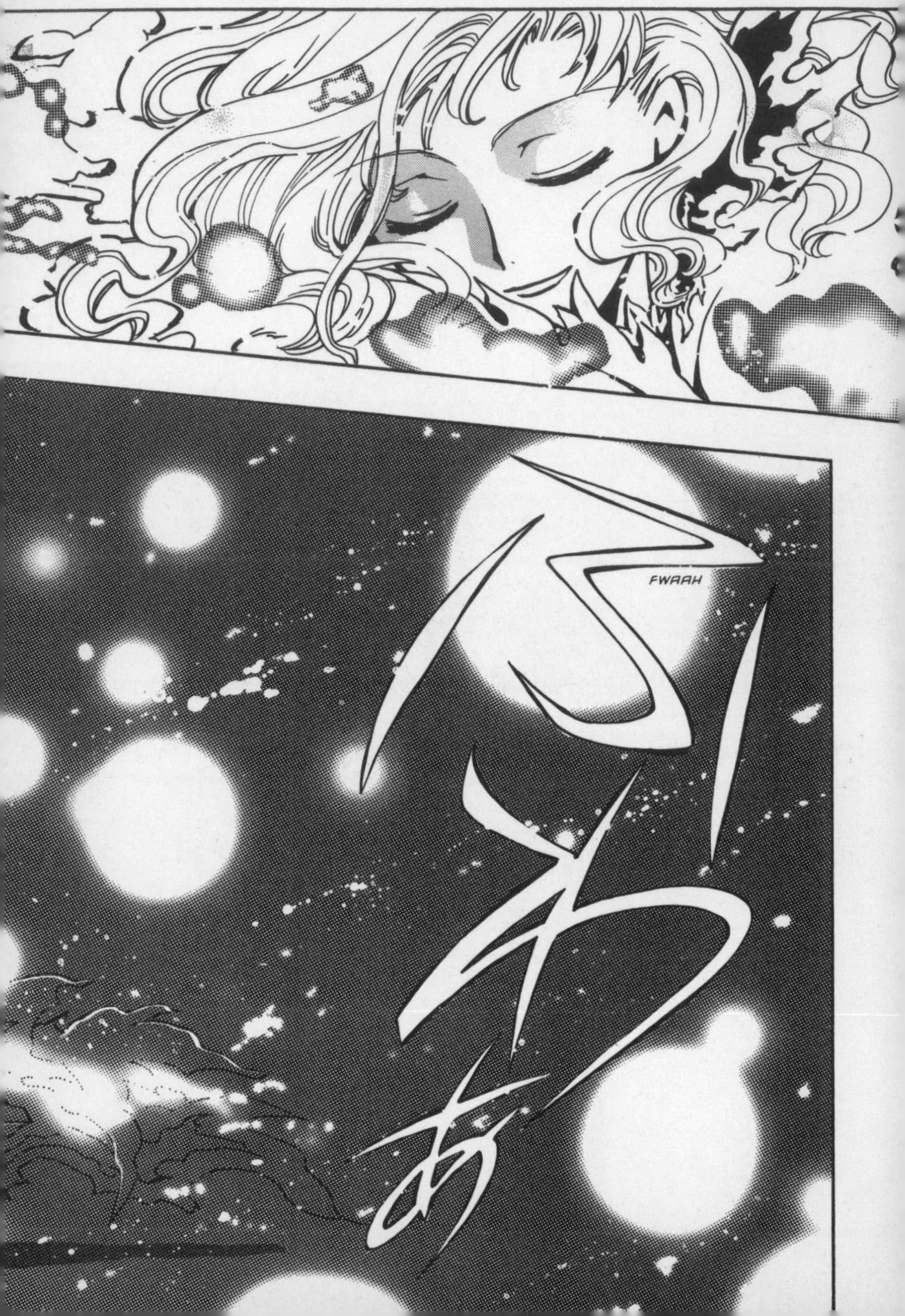
FWAAH

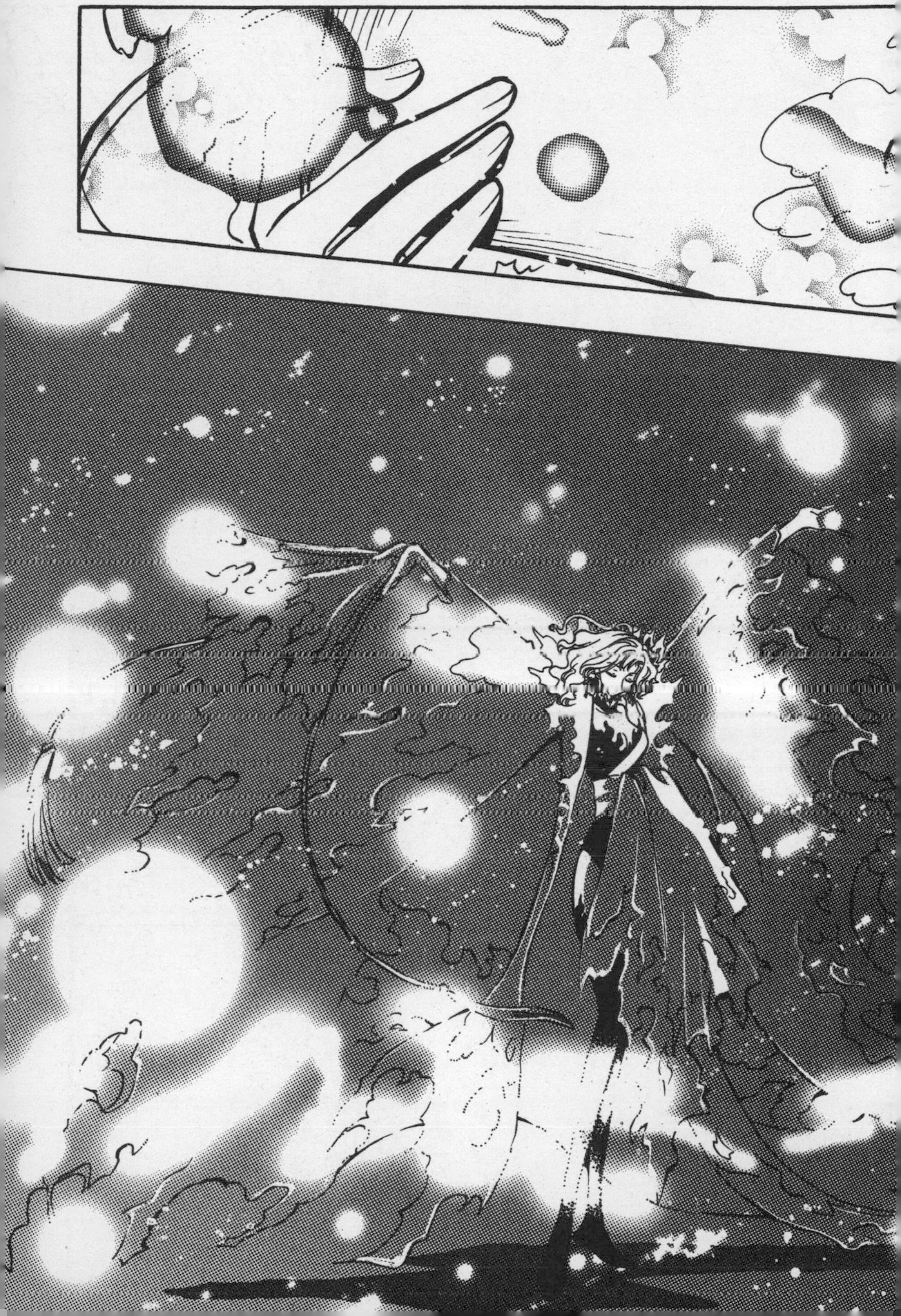

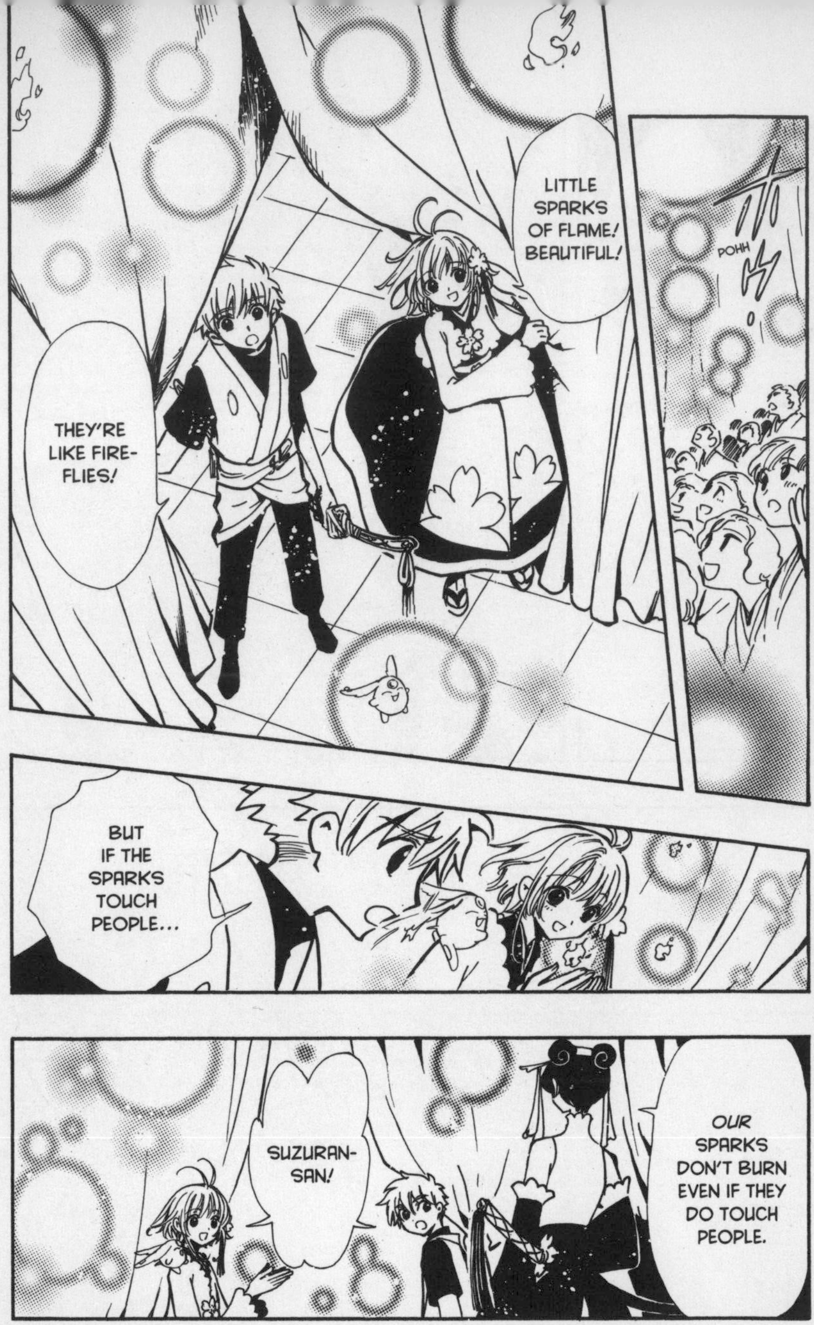
POHH
LITTLE SPARKS OF FLAME! BEAUTIFUL!
THEY'RE LIKE FIRE-FLIES!
BUT IF THE SPARKS TOUCH PEOPLE...
OUR SPARKS DON'T BURN EVEN IF THEY DO TOUCH PEOPLE.
SUZURAN-SAN!

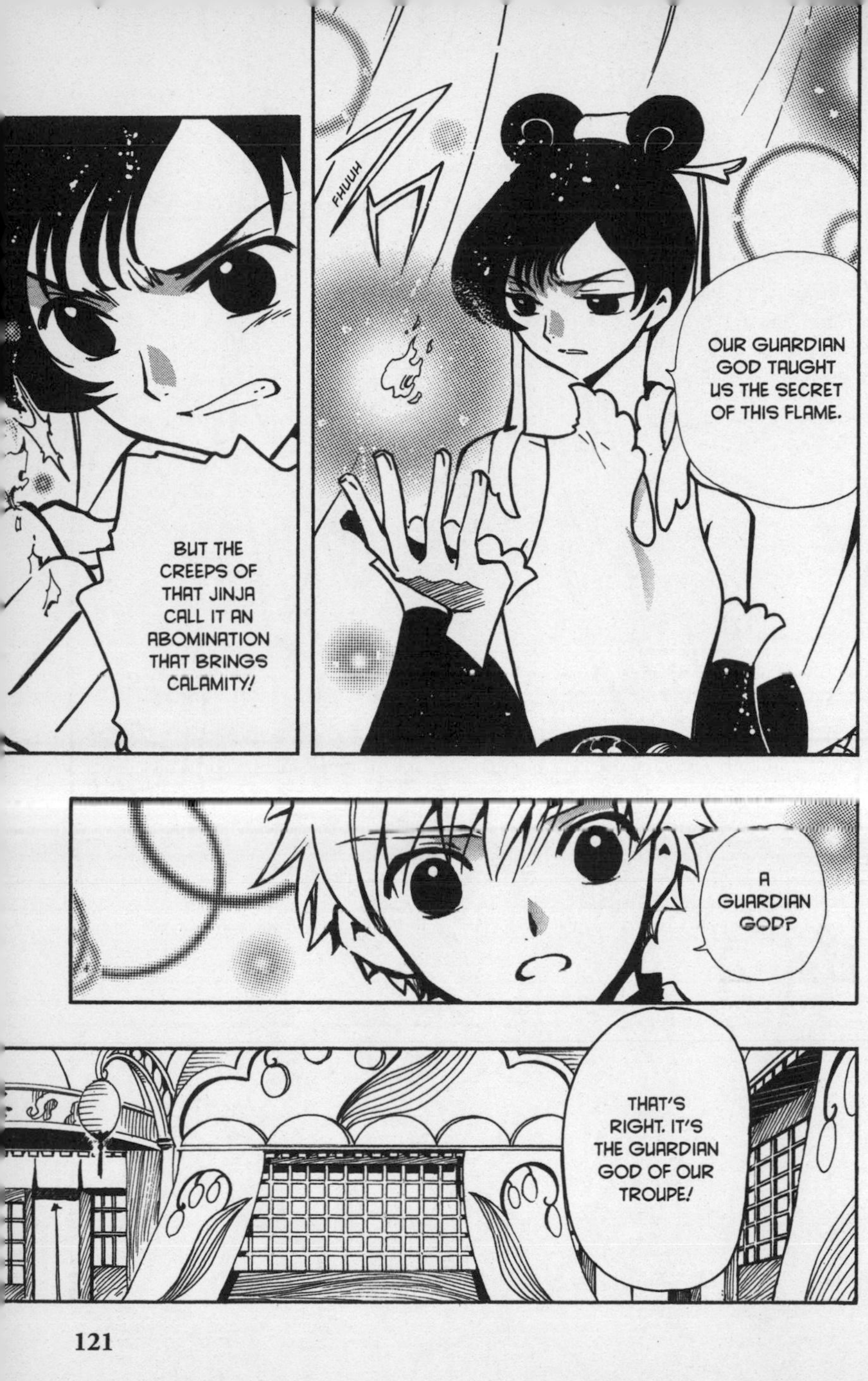
FHUUH
OUR GUARDIAN GOD TAUGHT US THE SECRET OF THIS FLAME.
BUT THE CREEPS OF THAT JINJA CALL IT AN ABOMINATION THAT BRINGS CALAMITY!
A GUARDIAN GOD?
THAT'S RIGHT. IT'S THE GUARDIAN GOD OF OUR TROUPE!

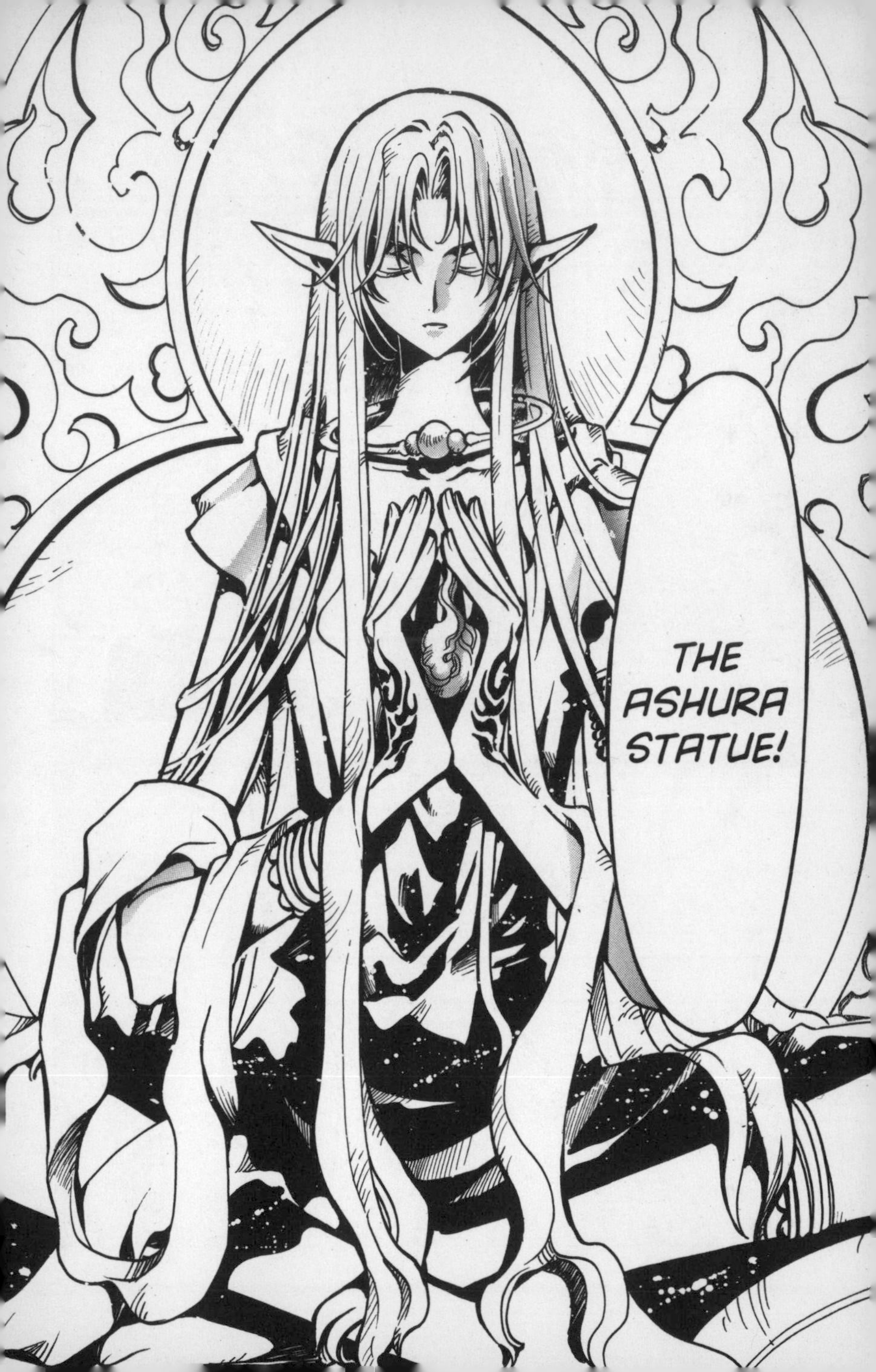
THE ASHURA STATUE!

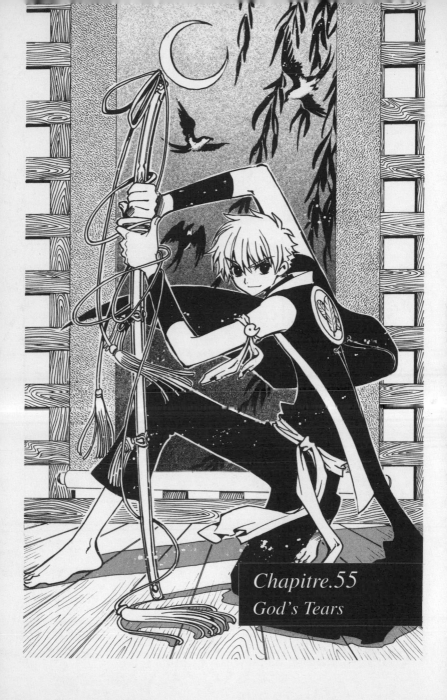

Chapitre.55
God's Tears

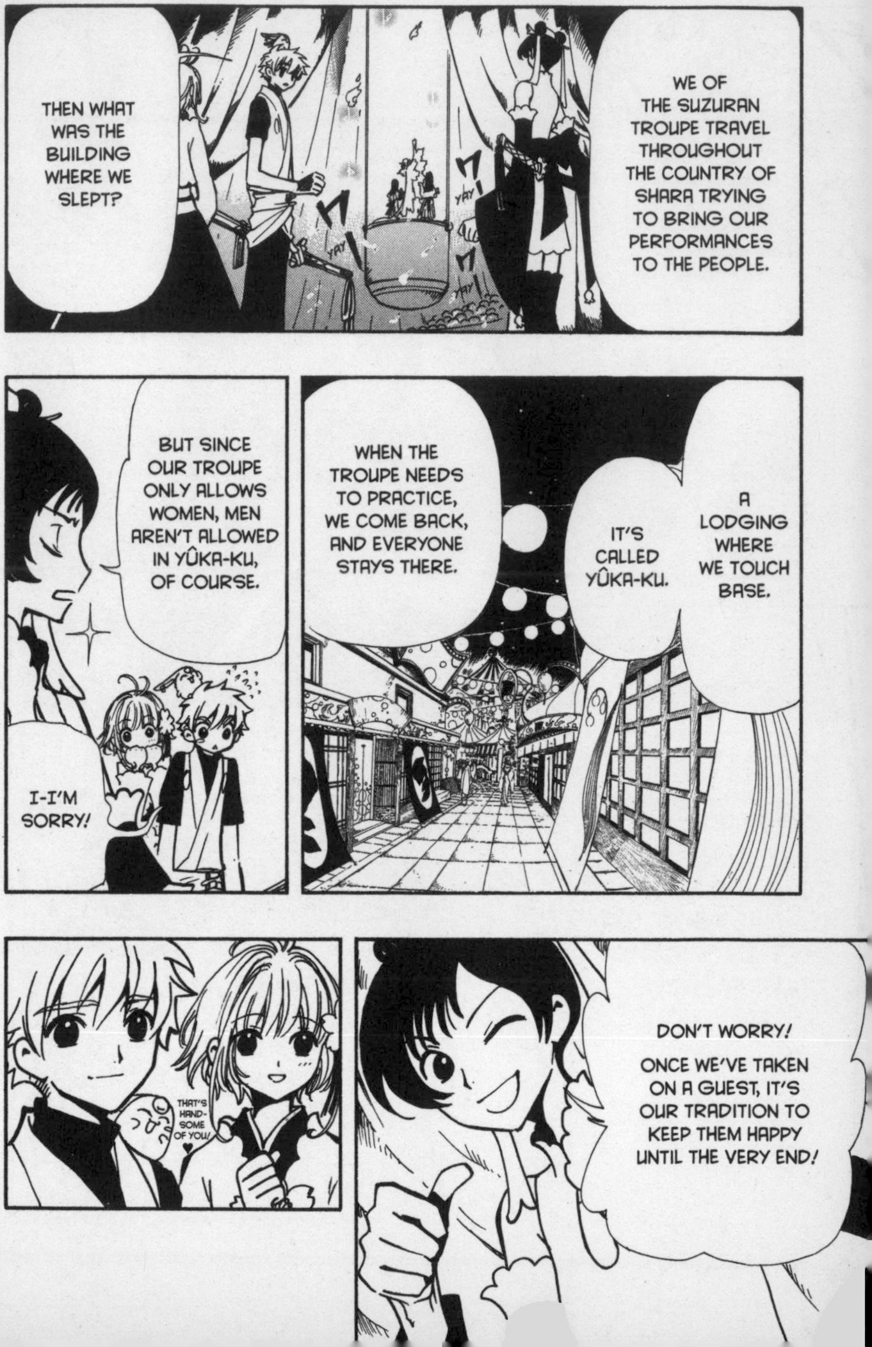
WE OF THE SUZURAN TROUPE TRAVEL THROUGHOUT THE COUNTRY OF SHARA TRYING TO BRING OUR PERFORMANCES TO THE PEOPLE.
YAY
YAY
YAY
THEN WHAT WAS THE BUILDING WHERE WE SLEPT?
A LODGING WHERE WE TOUCH BASE.
IT'S CALLED YÛKA-KU.
WHEN THE TROUPE NEEDS TO PRACTICE, WE COME BACK, AND EVERYONE STAYS THERE.
BUT SINCE OUR TROUPE ONLY ALLOWS WOMEN, MEN AREN'T ALLOWED IN YÛKA-KU, OF COURSE.
I-I'M SORRY!
DON'T WORRY!
ONCE WE'VE TAKEN ON A GUEST, IT'S OUR TRADITION TO KEEP THEM HAPPY UNTIL THE VERY END!
THAT'S HAND-SOME OF YOU! ♥

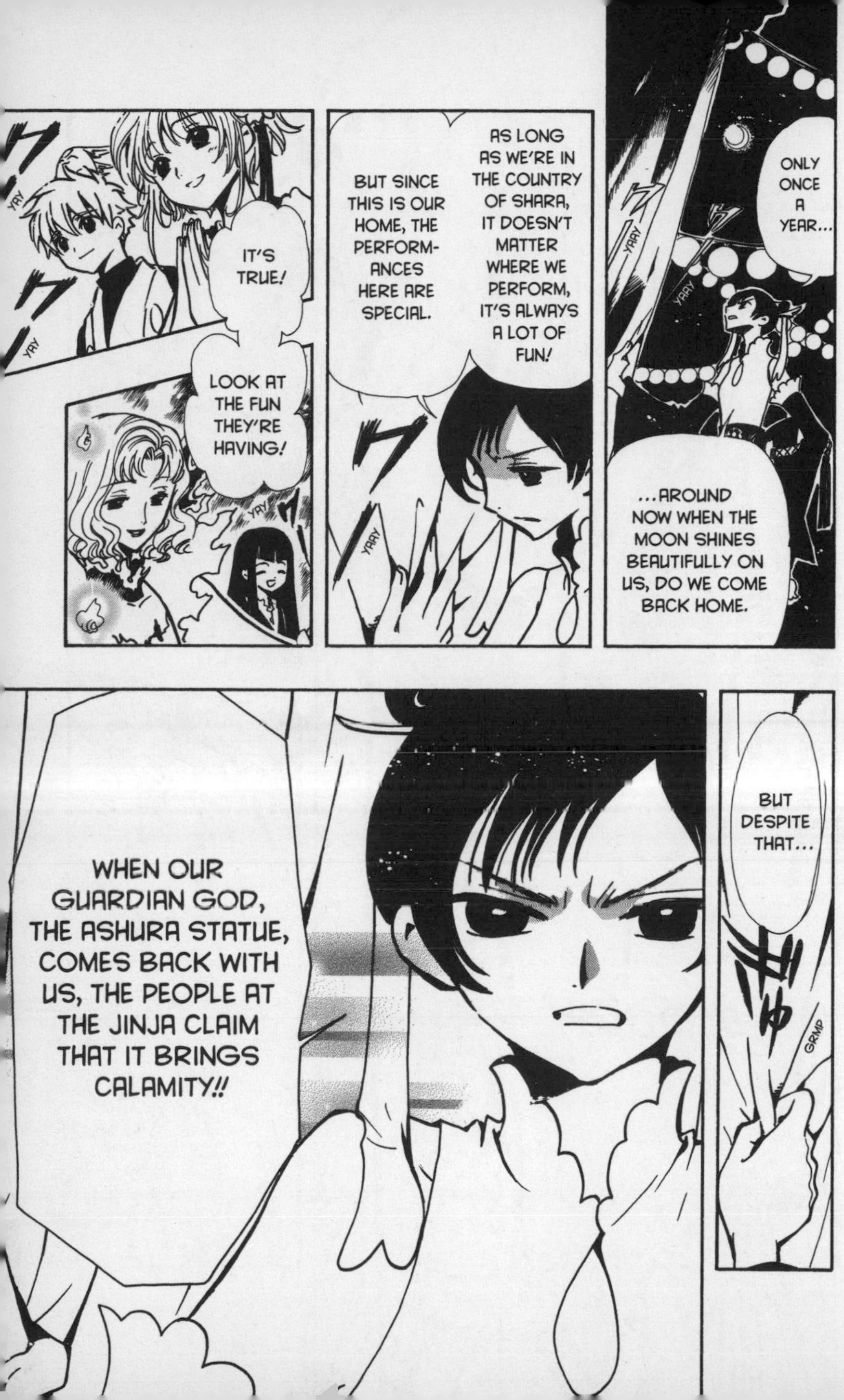
ONLY ONCE A YEAR...
YAAY
YAAY
...AROUND NOW WHEN THE MOON SHINES BEAUTIFULLY ON US, DO WE COME BACK HOME.
AS LONG AS WE'RE IN THE COUNTRY OF SHARA, IT DOESN'T MATTER WHERE WE PERFORM, IT'S ALWAYS A LOT OF FUN!
BUT SINCE THIS IS OUR HOME, THE PERFORM-ANCES HERE ARE SPECIAL.
YAAY
IT'S TRUE!
YAY
YAY
LOOK AT THE FUN THEY'RE HAVING!
YAY
BUT DESPITE THAT...
GRMP
WHEN OUR GUARDIAN GOD, THE ASHURA STATUE, COMES BACK WITH US, THE PEOPLE AT THE JINJA CLAIM THAT IT BRINGS CALAMITY!!

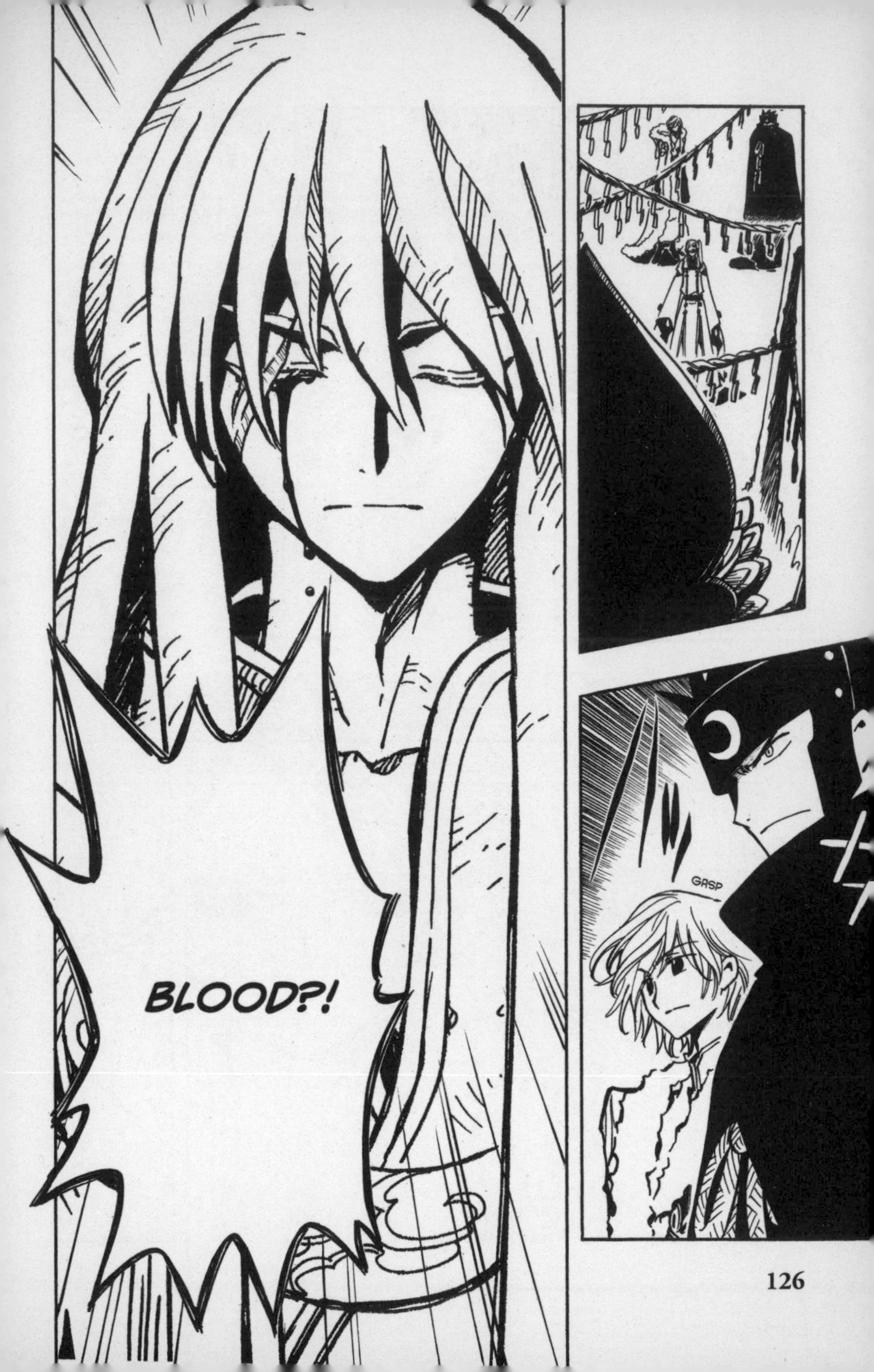
GASP
BLOOD?!

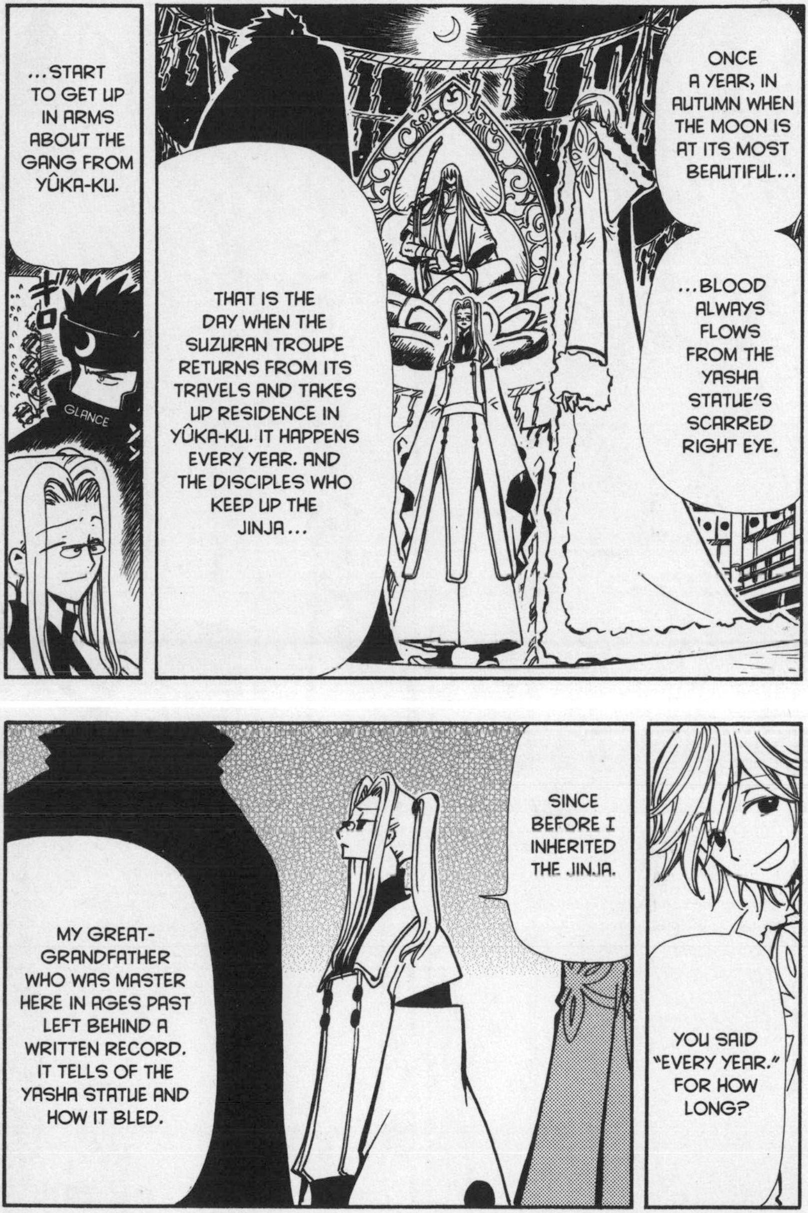
ONCE A YEAR, IN AUTUMN WHEN THE MOON IS AT ITS MOST BEAUTIFUL...
...BLOOD ALWAYS FLOWS FROM THE YASHA STATUE'S SCARRED RIGHT EYE.
THAT IS THE DAY WHEN THE SUZURAN TROUPE RETURNS FROM ITS TRAVELS AND TAKES UP RESIDENCE IN YÛKA-KU. IT HAPPENS EVERY YEAR. AND THE DISCIPLES WHO KEEP UP THE JINJA...
...START TO GET UP IN ARMS ABOUT THE GANG FROM YÛKA-KU.
ギロ
GLANCE
YOU SAID "EVERY YEAR." FOR HOW LONG?
SINCE BEFORE I INHERITED THE JINJA.
MY GREAT-GRANDFATHER WHO WAS MASTER HERE IN AGES PAST LEFT BEHIND A WRITTEN RECORD. IT TELLS OF THE YASHA STATUE AND HOW IT BLED.

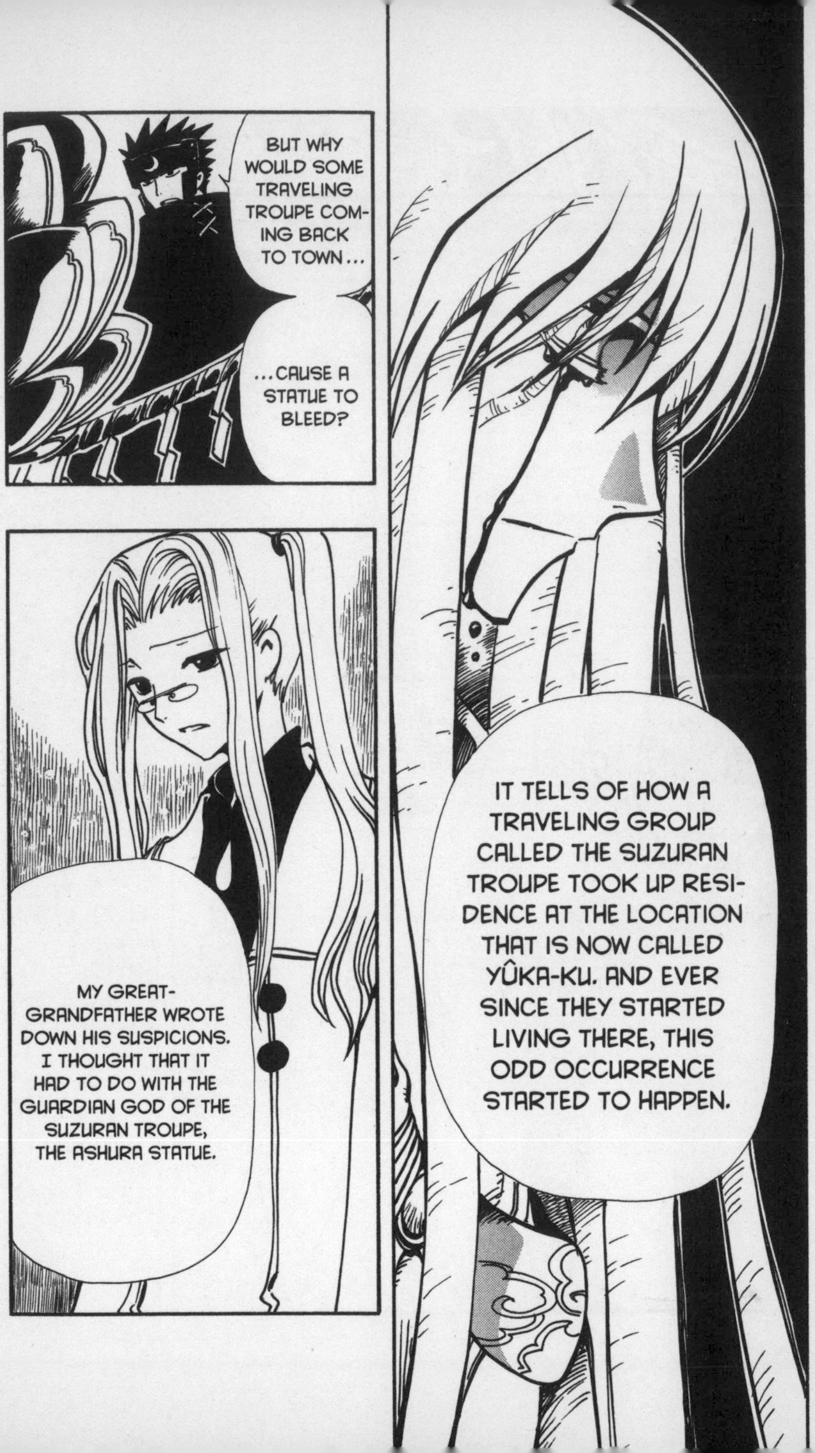
IT TELLS OF HOW A TRAVELING GROUP CALLED THE SUZURAN TROUPE TOOK UP RESI-DENCE AT THE LOCATION THAT IS NOW CALLED YÛKA-KU. AND EVER SINCE THEY STARTED LIVING THERE, THIS ODD OCCURRENCE STARTED TO HAPPEN.
BUT WHY WOULD SOME TRAVELING TROUPE COM-ING BACK TO TOWN...
...CAUSE A STATUE TO BLEED?
MY GREAT-GRANDFATHER WROTE DOWN HIS SUSPICIONS. I THOUGHT THAT IT HAD TO DO WITH THE GUARDIAN GOD OF THE SUZURAN TROUPE, THE ASHURA STATUE.

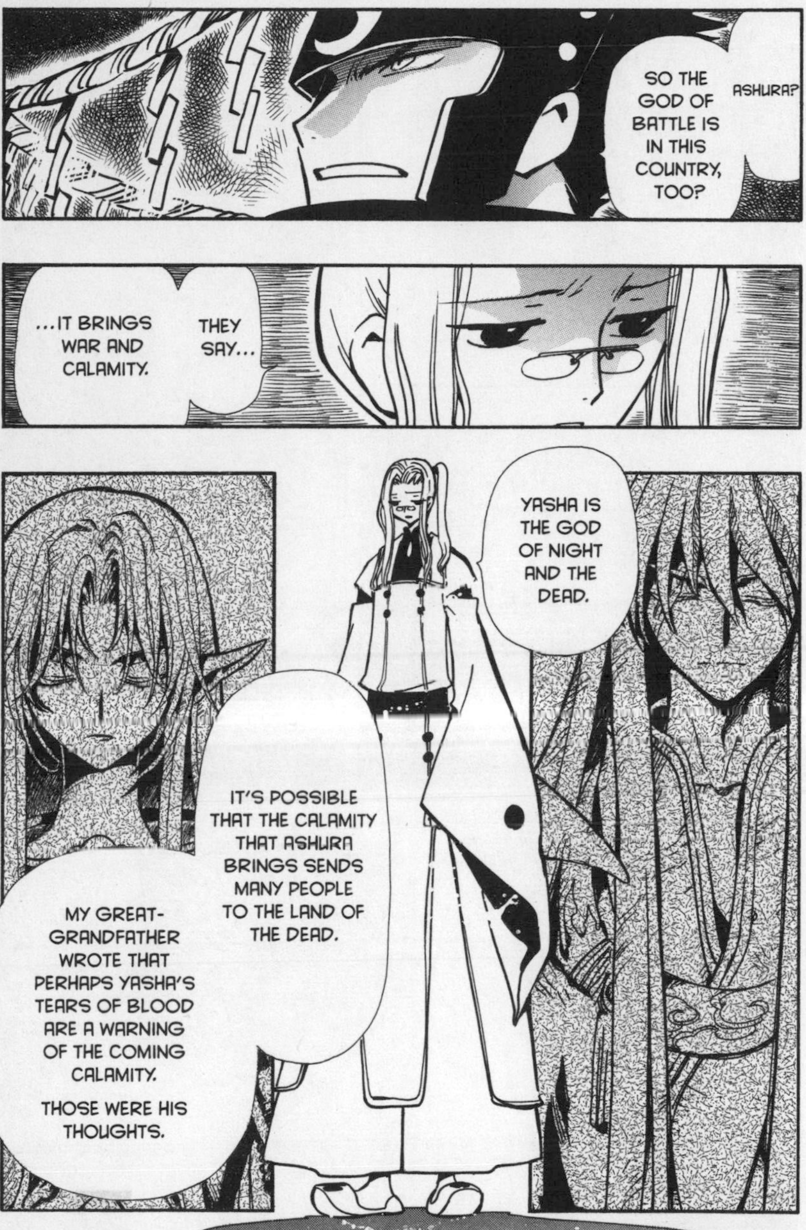
ASHURA?
SO THE GOD OF BATTLE IS IN THIS COUNTRY, TOO?
THEY SAY...
...IT BRINGS WAR AND CALAMITY.
YASHA IS THE GOD OF NIGHT AND THE DEAD.
IT'S POSSIBLE THAT THE CALAMITY THAT ASHURA BRINGS SENDS MANY PEOPLE TO THE LAND OF THE DEAD.
MY GREAT-GRANDFATHER WROTE THAT PERHAPS YASHA'S TEARS OF BLOOD ARE A WARNING OF THE COMING CALAMITY.
THOSE WERE HIS THOUGHTS.

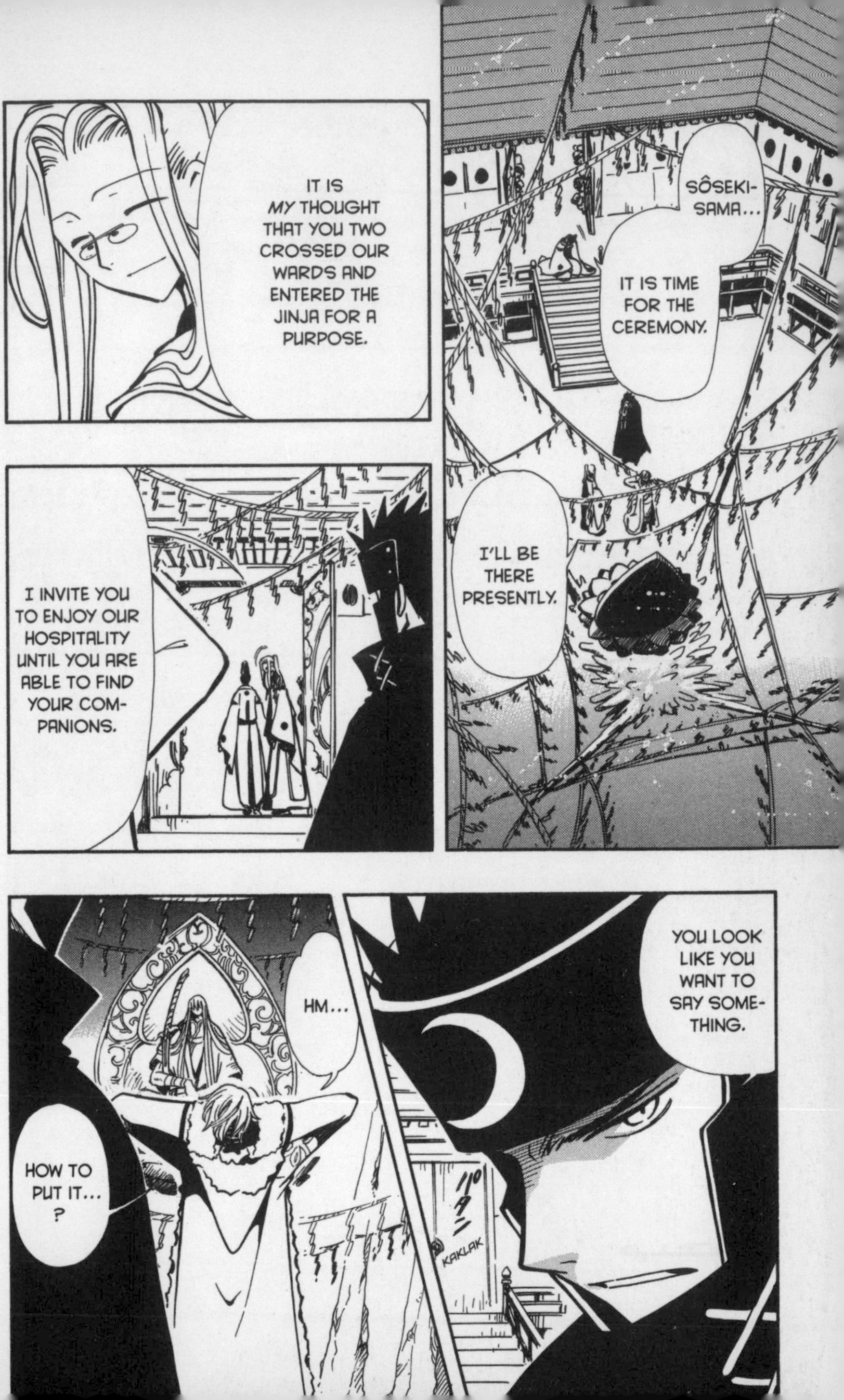
SÔSEKI-SAMA...
IT IS TIME FOR THE CEREMONY.
I'LL BE THERE PRESENTLY.
IT IS *MY* THOUGHT THAT YOU TWO CROSSED OUR WARDS AND ENTERED THE JINJA FOR A PURPOSE.
I INVITE YOU TO ENJOY OUR HOSPITALITY UNTIL YOU ARE ABLE TO FIND YOUR COM-PANIONS.
YOU LOOK LIKE YOU WANT TO SAY SOME-THING.
KAKLAK
HM...
HOW TO PUT IT... ?

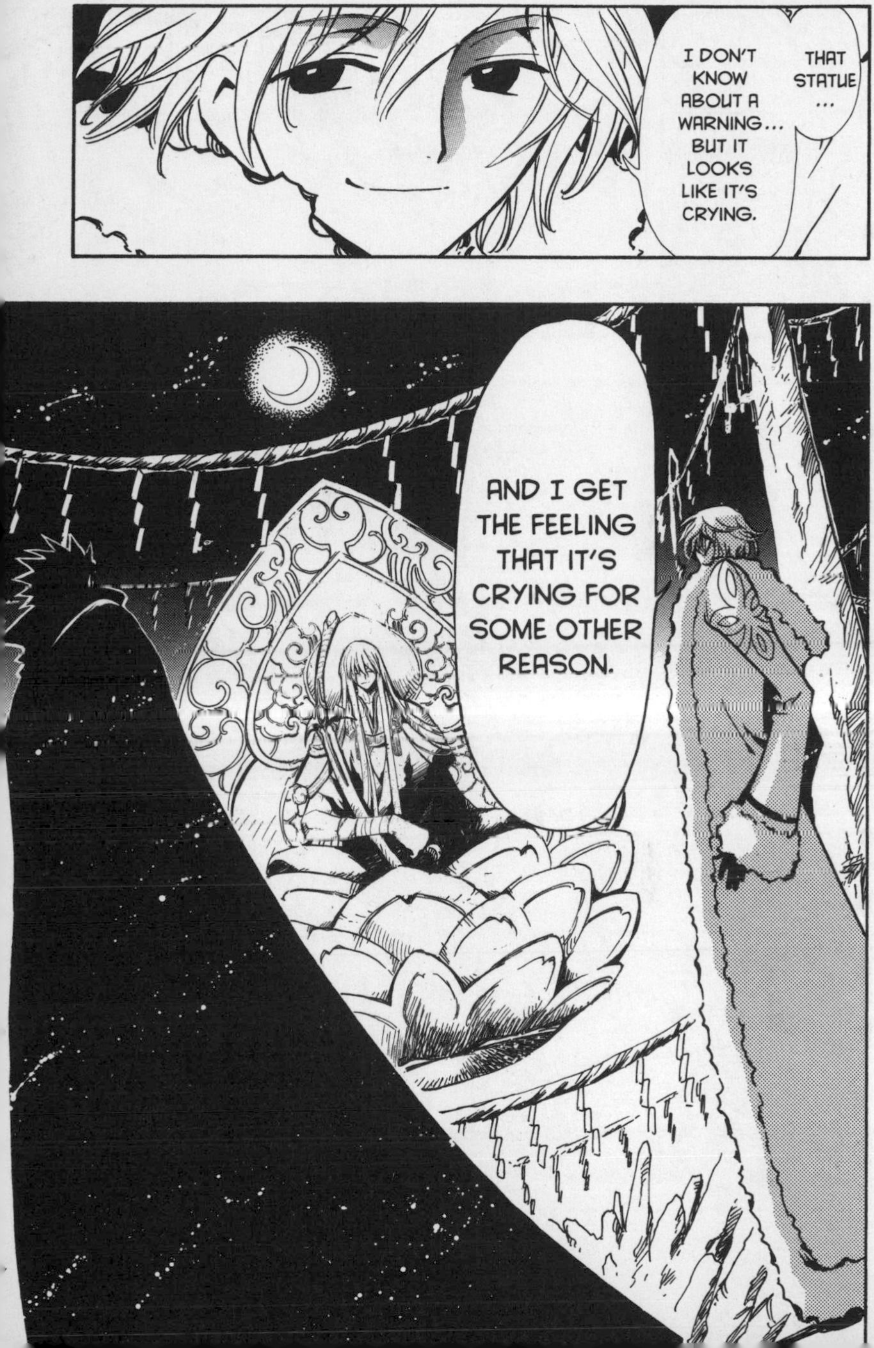
THAT STATUE ...
I DON'T KNOW ABOUT A WARNING... BUT IT LOOKS LIKE IT'S CRYING.
AND I GET THE FEELING THAT IT'S CRYING FOR SOME OTHER REASON.

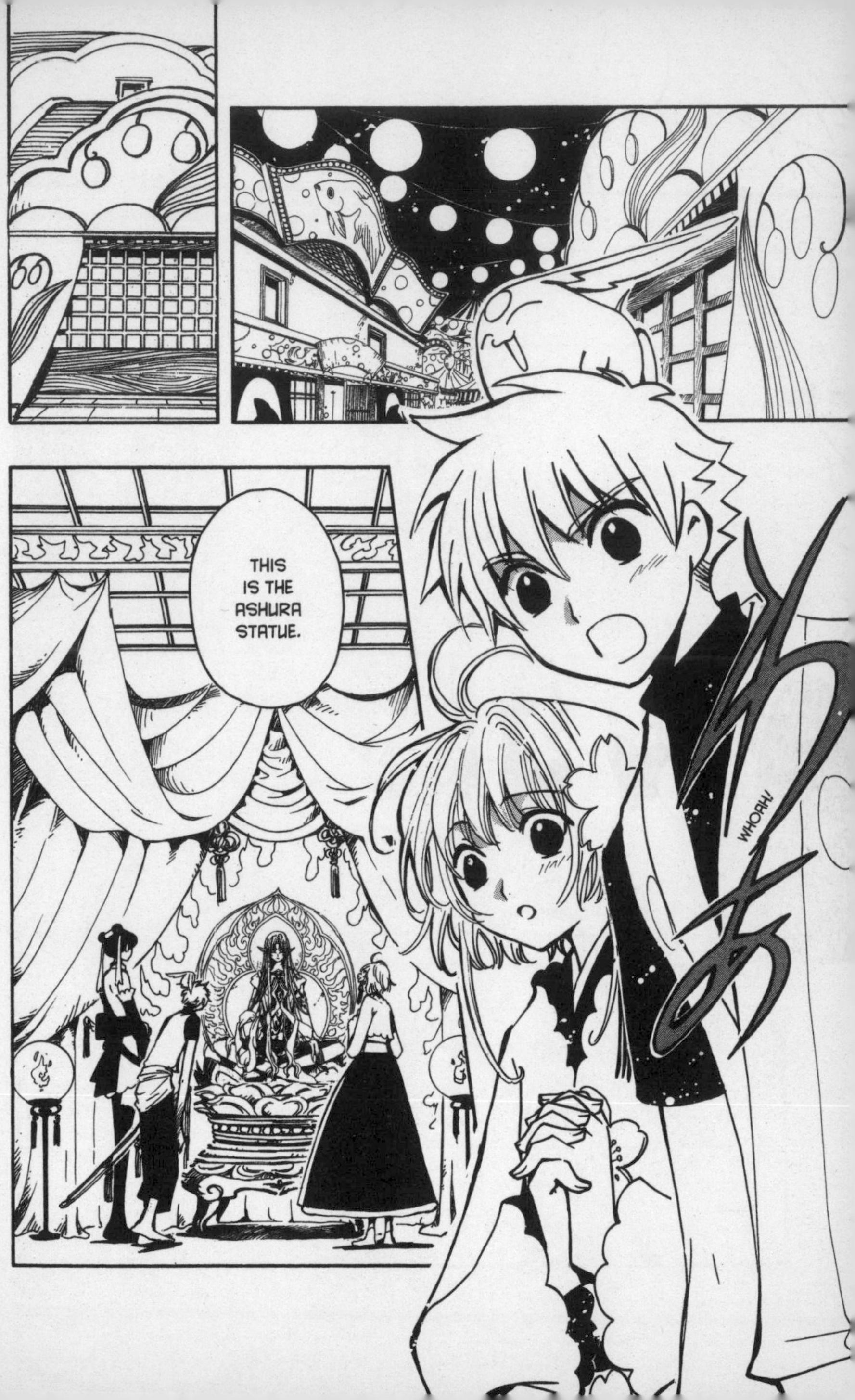
THIS IS THE ASHURA STATUE.
WHOAH!

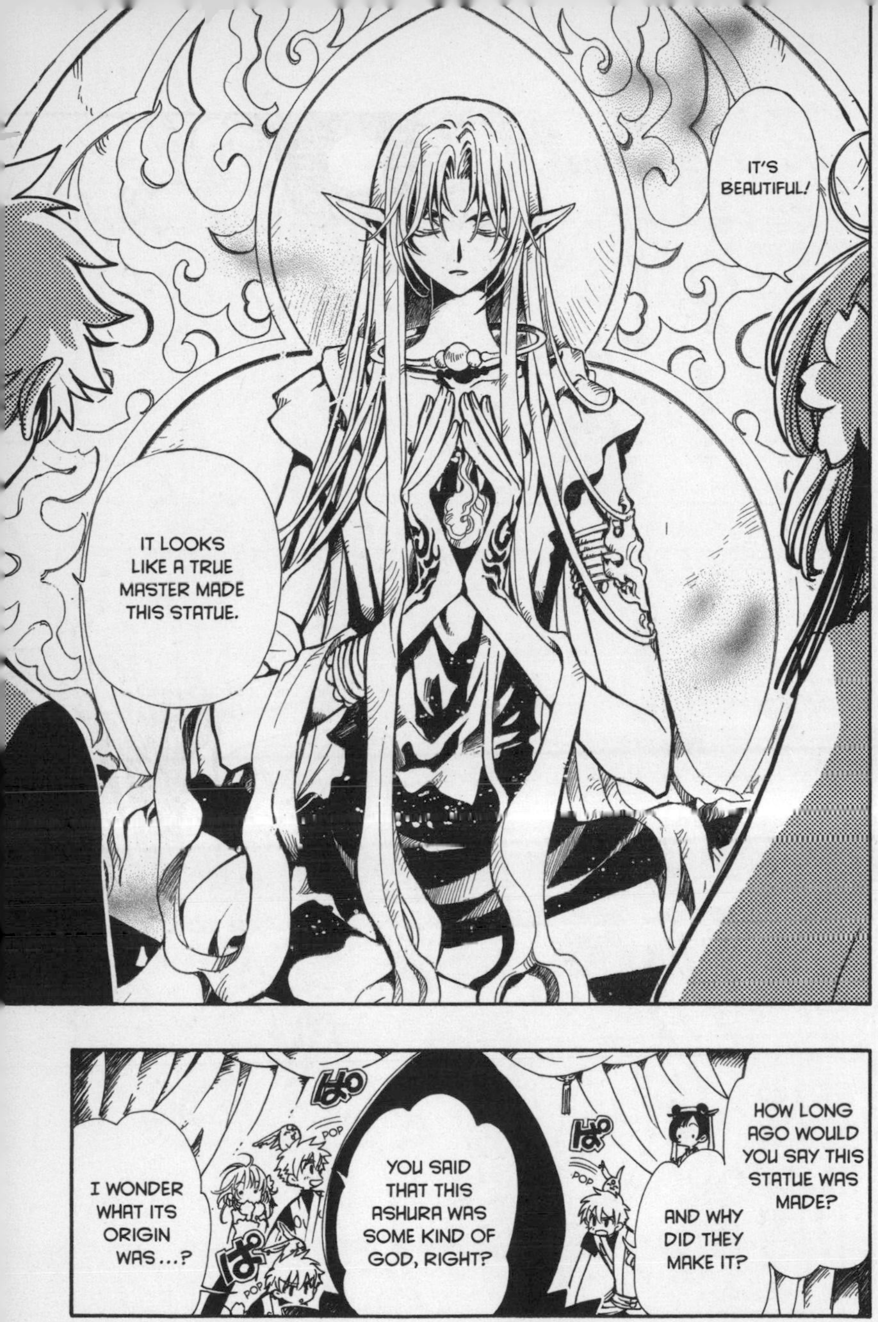
IT'S BEAUTIFUL!
IT LOOKS LIKE A TRUE MASTER MADE THIS STATUE.
HOW LONG AGO WOULD YOU SAY THIS STATUE WAS MADE?
AND WHY DID THEY MAKE IT?
POP
YOU SAID THAT THIS ASHURA WAS SOME KIND OF GOD, RIGHT?
POP
I WONDER WHAT ITS ORIGIN WAS...?
POP

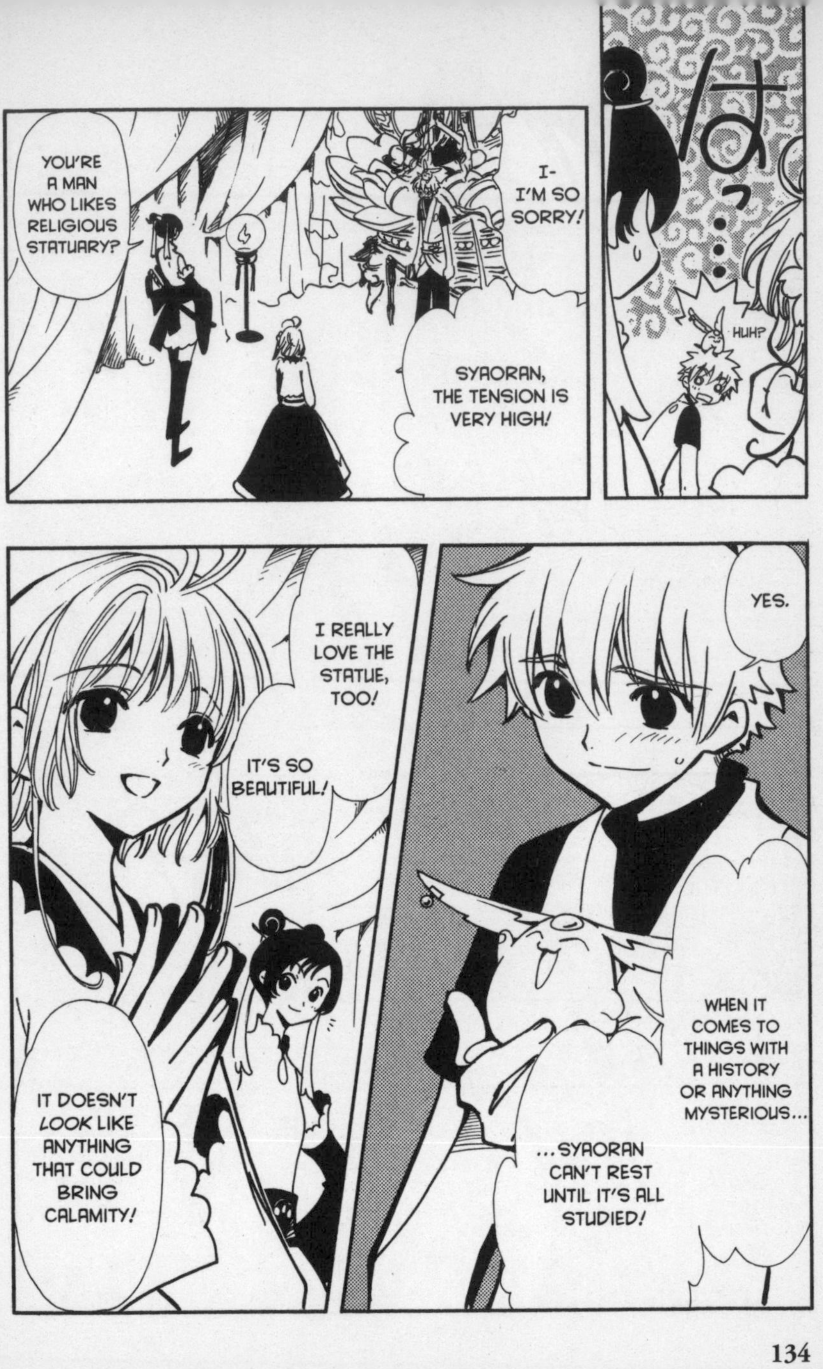
はっ…
HUH?
I- I'M SO SORRY!
YOU'RE A MAN WHO LIKES RELIGIOUS STATUARY?
SYAORAN, THE TENSION IS VERY HIGH!
YES.
WHEN IT COMES TO THINGS WITH A HISTORY OR ANYTHING MYSTERIOUS...
...SYAORAN CAN'T REST UNTIL IT'S ALL STUDIED!
I REALLY LOVE THE STATUE, TOO!
IT'S SO BEAUTIFUL!
IT DOESN'T *LOOK* LIKE ANYTHING THAT COULD BRING CALAMITY!

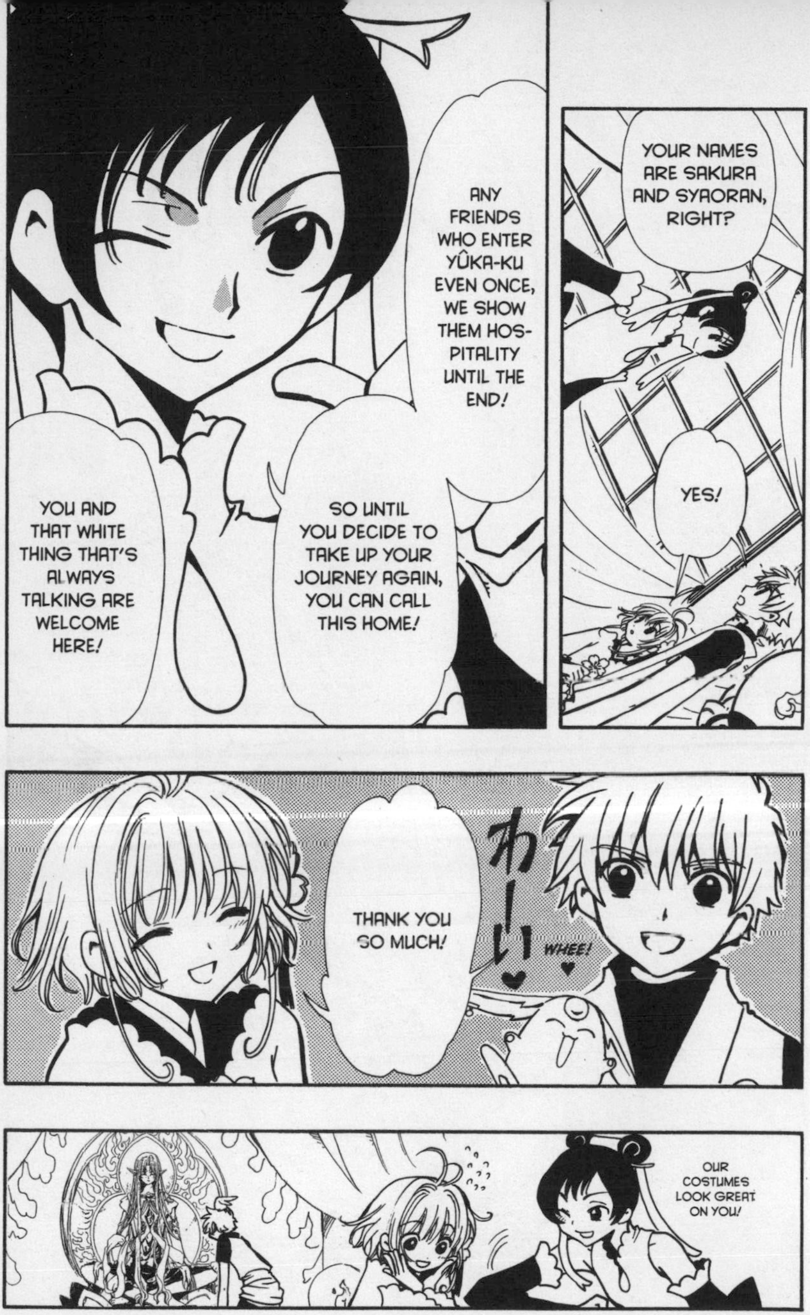
YOUR NAMES ARE SAKURA AND SYAORAN, RIGHT?
YES!
ANY FRIENDS WHO ENTER YÛKA-KU EVEN ONCE, WE SHOW THEM HOS-PITALITY UNTIL THE END!
SO UNTIL YOU DECIDE TO TAKE UP YOUR JOURNEY AGAIN, YOU CAN CALL THIS HOME!
YOU AND THAT WHITE THING THAT'S ALWAYS TALKING ARE WELCOME HERE!
わーい
WHEE!
THANK YOU SO MUCH!
OUR COSTUMES LOOK GREAT ON YOU!

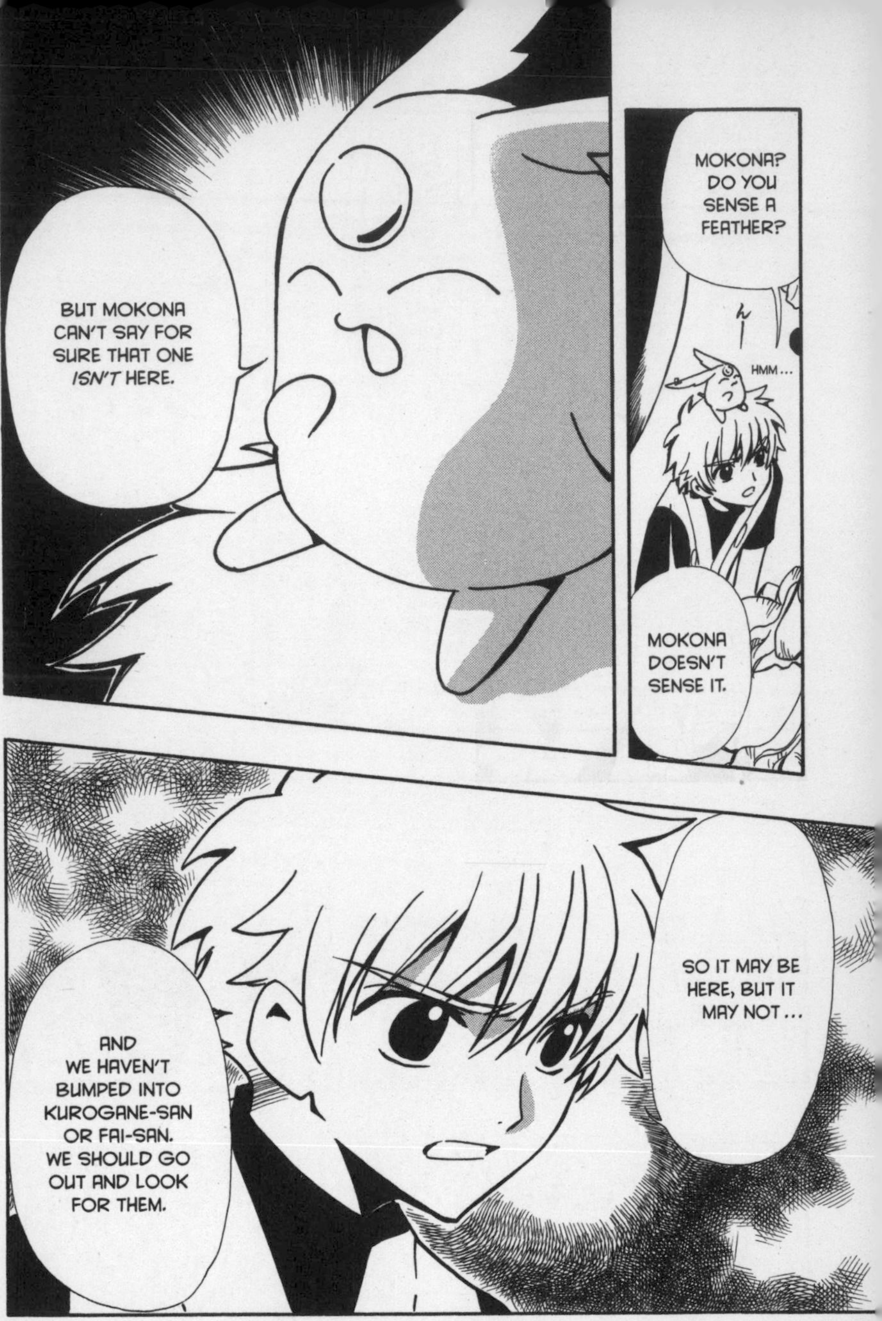
MOKONA? DO YOU SENSE A FEATHER?
ん
HMM...
MOKONA DOESN'T SENSE IT.
BUT MOKONA CAN'T SAY FOR SURE THAT ONE *ISN'T* HERE.
SO IT MAY BE HERE, BUT IT MAY NOT...
AND WE HAVEN'T BUMPED INTO KUROGANE-SAN OR FAI-SAN. WE SHOULD GO OUT AND LOOK FOR THEM.

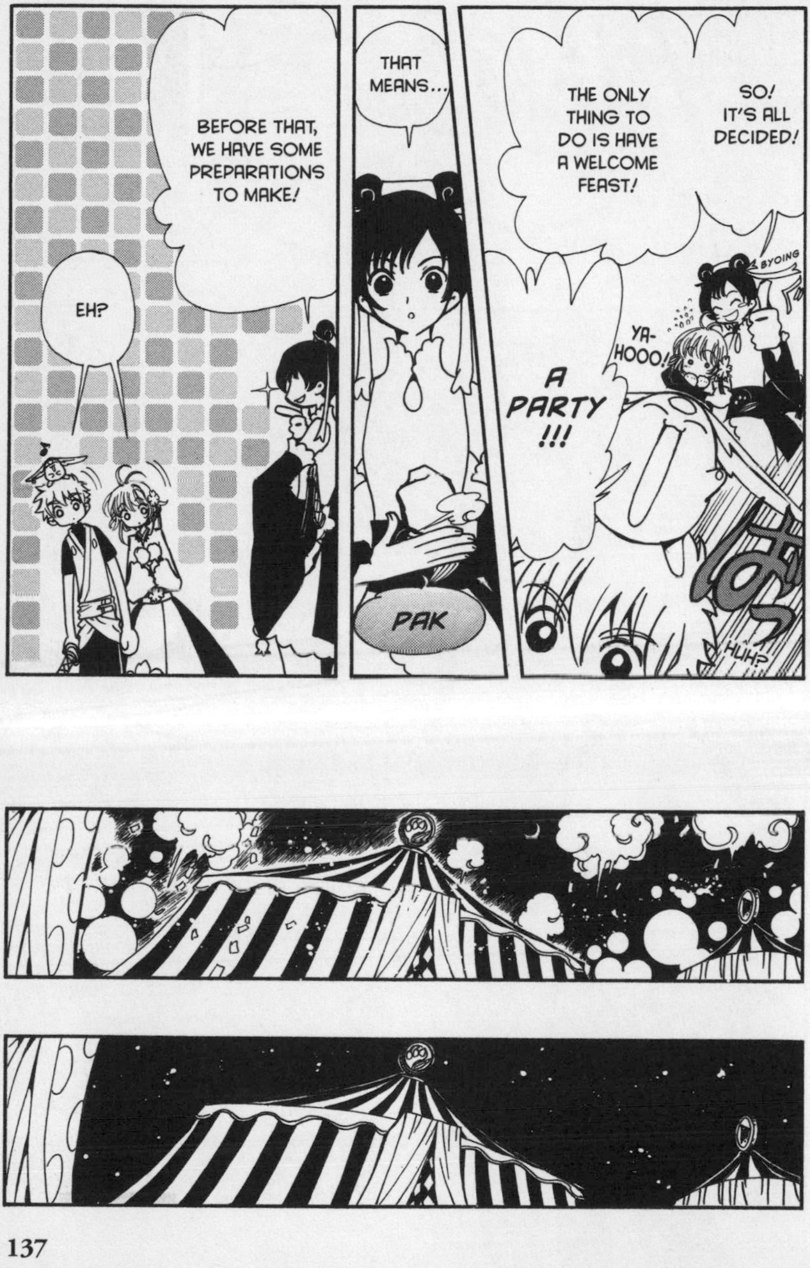
SO! IT'S ALL DECIDED!
THE ONLY THING TO DO IS HAVE A WELCOME FEAST!
BYOING
YA-HOOO!
A PARTY!!!
HUH?
THAT MEANS...
PAK
BEFORE THAT, WE HAVE SOME PREPARATIONS TO MAKE!
EH?

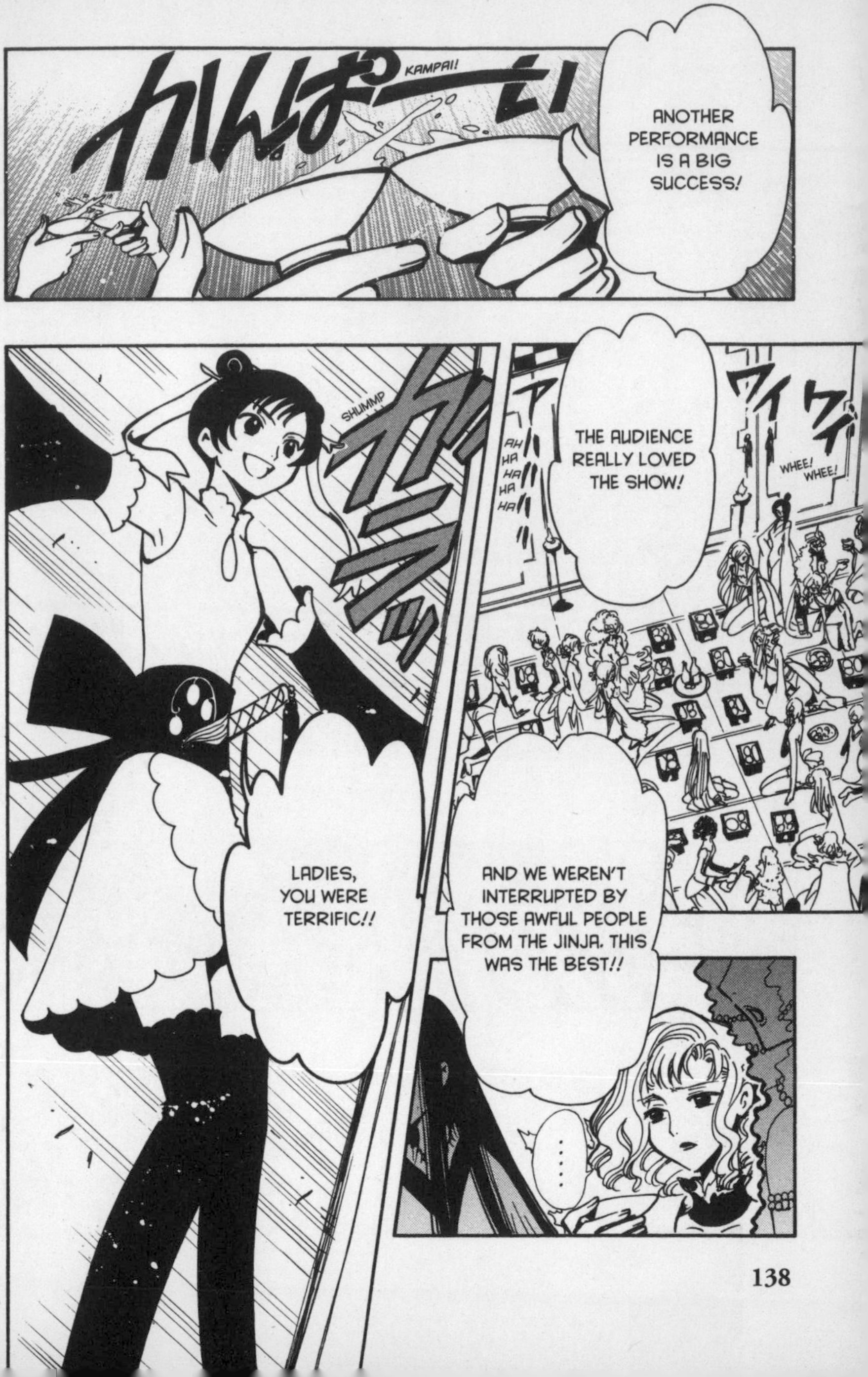
KAMPAI!
ANOTHER PERFORMANCE IS A BIG SUCCESS!
THE AUDIENCE REALLY LOVED THE SHOW!
AH HA HA HA HA
WHEE! WHEE!
SHUMMP
LADIES, YOU WERE TERRIFIC!!
AND WE WEREN'T INTERRUPTED BY THOSE AWFUL PEOPLE FROM THE JINJA. THIS WAS THE BEST!!
.....

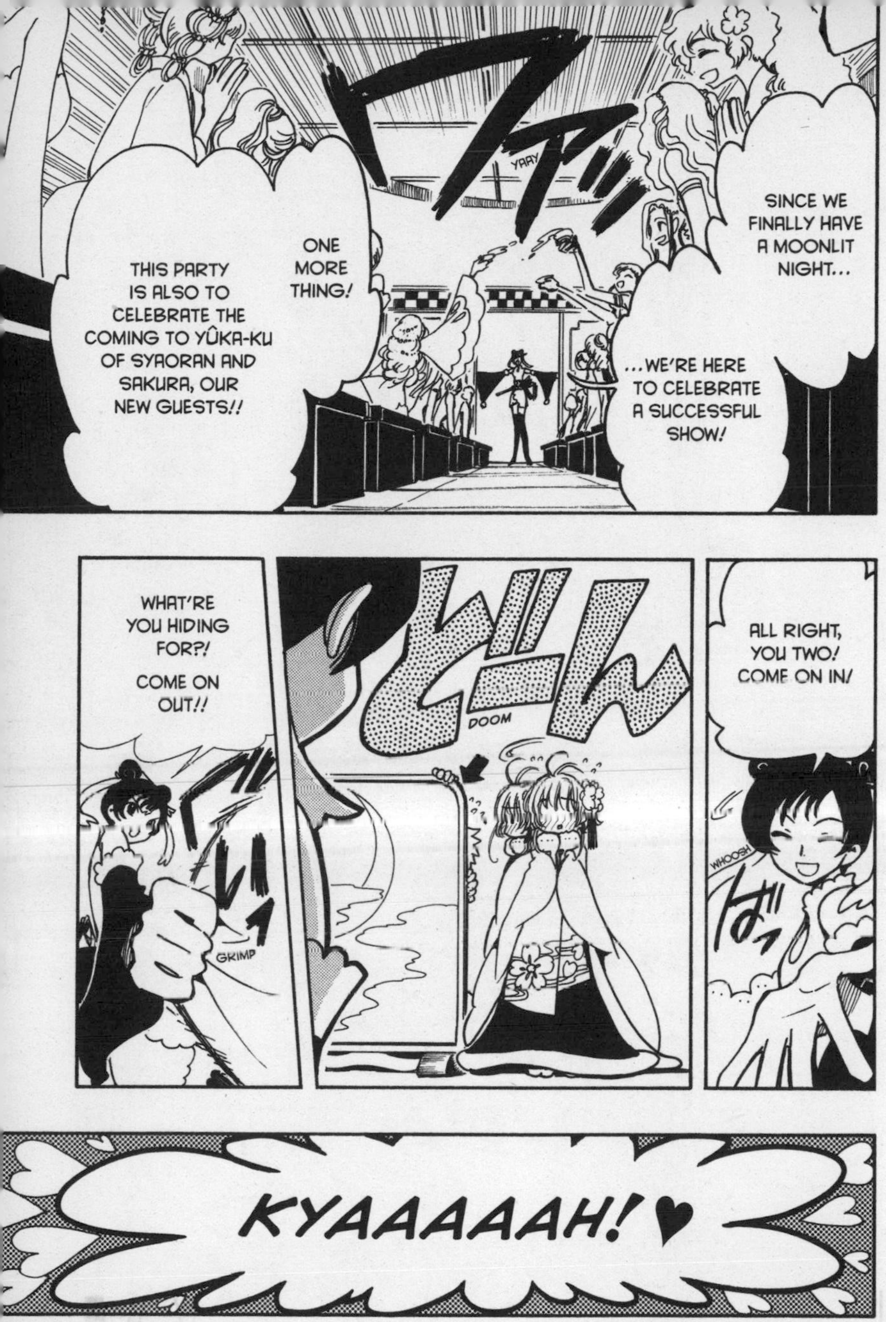
SINCE WE FINALLY HAVE A MOONLIT NIGHT...
...WE'RE HERE TO CELEBRATE A SUCCESSFUL SHOW!
YAAY
ONE MORE THING!
THIS PARTY IS ALSO TO CELEBRATE THE COMING TO YÛKA-KU OF SYAORAN AND SAKURA, OUR NEW GUESTS!!
ALL RIGHT, YOU TWO! COME ON IN!
WHOOSH
DOOM
WHAT'RE YOU HIDING FOR?!
COME ON OUT!!
GRIMP
KYAAAAAAH! ♥

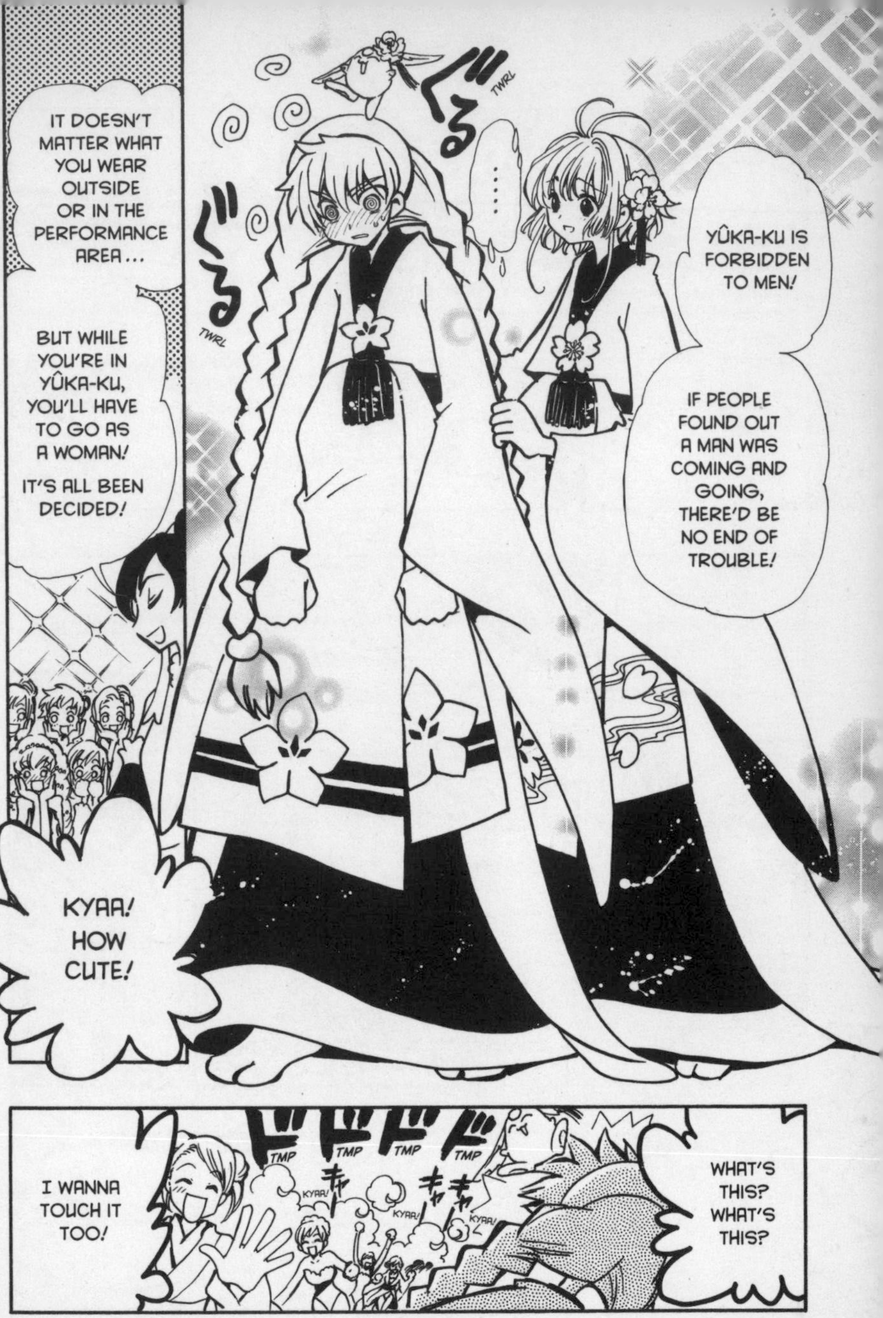
YÛKA-KU IS FORBIDDEN TO MEN!
IF PEOPLE FOUND OUT A MAN WAS COMING AND GOING, THERE'D BE NO END OF TROUBLE!
ぐる TWRL
……
ぐる TWRL
IT DOESN'T MATTER WHAT YOU WEAR OUTSIDE OR IN THE PERFORMANCE AREA...
BUT WHILE YOU'RE IN YÛKA-KU, YOU'LL HAVE TO GO AS A WOMAN!
IT'S ALL BEEN DECIDED!
KYAA! HOW CUTE!
WHAT'S THIS? WHAT'S THIS?
TMP TMP TMP TMP
KYAA! KYAA! KYAA!
I WANNA TOUCH IT TOO!

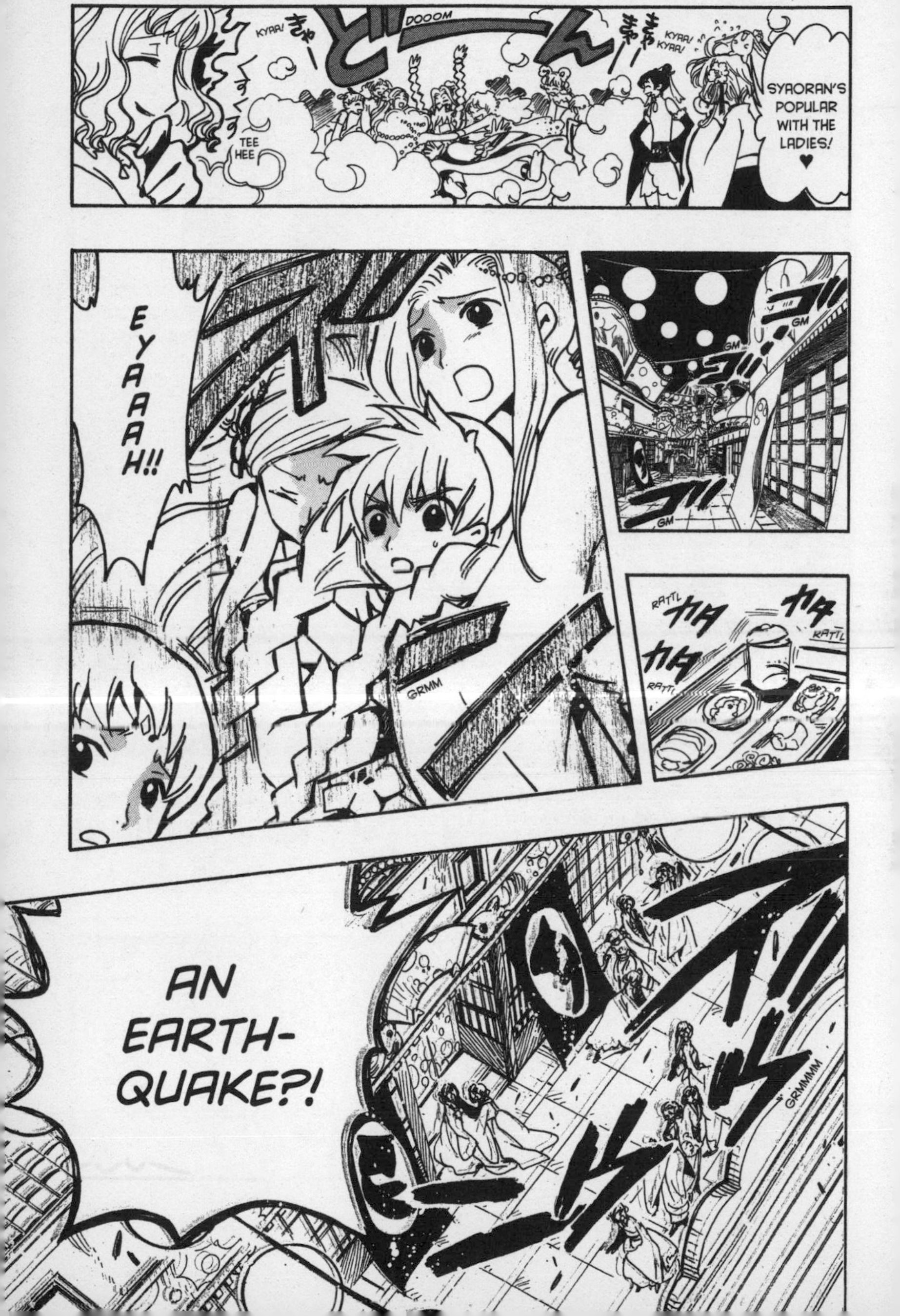

SYAORAN'S POPULAR WITH THE LADIES! ♥
KYAA! KYAA!
DOOOM
KYAA!
TEE HEE
GM GM GM
RATTL RATTL RATTL
EYAAAAH!!
GRMM
AN EARTH-QUAKE?!
GRMMMM

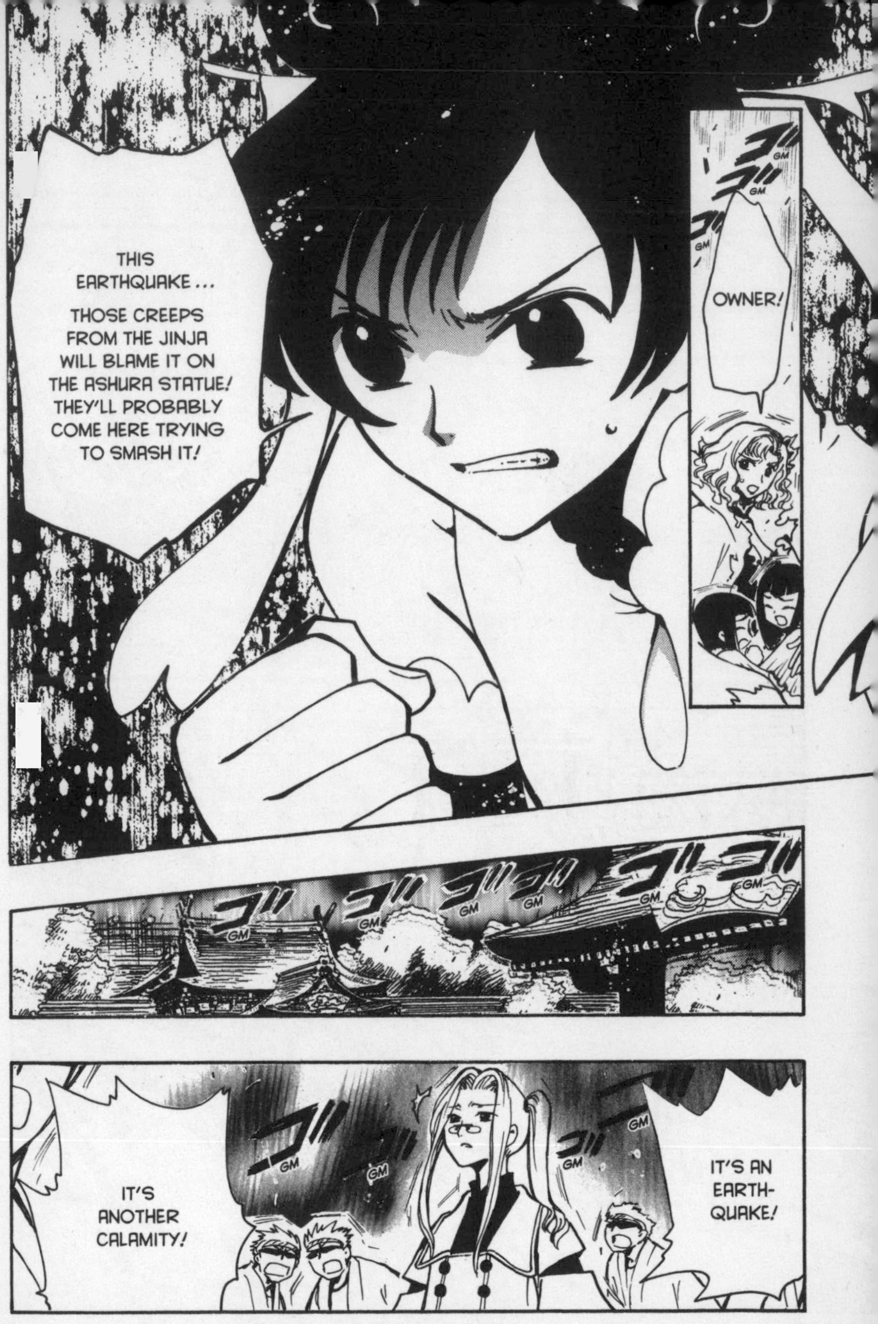
GM GM GM
OWNER!
THIS EARTHQUAKE...
THOSE CREEPS FROM THE JINJA WILL BLAME IT ON THE ASHURA STATUE! THEY'LL PROBABLY COME HERE TRYING TO SMASH IT!
GM GM GM GM GM GM
GM GM GM GM
IT'S AN EARTH-QUAKE!
IT'S ANOTHER CALAMITY!

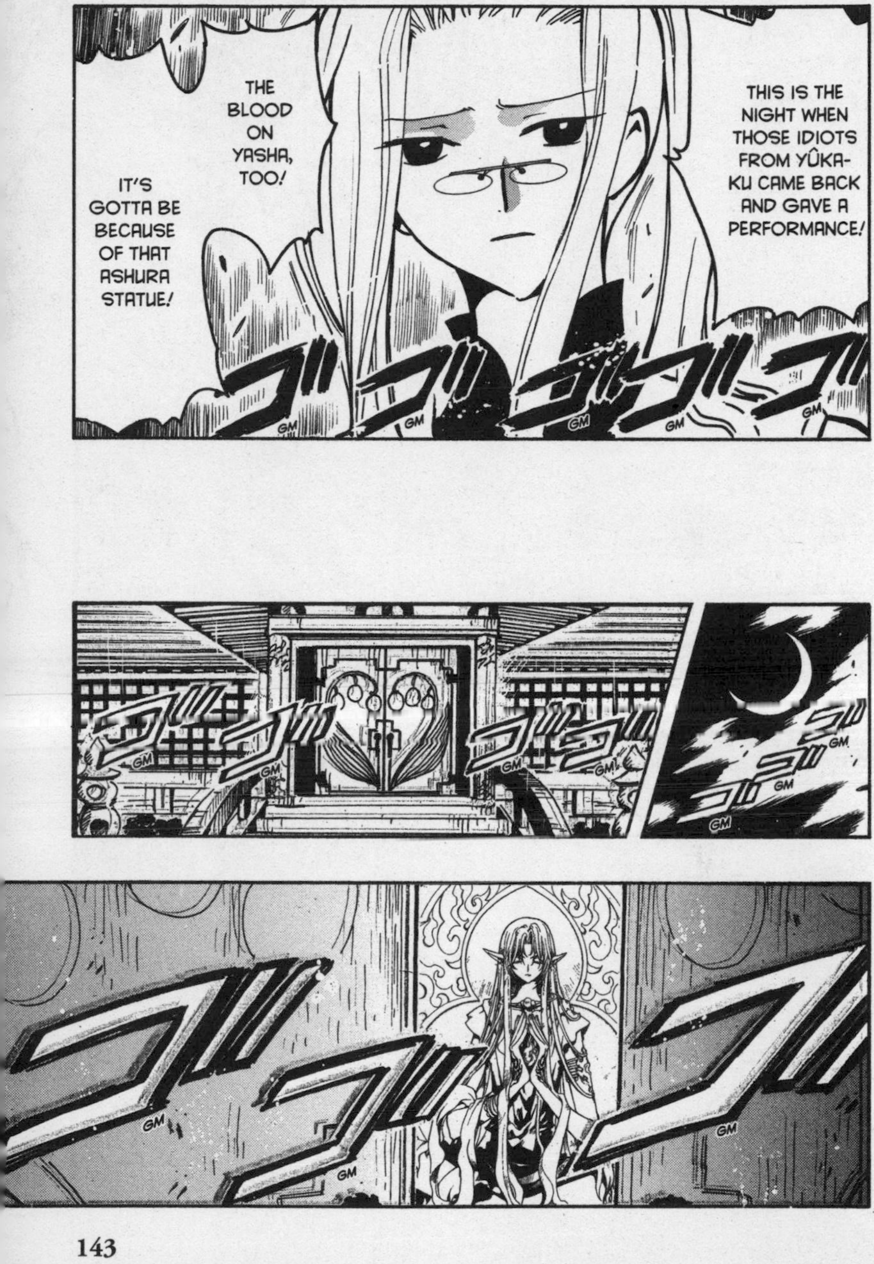
THIS IS THE NIGHT WHEN THOSE IDIOTS FROM YÛKA-KU CAME BACK AND GAVE A PERFORMANCE!
THE BLOOD ON YASHA, TOO!
IT'S GOTTA BE BECAUSE OF THAT ASHURA STATUE!
GM
GM
GM
GM
GM
GM
GM
GM
GM
GM
GM
GM
GM
GM
GM
GM

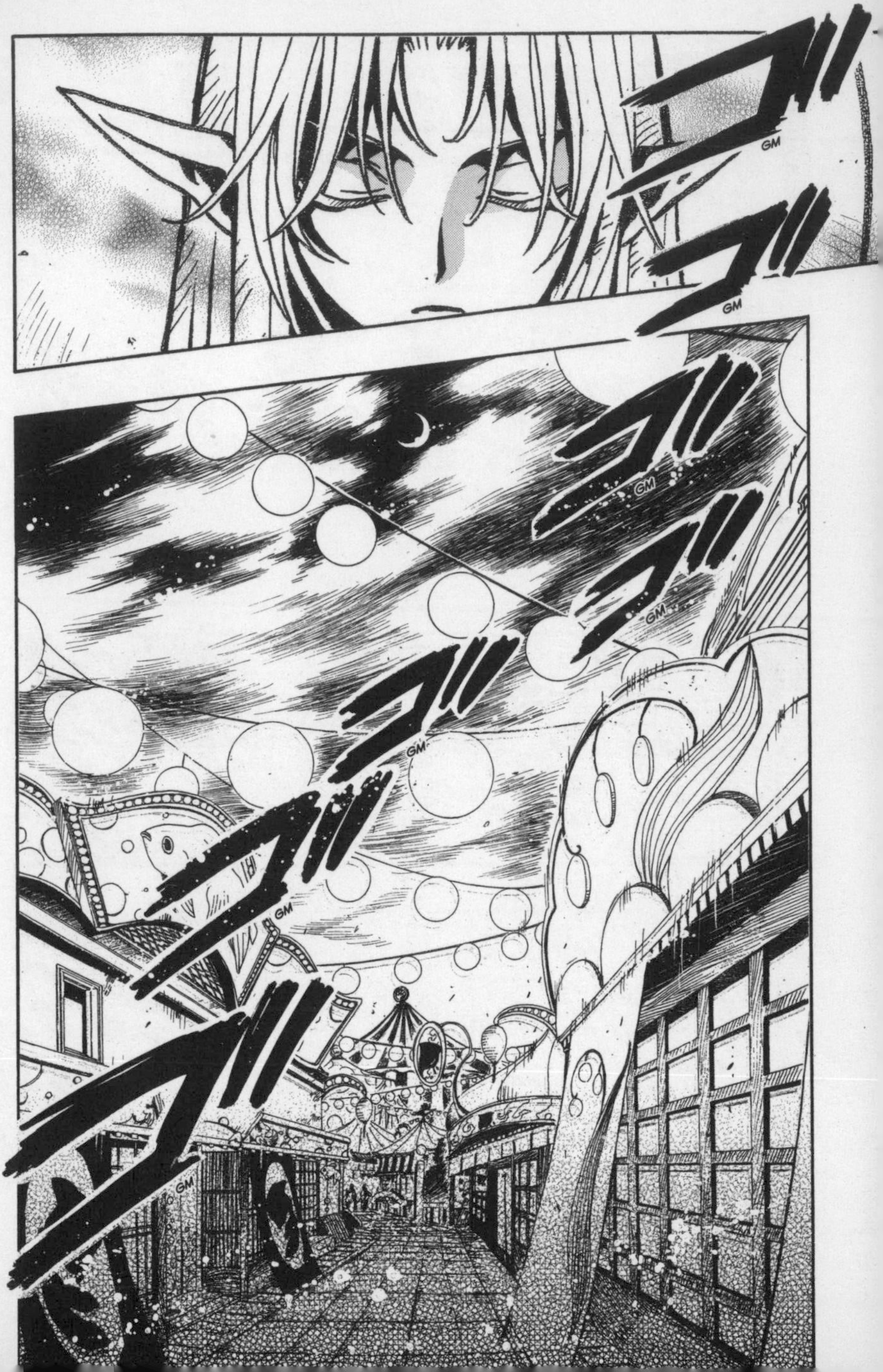
GM
GM
GM
GM
GM
GM
GM

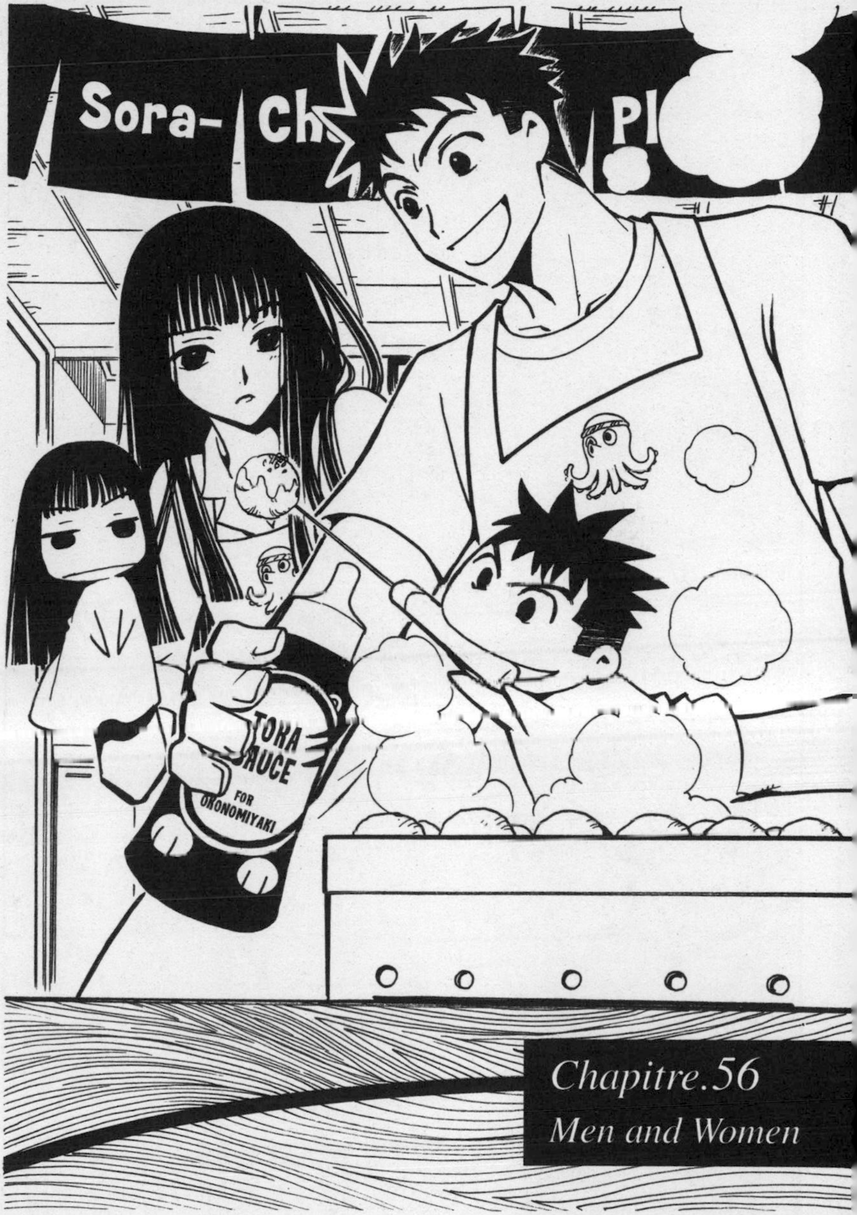
Sora-
TORA
FOR OKONOMIYAKI

Chapitre.56
Men and Women

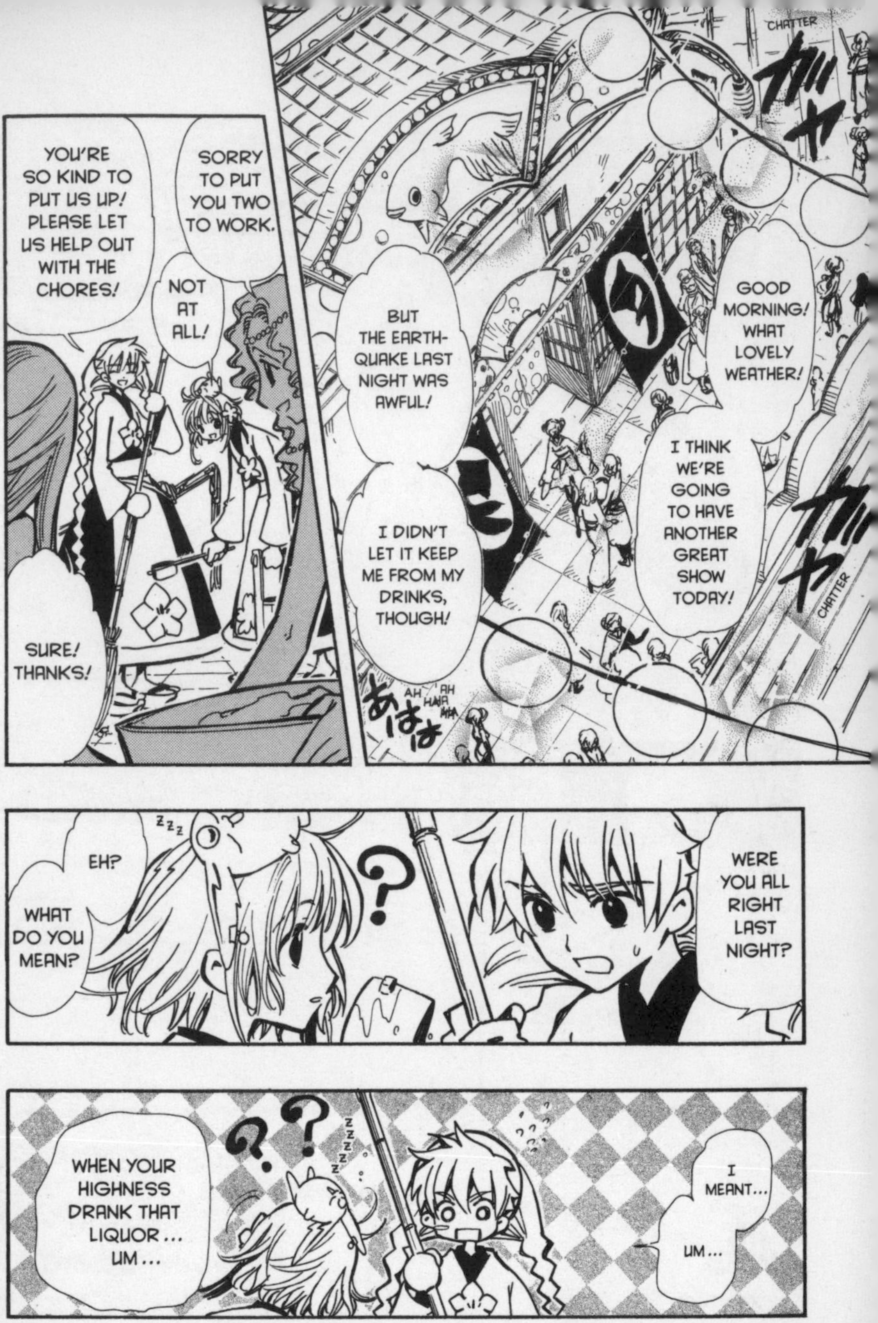
CHATTER
GOOD MORNING! WHAT LOVELY WEATHER!
I THINK WE'RE GOING TO HAVE ANOTHER GREAT SHOW TODAY!
CHATTER
BUT THE EARTHQUAKE LAST NIGHT WAS AWFUL!
I DIDN'T LET IT KEEP ME FROM MY DRINKS, THOUGH!
あはは
AH HAHA AH HAHA
SORRY TO PUT YOU TWO TO WORK.
YOU'RE SO KIND TO PUT US UP! PLEASE LET US HELP OUT WITH THE CHORES!
NOT AT ALL!
SURE! THANKS!
WERE YOU ALL RIGHT LAST NIGHT?
EH?
WHAT DO YOU MEAN?
I MEANT...
UM...
WHEN YOUR HIGHNESS DRANK THAT LIQUOR... UM...

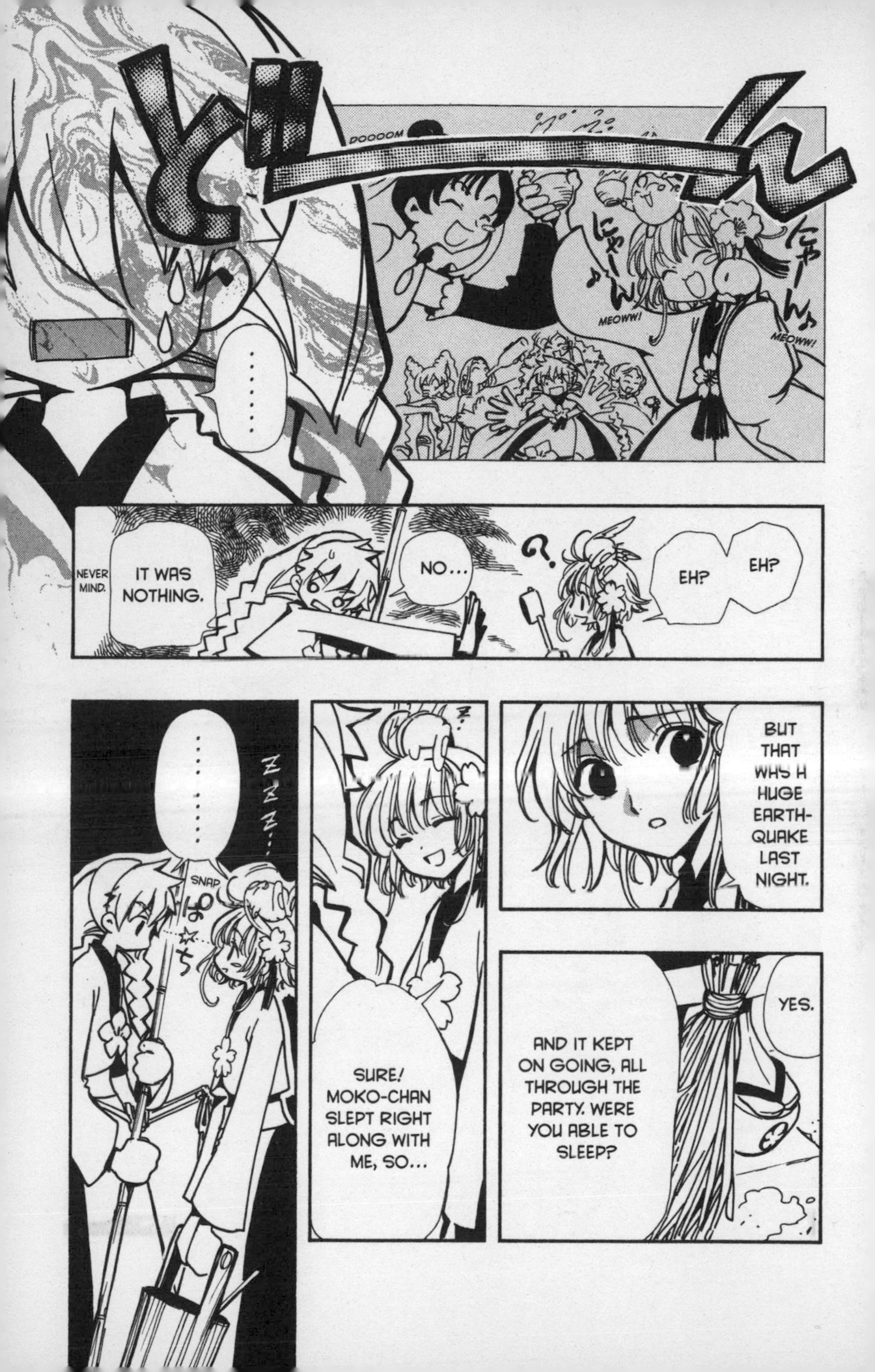
DOOOOM
MEOWW!
MEOWW!
......
EH?
EH?
NO...
IT WAS NOTHING.
NEVER MIND.
BUT THAT WAS A HUGE EARTH-QUAKE LAST NIGHT.
YES.
AND IT KEPT ON GOING, ALL THROUGH THE PARTY. WERE YOU ABLE TO SLEEP?
SURE! MOKO-CHAN SLEPT RIGHT ALONG WITH ME, SO...
......
Z Z Z...
SNAP

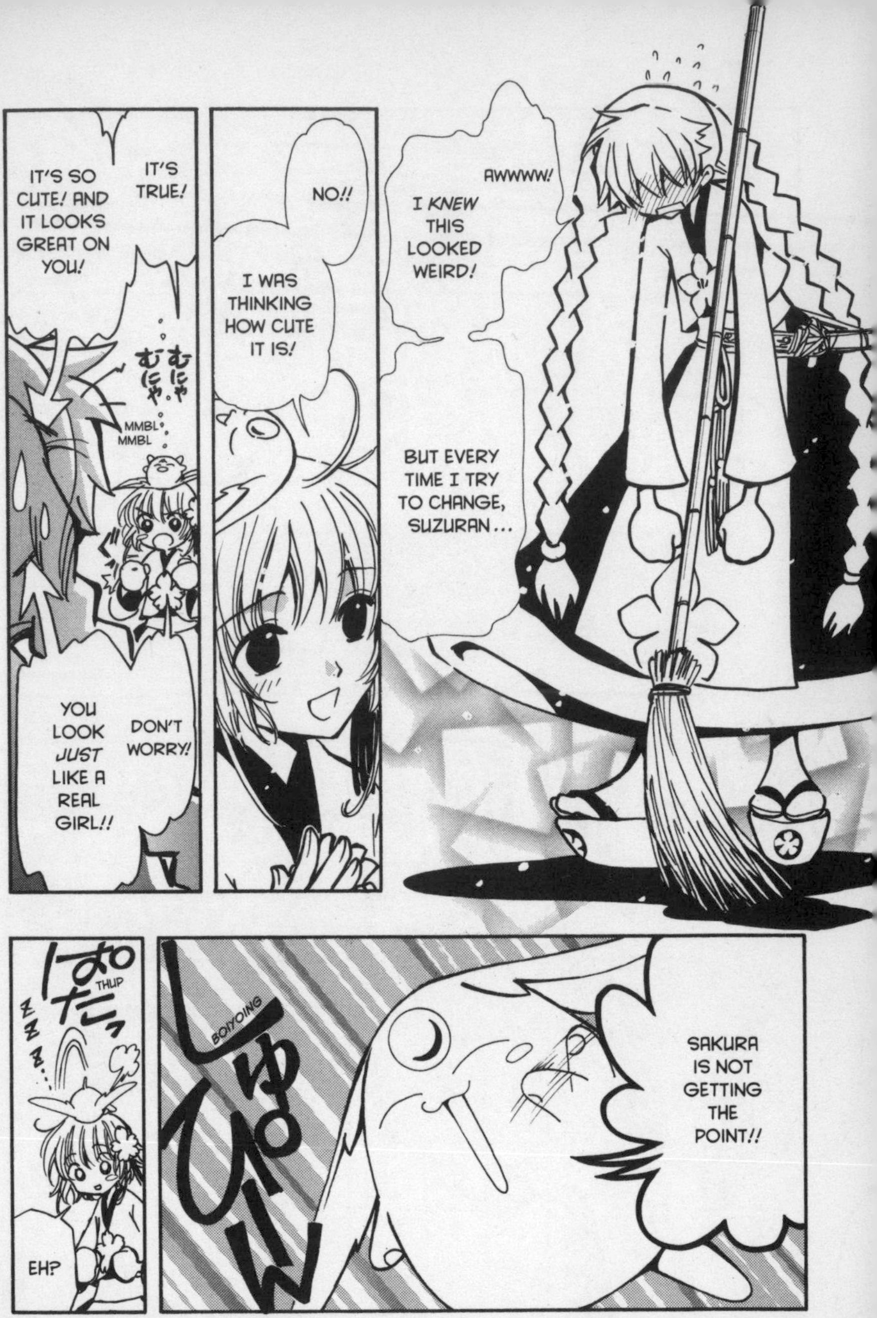
AWWWW!
I KNEW THIS LOOKED WEIRD!
BUT EVERY TIME I TRY TO CHANGE, SUZURAN...
NO!!
I WAS THINKING HOW CUTE IT IS!
IT'S TRUE!
IT'S SO CUTE! AND IT LOOKS GREAT ON YOU!
むにゃむにゃ
MMBL MMBL
DON'T WORRY!
YOU LOOK JUST LIKE A REAL GIRL!!
SAKURA IS NOT GETTING THE POINT!!
BOIYOING
ぽたっ
THUP
Z Z Z...
EH?

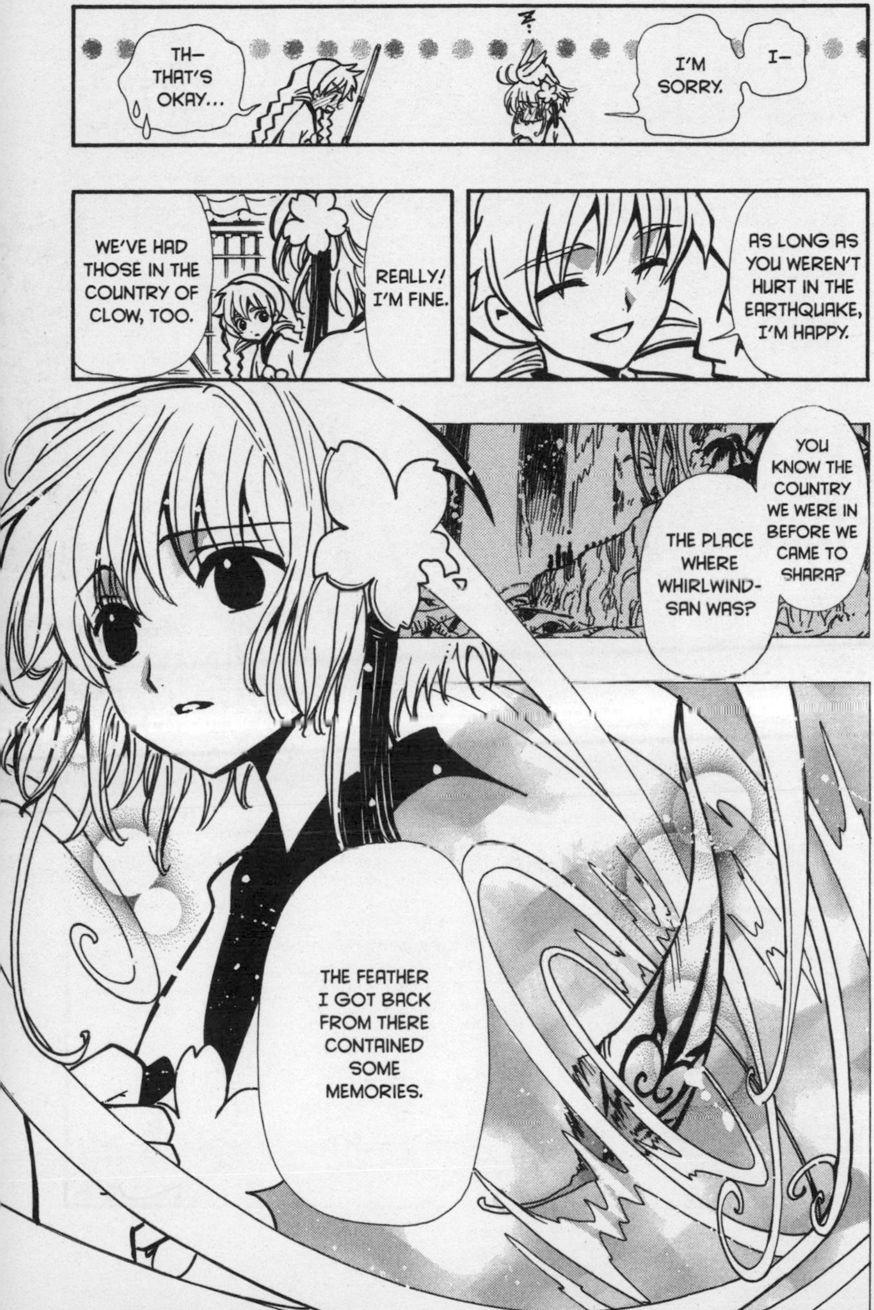
I—
I'M SORRY.
TH— THAT'S OKAY...
AS LONG AS YOU WEREN'T HURT IN THE EARTHQUAKE, I'M HAPPY.
REALLY! I'M FINE.
WE'VE HAD THOSE IN THE COUNTRY OF CLOW, TOO.
YOU KNOW THE COUNTRY WE WERE IN BEFORE WE CAME TO SHARA?
THE PLACE WHERE WHIRLWIND-SAN WAS?
THE FEATHER I GOT BACK FROM THERE CONTAINED SOME MEMORIES.

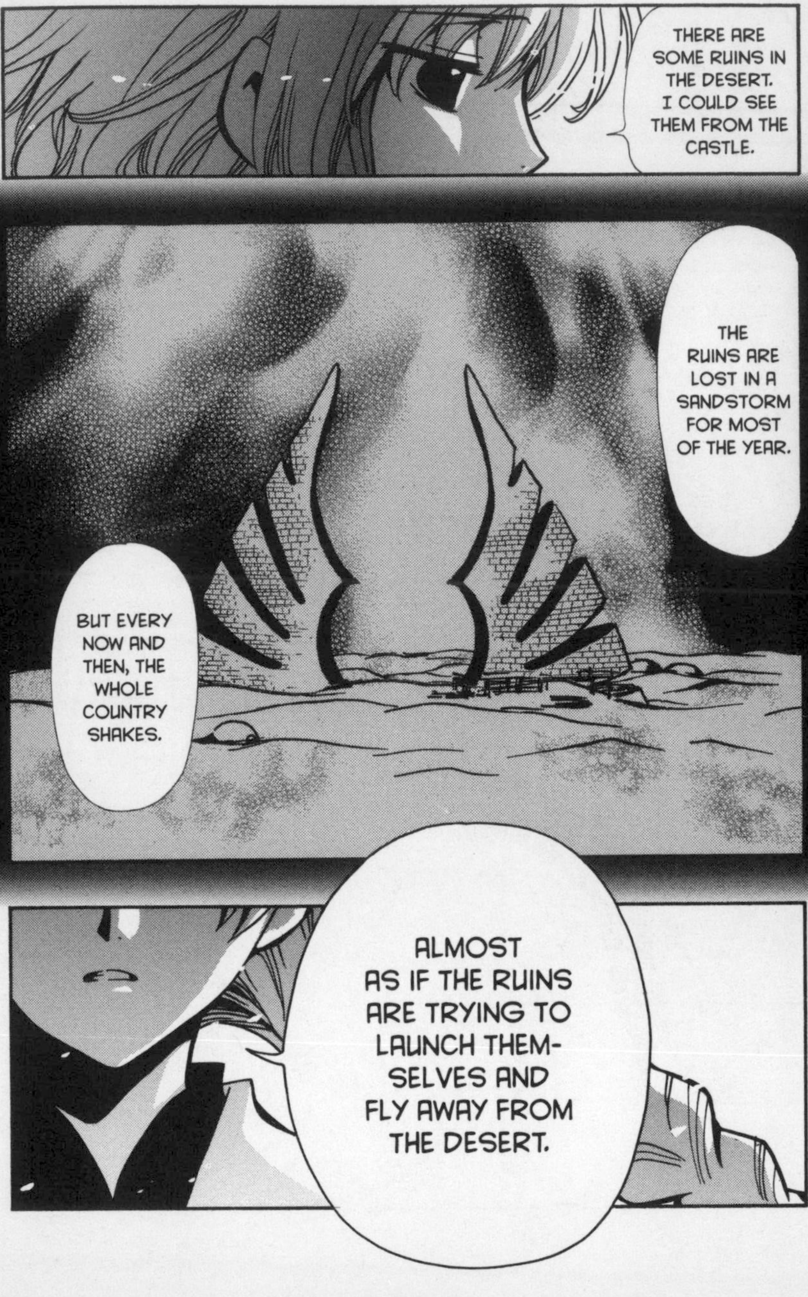
THERE ARE SOME RUINS IN THE DESERT. I COULD SEE THEM FROM THE CASTLE.
THE RUINS ARE LOST IN A SANDSTORM FOR MOST OF THE YEAR.
BUT EVERY NOW AND THEN, THE WHOLE COUNTRY SHAKES.
ALMOST AS IF THE RUINS ARE TRYING TO LAUNCH THEM-SELVES AND FLY AWAY FROM THE DESERT.

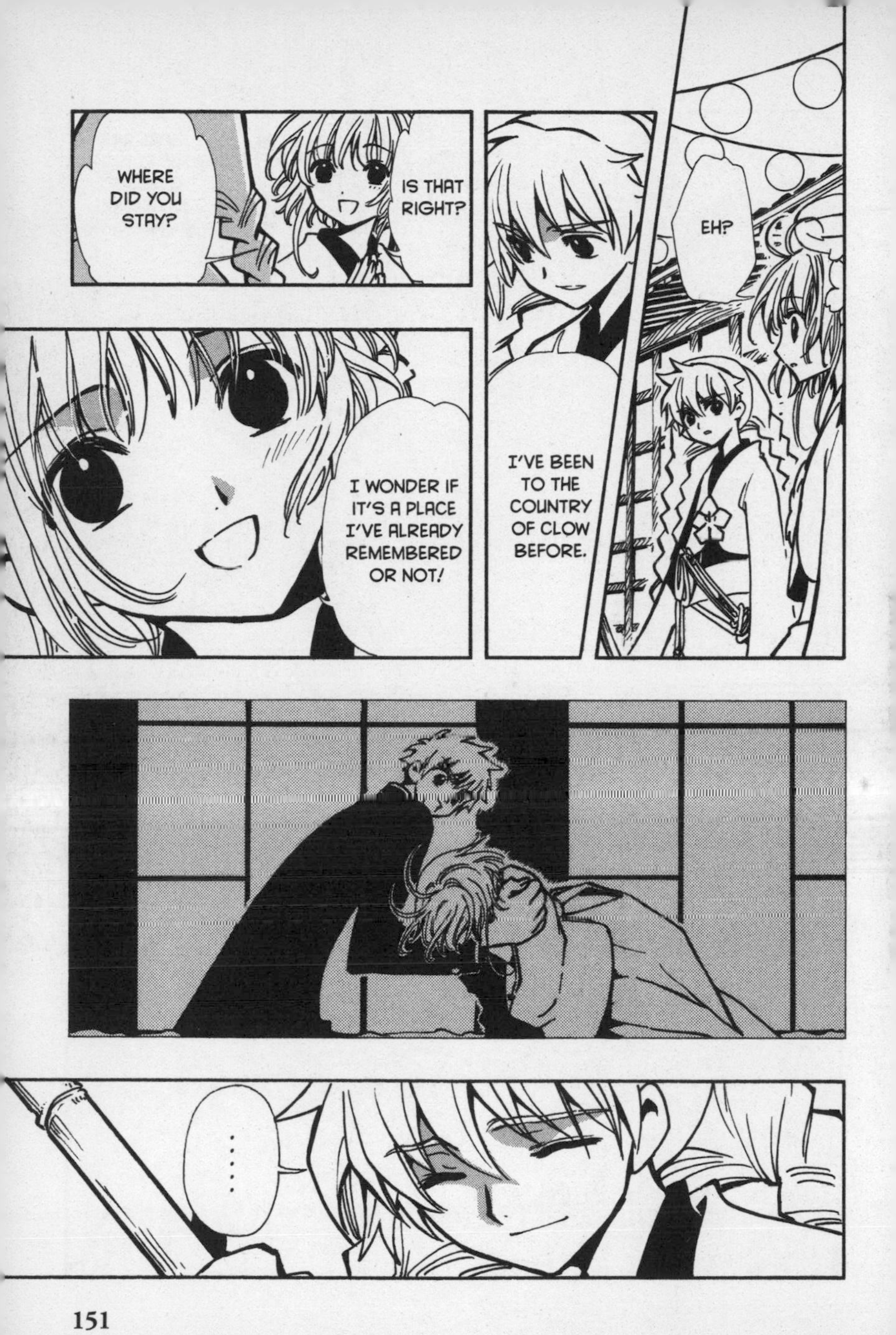
EH?
I'VE BEEN TO THE COUNTRY OF CLOW BEFORE.
IS THAT RIGHT?
WHERE DID YOU STAY?
I WONDER IF IT'S A PLACE I'VE ALREADY REMEMBERED OR NOT!
.....

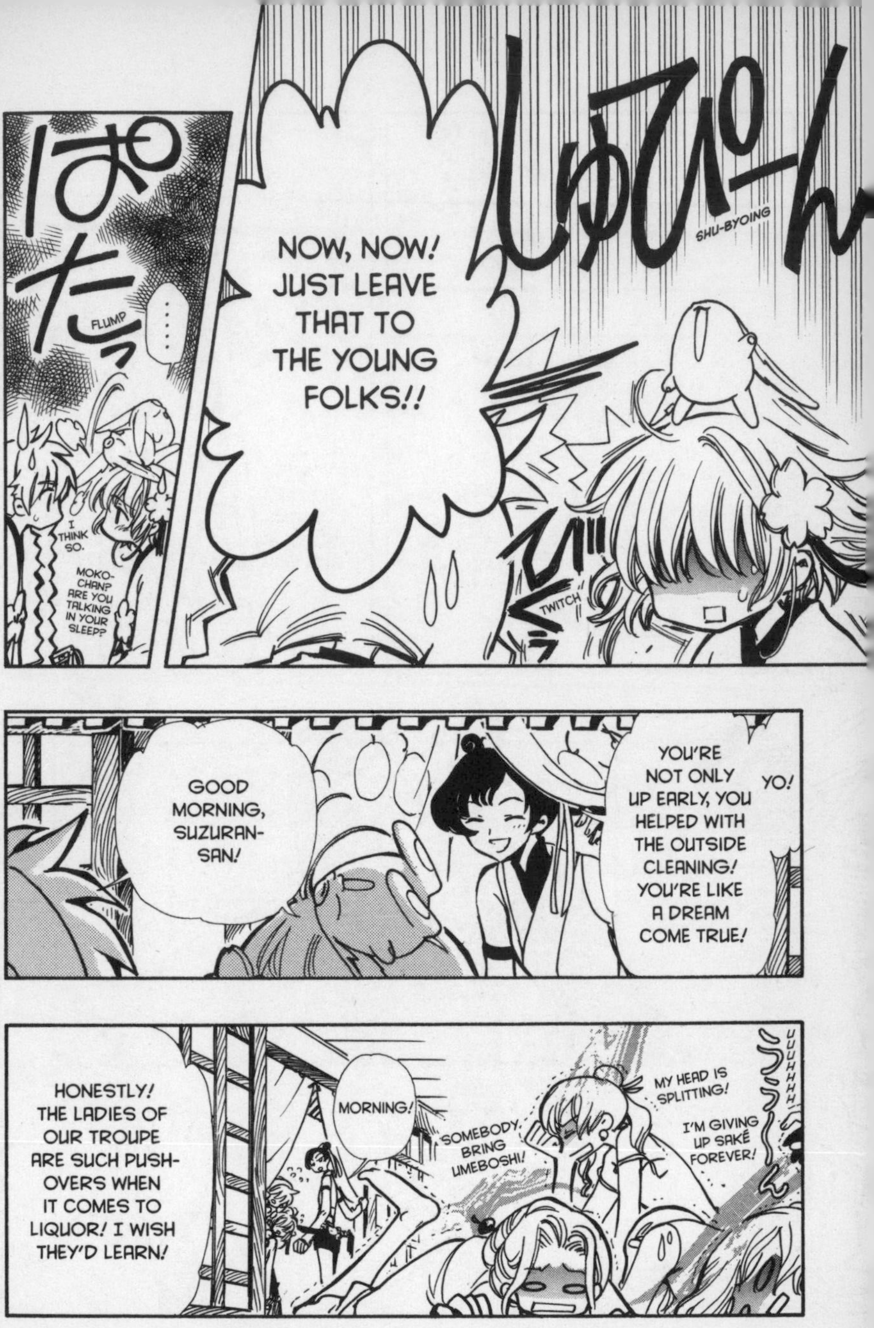
SHU-BYOING
NOW, NOW! JUST LEAVE THAT TO THE YOUNG FOLKS!!
TWITCH
FLUMP
......
MOKO-CHAN? ARE YOU TALKING IN YOUR SLEEP?
I THINK SO.
YO!
YOU'RE NOT ONLY UP EARLY, YOU HELPED WITH THE OUTSIDE CLEANING! YOU'RE LIKE A DREAM COME TRUE!
GOOD MORNING, SUZURAN-SAN!
UUUHHHH
I'M GIVING UP SAKÉ FOREVER!
MY HEAD IS SPLITTING!
SOMEBODY BRING UMEBOSHI!
MORNING!
HONESTLY! THE LADIES OF OUR TROUPE ARE SUCH PUSH-OVERS WHEN IT COMES TO LIQUOR! I WISH THEY'D LEARN!

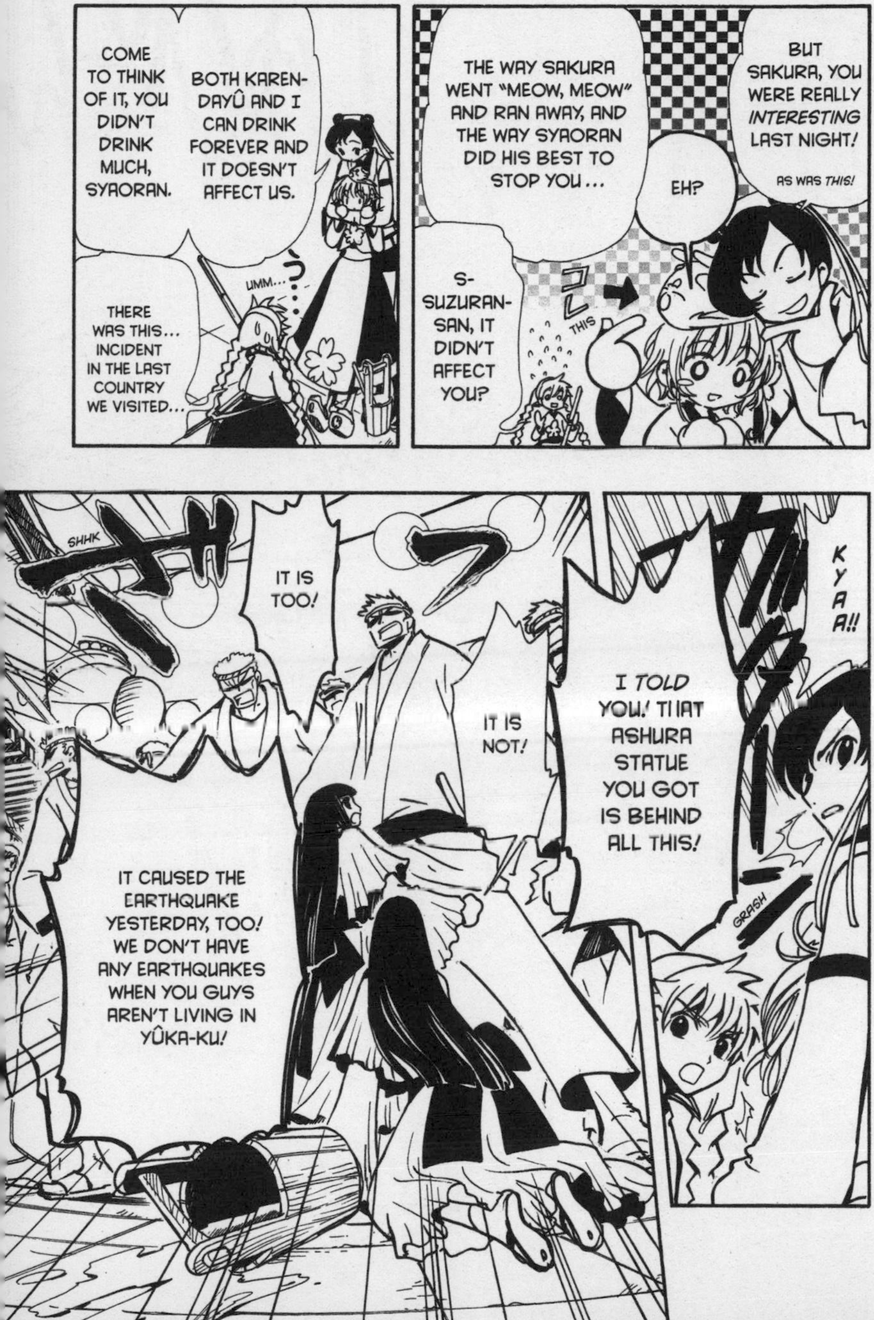

BUT SAKURA, YOU WERE REALLY *INTERESTING* LAST NIGHT!
AS WAS *THIS!*
THE WAY SAKURA WENT "MEOW, MEOW" AND RAN AWAY, AND THE WAY SYAORAN DID HIS BEST TO STOP YOU . . .
EH?
THIS
S-SUZURAN-SAN, IT DIDN'T AFFECT YOU?
BOTH KAREN-DAYÛ AND I CAN DRINK FOREVER AND IT DOESN'T AFFECT US.
COME TO THINK OF IT, YOU DIDN'T DRINK MUCH, SYAORAN.
UMM...
THERE WAS THIS... INCIDENT IN THE LAST COUNTRY WE VISITED...
KYAA!!
I *TOLD* YOU! THAT ASHURA STATUE YOU GOT IS BEHIND ALL THIS!
IT IS NOT!
IT IS TOO!
SHHK
IT CAUSED THE EARTHQUAKE YESTERDAY, TOO! WE DON'T HAVE ANY EARTHQUAKES WHEN YOU GUYS AREN'T LIVING IN YÛKA-KU!
CRASH

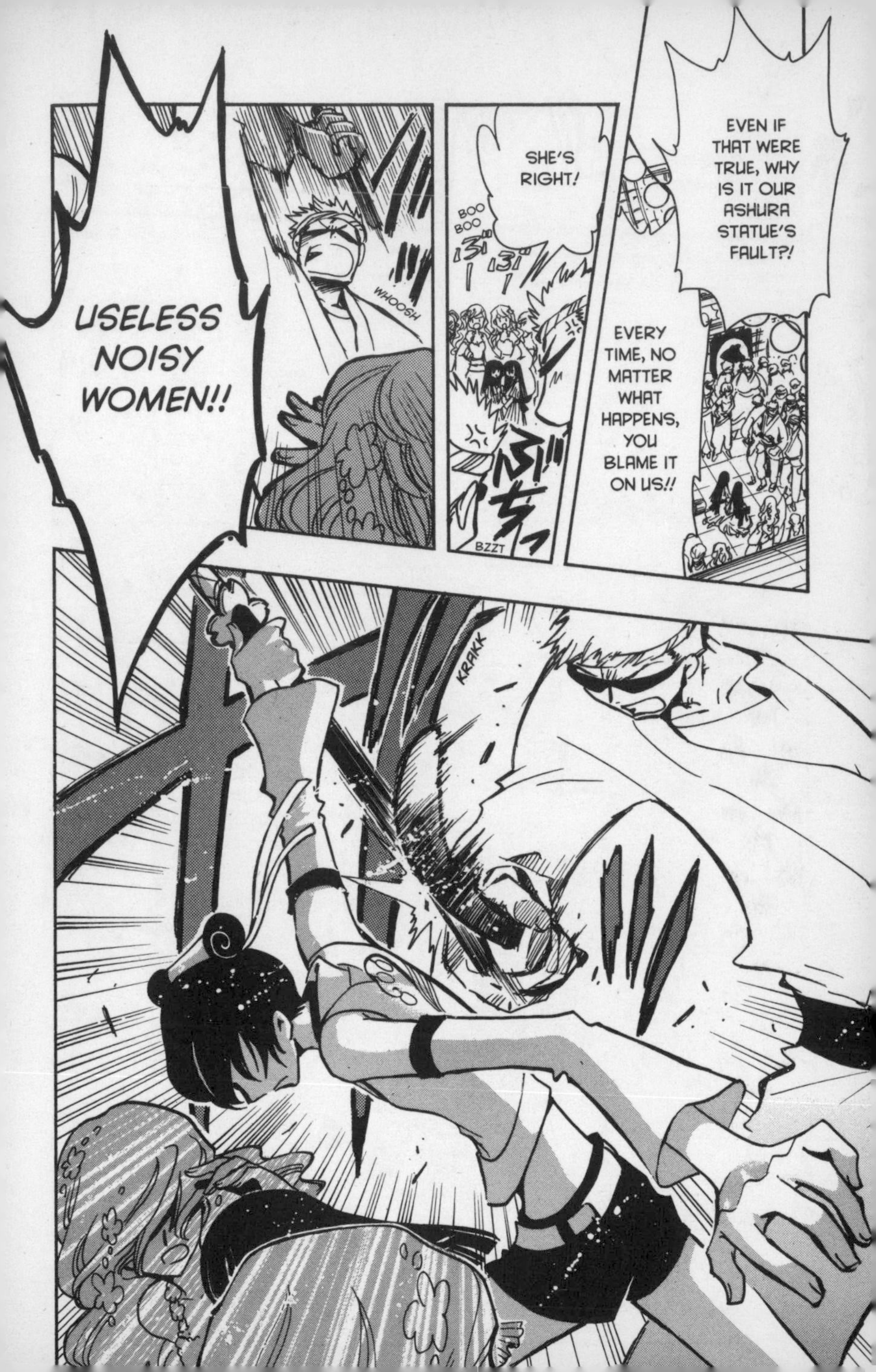
EVEN IF THAT WERE TRUE, WHY IS IT OUR ASHURA STATUE'S FAULT?!
EVERY TIME, NO MATTER WHAT HAPPENS, YOU BLAME IT ON US!!
SHE'S RIGHT!
BOO BOO
BZZT
WHOOSH
USELESS NOISY WOMEN!!
KRAKK

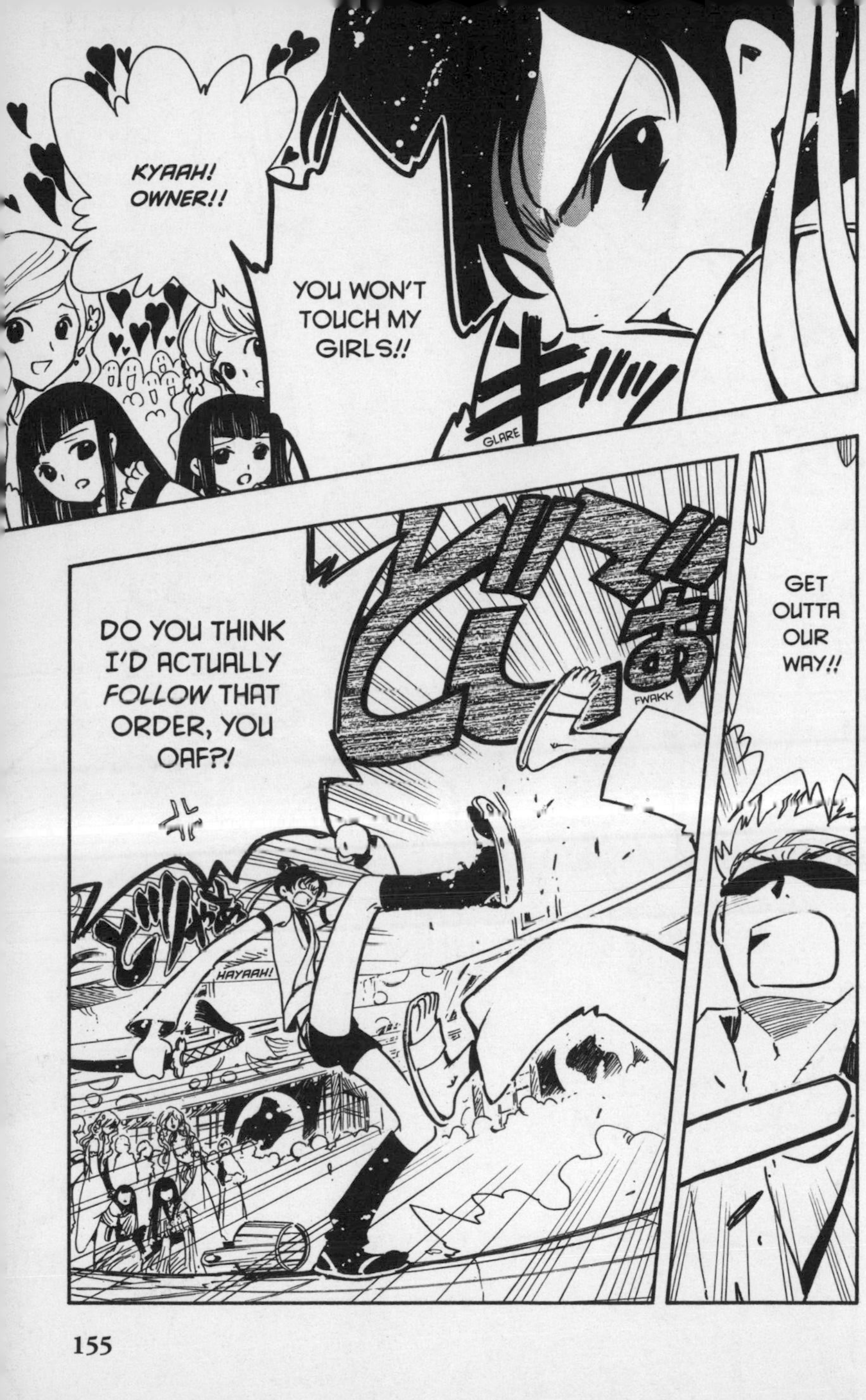
YOU WON'T TOUCH MY GIRLS!!
GLARE
KYAAH! OWNER!!
GET OUTTA OUR WAY!!
FWAKK
DO YOU THINK I'D ACTUALLY FOLLOW THAT ORDER, YOU OAF?!
HAYAAH!

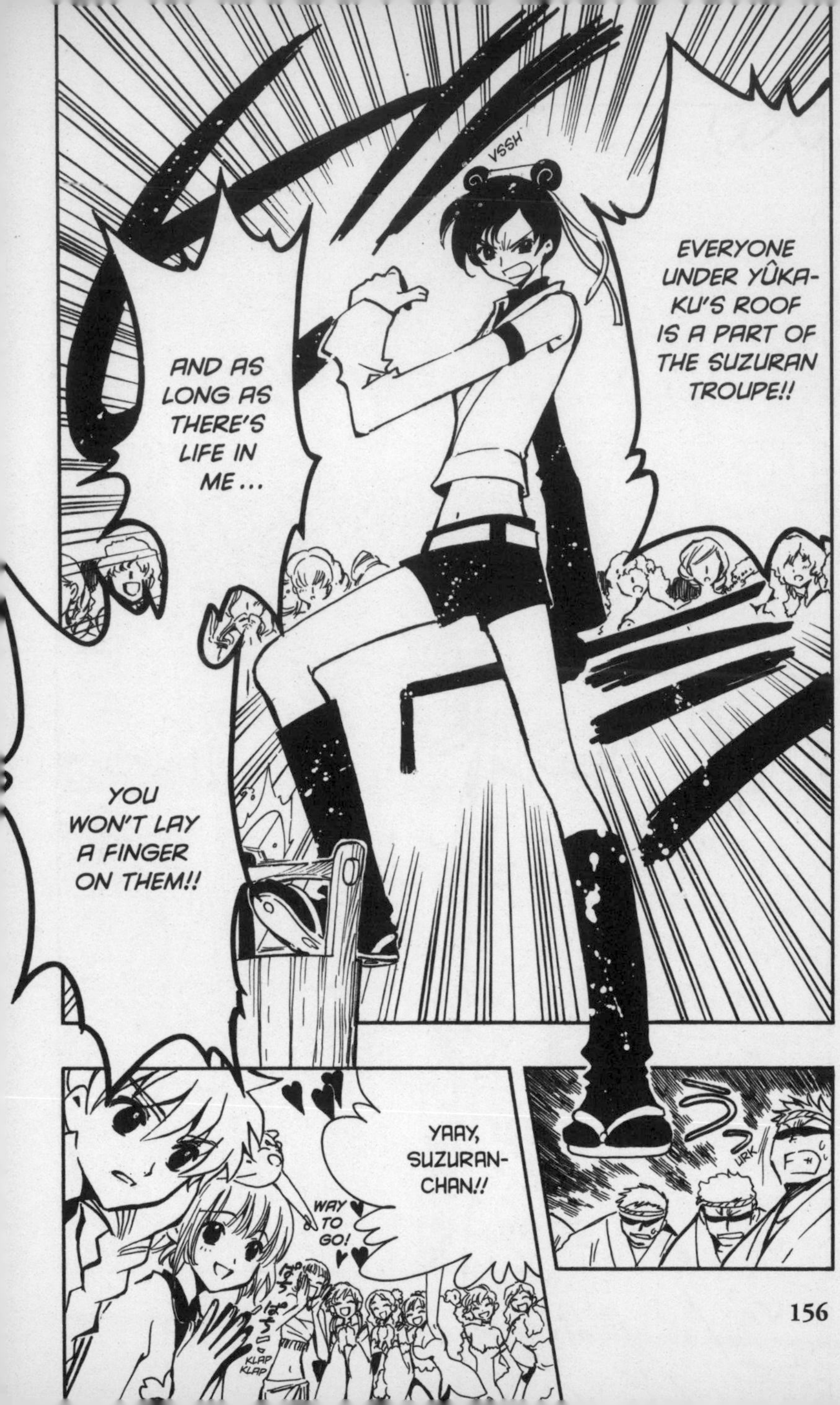
VSSH
EVERYONE UNDER YÛKA-KU'S ROOF IS A PART OF THE SUZURAN TROUPE!!
AND AS LONG AS THERE'S LIFE IN ME...
YOU WON'T LAY A FINGER ON THEM!!
URK
YAAY, SUZURAN-CHAN!!
WAY TO GO!
KLAP KLAP

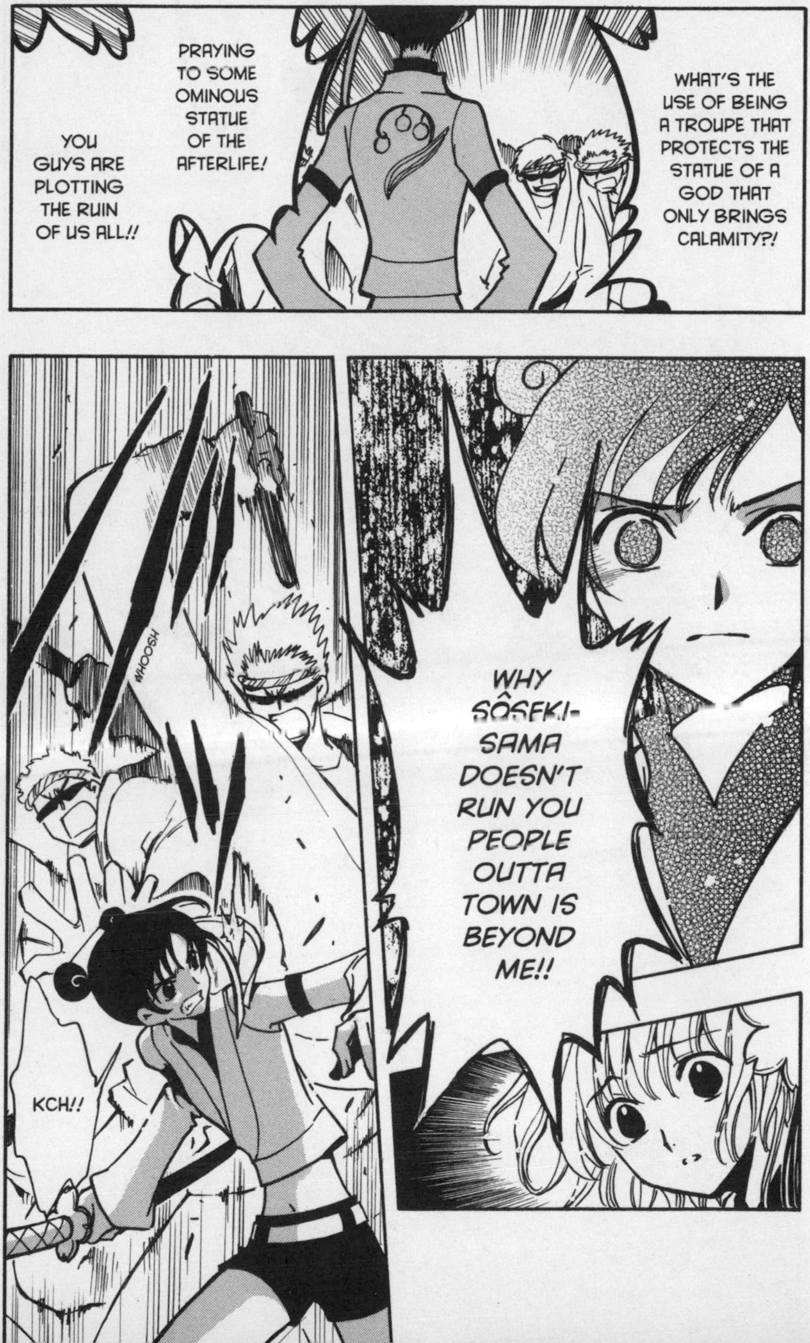
WHAT'S THE USE OF BEING A TROUPE THAT PROTECTS THE STATUE OF A GOD THAT ONLY BRINGS CALAMITY?!
PRAYING TO SOME OMINOUS STATUE OF THE AFTERLIFE!
YOU GUYS ARE PLOTTING THE RUIN OF US ALL!!
WHY SÔSEKI-SAMA DOESN'T RUN YOU PEOPLE OUTTA TOWN IS BEYOND ME!!
WHOOSH
KCH!!

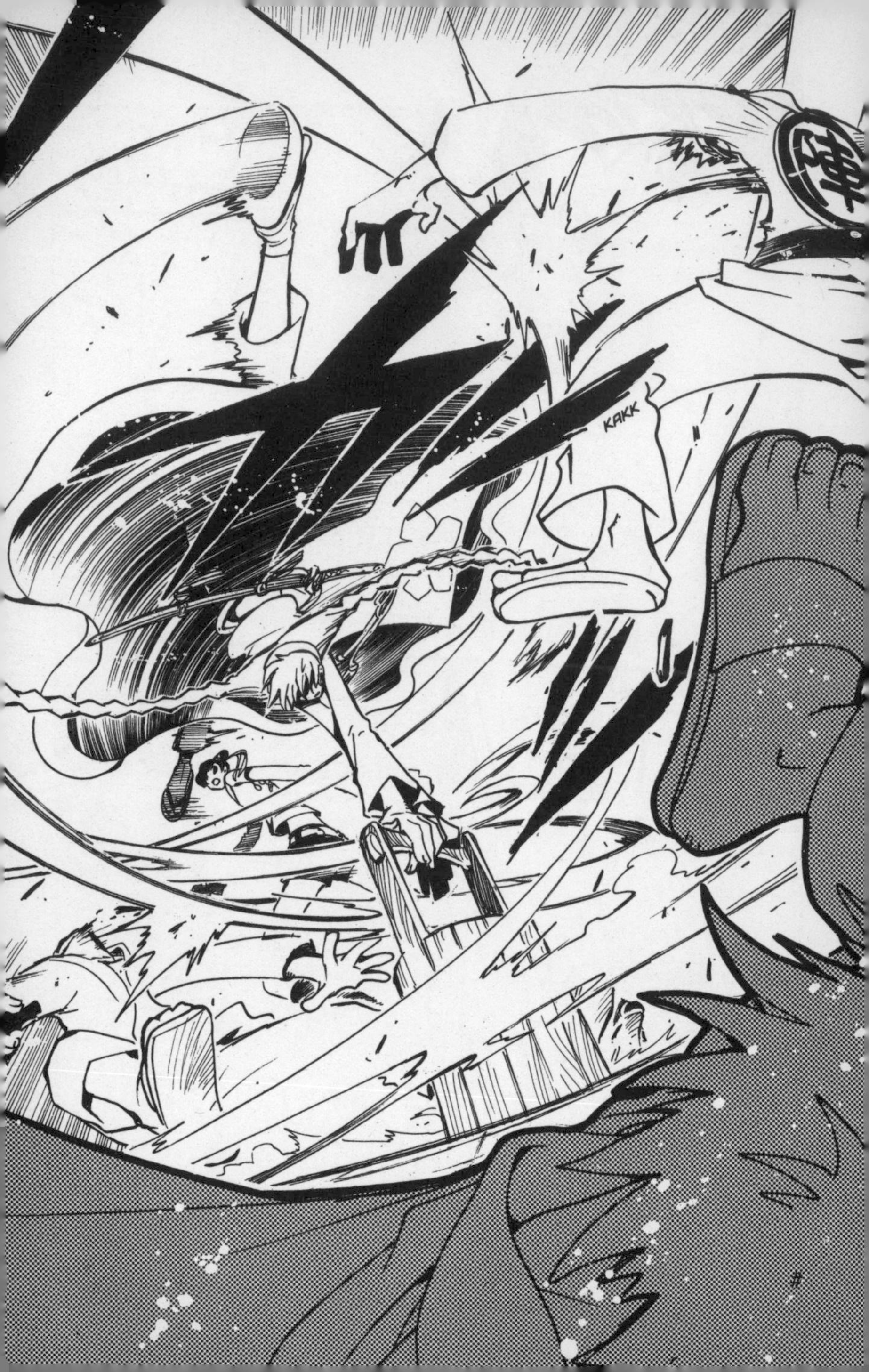
KAKK

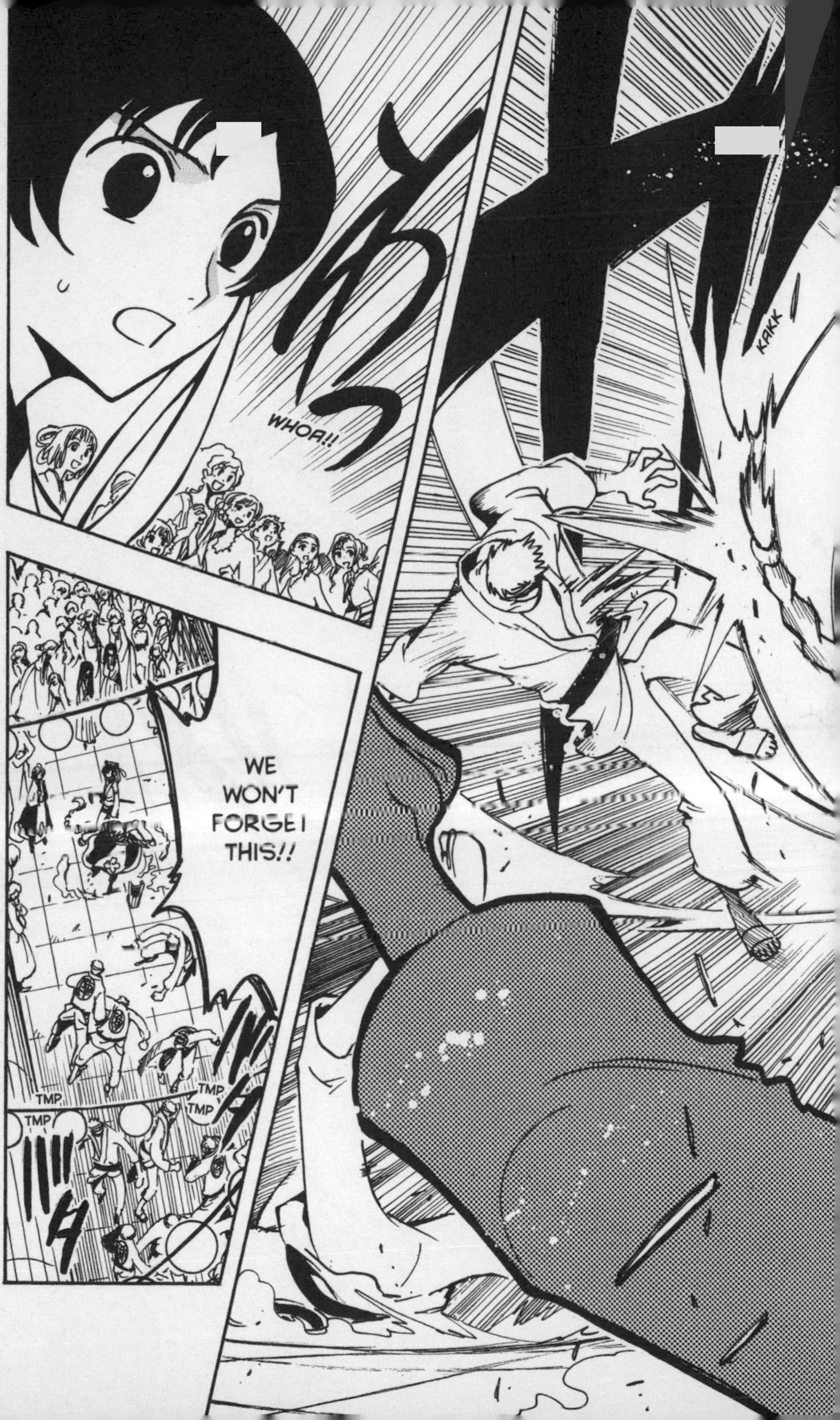
KAKK
WHOA!!
WE WON'T FORGET THIS!!
TMP
TMP
TMP
TMP

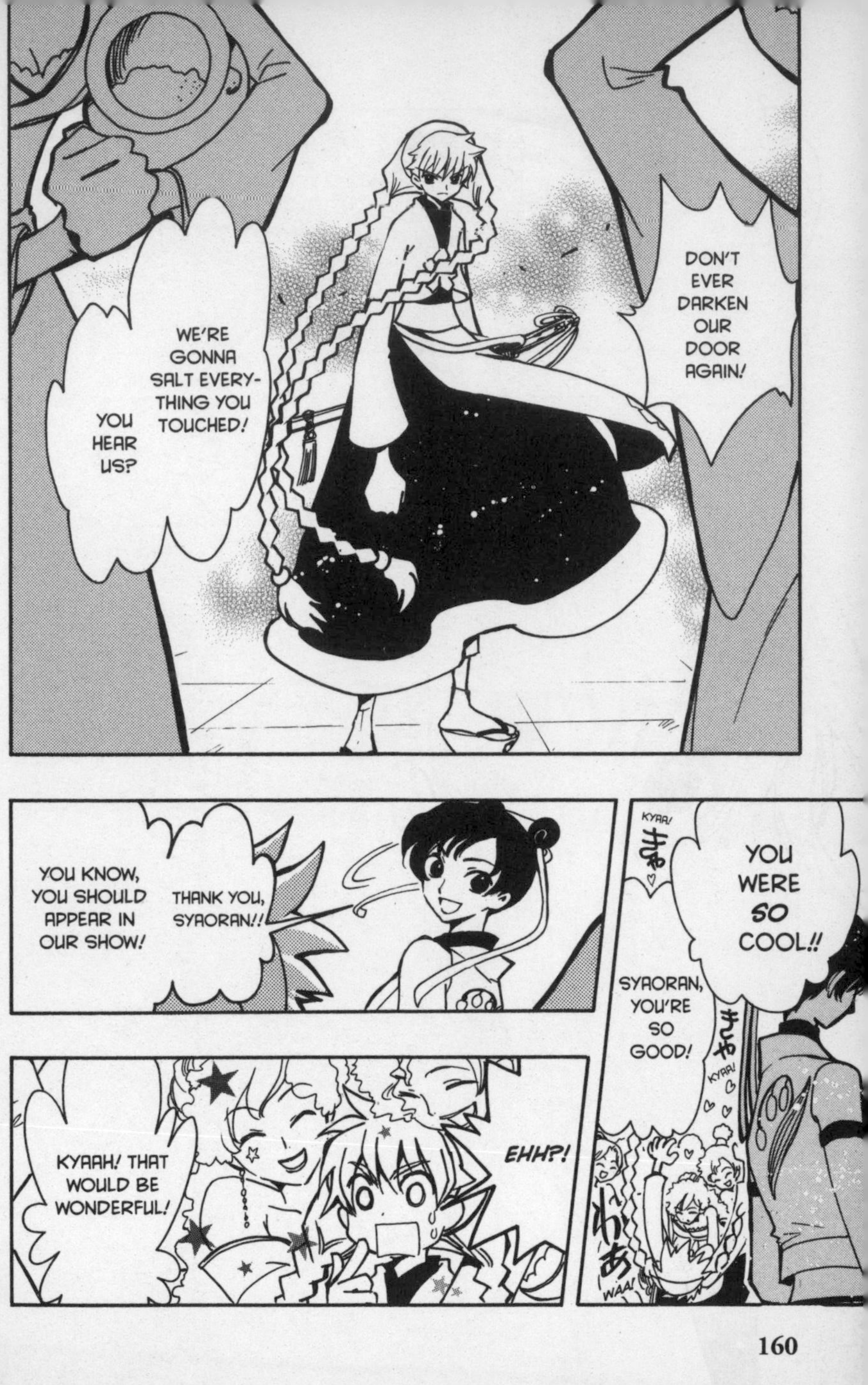
DON'T EVER DARKEN OUR DOOR AGAIN!
WE'RE GONNA SALT EVERY-THING YOU TOUCHED!
YOU HEAR US?
KYAA!
きゃ
YOU WERE SO COOL!!
SYAORAN, YOU'RE SO GOOD!
きゃ
KYAA!
わあ
WAA!
THANK YOU, SYAORAN!!
YOU KNOW, YOU SHOULD APPEAR IN OUR SHOW!
EHH?!
KYAAH! THAT WOULD BE WONDERFUL!

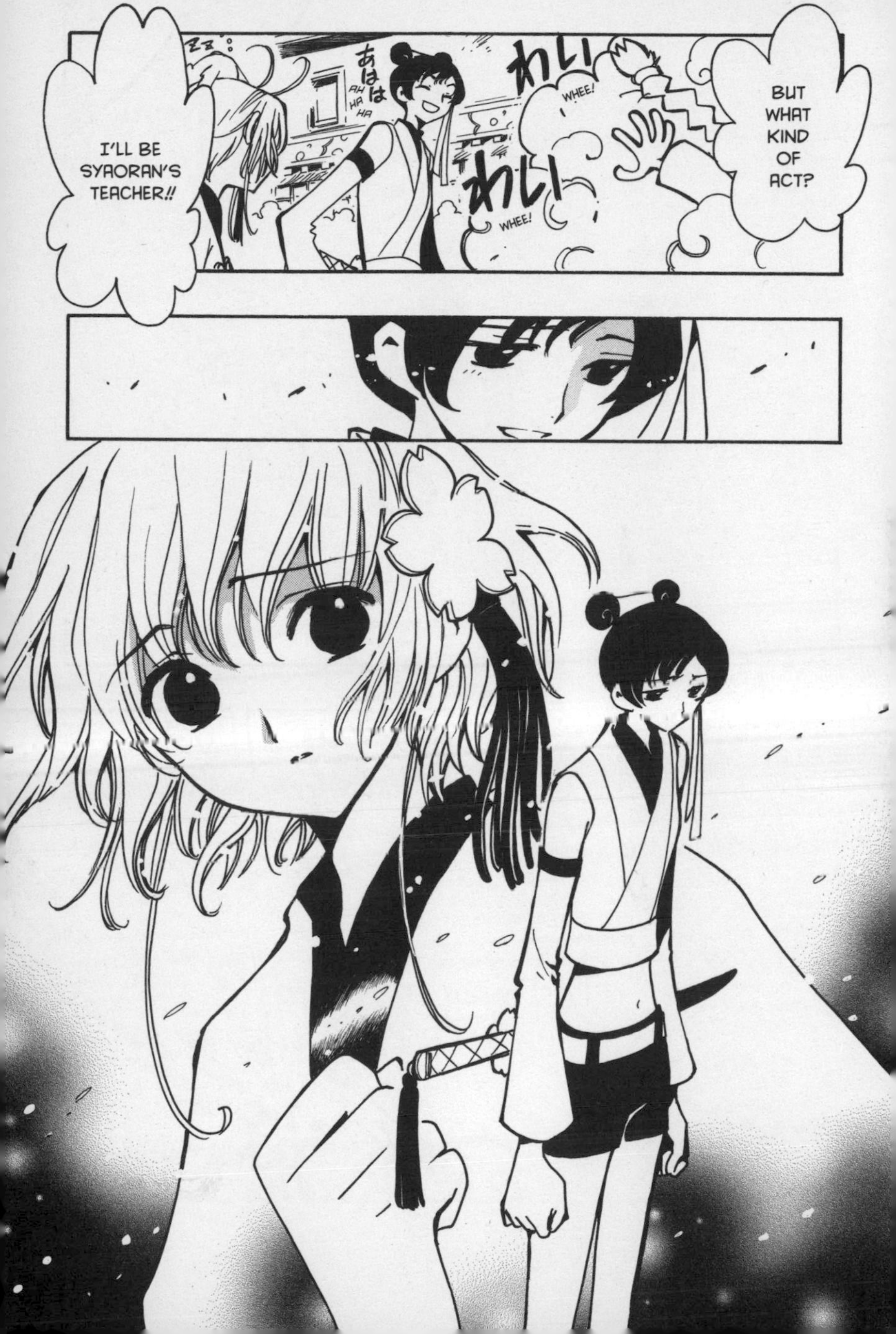
BUT WHAT KIND OF ACT?
わい
WHEE!
わい
WHEE!
あはは
AH HA HA
I'LL BE SYAORAN'S TEACHER!!

ツバサ

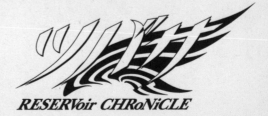

RESERVoir CHRoNiCLE

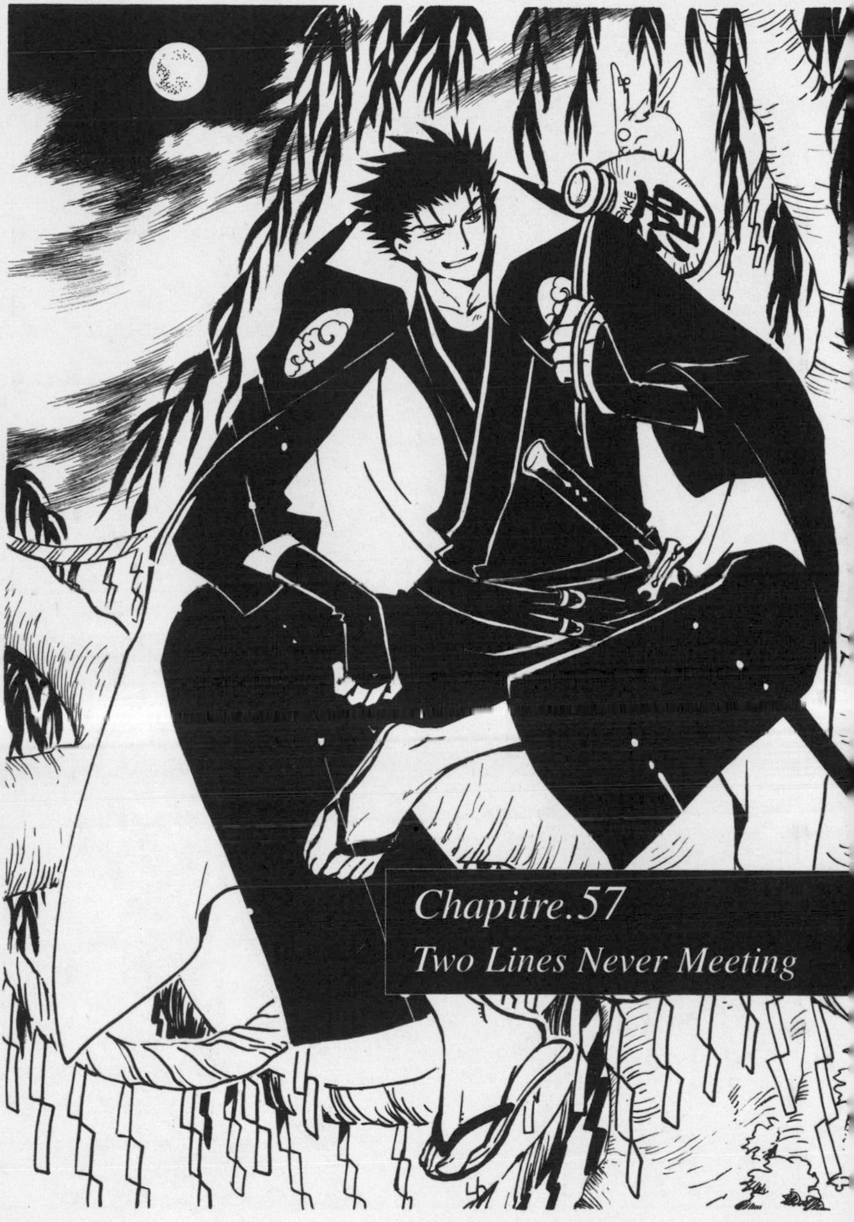
SAKE
Chapitre.57
Two Lines Never Meeting

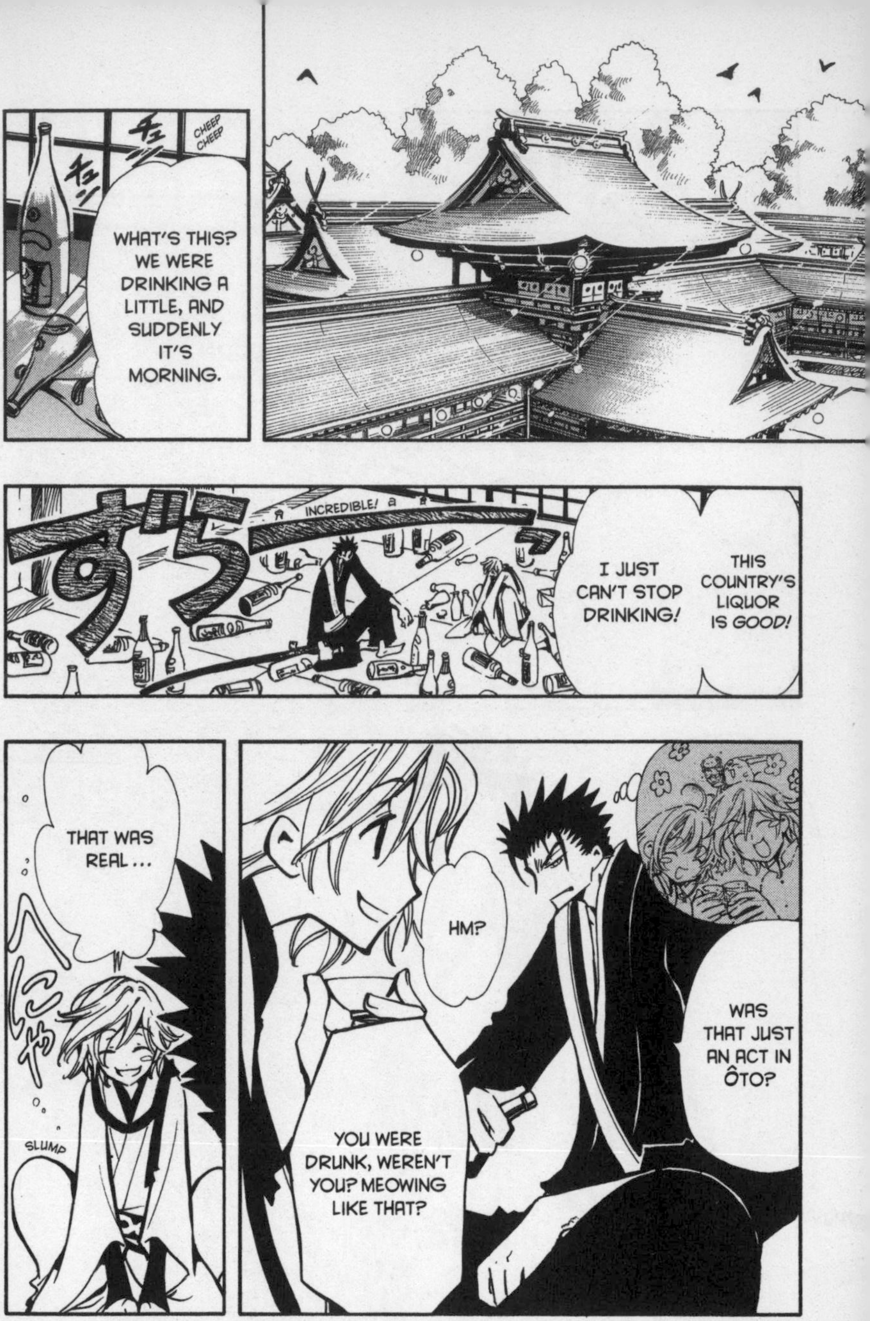
CHEEP CHEEP
WHAT'S THIS? WE WERE DRINKING A LITTLE, AND SUDDENLY IT'S MORNING.
THIS COUNTRY'S LIQUOR IS *GOOD!*
I JUST CAN'T STOP DRINKING!
INCREDIBLE!
WAS THAT JUST AN ACT IN ÔTO?
HM?
YOU WERE DRUNK, WEREN'T YOU? MEOWING LIKE THAT?
THAT WAS REAL...
SLUMP

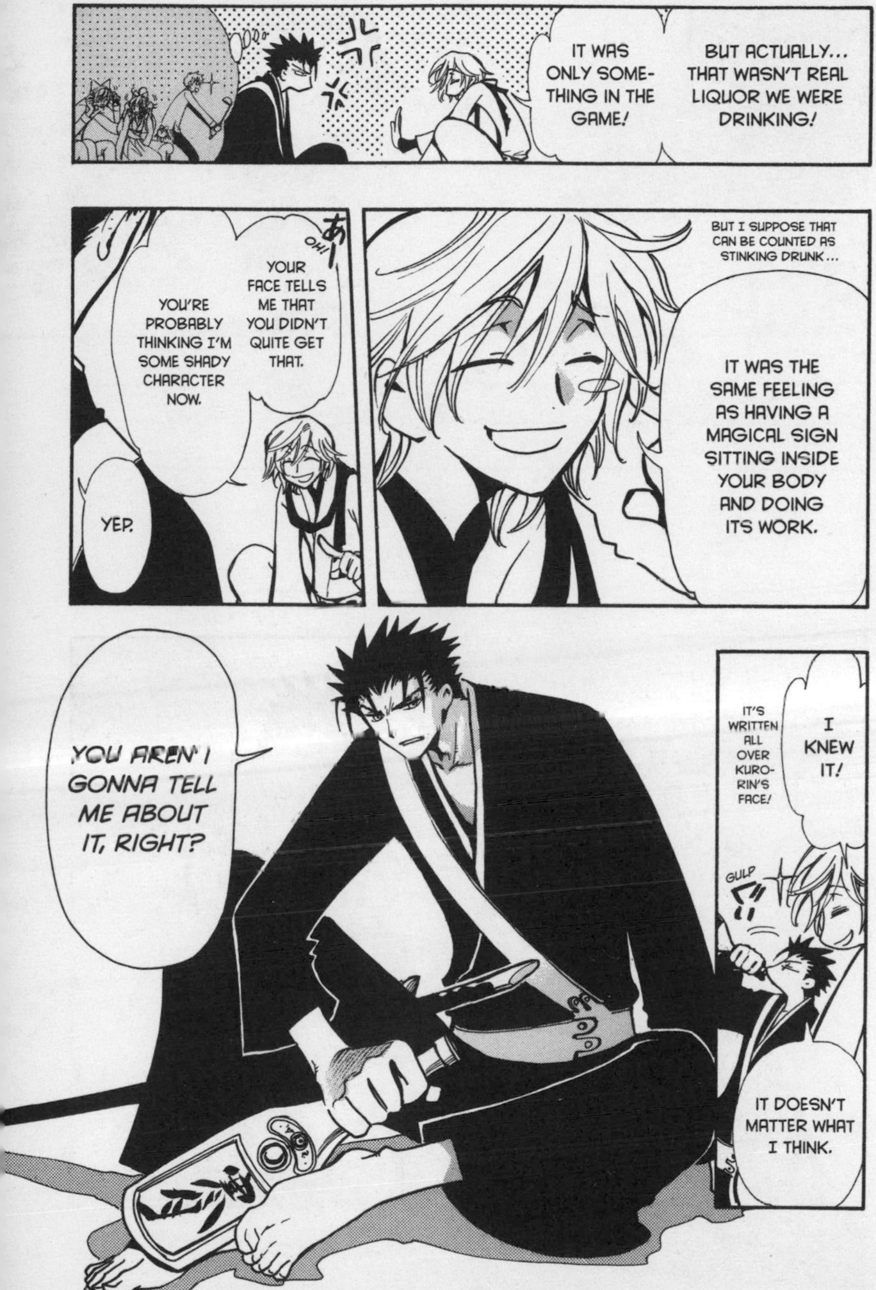
BUT ACTUALLY... THAT WASN'T REAL LIQUOR WE WERE DRINKING!
IT WAS ONLY SOMETHING IN THE GAME!
BUT I SUPPOSE THAT CAN BE COUNTED AS STINKING DRUNK...
IT WAS THE SAME FEELING AS HAVING A MAGICAL SIGN SITTING INSIDE YOUR BODY AND DOING ITS WORK.
あ
OH!
YOUR FACE TELLS ME THAT YOU DIDN'T QUITE GET THAT.
YOU'RE PROBABLY THINKING I'M SOME SHADY CHARACTER NOW.
YEP.
I KNEW IT!
IT'S WRITTEN ALL OVER KURORIN'S FACE!
GULP
IT DOESN'T MATTER WHAT I THINK.
YOU AREN'T GONNA TELL ME ABOUT IT, RIGHT?

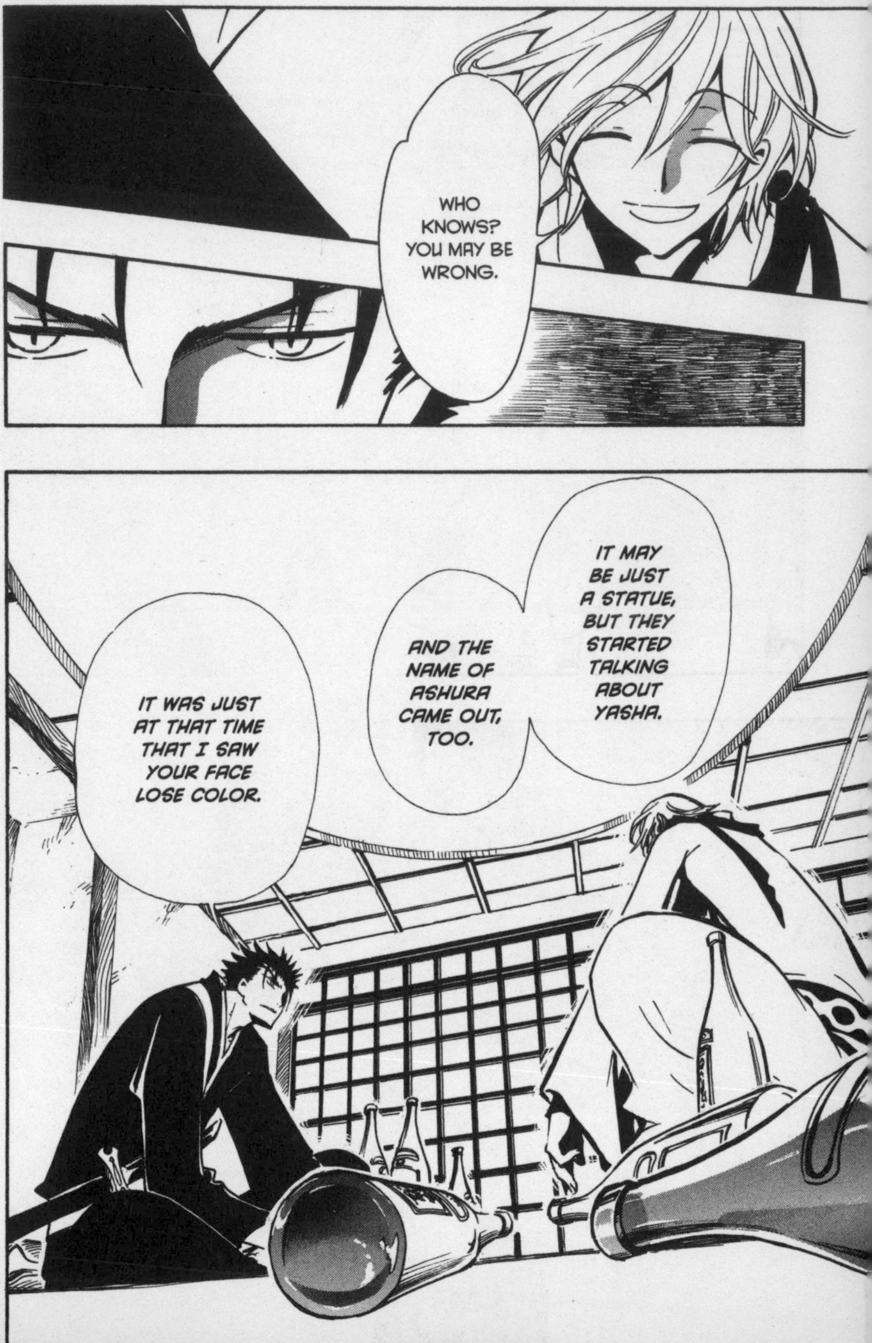
WHO KNOWS? YOU MAY BE WRONG.
IT MAY BE JUST A STATUE, BUT THEY STARTED TALKING ABOUT YASHA.
AND THE NAME OF ASHURA CAME OUT, TOO.
IT WAS JUST AT THAT TIME THAT I SAW YOUR FACE LOSE COLOR.

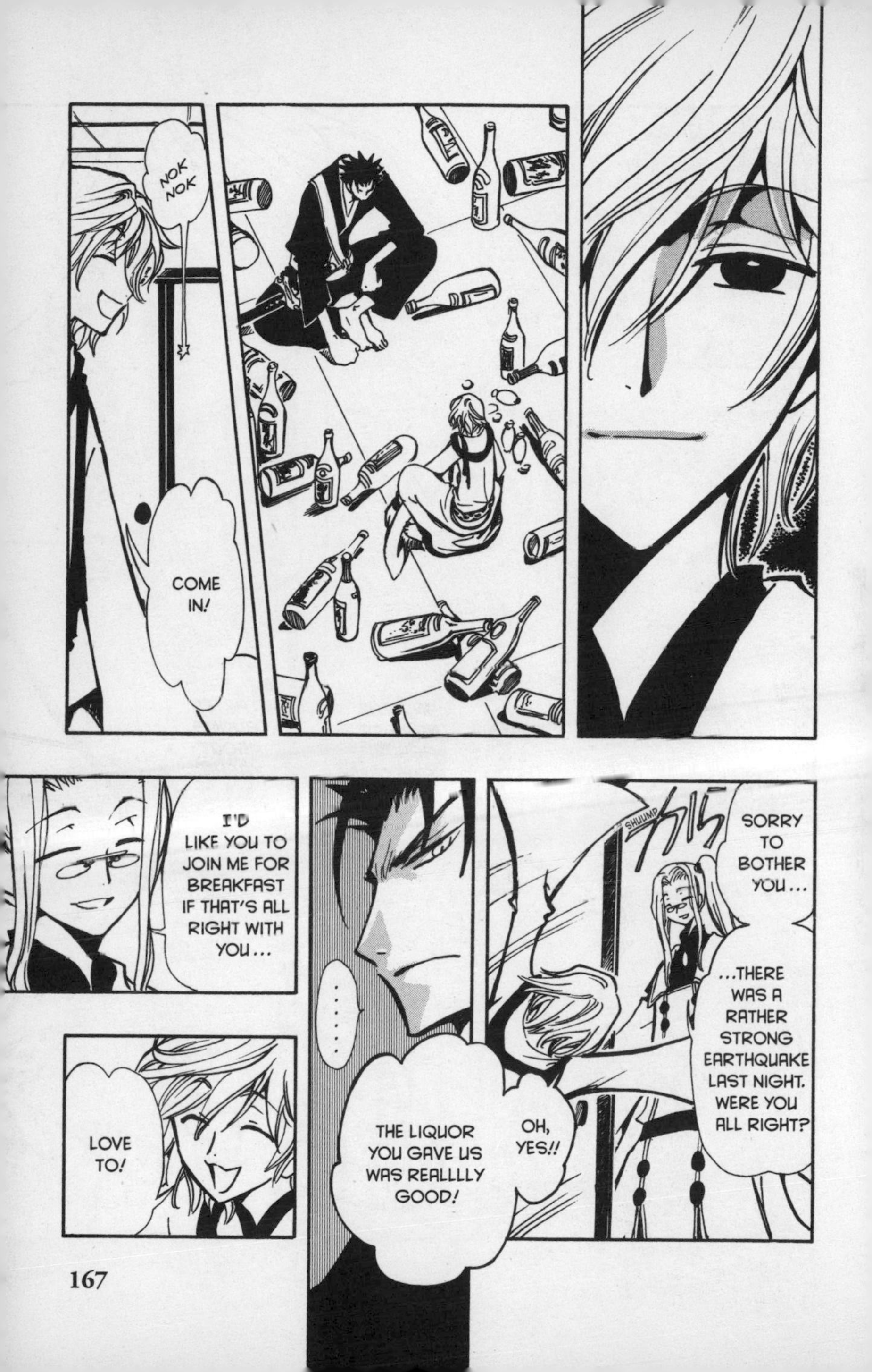
NOK NOK
COME IN!
SHUUMP
から
SORRY TO BOTHER YOU...
...THERE WAS A RATHER STRONG EARTHQUAKE LAST NIGHT. WERE YOU ALL RIGHT?
OH, YES!!
......
THE LIQUOR YOU GAVE US WAS REALLLLY GOOD!
I'D LIKE YOU TO JOIN ME FOR BREAKFAST IF THAT'S ALL RIGHT WITH YOU...
LOVE TO!

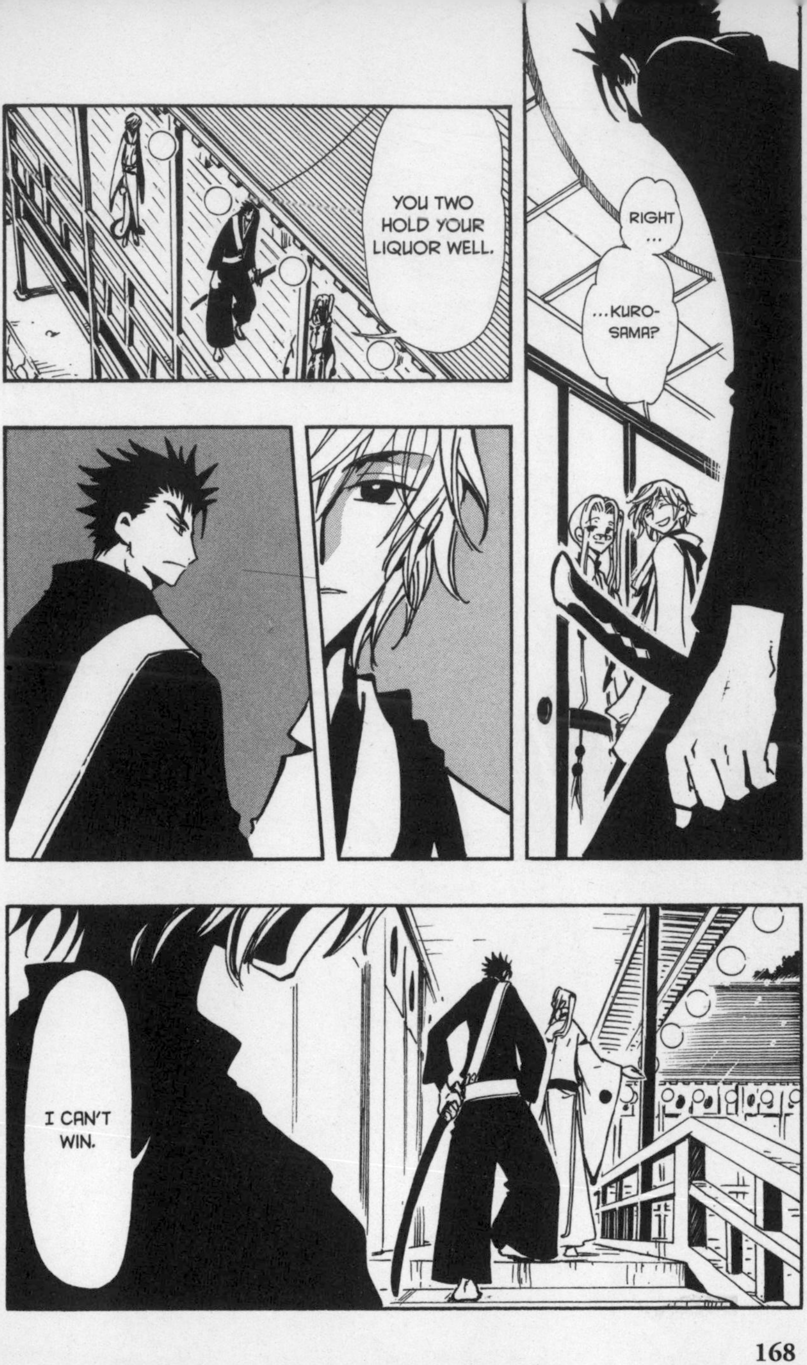
RIGHT ...
...KURO-SAMA?
YOU TWO HOLD YOUR LIQUOR WELL.
I CAN'T WIN.

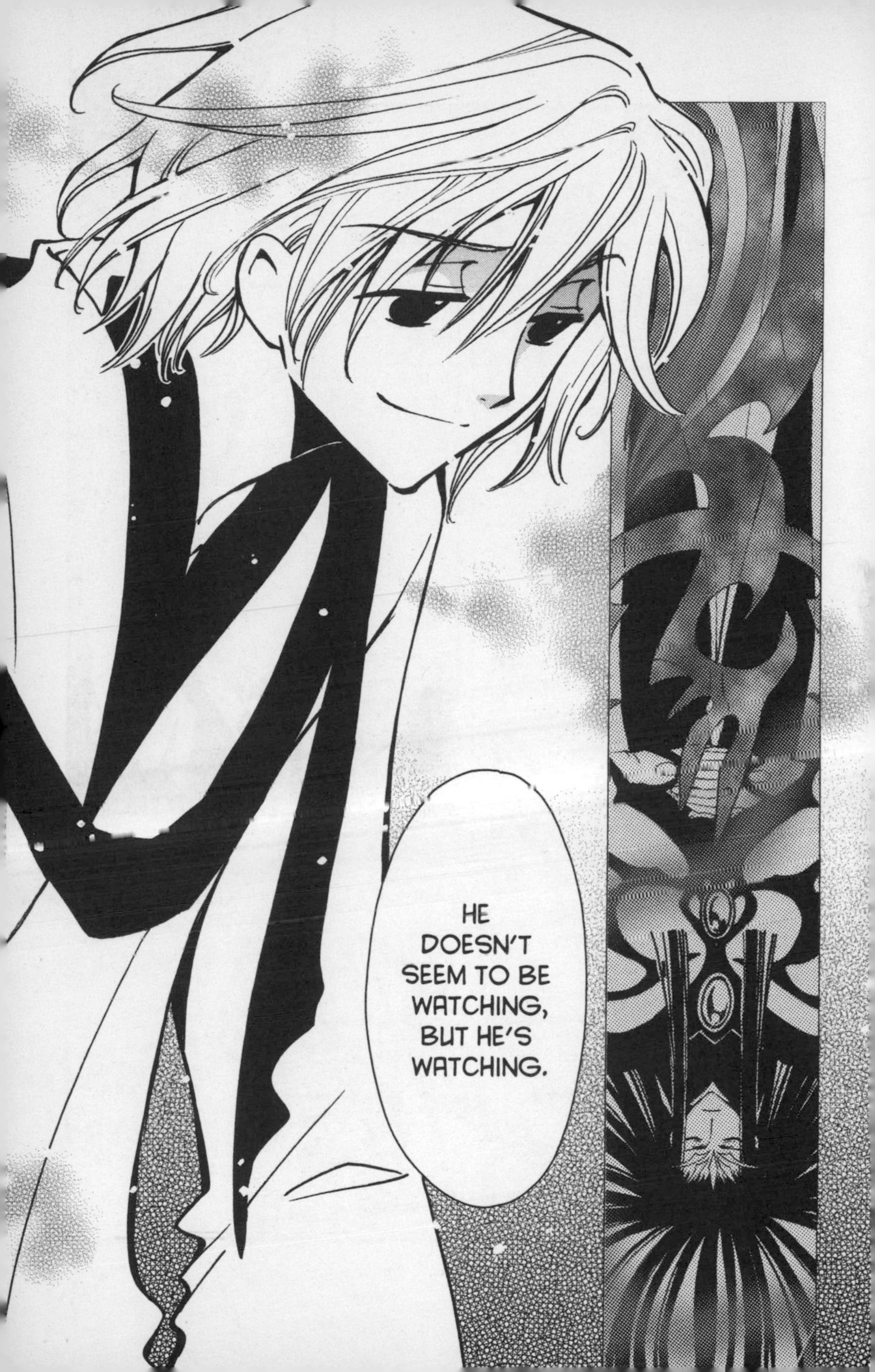
HE DOESN'T SEEM TO BE WATCHING, BUT HE'S WATCHING.

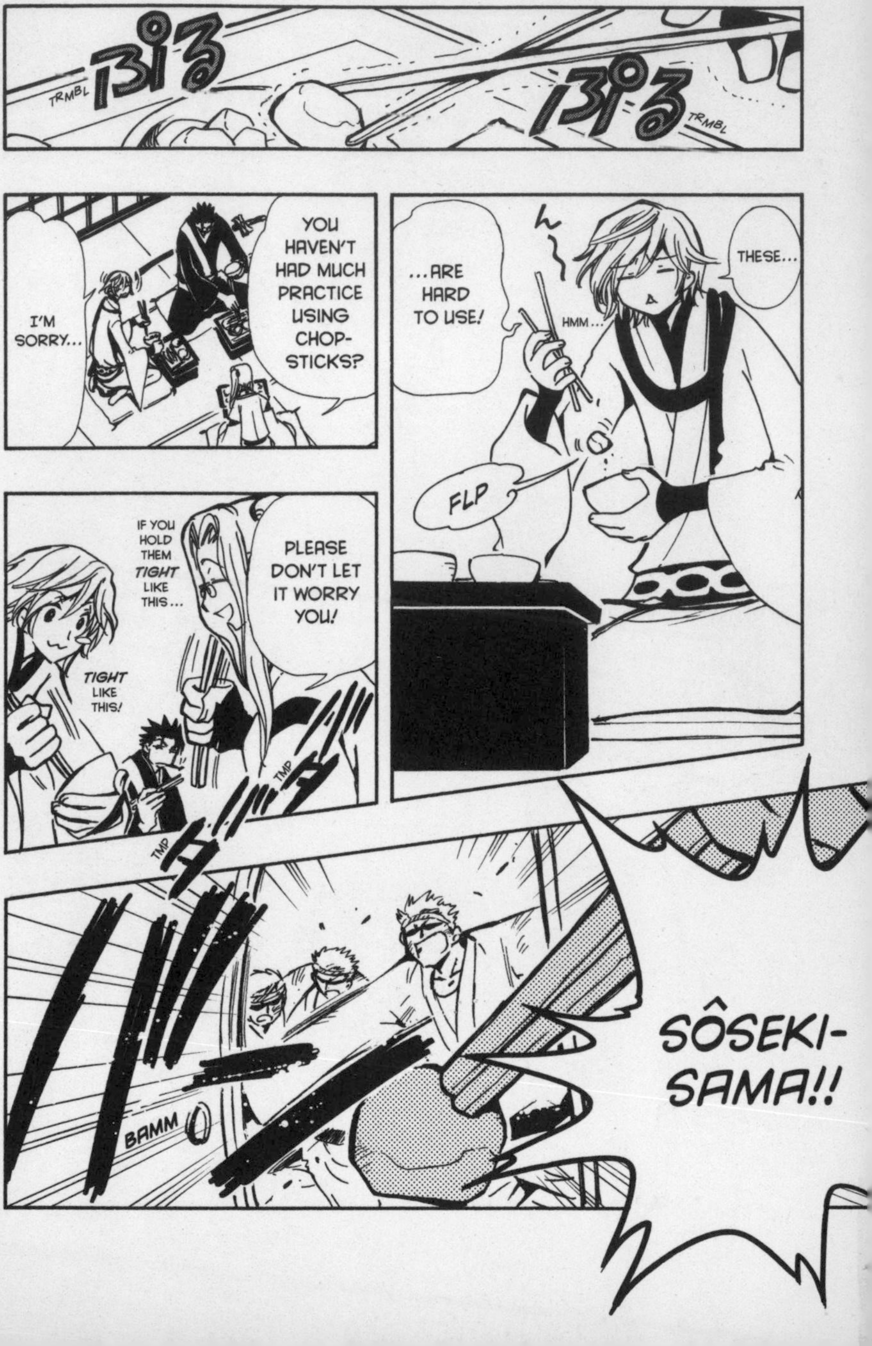
ぷる
TRMBL
ぷる
TRMBL
THESE...
HMM...
...ARE HARD TO USE!
FLP
YOU HAVEN'T HAD MUCH PRACTICE USING CHOP-STICKS?
I'M SORRY...
PLEASE DON'T LET IT WORRY YOU!
IF YOU HOLD THEM TIGHT LIKE THIS...
TIGHT LIKE THIS!
TMP
TMP
SÔSEKI-SAMA!!
BAMM

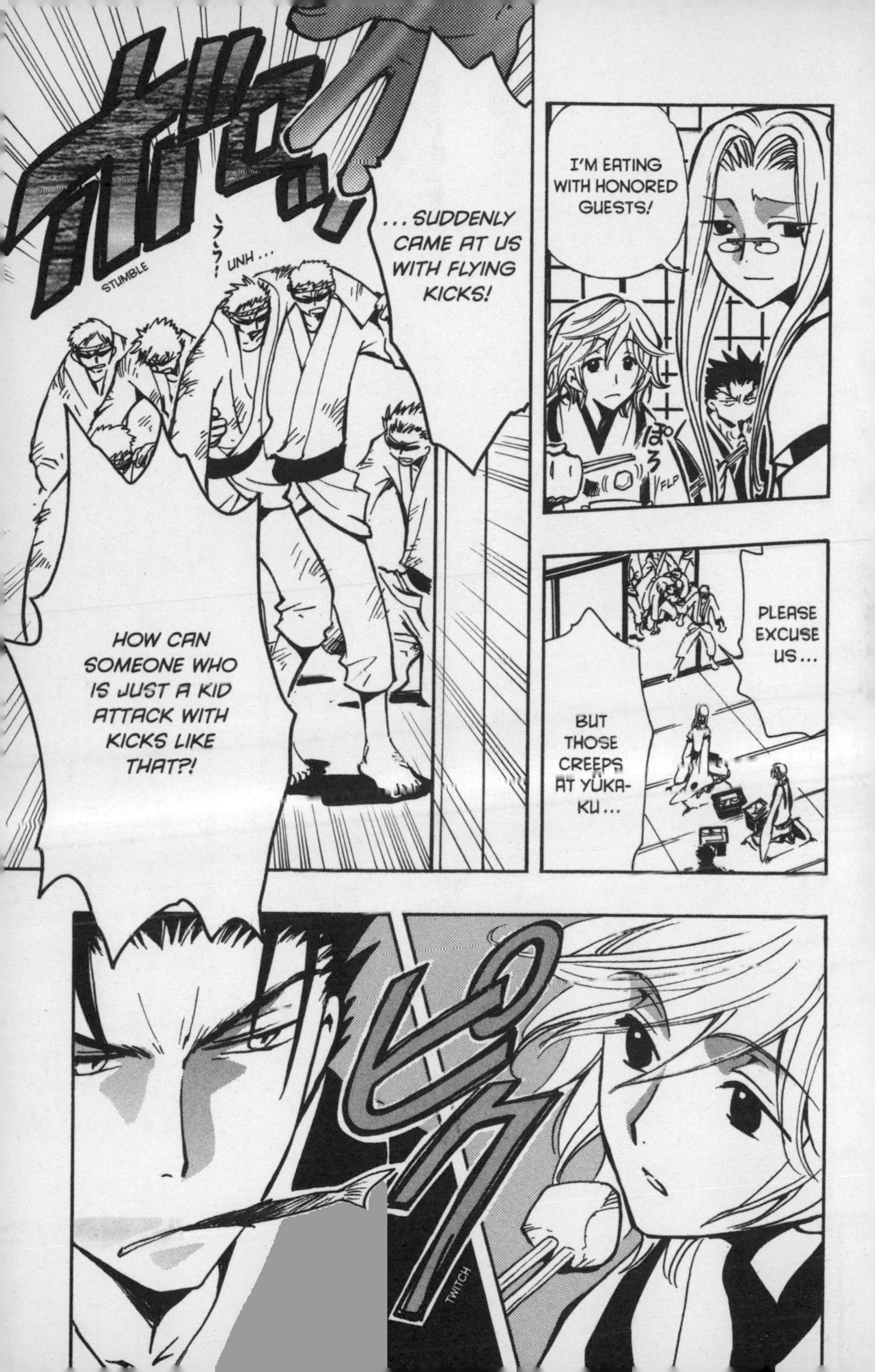
I'M EATING WITH HONORED GUESTS!
ぽろ
FLP
PLEASE EXCUSE US...
BUT THOSE CREEPS AT YUKAKU...
...SUDDENLY CAME AT US WITH FLYING KICKS!
UNH...
STUMBLE
HOW CAN SOMEONE WHO IS JUST A KID ATTACK WITH KICKS LIKE THAT?!
TWITCH

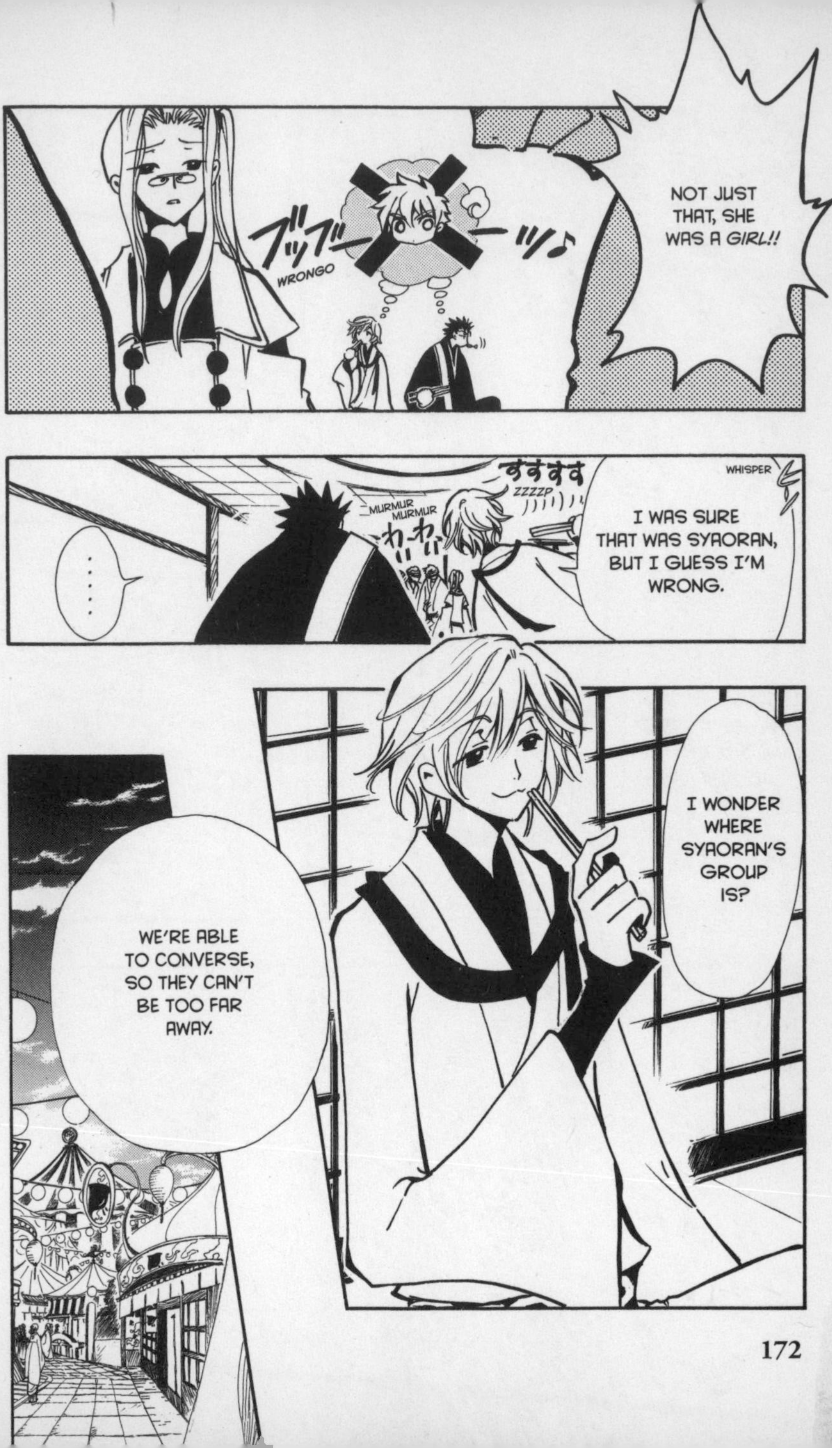
NOT JUST THAT, SHE WAS A *GIRL*!!
ブッブーッ♪
WRONGO
WHISPER
I WAS SURE THAT WAS SYAORAN, BUT I GUESS I'M WRONG.
すすすす
ZZZZP
MURMUR MURMUR
わいわい
.....
I WONDER WHERE SYAORAN'S GROUP IS?
WE'RE ABLE TO CONVERSE, SO THEY CAN'T BE TOO FAR AWAY.

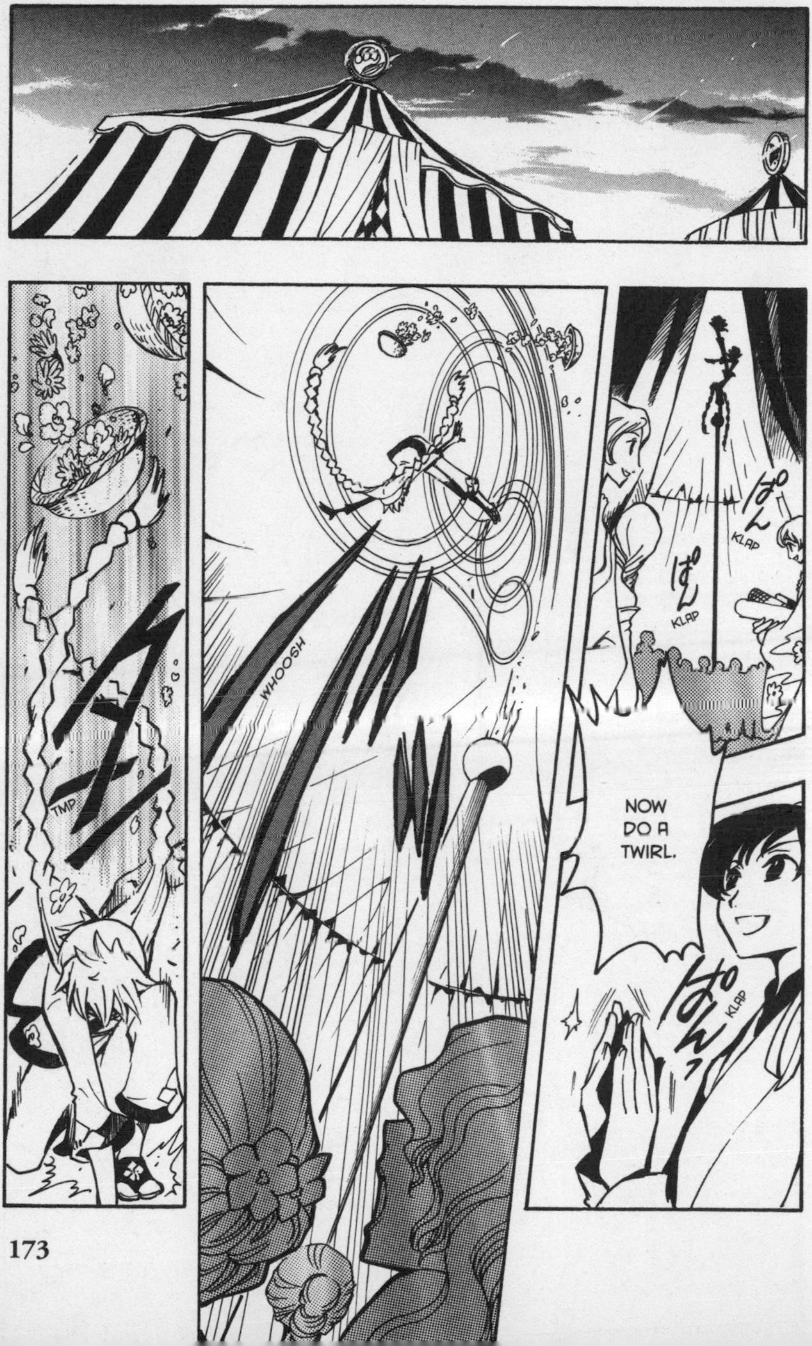
ぱん
KLAP
ぱん
KLAP
NOW DO A TWIRL.
ぱんっ
KLAP
WHOOSH
TMP

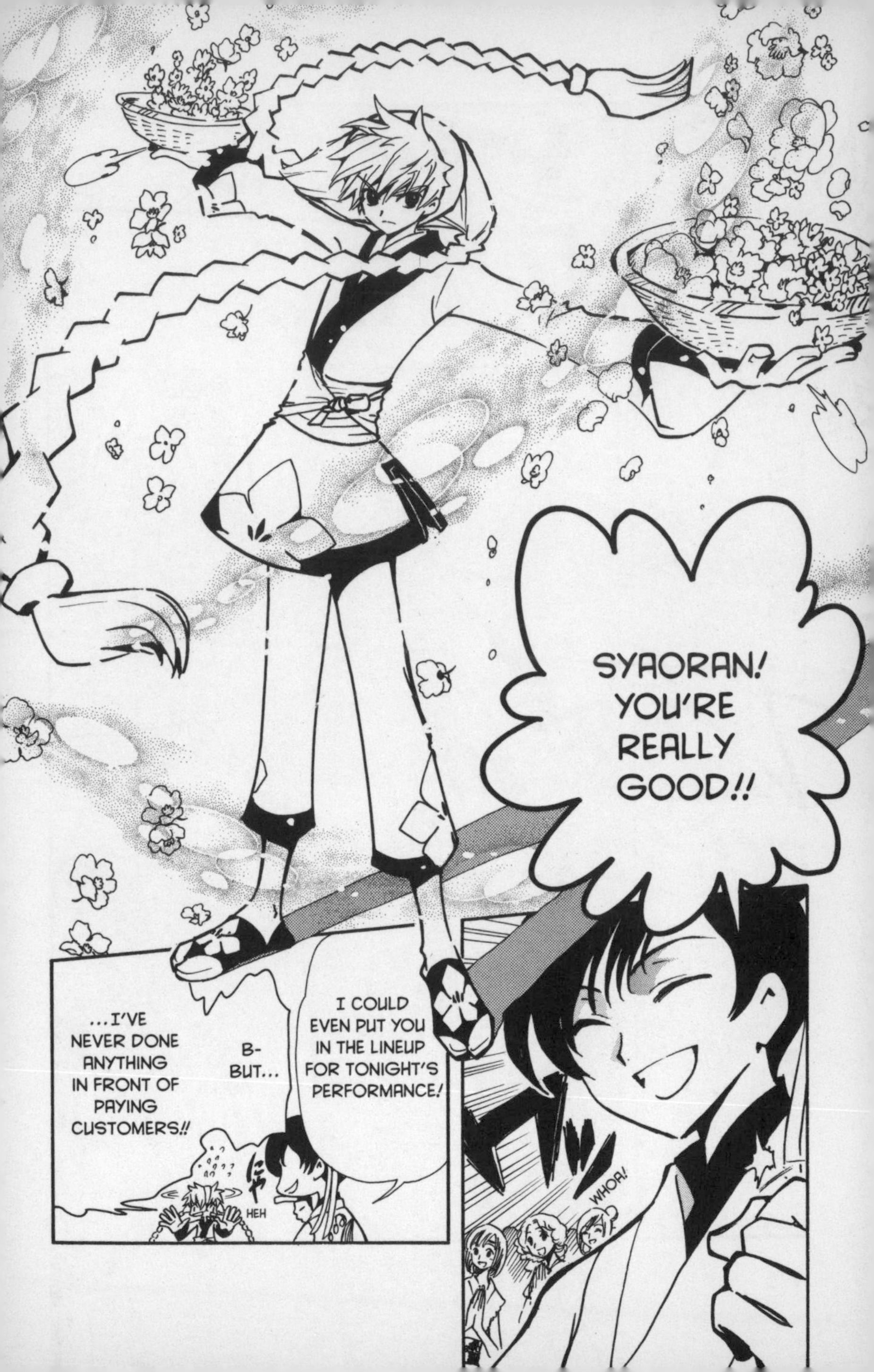
SYAORAN! YOU'RE REALLY GOOD!!
WHOA!
I COULD EVEN PUT YOU IN THE LINEUP FOR TONIGHT'S PERFORMANCE!
B-BUT...
...I'VE NEVER DONE ANYTHING IN FRONT OF PAYING CUSTOMERS!!
HEH

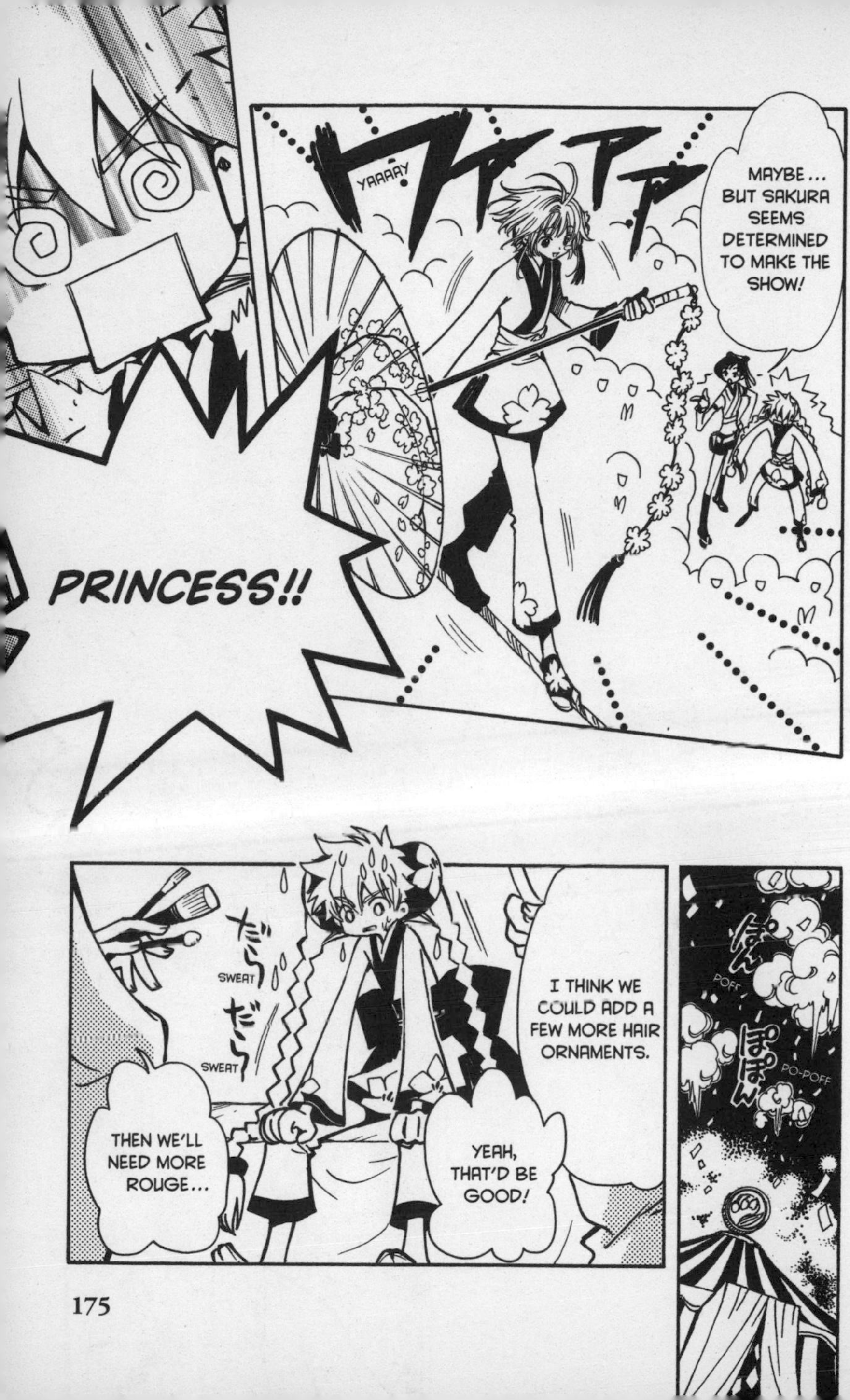
ワァァァ
YAAAAY
MAYBE... BUT SAKURA SEEMS DETERMINED TO MAKE THE SHOW!
PRINCESS!!
ぽん
POFF
ぽぽん
PO-POFF
I THINK WE COULD ADD A FEW MORE HAIR ORNAMENTS.
YEAH, THAT'D BE GOOD!
THEN WE'LL NEED MORE ROUGE...
だら
SWEAT
だら
SWEAT

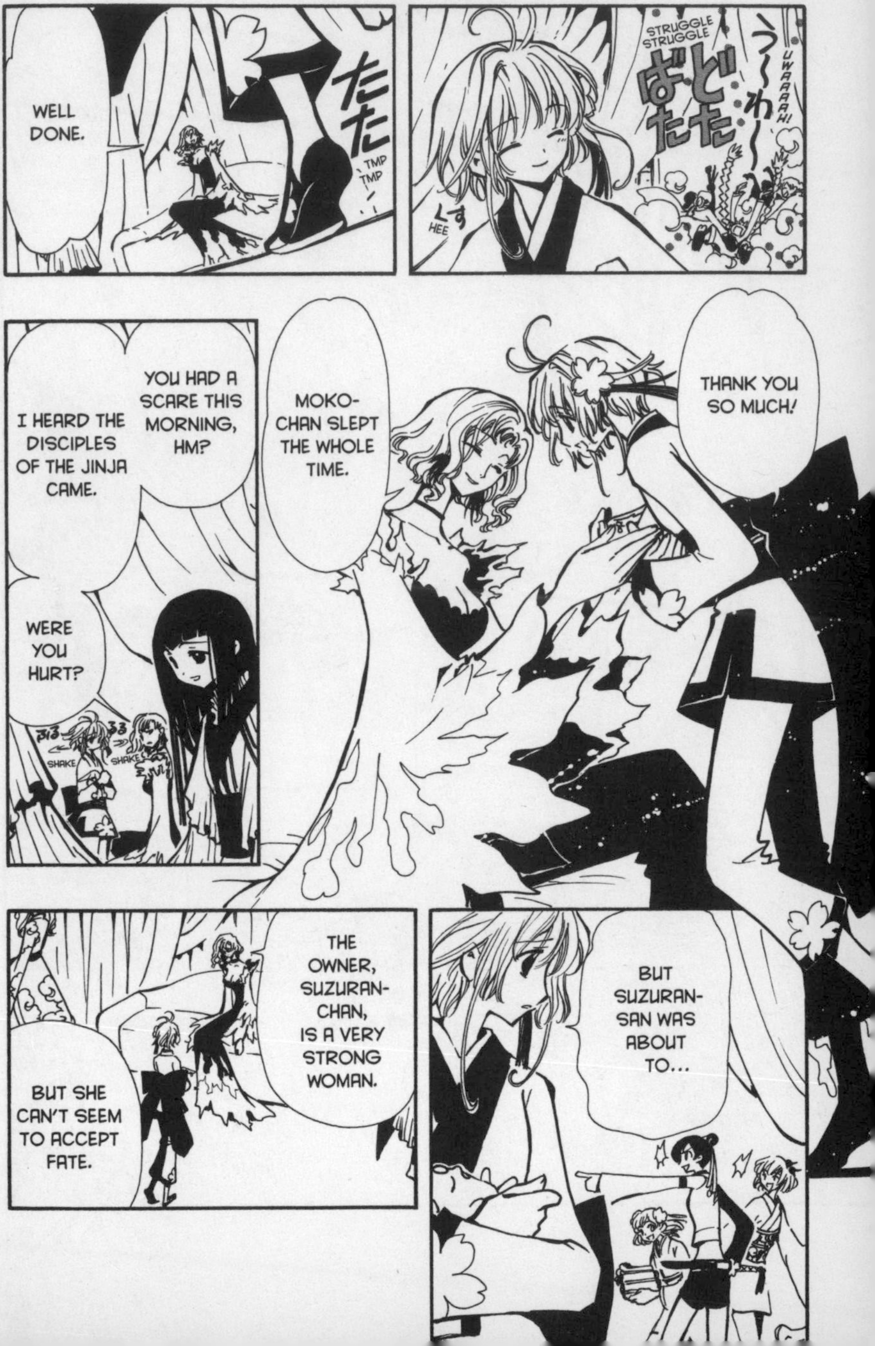
STRUGGLE STRUGGLE
UWAAAAH!
HEE
WELL DONE.
たた
TMP TMP
THANK YOU SO MUCH!
MOKO-CHAN SLEPT THE WHOLE TIME.
YOU HAD A SCARE THIS MORNING, HM?
I HEARD THE DISCIPLES OF THE JINJA CAME.
WERE YOU HURT?
SHAKE
SHAKE
BUT SUZURAN-SAN WAS ABOUT TO...
THE OWNER, SUZURAN-CHAN, IS A VERY STRONG WOMAN.
BUT SHE CAN'T SEEM TO ACCEPT FATE.

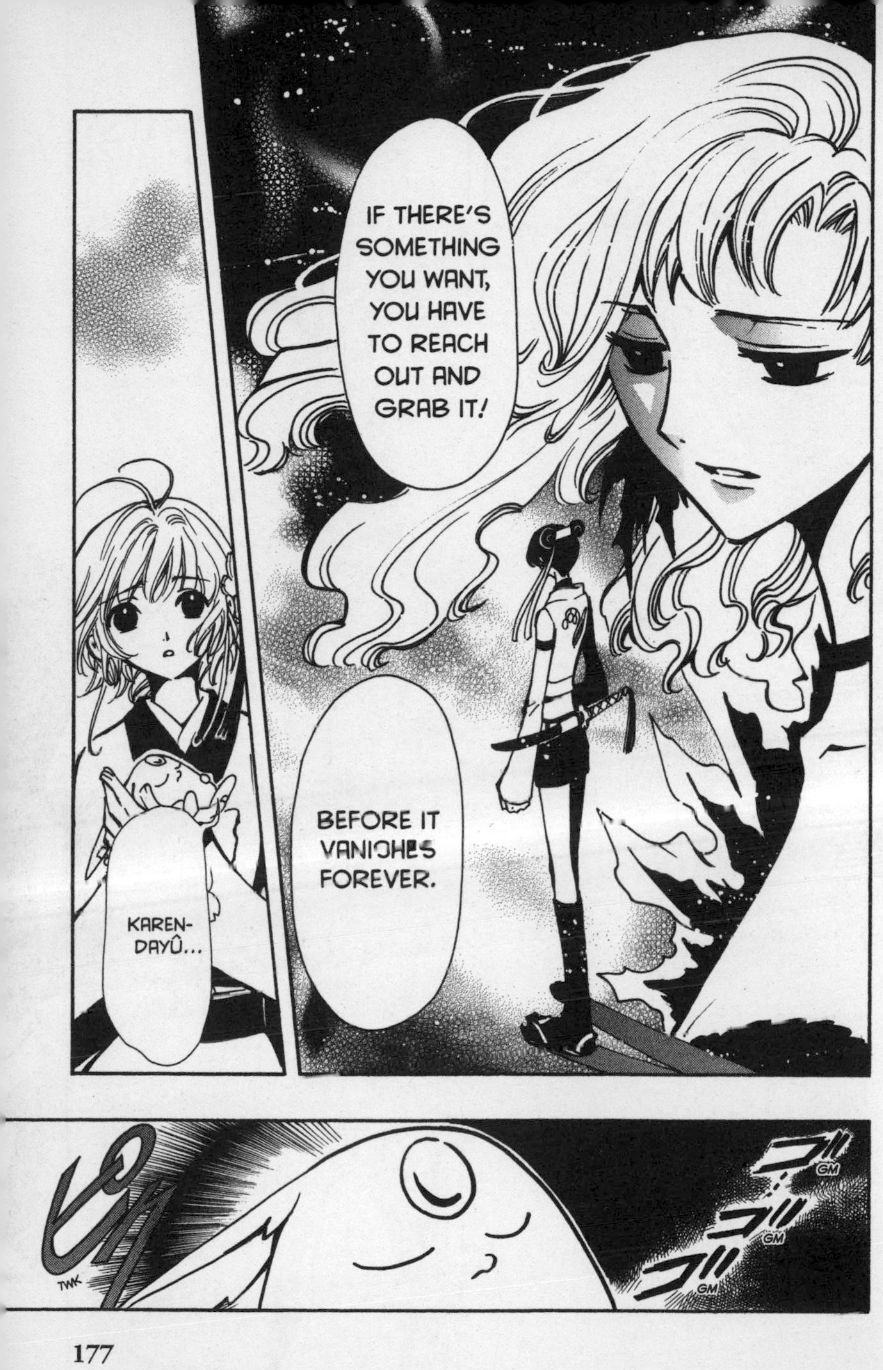
IF THERE'S SOMETHING YOU WANT, YOU HAVE TO REACH OUT AND GRAB IT!
BEFORE IT VANISHES FOREVER.
KAREN-DAYÛ...
GM
GM
GM
TWK

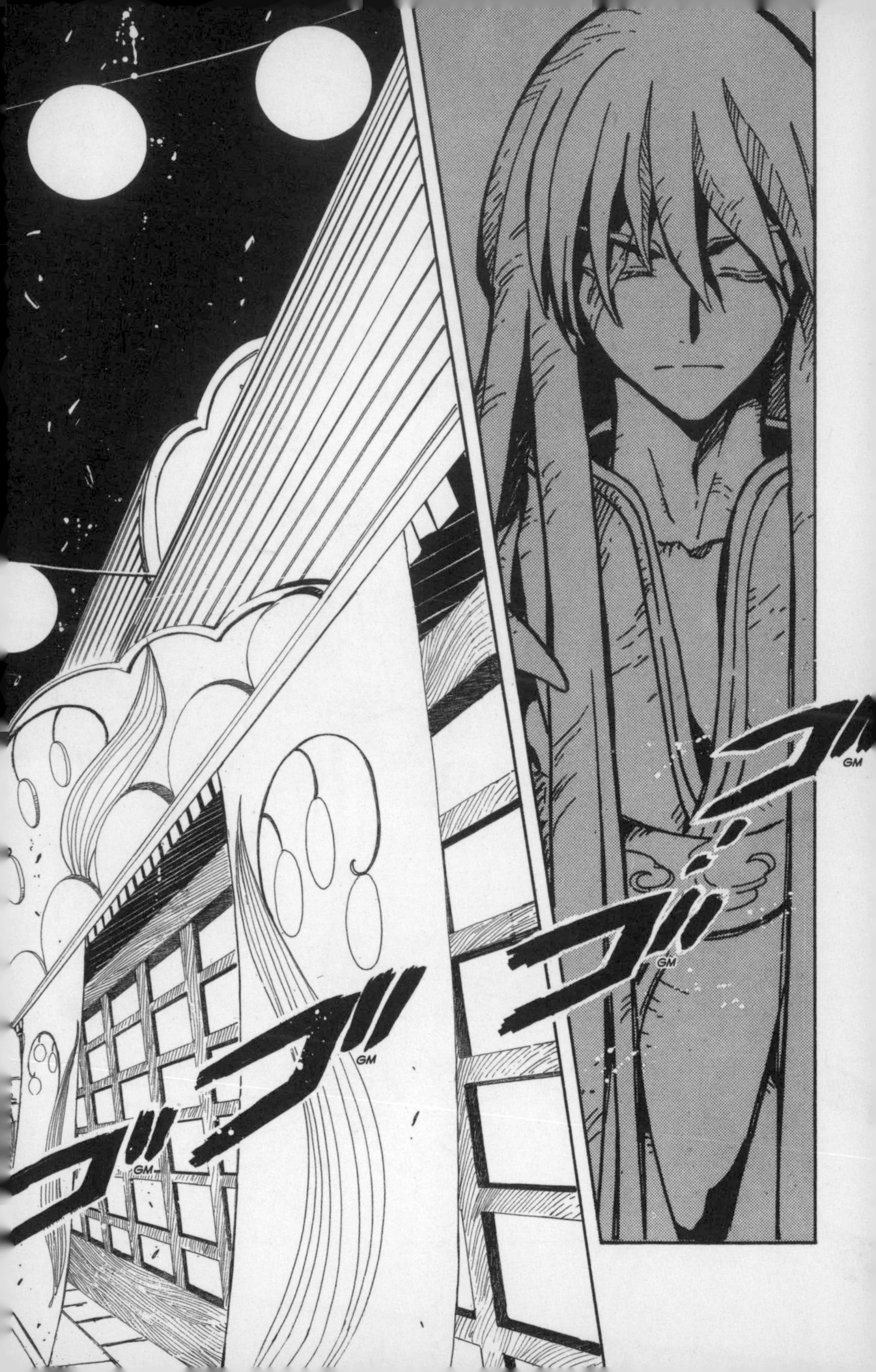
ゴ
GM
ゴ
GM
ゴ
GM
ゴ
GM

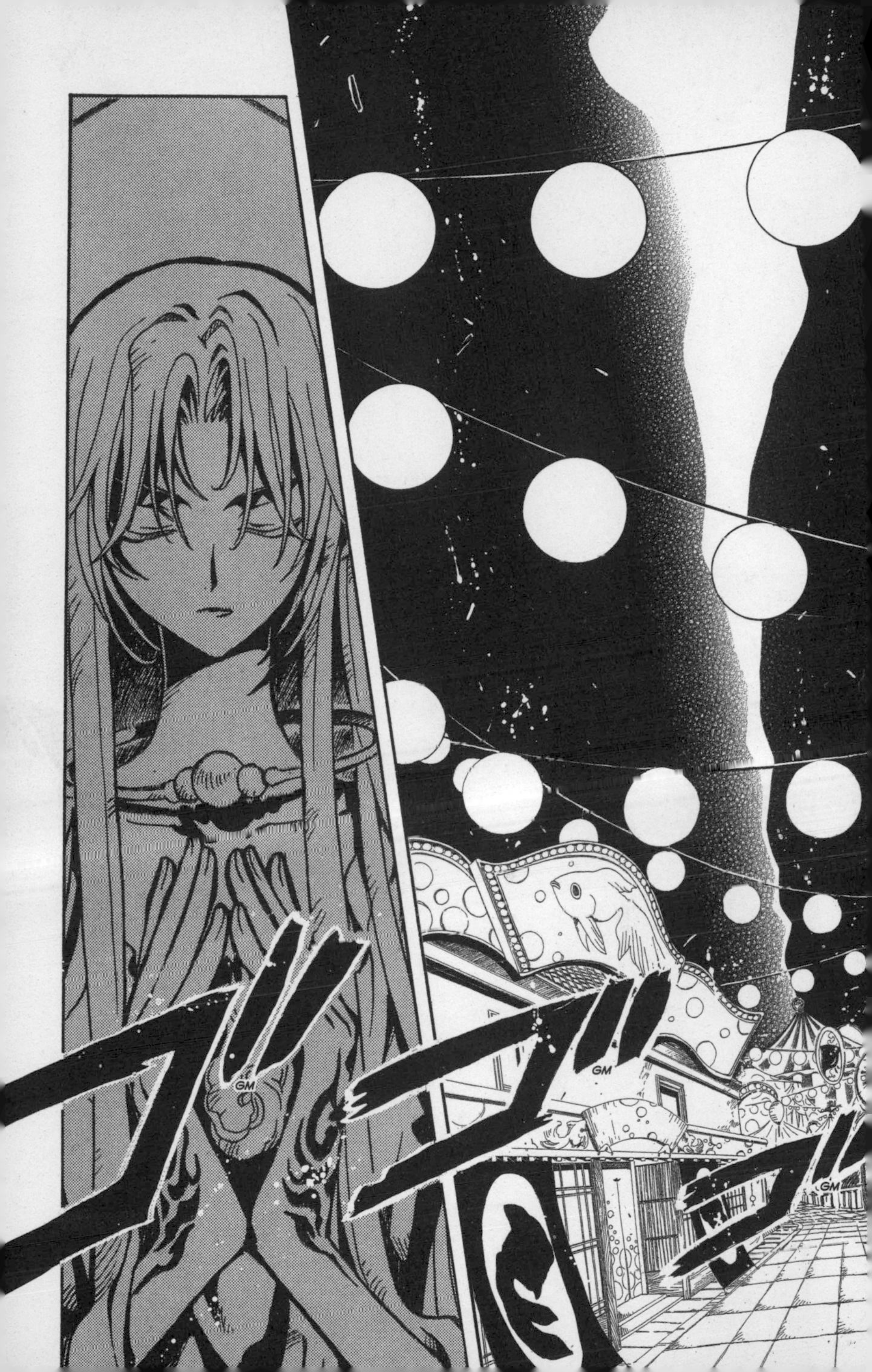

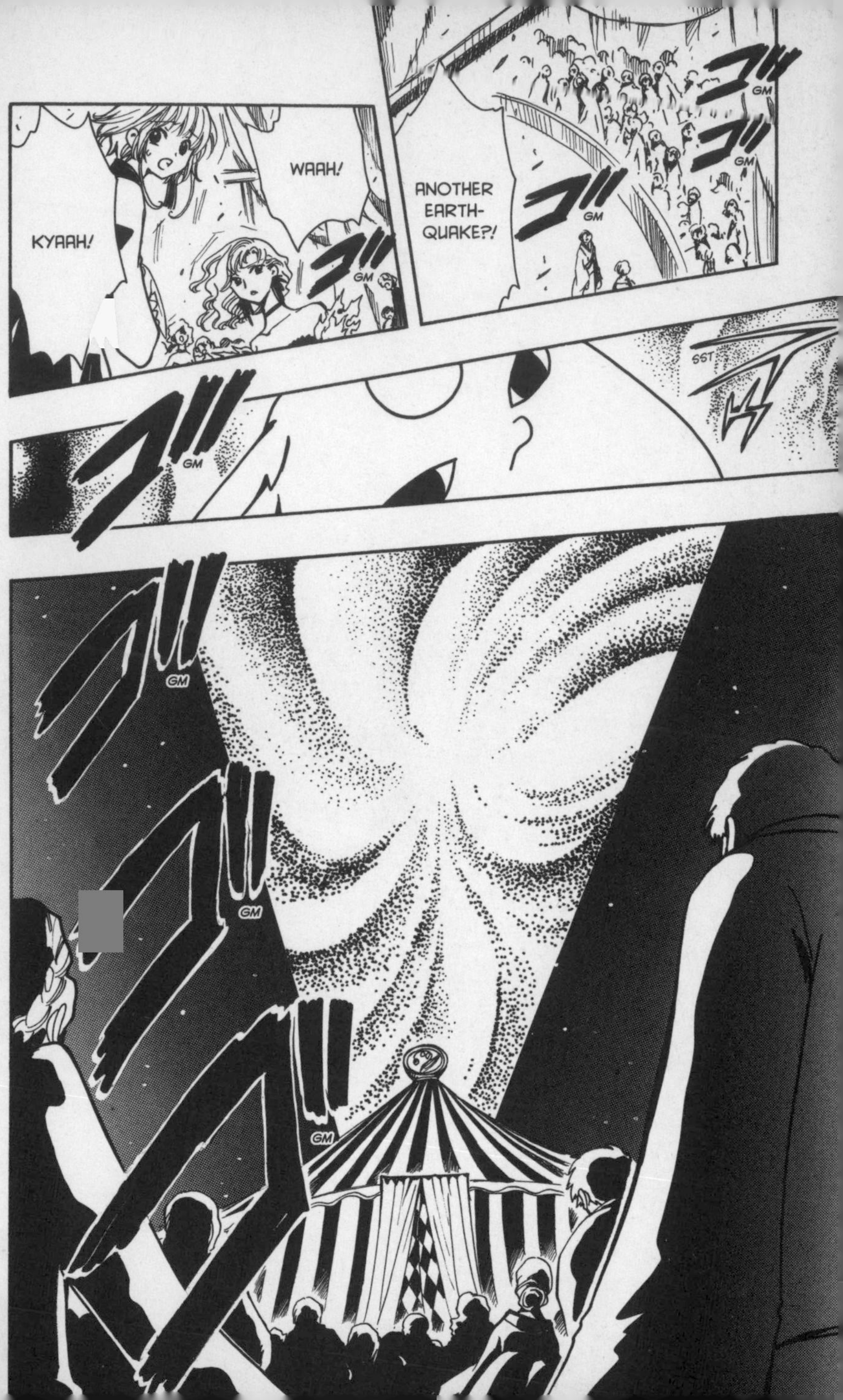
GM
GM
ANOTHER EARTH-QUAKE?!
GM
WAAH!
KYAAH!
GM
SST
GM
GM
GM
GM

To Be Continued

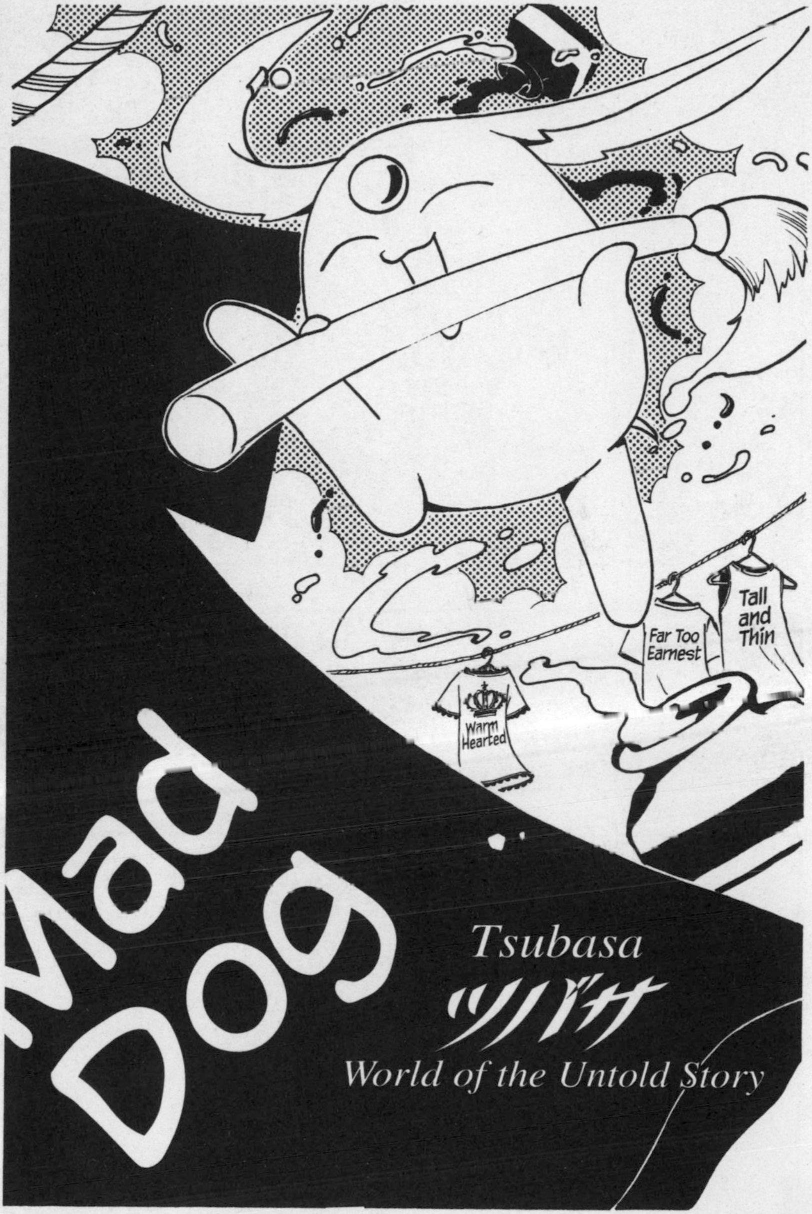
Tall and Thin
Far Too Earnest
Warm Hearted
Mad Dog
Tsubasa
ツバサ
World of the Untold Story

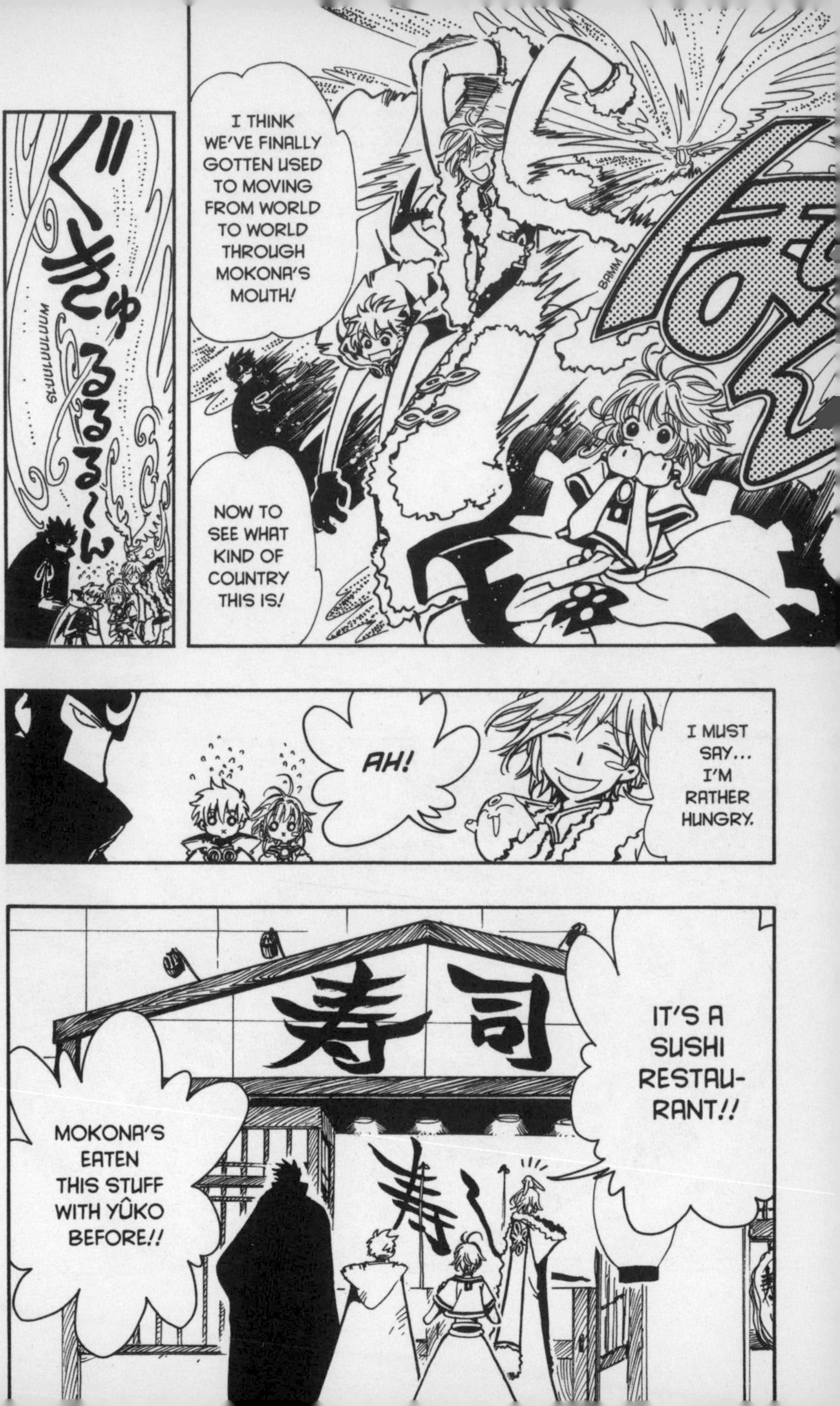
I THINK WE'VE FINALLY GOTTEN USED TO MOVING FROM WORLD TO WORLD THROUGH MOKONA'S MOUTH!
BAMM
NOW TO SEE WHAT KIND OF COUNTRY THIS IS!
ぐきゅるるるる〜ん
I MUST SAY... I'M RATHER HUNGRY.
AH!
寿司
IT'S A SUSHI RESTAURANT!!
MOKONA'S EATEN THIS STUFF WITH YÛKO BEFORE!!

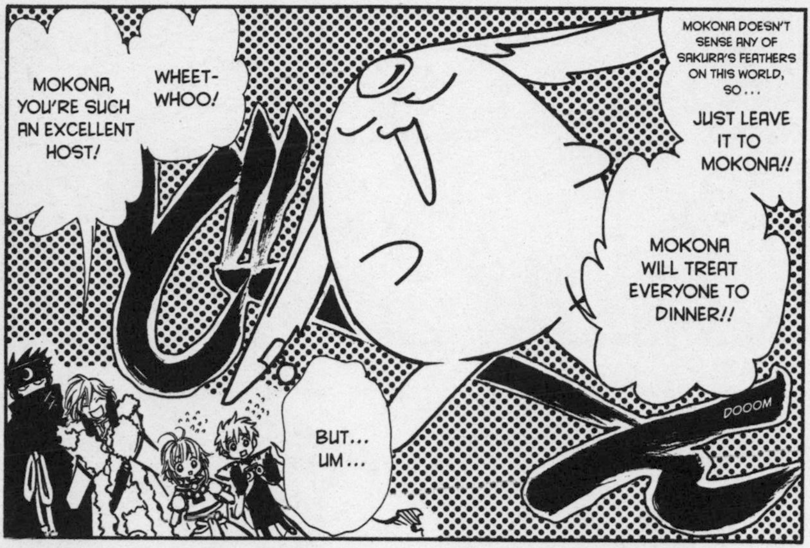
MOKONA DOESN'T SENSE ANY OF SAKURA'S FEATHERS ON THIS WORLD, SO...
JUST LEAVE IT TO MOKONA!!
MOKONA WILL TREAT EVERYONE TO DINNER!!
DOOOM
WHEET-WHOO!
MOKONA, YOU'RE SUCH AN EXCELLENT HOST!
BUT... UM...

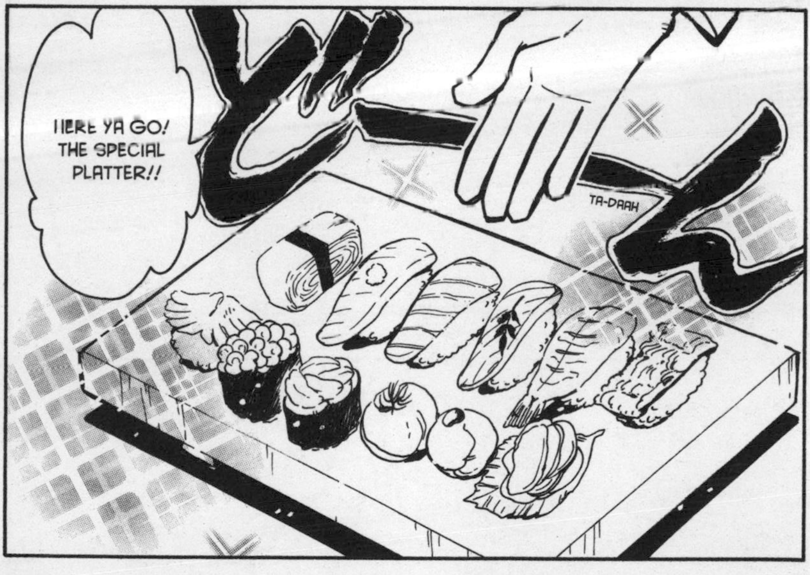
TA-DAAH
HERE YA GO! THE SPECIAL PLATTER!!

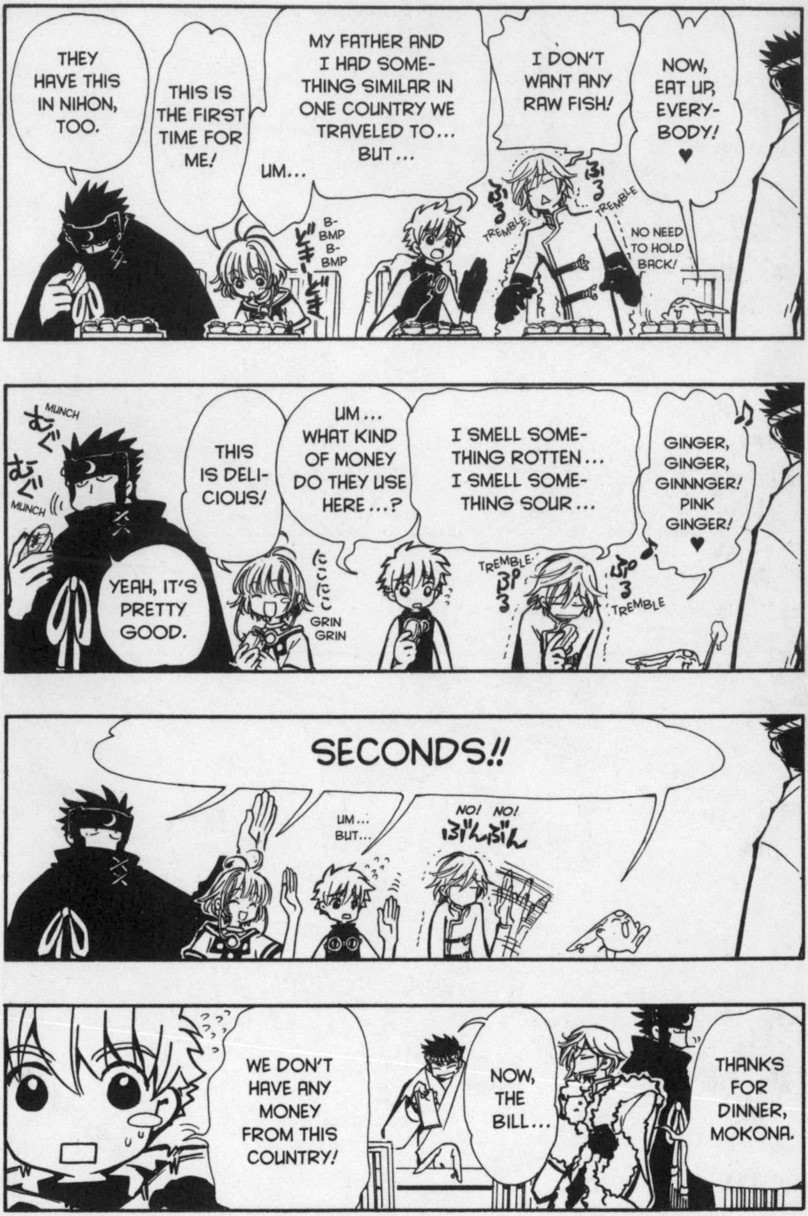
NOW, EAT UP, EVERY-BODY! ♥
NO NEED TO HOLD BACK!
I DON'T WANT ANY RAW FISH!
TREMBLE TREMBLE
MY FATHER AND I HAD SOME-THING SIMILAR IN ONE COUNTRY WE TRAVELED TO... BUT...
UM...
B-BMP B-BMP
THIS IS THE FIRST TIME FOR ME!
THEY HAVE THIS IN NIHON, TOO.
GINGER, GINGER, GINNNGER! PINK GINGER! ♥
TREMBLE TREMBLE
I SMELL SOME-THING ROTTEN... I SMELL SOME-THING SOUR...
UM... WHAT KIND OF MONEY DO THEY USE HERE...?
GRIN GRIN
THIS IS DELI-CIOUS!
YEAH, IT'S PRETTY GOOD.
MUNCH MUNCH
SECONDS!!
NO! NO!
UM... BUT...
THANKS FOR DINNER, MOKONA.
NOW, THE BILL...
WE DON'T HAVE ANY MONEY FROM THIS COUNTRY!

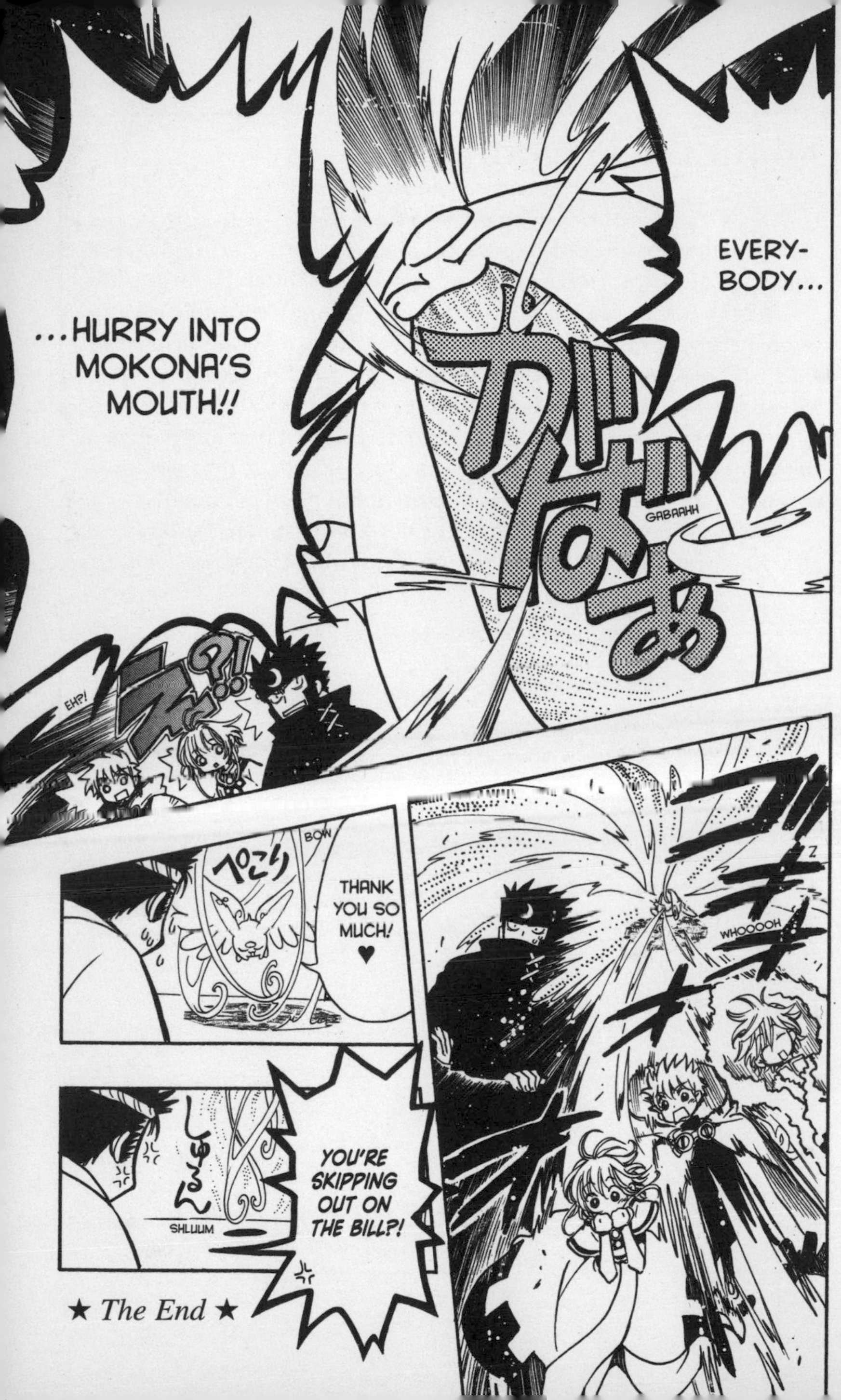
EVERY-BODY...
...HURRY INTO MOKONA'S MOUTH!!
GABAAHH
?!
EHP!
WHOOOOH
BOW
THANK YOU SO MUCH! ♥
SHLUUM
YOU'RE SKIPPING OUT ON THE BILL?!

★ *The End* ★

About the Creators

CLAMP is a group of four women who have become the most popular manga artists in America—Ageha Ohkawa, Mokona, Satsuki Igarashi, and Tsubaki Nekoi. They started out as doujinshi (fan comics) creators, but their skill and craft brought them to the attention of publishers very quickly. Their first work from a major publisher was *RG Veda*, but their first mass success was with *Magic Knight Rayearth*. From there, they went on to write many series, including *Cardcaptor Sakura* and *Chobits*, two of the most popular manga in the United States. Like many Japanese manga artists, they prefer to avoid the spotlight, and little is known about them personally.

CLAMP is currently publishing three series in Japan: *Tsubasa* and *xxxHOLiC* with Kodansha and *Gohou Drug* with Kadokawa.

Translation Notes

Japanese is a tricky language for most Westerners, and translation is often more art than science. For your edification and reading pleasure, here are notes on some of the places where we could have gone in a different direction in our translation of the work, or where a Japanese cultural reference is used.

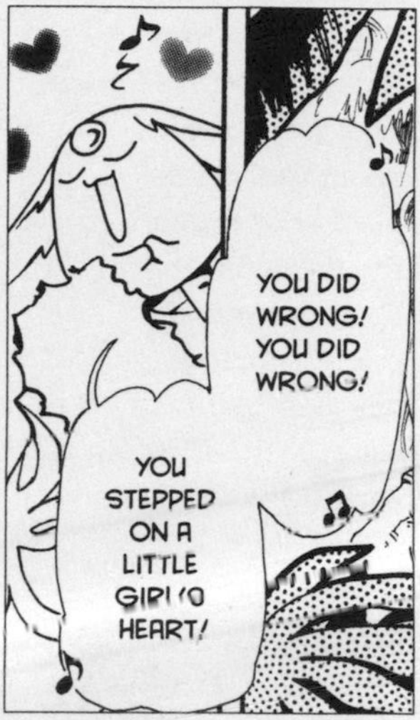
YOU DID WRONG! YOU DID WRONG!
YOU STEPPED ON A LITTLE GIRL'S HEART!

You did wrong! (*Ikenai-nda! Ikenai-nda!*) page 14

Some Americans might remember hearing a little sing-song chant in elementary school when one happened go a bit beyond the school rules, and the other children sang out, "You're gonna get it!" The Japanese version, *Ikenai-nda, ikenai-nda!* is exactly the same. Children chant it with the glee of schadenfreude when they know punishment is coming to someone else from a teacher or parent. Mokona also adds the oft-forgotten second phrase of the song.

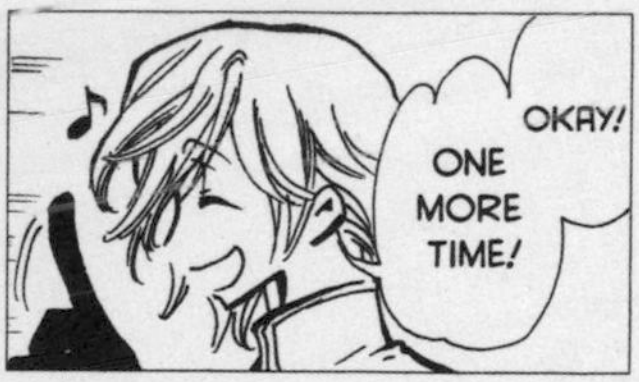
OKAY!
ONE MORE TIME!

***Se-no* . . . (One, two . . .), page 68**

This is how Japanese people time things so that they all start on the same beat. People in the West usually chant "One, two, three . . . ," starting off all together on the next beat. In Japan, they do it by counting to two with the words *se, no,* and then, on the third beat, they start together.

The Game of Telephone (*Dengon*), page 68

The origin of this children's game is lost, and considering that it has appeared in many cultures, it probably has more than one origin. Children are lined up and the first whispers a message to the second. The second whispers the message to the third, and so on down the line.

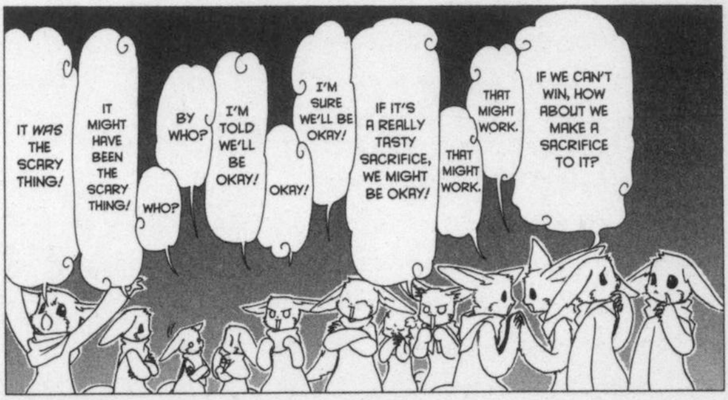
IF WE CAN'T WIN, HOW ABOUT WE MAKE A SACRIFICE TO IT?
THAT MIGHT WORK.
THAT MIGHT WORK.
IF IT'S A REALLY TASTY SACRIFICE, WE MIGHT BE OKAY!
I'M SURE WE'LL BE OKAY!
OKAY!
I'M TOLD WE'LL BE OKAY!
BY WHO?
WHO?
IT MIGHT HAVE BEEN THE SCARY THING!
IT *WAS* THE SCARY THING!

At the end, the final child tells the group what the message is, and everyone compares notes as to how much the message has changed in the telling. It has also been called Gossip, Chinese Whispers, Whisper Down the Lane, *Stille Post* (German for "silent mail") and foreign-language variations on Telephone. The Japanese word *dengon* translates as "message."

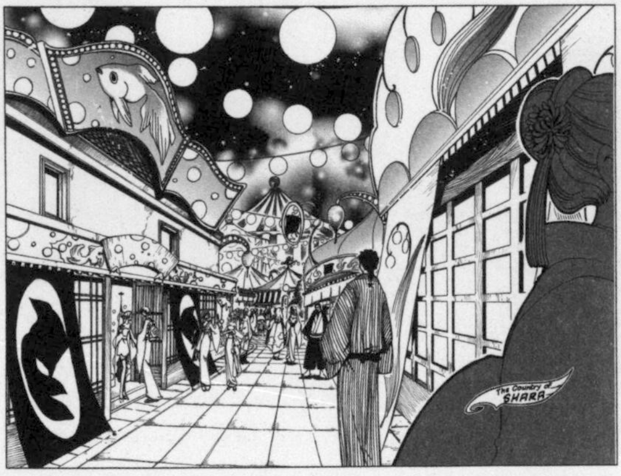
The Country of SHARA

Shara no Kuni (The Country of Shara), page 86

So far in *Tsubasa* we've visited several countries based on Japan of different eras, such as Ôto, based on the Japan of the early twentieth century; the Hanshin Republic, based on Osaka of today; Kurogane's world, based on feudal Japan; and now Shara (the *kanji* of which might translate to "gossamer silk"), which is based on the opposition between the floating world (pleasure quarters) of Edo period Japan (1603–1867) and the pious, religious culture of the temples and shrines. The floating world is the world of geisha, restaurants, inns, and other carnival-like entertainments. The life was raucous, rough, and full of energy. Much of the floating-world lifestyle of these districts is found in the famous *Ukio-e* wood-block prints of Edo-period Japan. The religious culture was polite, contemplative, and aesthetic at best; political and overbearing at its worst.

Tayû, page 91

This is a high rank for actors in *Noh* drama, entertainers, and courtesans. In *Kabuki*, it refers to the male actor who plays the female roles. In this case, Karen (who shares an identity with the sultry ally of Kamui in *X*) is the highest-ranked entertainer in Suzuran's business. Phonetically, the voiced "n" sound in Karen's name, forces the "t" to be voiced and become a "d" when used as Karen's title. Thus *Tayû* becomes *Dayû*.

KAREN-DAYÛ!

THIS JINJA IS SACRED GROUND!

Jinja, page 98

Normally, *Jinja* is spelled with two *kanji*, one that stands for god and the other for shrine, and it means a shrine to the Shinto gods. In this case, the *Jin* part is for a different *kanji* that sounds the same but means army or troops, so it comes off sounding like a shrine dedicated to the military arts.

***Kannushi*, page 109**

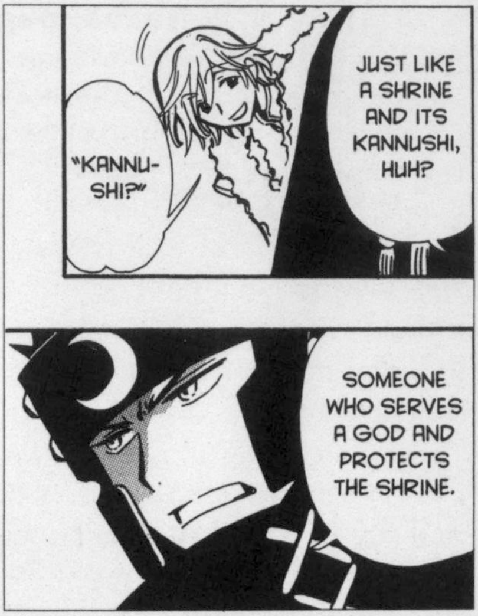
JUST LIKE A SHRINE AND ITS KANNUSHI, HUH?
"KANNU-SHI?"
SOMEONE WHO SERVES A GOD AND PROTECTS THE SHRINE.

Kannushi isn't just legends from Kurogane's world. In ours as well, the word means a Shinto priest and one who protects a shrine. The word is also used for a card in the Magic the Gathering® card game.

***Miko*, page 109**

In this case, the word would refer to a virgin priestess in the Shinto religion. Although these days *miko* are nothing more than lowly priest's assistants (usually the daughters of Shinto priests), in a small section of *Romance of the Three Kingdoms* (a Chinese epic), the country, Yamatai, that was the central power in the land of Wa (Japan), was ruled by a Queen/Miko by the name of Himiko. This precedent has led to many stories of women who are powerful priestess/rulers.

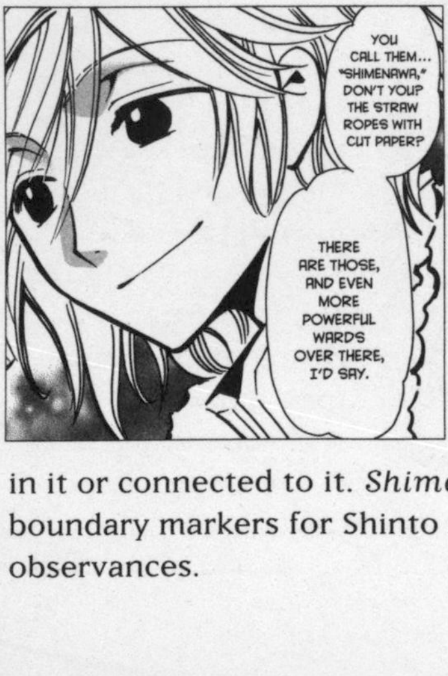
YOU CALL THEM... "SHIMENAWA," DON'T YOU? THE STRAW ROPES WITH CUT PAPER?
THERE ARE THOSE, AND EVEN MORE POWERFUL WARDS OVER THERE, I'D SAY.

***Shimenawa*, page 110**

Shimenawa is a rough rope decorated with strips of folded and cut white paper. It is usually placed around holy sites, and especially on old or prominent parts of nature such as locally significant rocks or old trees. The *shimenawa* indicates that the locals respect that piece of nature as having a *kami* residing in it or connected to it. *Shimenawa* can also be used as wards or boundary markers for Shinto shrines and other religious observances.

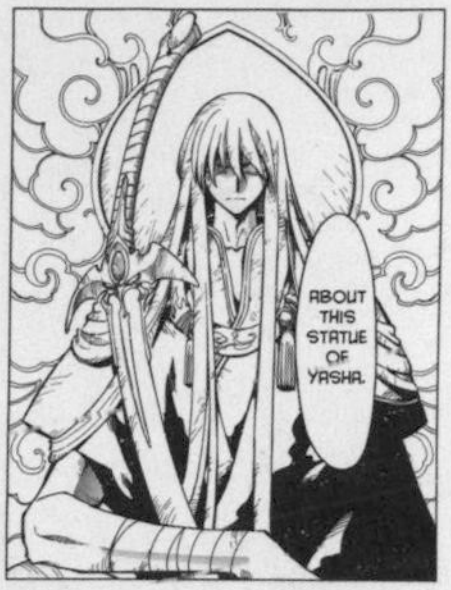
ABOUT THIS STATUE OF YASHA.

Yasha, page 112
RG Veda fans will be familiar with Yasha-ô (Lord Yasha), one of the tragic main characters of the *RG Veda* manga and anime videos.

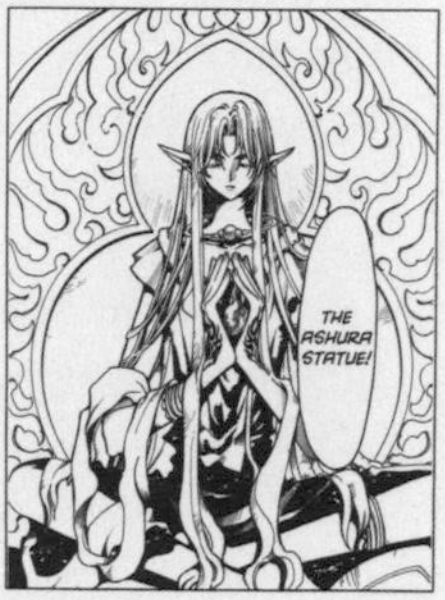
THE ASHURA STATUE!

Ashura, page 122
RG Veda fans will also be familiar with Ashura, the other tragic main character of the manga and anime videos.

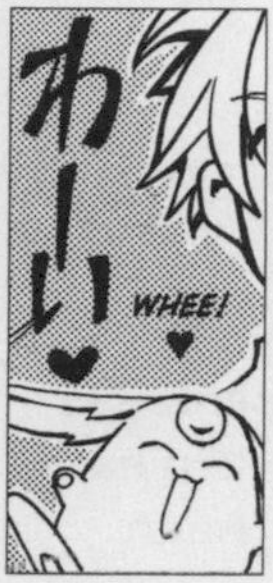
わーい!
WHEE!

Wai! (Whee!), page 135
Wai is the cry of delight for a baby or very young child in Japan. And because of the cuteness craze that seems to be a Japanese staple, when someone older wants to appear cute, they have been known to cry *wai-wai* as well.

Kampai!, page 138
(Alternatively spelled Kanpai) This toast literally means empty glass, but for all intents and purposes, its direct translation would be the English "Cheers!"

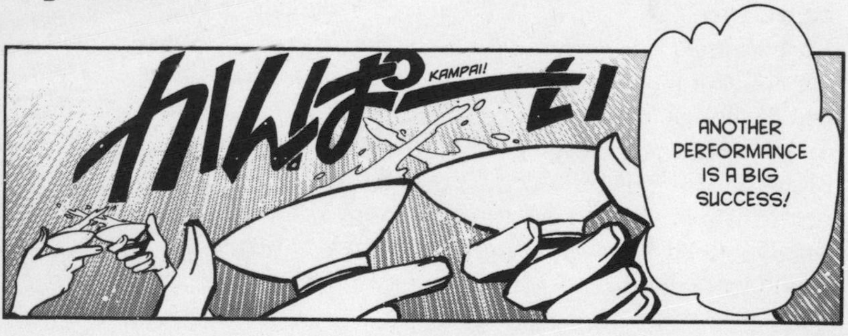
ANOTHER PERFORMANCE IS A BIG SUCCESS!
かんぱーい
KAMPAI!

Umeboshi as a Hangover Remedy, page 152

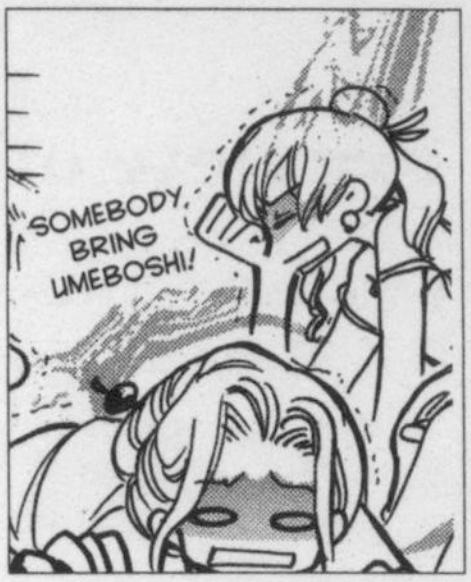
SOMEBODY BRING UMEBOSHI!

Umeboshi is usually described as a pickled plum, but it is actually in the apricot family, and has many uses. One of the main uses is to add a tart flavor to rice balls, but another use is to help with hangovers. *Umeboshi* contains picric acid, a substance that is said to stimulate the liver and clean artificial chemicals out of the body. Other uses for *Umeboshi* include preventing fatigue, constipation, and bad breath, and serving as a morning-sickness remedy.

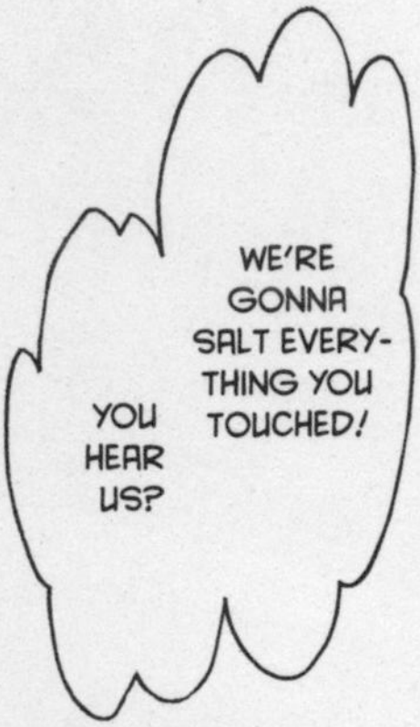
WE'RE GONNA SALT EVERY-THING YOU TOUCHED!
YOU HEAR US?

Sprinkling Salt, page 160

One of the rites of Shinto purification is to sprinkle salt on ground that has been made impure. One can see this just before a sumo match when the wrestlers sprinkle salt on the ring to purify it.

How to Hold Chopsticks, page 170

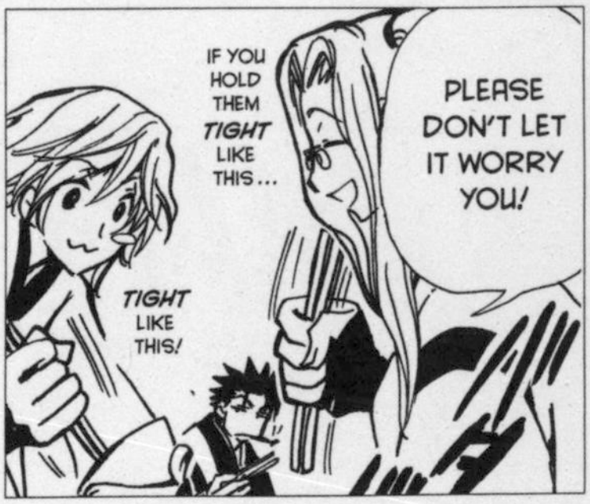
PLEASE DON'T LET IT WORRY YOU!
IF YOU HOLD THEM TIGHT LIKE THIS...
TIGHT LIKE THIS!

Master Sôseki was teaching Fai the method that Japanese children use before they gain enough dexterity to use chopsticks properly. Basically, you grasp both sticks tightly in your fist and use them as a shovel to push rice into your mouth from the lip of the bowl.

Preview of Volume 9

We're pleased to present you a preview from volume 9. This volume is available in English now!

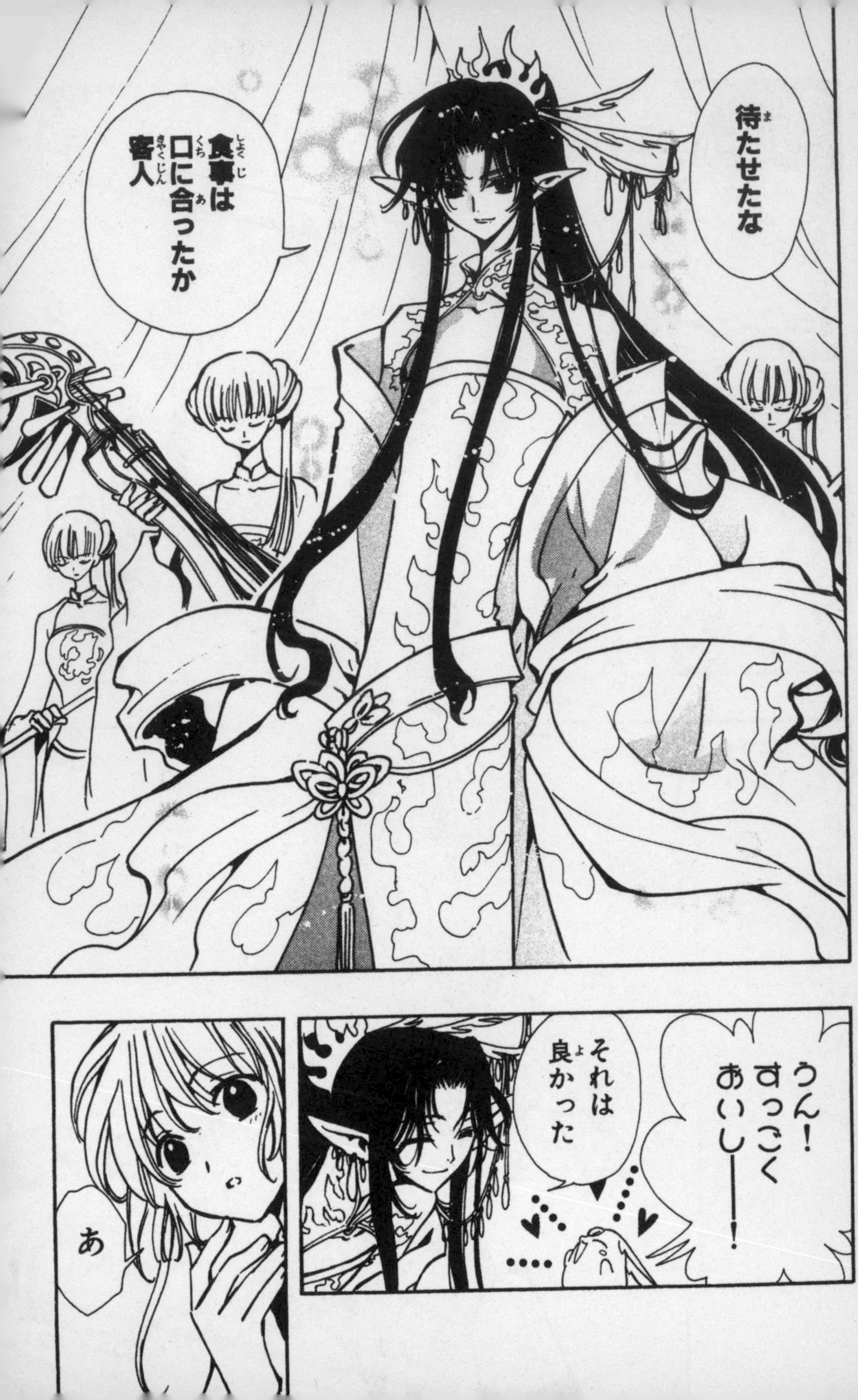
待たせたな
食事は口に合ったか客人
うん！すっごくおいしーー！
それは良かった
‥‥
あ

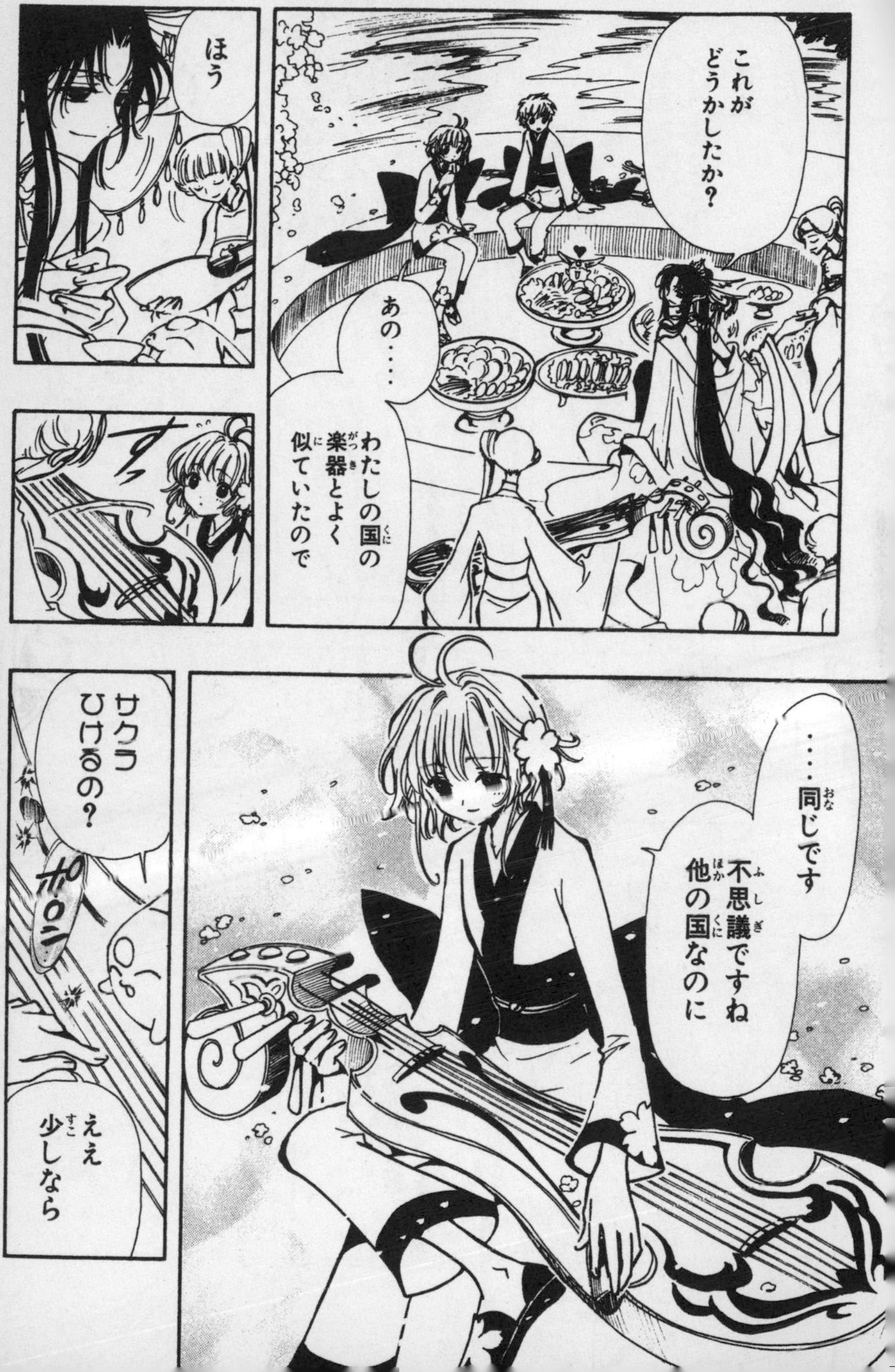
これが
どうかしたか？
あの……
わたしの国の楽器とよく似ていたので
ほう
す
……同じです
不思議ですね
他の国なのに
サクラ
ひけるの？
ポロン
ええ
少しなら

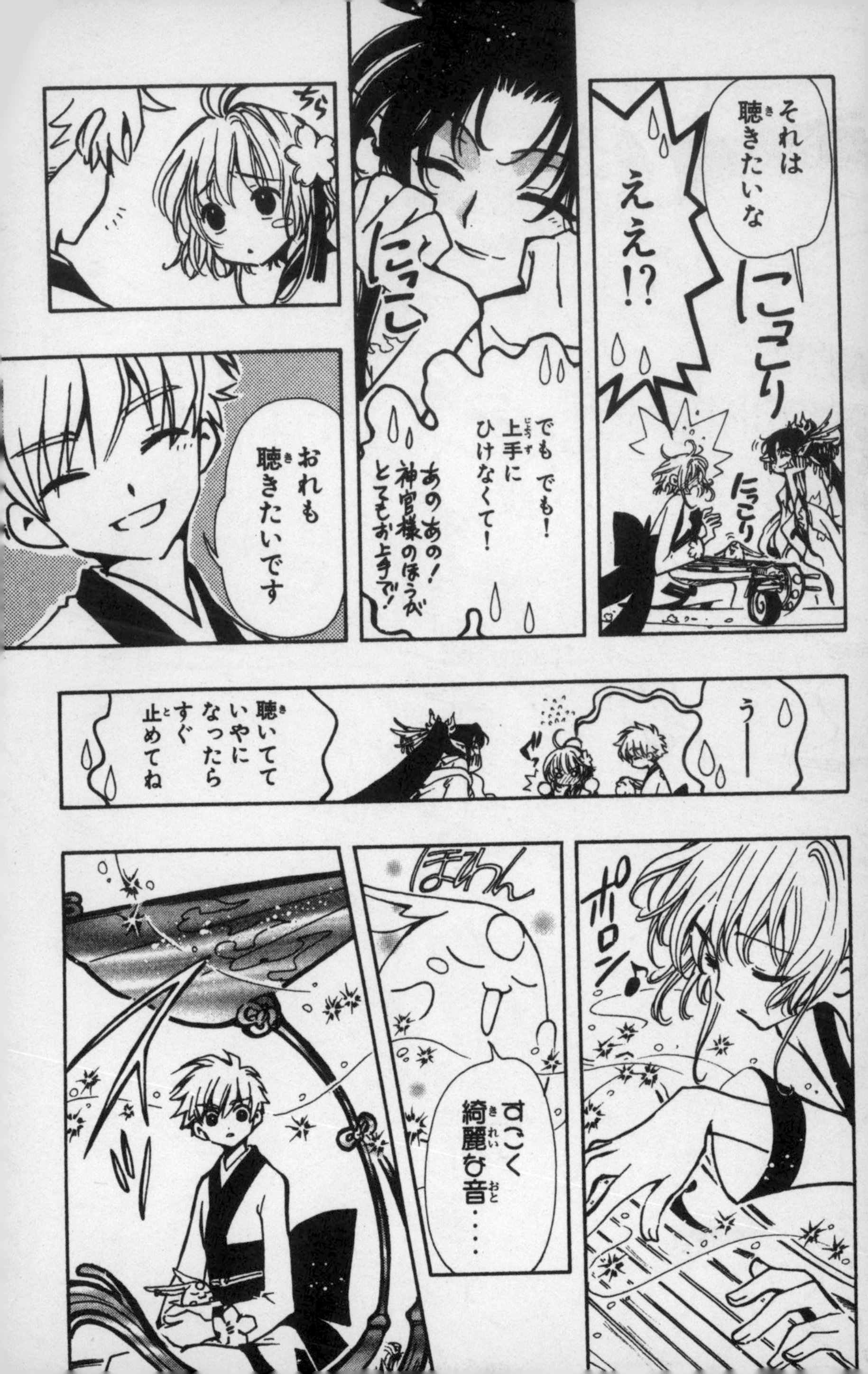
それは聴きたいな
にっこり
ええ!?
にっこり
にこ
でも でも! 上手にひけなくて!
あの あの! 神官様のほうがとてもお上手で!
ちら
おれも聴きたいです
うー
聴いてていやになったらすぐ止めてね
ポロン♪
ほわん
すごく綺麗な音……

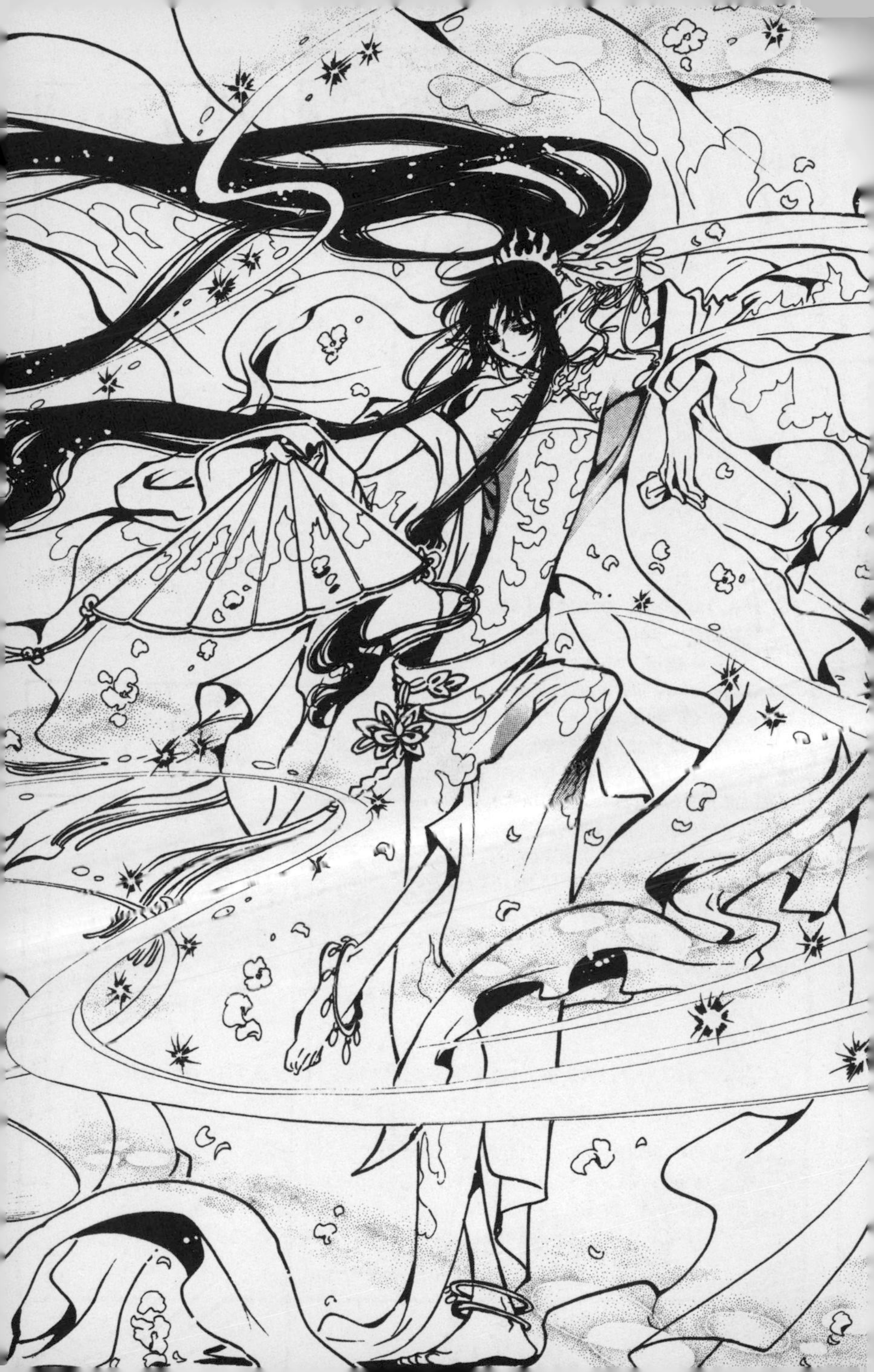

BY MINORU TOYODA

A fun, romantic comedy, Love Roma is about the simple kind of relationships we all longed for when we were young. It's a story of love at first sight—literally. When Hoshino sees Negishi for the first time, he asks her to be his girlfriend. Shocked, Negishi nevertheless agrees to allow Hoshino to walk her home, while he explains why he is in love with her. Touched, Negishi begins to feel something for this strange young boy from her school.

Ages: 16+

Special extras in each volume! Read them all!

Sugar Sugar Rune

BY MOYOCO ANNO VOLUME 1

QUEEN OF HEARTS

Little witch-girls Chocolat and Vanilla are best friends, but only one of them can be Queen of the Magic World. To determine who deserves the title, they must go to the Human World and enter a strange competition. Whoever attracts the most human boys wins!

Here's how it works: When a boy falls for a witch-girl, she utters a few mystic words and the boy's heart will be hers in jewel-like form. It may sound simple, but winning hearts is tricky business. While Chocolat had no problem enticing witch-boys with her forthright personality, human boys seem to be drawn to shy and modest girls like Vanilla. And to make matters worse, Chocolat is finding herself increasingly drawn to the cool and mysterious Pierre—who feels nothing for her! The girls had planned to be best friends forever, but both of them want to be Queen. Will their rivalry ruin their friendship?

Ages: 10 +

Includes special extras after the story!

VOLUME 1: On sale September 27, 2005

For more information and to sign up for Del Rey's manga e-newsletter, visit www.delreymanga.com

TOMARE!

[STOP!]

You're going the wrong way!

Manga is a completely different type of reading experience.

To start at the *beginning*, go to the *end*!

That's right! Authentic manga is read the traditional Japanese way—from right to left. Exactly the *opposite* of how American books are read. It's easy to follow: Just go to the other end of the book, and read each page—and each panel—from right side to left side, starting at the top right. Now you're experiencing manga as it was meant to be.